1/95

 St. Louis Community College

Forest Park
Florissant Valley
Meramec

Instructional Resources
St. Louis, Missouri

GAYLORD

CAT MONSTERS AND HEAD POTS

CAT MONSTERS

The Archaeology

AND **HEAD POTS**

of Missouri's Pemiscot Bayou

Michael J. O'Brien

with contributions by

Gregory L. Fox

Thomas D. Holland

Richard A. Marshall

J. Raymond Williams

UNIVERSITY OF MISSOURI PRESS

Columbia and London

Library of Congress Cataloging-in-Publication Data

O'Brien, Michael J. (Michael John), 1950–

   Cat monsters and head pots : the archaeology of Missouri's

   Pemiscot Bayou / Michael J. O'Brien with contributions by Gregory L. Fox . . . [et al.].

      p.   cm.

      Includes bibliographical references and index.

      ISBN 0-8262-0969-6 (cloth : alk. paper)

      1. Mississippian culture—Missouri—Pemiscot County.

   2. Excavations (Archaeology)—Missouri—Pemiscot County.

   3. Pemiscot County (Mo.)—Antiquities.   I. Title.

   E99.M6815034   1994

   977.8'996—dc20   94-20119

                                                                        CIP

∞™   This paper meets the requirements of the
American National Standard for Permanence of
Paper for Printed Library Materials, Z39.48, 1984.

Designer: Kristie Lee
Typesetter: Cornerstone Composition Services
Printer and binder: Thomson-Shore, Inc.
Typefaces: Garamond #3, Garamond #3 SC & OSF
            Lithos Bold, Eras Demi

To my dad, who taught me the difference between genius and hard work.

CONTENTS

ILLUSTRATIONS

Plates

Figures

TABLES

PREFACE

My purpose in producing this volume is to assemble in one place what is known about late-prehistoric (ca. A.D. 1350 to at least 1541) settlements along an ancient crevasse channel of the Mississippi River in Pemiscot County, Missouri. Why, one might ask, when so many articles and books have been written on the archaeology of the central Mississippi Valley, would someone produce yet another volume, especially one that is so limited in time and space? My answer to this question is that the late portion of the archaeological record along the ancient channel—historically known as Pemiscot Bayou—has figured prominently in central Mississippi River valley archaeology since the late nineteenth century, yet despite such prominence, built in part on several decades of intermittent archaeological survey and excavation but primarily on intensive relic hunting, no comprehensive examination of the late-period archaeological record of the Pemiscot Bayou locality has ever appeared. A lack of scientific analysis and an uncritical reliance on hearsay evidence have led to erroneous conclusions about the origin and nature of the Pemiscot Bayou settlements and about their role in the prehistory of the region—archaeological myths that have been perpetuated because no one has questioned them. My intent, and that of my coauthors, is to correct that situation and to present an important set of materials in a new light.

Various factors have contributed to a sustained interest in the Pemiscot Bayou sites, the most significant being the incredible richness of the archaeological record, especially in terms of its pottery. Beginning around 600 B.C.—perhaps slightly earlier in some areas, later in others—prehistoric groups residing in the central Mississippi Valley made and used a variety of cooking and storage vessels, some of which eventually made their way into the ground intact as funerary offerings. During most of this ceramic period the containers were rather plain in appearance, certainly in contrast to many of the vessels—especially bottles—produced after ca. A.D. 1350-1400 in the region centered on northeastern Arkansas, northwestern Tennessee, and Pemiscot County, Missouri. These beautifully decorated pieces, which took on a wide variety of shapes and decorative features, have always appealed to archaeologists as well as to antiquarians and art collectors. By the late 1800s thousands of vessels had been removed from the tristate region—

many of them from Pemiscot County—some placed in museums but most ending up in the hands of private collectors.

One cannot pick up a book or article on the late-period archaeology of the central Mississippi River valley without finding reference to one or more of the Pemiscot Bayou sites. For reasons discussed in Chapter 1, the locale has developed a certain mystique in archaeological circles, primarily because of the possibility, heretofore unproven, that a party connected with the de Soto entrada of 1541 actually visited a community located on the edge of the bayou. In addition, several sites have produced upwards of a thousand ceramic vessels each, including elaborately incised and painted jars, bottles, and bowls, as well as a large number of human skeletons. Very few of these items carry more than the barest of provenience information, which is made all the more unfortunate by the rapid destruction of sites in the region by land leveling and, until recent enactment of state laws, by looting.

Fortunately, sizable collections of provenienced artifacts do exist from a few of the known late-period sites, primarily those disturbed by land-leveling activities. Small grants provided to the University of Missouri by the National Park Service allowed field crews to spend several seasons during the 1960s and early 1970s salvaging material from select sites in southeastern Missouri, including some in Pemiscot County. Most excavations lasted a few weeks, others occurred over several seasons. The results of those efforts are evident in the several thousand boxes of archaeological materials from southeastern Missouri housed at the University of Missouri. But boxes of unanalyzed artifacts contribute little or nothing to advancing the knowledge of a region beyond that obtained through hearsay or from vague recollections. Thus it has been with materials from southeastern Missouri. Site destruction was so severe across the region that efforts were directed primarily at getting artifacts out of the ground, as opposed to analyzing the remains and writing comprehensive reports. Summaries of some of the excavations were produced and for the most part have served as the final word on the regional archaeology.

Interest in southeastern Missouri on the part of university archaeology faculty and students waned after 1972, with salvage efforts being focused on other regions of the state. Many members of the archaeological staff who had spent a decade or more working in Pemiscot, New Madrid, and Mississippi counties moved on to other positions, leaving a void that would remain unfilled for almost another two decades. Meanwhile, notes and artifacts from the excavations were stored in various buildings on campus, where they joined thousands of other boxes of material from around the state. In 1989, partly in response to growing concern over the state of curation at the university and partly because of resurgent interest in the archaeology of southeastern Missouri, the university's Museum of Anthropology applied for and received a systematics grant from the National Science Foundation to conserve and properly curate archaeological notes and collections from five southeastern Missouri counties. Our purpose in applying for the grant was twofold. First, it would provide for proper disposition of the materials, for which the university had responsibility, and second, it would allow us to inventory the enormous holding to determine what it contained. The results of the inventory were astounding, for we became aware for the first time of the significance of the collections in terms of both their breadth and their depth. Materials from hundreds of sites were cataloged, many of which were unique items that had never been described and photographed. Some of the largest collections were from sites located along and near Pemiscot Bayou.

Another event led to the analysis described in this volume. In 1987 Carl Chapman, whose entire professional career as professor of anthropology at the University of Missouri was dedicated to Missouri archaeology, was killed, along with his wife, Eleanor, in a traffic accident in Florida. Chapman's tragic and untimely death resulted in almost 50 years of archaeological records being turned over to the university for inventory and curation. Inspection of the archives produced volumes of notes related to the archaeology of southeastern Missouri, which would have formed the basis for volume 3 of Chapman's *The Archaeology of Missouri*. It took several years to acquaint ourselves with exactly what was in Chapman's archives, but by 1989 it was apparent that the records pertaining to the Pemiscot Bayou sites were extensive. Many of the notes and plans, we found out later, were incomplete, but in many cases the missing portions were found housed in boxes with the corresponding artifacts. We realized that we had an opportunity to analyze a unique set of materials and to publish a volume that highlighted their significance. This volume was the result of that realization.

The most difficult aspect of producing the volume was deciding on an organizational outline that presented the information in a clear, logical progression. Two problems became rather obvious early on: (1) the discussion requires at least a moderate background in central Mississippi Valley archaeology and (2) several topics are so interrelated that it is difficult to separate them into chapters. The final product was a compromise that I hope makes sense out of complex issues. Chapter 1 is an introduction to the Pemiscot Bayou locality in terms of the archaeological sites, their significance to regional prehistory, and the people who were responsible for the surveys and excavations discussed in chapters 5 through 7.

Attempting to understand the differences and similarities among the Pemiscot Bayou sites without at least a passing knowledge of how they fit into a regional chronological framework is confusing even to archaeologists familiar with the region. The list of phases proposed for Mississippian-period (post–a.d. 900) remains in southeastern Missouri and adjacent areas has grown over the years, as has the list of ceramic types used to construct the phases. In Chapter 2 Greg Fox and I discuss the historical development of a chronological framework for the middle and late portions of the Mississippian period and illustrate some of the more chronologically important ceramic types that are referred to throughout the volume.

In Chapter 3 Fox and I focus on identifying similarities and differences in the ceramic assemblages from Pemiscot Bayou sites. The reader should note that the data used in Chapter 3 are derived from tables presented in later chapters, where we discuss the individual assemblages in greater depth. This is one of the organizational problems mentioned above, but there appeared to be no way around it. We wanted to make clear early on in the book what some of the similarities and dissimilarities were among the Pemiscot Bayou sites themselves and what the differences were between those sites and other Mississippian-period sites from southeastern Missouri. The chapter is divided into four sections. In the first section we assess the effects of biases in the assemblages—introduced in part by sample size and in part by repeated collecting of the sites over the years by artifact hunters. In the second section we examine the issue of sample diversity in terms of its two components, evenness and richness. In the third section we turn attention to collections from 18 sites—12 in Pemiscot County (10 of which are late Mississippian period sites), 5 in Mississippi County, and 1 in northeastern Arkansas—to determine if the Pemiscot Bayou sites can be distinguished from other Mississippian-period sites in southeastern Missouri in terms of artifact content. The fourth section focuses exclusively on the Pemiscot County sites in terms of similarity/dissimilarity and how the sites relate to each other in terms of space and/or time.

Chapter 4 is an overview of the physical environment. Instead of focusing exclusively on the Pemiscot Bayou locality, I attempt to place its environment and its history of environmental change into a larger framework that includes the upper half of the central Mississippi River valley. It is impossible to understand the prehistory of any portion of southeastern Missouri without a fairly detailed understanding of how the landscape evolved. Few regions of North America underwent such rapid landscape evolution over the last 12,000 years as did the central Mississippi River valley, and these changes had profound effects on how and where people carried out their activities. The landscape that was a backdrop to the activities of the late-period inhabitants of the Pemiscot Bayou communities was a complex mosaic of low floodplain features that formed and reformed over thousands of years as the Mississippi River carved new channels and then backfilled them as it migrated across its floodplain. Dense forests of cottonwood and box elder covered the landscape, and extensive lakes and swamps filled old river channels. To understand the human response to that landscape necessitates not only an in-depth understanding of the nature of the landscape but knowledge of the geographic positioning of its components as well.

In Chapter 5 Dick Marshall and I examine two sites—Kersey and Murphy—that were antecedents to the late Mississippian period Pemiscot Bayou sites. Kersey completely predated the sites that are the focus of this volume; Murphy was founded well before the late sites, but, based on stylistic similarities with other late sites, its occupation lasted well past A.D. 1400. Several large areas were excavated at each site, which produced large quantities of archaeological materials.

The large sizes of the assemblages from the two sites will contribute to our eventual ability to document changes in specific groups of materials through time. However, analysis of the majority of materials from Kersey and Murphy—literally tens of thousands of sherds—is well beyond the scope of this volume. We concentrate instead on burial programs at the two sites and on how these interment practices changed through time. The types of burials evident at Kersey and in the pre–A.D. 1400 component at Murphy are unduplicated at the other sites and allow us to extend our investigation of mortuary programs back to ca. A.D. 900–1000.

In Chapter 6 Tom Holland and I discuss what might be considered the archaeological centerpiece of the Pemiscot Bayou settlements, the Campbell site, which has produced the largest skeletal series and probably the most grave goods known from southeastern Missouri. No discussion of the late-period archaeological record of the central Mississippi Valley is complete without mentioning Campbell, not only because of the amount of material it has produced but also because of what it has produced: an abundance of head pots and other elaborately decorated vessels as well as items manufactured in Europe. Campbell is often cited as a community directly contacted by members of the de Soto expedition, though it is just as conceivable that the items were traded into the community. Regardless, Campbell has produced (to our knowledge) more Spanish material than any other site in southeastern Missouri or northeastern Arkansas. These items include 24 glass chevron beads, a brass book clasp with powdered glass inset to resemble cloisonné, several Clarksdale bells, and miscellaneous pieces of iron and brass. No photographs of these pieces have previously been published.

In Chapter 7 Ray Williams and I summarize what is known about other late-period sites in the Pemiscot Bayou locality, including Berry, Berry II, Braggadocio, Brooks, Cagle Lake, Denton Mounds, Dorrah, Holland, Kinfolk Ridge, McCoy, Nora Tucker, and State Line. The amount of known material from these sites is considerably less than that from Campbell, but the materials are by no means insignificant. Artifacts from these sites document the presence of numerous contemporary communities in the Pemiscot Bayou locality during the late Mississippian period as well as the existence of a fairly standardized ceramic tradition. Brooks is particularly significant because it is a second site that has produced Spanish goods—a fact not reported previously. Cagle Lake and Denton Mounds are important because they are the only sites that have produced data on prehistoric houses.

In Chapter 8, Holland presents an analysis of skeletal data from the sites, with an emphasis on material from Campbell excavated by Leo Anderson, an amateur archaeologist from Van Buren, Missouri. The skeletal remains offer a rare opportunity to examine the health and physical characteristics of late Mississippian period groups in the central Mississippi River valley. Holland makes comparisons between the inhabitants of the Pemiscot Bayou locality and those of the contemporary site of Nodena, located a short distance to the south in Mississippi County, Arkansas.

In Chapter 9 I synthesize our current knowledge of the late prehistory of the Pemiscot Bayou locality and attempt to place the remains in a larger regional perspective. I also discuss some of the directions that future research on materials both from the Pemiscot Bayou locality and from the adjoining portions of northeastern Arkansas and northwestern Tennessee might take. To be sure, significant gaps in our knowledge still exist, but at least we know what important issues remain unresolved and what kinds of information are needed to address those issues. Previously, we were caught somewhere between fact and fiction. Archaeological materials from the Pemiscot Bayou sites may have received little or no systematic analysis, but there is no shortage of accounts that have grown up about the role of the communities in the late-period prehistory of the central Mississippi River valley and what the sociopolitical systems of their inhabitants were. The accounts, while entertaining, are, to borrow Kipling's words, just-so stories—neat concoctions that tell us "things were so, just so, a little time ago."

Unfortunately, archaeological analysis can rarely tell us that things were "just so." The archaeological record is a historical accounting of products that people manufactured, used, and discarded, but it is an incomplete accounting. It rarely tells us, at least in a direct way, much about anything other than, again, what people made, used, and then threw away. We often tend to forget this. Other things that can be learned usually must be inferred from the objects and the contexts in which they are found—a process that opens up an endless number of possibilities but also imposes a certain degree of risk. Using inference can be like building a house of cards: No matter how carefully one adds cards, if one basic inference can be shown to be incorrect, it must be removed, and the whole house is liable to crumble. I want to dismantle the house of cards for Pemiscot Bayou and construct a new one in its place, but I want to build it using a minimum of inference. I want to present the archaeological record, at least the portion that is now known, in clear terms and without much speculation about such things as religious beliefs, political alliances, or social organization. Although in Chapter 9 I entertain the notion that archaeological materials from Pemiscot Bayou and adjoining regions might some day, at least conceivably, be linked to ethnohistorically known groups that resided in the central Mississippi Valley, I do not use ethnohistorical data in the discussion. Although certainly some parallels existed between those groups and previous groups living in the region—some of whom undoubtedly were ancestral to later peoples—little or no evidence exists to assist us in evaluating scenarios constructed using ethnohistorical data. This may prove annoying to those who want cultural reconstructions and discussions of such things as chiefdoms and social systems, but my position is that the archaeological remains are interesting enough in their own right that they do not have to be dressed up in a mantle of speculation.

ACKNOWLEDGMENTS

Several people contributed to this project in important ways. Robert Hoard and James Cogswell served as project manager and assistant manager, respectively, of the National Science Foundation–sponsored systematics-collection project, which led to construction of the database used here. Unless otherwise noted, artifact photographs were taken by Lynden Steele, who by the end of the project had turned into a photographic wizard. The great majority of line drawings were done by Mike Lindsey, who could always find a better method of visually presenting data than what was given to him in rough form. Ceramic type specimens were drawn by Jerry Brightwell. I also thank Ty Martin, Bryce Hurst, Peggy Loy, and Sam Kincaid for their assistance with various aspects of the project. Roger Saucier and Peggy Guccione provided detailed comments on various drafts of the chapter on the physical environment, and both provided additional information, some unpublished. I also thank Beverly Jarrett, Jane Lago, and especially Gloria Thomas of the University of Missouri Press for all the assistance they provided in shepherding the manuscript through various phases of production.

Documentation of the immense variation in late Mississippian period ceramic vessels was greatly enhanced by Kenneth Berry of Holland, Missouri; Alan Banks, Joe Kinker, Mike Miller, and Chuck Adam of metropolitan St. Louis; Tom Campbell and the Brown family of Cooter, Missouri; Clem Caldwell of Danville, Kentucky; Jim Cherry of Springdale, Arkansas; and Roy Hathcock of West Plains, Missouri, all of whom graciously allowed us to photograph materials in their collections. Needless to say, the aesthetic aspect of the volume was also greatly enhanced through the addition of the photographs. I am especially indebted to Kinker, Hathcock, and Cherry for spending long hours with me, discussing not only their collections but also the nature of relic collecting in Pemiscot County. They also freely shared their ideas about stylistic variation and the technological aspects of vessel production. In addition, Cherry allowed me to cite some of his soon-to-be-published data on head-pot distributions. I offer my sincere thanks to all three and look forward to future collaborations.

I greatly appreciate the long hours that Robert Dunnell spent reviewing the manuscript. He forced me to rethink several important issues, especially the issue of sample size, and caught numerous silly errors that would have detracted from the seriousness of the arguments. His work in southeastern Missouri particularly and in archaeological method and theory generally has influenced my thinking considerably over the years.

I also thank my boss, Larry Clark, dean of the College of Arts and Science at the University of Missouri, for allowing me the time to pursue this project. He provided a role model as someone who could administer a large and diverse college and still maintain high scholarly achievement personally. Finally, I thank my wife, Beverly, and my son Aaron, who provided me with unflagging support and encouragement. Their understanding of the long hours involved in analysis and writing made a difficult project more tolerable.

CAT MONSTERS AND HEAD POTS

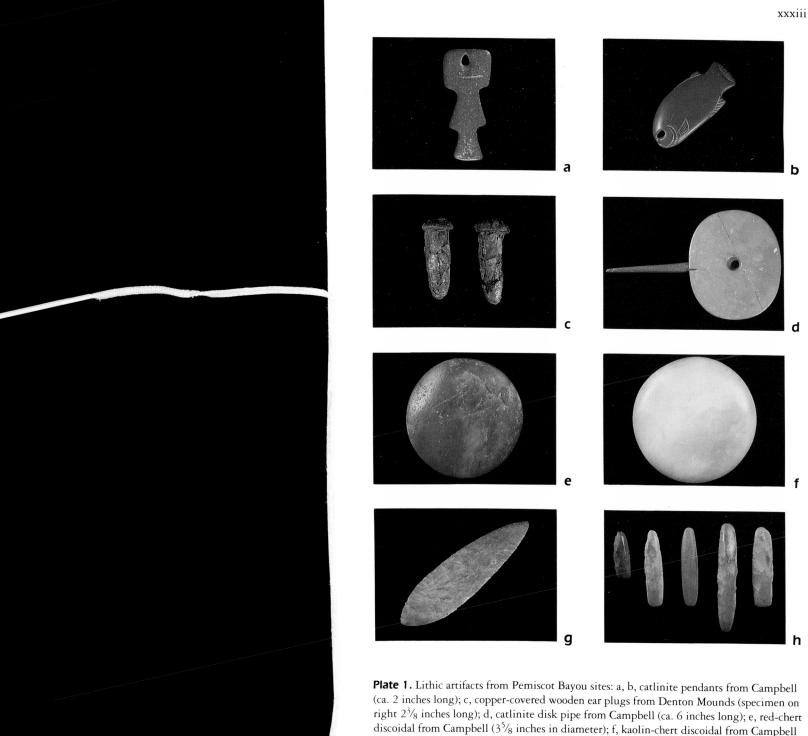

Plate 1. Lithic artifacts from Pemiscot Bayou sites: a, b, catlinite pendants from Campbell (ca. 2 inches long); c, copper-covered wooden ear plugs from Denton Mounds (specimen on right 2⅜ inches long); d, catlinite disk pipe from Campbell (ca. 6 inches long); e, red-chert discoidal from Campbell (3⅝ inches in diameter); f, kaolin-chert discoidal from Campbell (3¼ inches in diameter); g, Kay County–chert blade from Braggadocio (ca. 7 inches long); h, chert adzes from Denton Mounds (specimen second from right 7¼ inches long). All from Hathcock collection.

Plate 2. Ceramic artifacts from Pemiscot County sites: a, red-and-white human-effigy bottle (site unknown; ca. 8 inches high); b, red-slipped (interior) and white-slipped (exterior) conch-shell-effigy bowl from Campbell (ca. 5 inches high); c, human-effigy bottle from Campbell (8¾ inches high); d, red-slipped dog-effigy bottle from Campbell burial 19 (the "shaman" burial; 6¼ inches high); e, red-slipped (interior) and white-slipped (exterior) bowl sherd from Cagle Lake; f, cat-monster bottle with traces of red slip from Campbell (ca. 8 inches high). Specimens a and f from Kinker collection; b from Brown family collection; c from Hathcock collection; d and e from MU collection.

a

b

c

d

Plate 3. Ceramic vessels from Campbell: a, Campbell punctated bottle (5⅝ inches high); b, Campbell punctated jar (3⅞ inches high; burial 55 [same vessel as in Figure 6.17b]); c, Neeley's Ferry plain bowl (3⅜ inches high); d, Rhodes incised bowl (3⅛ inches high). All from Banks collection (specimen b originally from Anderson collection).

a

b

c

d

Plate 4. Ceramic vessels from Pemiscot County sites: a, b, red-slipped bottle from Brooks (5½ inches high); c, Campbell punctated bottle from Campbell (3⅝ inches high); d, red-slipped bowl from Campbell burial 59 containing a serrated mussel-shell "spoon" (2¼ inches high). All from Banks collection (specimen d originally from Anderson collection).

a   b

c   d

Plate 5. Ceramic vessels from Pemiscot County sites: a, red-slipped (interior) and white-slipped (exterior) fish-effigy bowl from Braggadocio (4½ inches high); b, red-slipped (interior) and white-slipped (exterior) conch-shell-effigy bowl from Braggadocio (3½ inches high); c, red-slipped compound bottle-jar from Campbell (9 inches high); d, red-slipped (interior) and white-slipped (exterior) bat-effigy bowl from Campbell (3½ inches high). All from Hathcock collection.

Plate 6. Slipped bottles from Pemiscot County sites: a, Carson red-on-buff from Denton Mounds (7$\frac{1}{8}$ inches high); b, Nodena red-and-white from Denton Mounds (ca. 8 inches high); c, red-slipped from Campbell (ca. 9 inches high); d, Nodena red-and-white from Brooks (7 inches high); e, Nodena red-and-white from Braggadocio (5$\frac{3}{4}$ inches high); f, Nodena red-and-white from Campbell (ca. 9 inches high). Specimen a from MU collection; specimens d and f from Kinker collection; specimens b, c, and e from Hathcock collection.

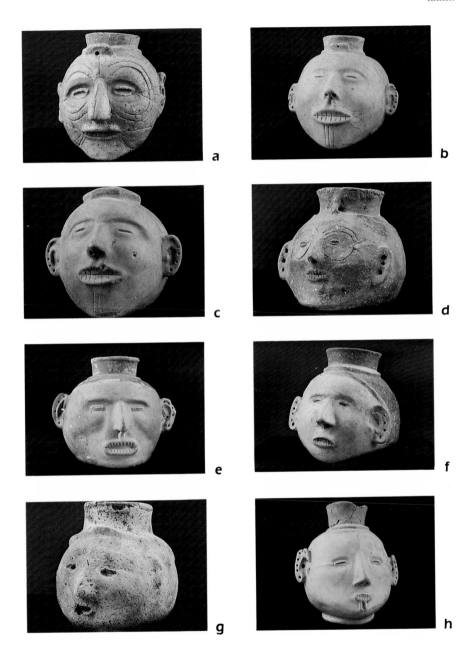

Plate 7. Head pots from Pemiscot County sites: a, Campbell (5³⁄₈ inches high); b, Berry (6¹⁄₄ inches high); c, Campbell (4³⁄₄ inches high); d, Braggadocio (3¹⁄₂ inches high); e, Brooks (6¹⁄₂ inches high); f, Campbell (5 inches high); g, State Line (3⁵⁄₈ inches high); h, unnamed site near Cooter (7 inches high). All from Cherry collection.

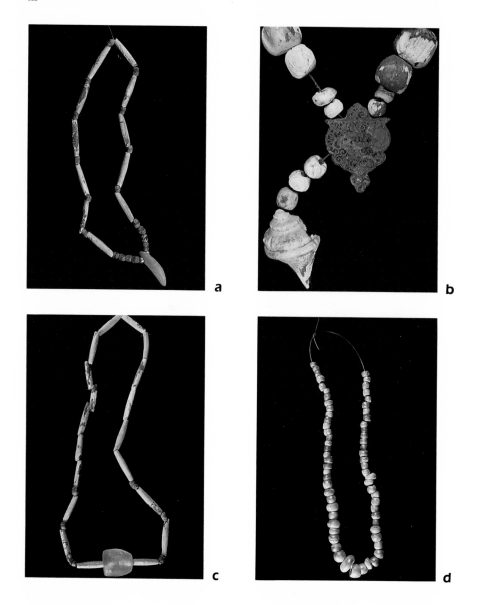

Plate 8. Necklaces from Campbell: a, c, glass chevron beads, bone beads, and (on c) quartz bead; b, shell beads and brass-and-powdered-glass ("cloisonné") book clasp made into a pendant; d, pearl beads. Photos courtesy of R. Hathcock.

1

INTRODUCTION

Michael J. O'Brien

The title of this book, *Cat Monsters and Head Pots,* will have significance for anyone who has at least a passing familiarity with the late Mississippian period (after ca. A.D. 1350) occupation of southeastern Missouri, especially the region drained by Pemiscot Bayou. In fact, no two other terms so adequately capture the essence of Mississippian symbolism as it was represented in formed clay by the prehistoric inhabitants of the dense forests and extensive swamps that covered the landscape in and around the bayou. *Cat monster* is the term commonly applied by archaeologists as well as relic collectors to a particular style of earthenware vessel in which an elongated bowl serves as the body of the monster and incised clay appliqués resting on the bowl rim form its head and tail (Figure 1.1). On other examples, the cat-monster design is incised into the exterior of the bottle, in one case with the cat monster resting on top of a coiled rattlesnake (Figure 1.2). *Head pots* are small clay bottles crafted in the shape of the human head, complete with facial features such as eyes, teeth, and ears, and often with scars and tattoos as well (Figure 1.3). The detailed nature of the faces has led numerous researchers to suggest that the bottles are portrait vessels carrying the likenesses of real people.

Although cat-monster vessels and head pots are two of the most well known features of the archaeological record of southeastern Missouri, they are only small parts of a staggering array of unusual ceramic items that the late-prehistoric inhabitants of the region used and then interred with their dead. On the one hand, the Mississippian-period vessels' beauty has attracted wide attention to the archaeological record of southeastern Missouri, but on the other hand, the objects' commercial value has led to massive destruction of archaeological sites by looters who have no interest in science.

1

Figure 1.1. Cat-monster bowl from Berry (8 inches high). Note the heavily modeled head and neck, including the triforked eye. The incised swirled design on the body is a typical motif on late Mississippian period bottles from the region. This particular specimen had been slipped completely in red. Berry collection.

And yet *science,* it could be argued, is a relative term that is time bound—what was "scientific" a century ago would hardly qualify as such today. Even that which qualified as "state-of-the-art" as recently as a few decades ago today might be looked upon as antiquarianism—the collecting of objects more for their aesthetic value than for anything they can tell us about prehistoric technology, function, or economic systems. And so it went with archaeological investigations in southeastern Missouri. The magnificent ceramic bowls, bottles, and jars that lay hidden in the large, late-prehistoric cemeteries along the St. Francis River and its neighboring Missouri and Arkansas streams such as the Little River and Pemiscot Bayou were a lure to numerous archaeologists (using the term loosely) throughout the late nineteenth and early twentieth centuries (see Chapman 1980: 184). In a few cases they came to the great pottery fields seeking answers to questions such as, Who were the people responsible for creating the large earthen mounds evident in the region? But more often they came to haphazardly mine the mounds and villages for pots. A. J. Conant, writing in *Transactions of the Academy of Science of St. Louis* in 1878, prosaically characterized the region as an archaeologist's paradise:

> There is, doubtless, now no richer field for archaeological research in this great basin of the Mississippi Valley than is to be found in the State of Missouri. The

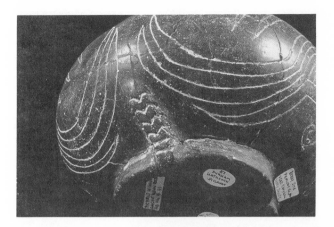

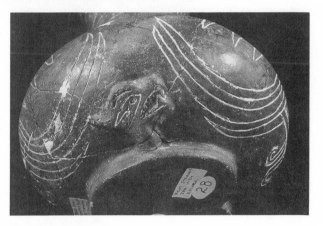

Figure 1.2. Cat-monster bottle from Berry ($7\frac{3}{4}$ inches high). This specimen is one of several bottles known from the Berry and Campbell assemblages, all of which have two engraved faces, one on each side of the vessel, and annular bases. This particular example has a coiled rattlesnake for the base, with the head and tail projecting from opposing sides. Note the familiar tri-lobed eye and the fretlike design on the neck of the vessel—both common late Mississippian period motifs. Kinker collection.

Figure 1.3. Head pot from Berry II (ca. 5½ inches high). Note the deathlike pose, especially the slit eyes and drawn lips. This specimen has tattooing around the eyes and mouth, though most specimens exhibit more extensive and complex tattooing, including a triforked design around the eyes. Note also the ear perforations—in which ear plugs might have hung—and the small node in the upper forehead, both of which are characteristic features. Almost all head pots were painted; the face was either left buff color (the natural color of the vessel) or painted white, while the ears, back of the head, and lower portion of the jaw were painted red. Berry collection.

> wonderful extent and variety of the ancient works and monuments therein, the relics they disclose, the huge burial mounds filled with the bones of the dead, disposed in orderly array, as though by loving hands, along with vessels of pottery of graceful forms and varied patterns, often, too, skillfully ornamented,—all bear witness to a settled and permanent condition of society and government and obedience to law, and to certain convictions of a future life. (Conant 1878: 353)

Conant is silent on how he was able to reconstruct these aspects of late-period prehistoric life, but we can be fairly certain that his insights were not the products of careful excavation. Although it was common practice in the nineteenth and early twentieth centuries to quarry archaeological sites for their pottery, it was not common practice to keep meticulous records of the contexts in which the vessels were found, that is, their depth, position, location within a mapped grid of the site, and any associated objects found with them. In some cases archaeologists were not even present in the field, instead hiring local crews to excavate the mounds and send the pottery back East to museums, where the vessels were exhibited. For the most part, the final reports of these "excavations" were little more than pottery descriptions, though in several instances they provide us with the only information available. For example, the great Bureau of American Ethnology archaeologist William H. Holmes had an intense interest in the prehistory of the Mississippi Valley and produced detailed descriptions and illustrations of ceramic vessels from myriad sites, many of which have been completely emptied of their prehistoric contents (Holmes 1886, 1903).

One exception to the general lack of control in early archaeological excavation was the work of the Bureau of Ethnology Division of Mound Exploration, which carried out a large-scale program of mapping and excavation in 23 states between 1881 and 1890 under the general direction of Cyrus Thomas (1894). B. D. Smith (1981) rightfully labels Thomas's work as the birth of American archaeology, though Meltzer and Dunnell (1992) make a rather convincing case that the title should belong to Holmes. As opposed to the indiscriminate excavations that were the usual practice, Thomas gave strict orders to his field crews on how to map the mounds, to record the strata observed in mound profiles, and to describe the artifacts recovered. Thomas's field parties spent considerable time in the St. Francis basin locating and excavating sites that he realized would be lost to agricultural practices and looting.

Perhaps the most extensive excavations in the region were undertaken during the first two decades of the twentieth century by a young Harvard graduate who traveled the waterways of the southeastern United States in his stern-wheeler, carrying with him a full crew of excavators. The young man, Clarence B. Moore, spent four seasons between 1908 and 1916 in the central Mississippi Valley, including the St. Francis basin. As Morse and Morse (1983: 21) note, "It has become almost traditional to deplore the work of Moore, because of his emphasis on recovery of fine specimens from burials." But as they also point out, he published his results immediately, usually with excellent illustrations, kept excavation records, cataloged his materials, and donated his collections to museums. Moore's primary interest was in obtaining pots, but he also had an interest in provenience:

> The St. Francis valley has yielded more examples of its ware than has any equal area in the United States, and while this pottery has shared in the full description which has been accorded the earthenware of the region to which it belongs, and while we can hope to shed but little new light upon the pottery itself, we shall try to describe in this report the conditions under which the vessels were placed with the dead and the burial customs of the aborigines who made the vessels, details which former seekers of aboriginal remains along the St. Francis have failed to make public. (Moore 1910: 259)

It is readily apparent from the reports of both Thomas (1894) and Moore (e.g., 1910, 1911) that the central Mississippi River valley, even in those early days, was witnessing wholesale destruction of its archaeological resources through activities connected with the commercial sale of prehistoric pottery:

> As the St. Francis (with the possible exception of the Mississippi, a river very many times the length of the St. Francis) long has had the reputation of being richer in aboriginal earthenware than is any other river in the United States, the territory through which the river passes has been for years the headquarters for collectors and for persons wishing to make a livelihood or to increase their means by the sale of Indian pottery, and these individuals have worked for long periods and with indefatigable zeal. (Moore 1910: 259)

Until the recent enactment of state laws to protect human burials, the "indefatigable zeal" to which Moore referred did not abate after his forays into the central Mississippi River valley were completed. If anything, the zeal accelerated throughout the twentieth century. It is anyone's guess as to the number of items actually removed from context during the last century, but based on conversations with numerous landowners in Pemiscot County, Missouri, it is not an unreasonable estimate that well over 5,000 pots have been excavated in that one county alone over the last 50 years. It would be one thing if the archaeological materials were available for study, but for the most part they are scattered across hundreds or thousands of private collections, usually with no accompanying documentation. This is not meant to imply that most collectors are unwilling to share information; quite to the contrary, they are more than willing to work with archaeologists, as I can attest. The problem for the archaeologist lies in tracking down items from a locality such as Pemiscot Bayou and establishing a provenience of origin. Often collectors think pieces in their collections might have come from Pemiscot County or even from a specific site, but they have no way of proving it. I was fortunate to work with collectors who had detailed knowledge not only of artifacts in their collections but of items in other collections as well—a phenomenon that is further testimony to the widespread appeal of late Mississippian period artifacts from Pemiscot County.

There were some attempts by professional archaeologists, often working in conjunction with interested amateurs, to salvage some information from sites in southeastern Missouri before they were destroyed through indiscriminate digging, agricultural development, or road construction. Compared to the wholesale destruction of archaeological resources in the region that occurred as a result of these activities, the amount of excavation was small, but it is not insignificant. For example, considerable work was undertaken in Pemiscot County on Mississippian-period (ca. A.D. 900–1541) sites, several of which contained late-period (after ca. A.D. 1350) components. But except for one short report (Chapman and Anderson 1955), none of the work on the late period has ever been published. This shortcoming, however, has not prevented archaeologists from referring extensively to the Pemiscot County sites in overviews of the region or from assigning the late-period components to phases—spatial-temporal units constructed on the basis of artifact similarity among individual sites or portions of sites. The one site for which a report was published, Campbell (Chapman and Anderson 1955), is highlighted in the literature on the archaeology of the central Mississippi Valley (e.g., D. F. Morse 1990; Morse and Morse 1983; G. P. Smith 1990) because of its late date (into the sixteenth century) and exceptional pottery—including numerous cat-monster vessels and head pots—though the report was preliminary and contains many factual errors.

This volume is an initial step in assembling what is known about the late Mississippian period archaeological record of one small portion of the central Mississippi River valley. In it I attempt to lay out what is known about the archaeological remains in terms of site location, artifacts that have been recovered, and biases in the collections. I also point out directions for future research. It is not intended as a compendium of all artifacts that have been found, which would be virtually impossible to compile, nor is it an exhaustive analysis of extant collections. It is, rather, a fairly intensive treatment of a series of small, late Mississippian period sites that appear to share a number of features in common. The nature of those shared similarities, as well as the differences among sites, is a topic that runs throughout this volume.

The Study Area

The modern boundaries of Pemiscot County, Missouri, the most southeastern of the state's 114 political divisions, form the basic outline of the study area (Figure 1.4). Within the confines of Pemiscot County, focus is narrowed to a series of sites in the southern third of the county—an area termed the Pemiscot Bayou locality after the sluggish, meandering waterway that drains the south-central portion of the county on its way south into Arkansas. The reasons for using geopolitical boundaries are purely practical and in no way should obscure the fact that the prehistoric groups who left the remains discussed here did not limit their activities to the region north of the 36th parallel or west of the Mississippi River. Although we can never be sure of how extensive an area was occupied or used by a prehistoric group or how extensive its kinship network was, enough similarities exist between contemporary archaeological assemblages from Pemiscot County and from surrounding counties, especially those in northeastern Arkansas and western Tennessee, to assume that the study-area limits are entirely arbitrary. My primary reasons for limiting discussion to Pemiscot County are: (a) archaeological remains from the county are well known and thus have figured prominently in discussions of the late-period occupation of the central Mississippi River valley, and (b) archaeological materials and site records from the county are housed at the University of Missouri and thus were easily accessible. Also, the Pemiscot Bayou collections were recently inventoried and the information computerized, which facilitated data retrieval.

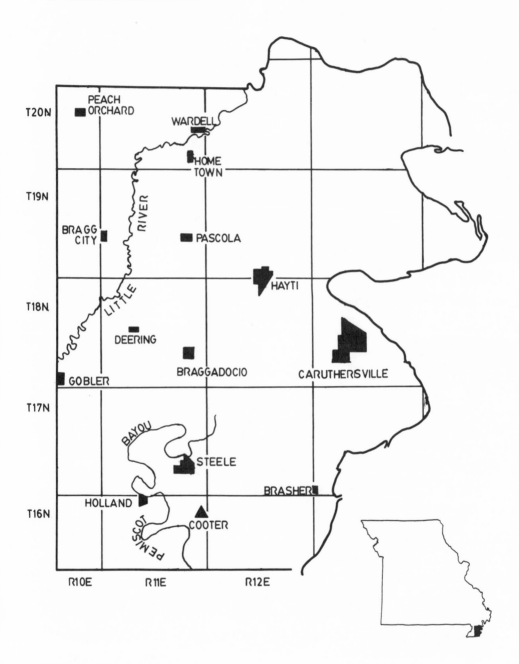

Figure 1.4. Map of Pemiscot County, Missouri, showing locations of towns and townships.

The Archaeological Survey of Missouri lists 11 Pemiscot County sites that have produced materials that appeared late (post–A.D. 1350) in the archaeological sequence of the central Mississippi River valley: Berry (23PM59), Brooks (23PM56), Cagle Lake (23PM13), Campbell (23PM5), Denton Mounds (23PM549), Dorrah (23PM11), Holland (23PM2), Kinfolk Ridge (23PM15), McCoy (23PM21), Murphy (23PM43), and Nora Tucker (23PM552) (Figure 1.5). At least 4 other sites—known to relic collectors as Braggadocio, State Line, an unnamed site near State Line, and what is referred to as Berry II—have produced contemporary remains, though very little information exists on these sites. Ray Williams and I discuss these in Chapter 7. For comparative purposes, Dick Marshall and I discuss in Chapter 5 both another Pemiscot County site—Kersey (23PM42), which dates pre–A.D. 1350—and the earlier Mississippian-period component at Murphy.

It is important to point out, primarily for the benefit of those with some knowledge of the Pemiscot Bayou sites, that the names that have been applied to the sites are confusing. Several sites go by different names, and in at least three cases the same name has been used for two different sites. I thought it wise to point out the inconsistencies so that the record would be set straight. For example, Holland has been referred to as both "Machlin" and "Cooter–Holland Junction" (Marshall 1965); Campbell as "Cooter" (S. Williams 1954); Denton Mounds as "Rhoades" (Hathcock 1988); McCoy as "Chute" (S. Williams 1954); Dorrah as "Matthews"; Cagle Lake as "Kersey" (Hathcock 1988), "Kersey II" (Leo Anderson's notes [Price and Price 1979]), and "Persimmon Grove" (S. Williams 1954); Murphy as "Caruthersville" (S. Williams 1954); and Kersey as "Canady." Repetition of the name *Kersey* has caused considerable confusion. Early on, I was baffled by the appearance of late Mississippian period vessels from Kersey, since none of the materials excavated by Marshall (1965, n.d. [see Chapter 5]) were that late. Hathcock (1988), for example, illustrates at least four vessels from "Kersey," one of which is a cylindrical container covered with an engraved rattlesnake motif. It was only after reading Leo Anderson's notes that I realized that what artifact collectors called "Kersey" was what is referred to in the literature (J. R. Williams 1968) as "Cagle Lake." I also was, for a while, unaware that two sites had the name *Berry*. The head pot shown in Figure 1.3 is labeled "Berry," but, based on what I now know, the site is located several miles away from the more famous site with the same name. I term the site "Berry II." S. Williams (1954: 188), incidentally, mentions a site that he calls "Frakes," which is listed in the archaeological survey as 23PM46. I was unable to locate the site, though the survey form, the information on which was taken directly from Williams's Lower Mississippi Valley Survey sheet, shows its location on Pemiscot Bayou, near where several late-period vessels reportedly were excavated prior to land leveling.

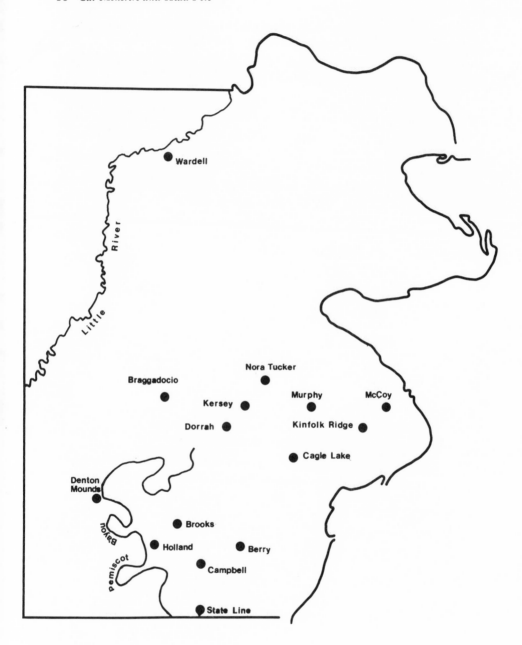

Figure 1.5. Locations of archaeological sites in the study area.

Archaeological Work in the Pemiscot Bayou Locality

The first modern archaeological work along Pemiscot Bayou was a survey of eight sites by Stephen Williams, undertaken as part of his doctoral dissertation field-work (S. Williams 1954). His general goals paralleled those established for the monumental survey of the lower Mississippi River valley conducted between 1940 and 1947 (Phillips et al. 1951) and for the more restricted Central Mississippi Valley Archaeological Survey begun in 1949 (Griffin and Spaulding 1952), namely, to record the locations of archaeological sites and to collect enough sherds to place the sites within a temporal framework. On the basis of surface collections, Williams assigned four of the Pemiscot Bayou sites to what he termed the "Pemiscot Bayou phase" and three of the sites to his chronologically later "Nodena phase" (discussed below). Morse and Morse (1983: 27) note that Williams's interpretation of the cultural sequence in terms of space and time is still the basis for what is published on southeastern Missouri.

In 1954 Leo Anderson, an avocational archaeologist from Van Buren, Missouri, began a series of visits to a locale just east of Cooter in Pemiscot County that was well known for the ceramic vessels it produced. The site has come to be known as "Campbell," though as mentioned above it was previously known as "Cooter" (e.g., S. Williams 1954). Over the next 15 years, Anderson would excavate 254 intact late Mississippian period vessels and 218 complete or nearly complete skeletons (only 132 were removed from the field), one of the largest skeletal collections from the central Mississippi River valley. Anderson was assisted by his wife, Mary Ellen, and, for part of the year 1954, by Carl and Eleanor Chapman (Figures 1.6 and 1.7). The Anderson-Chapman collaboration produced a preliminary report of the excavation in *The Missouri Archaeologist* (Chapman and Anderson 1955), but it was another 36 years before a comprehensive report was completed (Holland 1991; Chapter 6, this volume). Most of the vessels associated with the burials were either given to friends and landowners or placed on display in Anderson's small museum in Van Buren, though several vessels were given to the University of Missouri and several pieces were donated to the Peabody Museum of Archaeology and Ethnology at Yale University. Anderson's museum holdings subsequently were divided, and individual vessels were sold at auction. The only documentation of the vessels that exists is in the form of notes and photographs made by Cynthia and James Price (1979) just prior to the sale and in Anderson's field notes, which were copied by the Prices and placed in the University of Missouri Museum of Anthropology archives.

Figure 1.6. Excavators at Campbell, 1954: a, Leo Anderson; b, Mary Ellen Anderson; c, Mary Ellen Anderson with landowner C. V. Campbell; d, Eleanor Chapman.

Figure 1.7. Carl Chapman at Campbell, 1954.

In some respects, publication of the Campbell report (Chapman and Anderson 1955)—complete with Eleanor Chapman's rendition of the famous head pot from burial 10 on the cover (Figure 1.8)—ushered in an era of intense interest in the late Mississippian period remains along Pemiscot Bayou. Unfortunately, not all of this interest was shown by professional and amateur archaeologists. I calculate that the majority of looting of the Pemiscot Bayou sites occurred between 1956 and 1977, including the removal of burials located deep inside the mound at Campbell (Chapter 6). Prior to Anderson's work at Campbell, the Pemiscot Bayou sites appear to have escaped the ravages of pothunting that sites in northeastern Arkansas had been experiencing since the 1800s. The Pemiscot Bayou sites are on average smaller than those to the south, and they never contained large mounds; hence they may not have attracted much attention. By 1965, however, many of the Pemiscot Bayou sites must have looked as if they had been bombed, as pothunting reached a fever pitch throughout the locality. Anderson, who usually

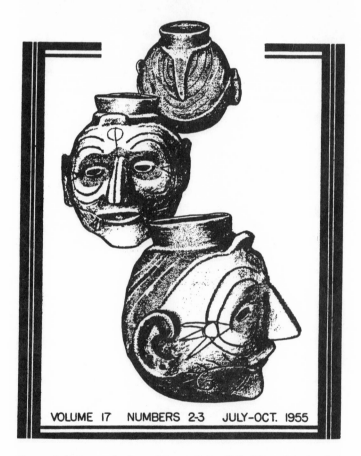

THE MISSOURI ARCHAEOLOGIST

VOLUME 17   NUMBERS 2-3   JULY-OCT. 1955

Figure 1.8. Cover of volume 17, nos. 2–3, of *The Missouri Archaeologist*, with drawings of the famous Campbell head pot associated with burial 10, excavated by Anderson. Other head pots have been found at Campbell, but Anderson's vessel is perhaps still the most famous.

kept notebooks on his work, spent part of 1965 working at Berry (Figure 1.5). However, because of the extensive looting that was taking place and his desire to outrace the pothunters, he could keep no records of his activities (Price and Price 1979: 113). Hence, as opposed to the information that exists for Campbell, there exist only unprovenienced vessels from Berry (Chapter 7).

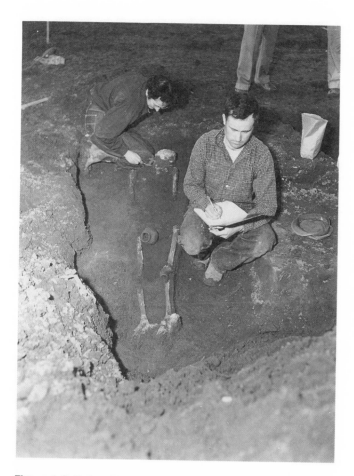

Figure 1.9. Robert T. Bray, research associate at the University of Missouri, working at Murphy, 1955, with Jean T. Hamilton in the background.

Chapman returned to Pemiscot County late in 1954 to begin an emergency salvage of Mississippian-period burials unearthed when a small rise was being leveled southwest of Caruthersville. The rise, part of the Murphy site (Chapter 5), turned out to be a man-made mound that contained a complex series of strata, numerous burials with associated grave goods, and the remains of several mortuary-related structures, that is, buildings in which bodies were prepared for interment. Work was completed in the spring of 1955. The Murphy excavation was an excellent example of Chapman's ability to rally amateurs and professionals to his archaeological causes. The excavation was directed by Robert Bray (Figure 1.9) and Richard Marshall (Figure 1.10a), with help from numerous nonprofessional members of the Missouri Archaeological Society, who, like Henry and Jean Hamilton (Figure 1.10b), gave up their Thanksgiving holidays, piled their children in the car, and raced down to Pemiscot County to help out. Unfortu-

a

b

Figure 1.10. Excavators working at Murphy, 1955: a, Richard A. Marshall, research associate at the University of Missouri; b, Carl H. Chapman (left) with Henry W. Hamilton and Jean T. Hamilton.

nately, despite the importance of the Murphy site for understanding the Mississippian-period sequence, no information on the excavation was produced aside from a brief and highly speculative note (Chapman 1957).

In the 1960s the University of Missouri–Columbia began several years of intensive fieldwork in southeastern Missouri geared toward salvaging information from sites slated for destruction through land leveling and road construction. Numerous reports, theses, and dissertations resulted from those concerted efforts (e.g., Hopgood 1969a, 1969b; Marshall 1965; J. R. Williams 1964, 1967, 1968, 1971, 1972, 1974), and while the works presented brief descriptive accounts of artifact classes, primarily ceramic materials, for the most part they were project- or site-specific, and their authors relied heavily on existing spatial-temporal frameworks to organize the materials. The reports also had extremely limited distribution. Work in Pemiscot County included a survey of Portage Open Bay—a drainage that forms part of the northern border of Pemiscot County (Hopgood 1969b)—and partial excavation of four sites along Pemiscot Bayou. Portions of McCoy and Cagle Lake were excavated in 1967 (J. R. Williams 1968; Chapter 7, this volume), Denton Mounds in 1968 (J. R. Williams 1972; Chapter 7, this volume), and Kersey in 1964 and 1965 (Marshall 1965, n.d.; Chapter 5, this volume). These were the last excavations by professional archaeologists undertaken in Pemiscot County.

Significance of the Pemiscot Bayou Sites

Although almost no published, or at least widely disseminated, information exists on the Pemiscot Bayou sites, this by no means implies that continued references to the sites are not made in the literature, especially that pertaining to the archaeological record of northeastern Arkansas (e.g., Lafferty and Cande 1989; D. F. Morse 1989, 1990; P. A. Morse 1981, 1990; Morse and Morse 1983; G. P. Smith 1990). As noted in the Preface, the archaeological renown of the Pemiscot Bayou sites stems in large part from their appearance late in the archaeological sequence—a time period just prior to or in some cases overlapping with European entradas into the region—and the recovery of Spanish trade goods at Campbell. Contributing to the significance of the sites is their geographic location—they form perhaps the most northern group of sites in the central Mississippi River valley that were occupied during the late fifteenth and sixteenth centuries. Proponents of what has become known as the "vacant-quarter hypothesis" (see below) maintain that a vast portion of the Mississippi River valley north of the Pemiscot Bayou locality—including the Cairo Lowland and the Western Lowlands (Chapter 4)—was essentially abandoned sometime during the late fourteenth or early fifteenth centuries, with the population moving south into southern Pemiscot County, northeastern Arkansas, and perhaps northwestern Tennessee (Morse and Morse 1983). Opponents of the vacant-quarter hypothesis maintain that the evidence is being misread and that the region was not abandoned. I certainly agree with Wesler (1991: 278), who notes that the post–A.D. 1400 occupation of the central Mississippi Valley is the "most vexing problem in the [regional] Mississippian period archaeology. . . . To a great extent this is an argument about chronology and sequence and about radiocarbon dates and horizon markers."

Abandonment and population movement, especially as they relate to the origin of the Pemiscot Bayou communities, are important topics that I take up in Chapter 9. To set the stage for that discussion, we can briefly examine the issues and the evidence for abandonment. The debate began with two papers presented by S. Williams in 1977 and 1978 (but published, in reverse order, in 1980 and 1983), in which he formulated a series of late-period markers (his Markala horizon) and commented on the geographical distribution of those markers. When the distribution was plotted, according to Williams (1983), a large void appeared in the center, which he termed the "vacant quarter." The area centers on the mouth of the Ohio River and includes eastern Missouri as far south as about New Madrid. Williams's use of the term *vacant* was not meant to imply that the region was completely void of people; rather, it refers to the desertion of large, fortified mound centers that occurred, according to Williams (1990: 173), between A.D. 1450 and 1550 (most archaeologists [e.g., Morse and Morse 1983] place the abandonment between about A.D. 1350 and 1400).

Williams's scheme has enjoyed widespread support among archaeologists working in the region (e.g., Morse and Morse 1983; D. F. Morse 1990; Price and Price 1990; B. D. Smith 1986), though Lewis (1986, 1990b) has raised objections to the proposal. Lewis's argument—that the evidence for the lack of late-period sites is not being recognized because of a bias on the part of the analysts—has considerable merit. That bias, according to Lewis (1990b), stems from the belief that all late-period evidence should look the same. In other words, late Mississippian period artifacts from the vacant quarter, if they were there, would look the same as artifacts from, say, the confluence of the Wabash and Ohio rivers or from the extreme southeastern Missouri–northeastern Arkansas region. In short, Lewis argues that the evidence of sizable populations is there, but we do not recognize it. Again, Wesler (1991: 279) sums up the problem nicely:

> Much of the argument arises from too few data, so that both sides have to argue negative cases. If there were a convincing explanation for a late prehistoric abandonment of a fertile environment, then the vacant-quarter hypothesis would be stronger. . . . On the other hand, Lewis's case for continued occupation until European disruption rests in part on the argument that late occupations have not been recognized, because little changed in artifact assemblages and settlement patterns after A.D. 1300. A further problem is that the debate polarized so quickly that alternative scenarios have not been considered adequately.

Regardless of how one views the archaeological record of the so-called vacant quarter, the Pemiscot Bayou locality, which, based on available evidence, never had large, fortified centers, continued to exhibit permanent settlements along its relict natural levees. I say "continued to exhibit" because, unless I am reading the archaeological record incorrectly, the Pemiscot Bayou locality contained numerous early and middle Mississippian period (pre–A.D. 1350) communities. This is not to say, however, that these same communities were occupied during the late Mississippian period; in fact, as noted throughout this volume, many of the artifact collections from late-period sites contain only small amounts of earlier material remains. Is this a result of collection bias, or, around A.D. 1350, was there, for whatever reason, a shift in community location? Or did ceramic vessels play a more important role during the late portion of the Mississippian period than they had earlier? Collection bias is discussed in some detail in the following section—and it is clear the collections are biased—but it is difficult to escape the facts that some large early and middle Mississippian period sites such as Kersey do not contain much if any later material (Murphy is an exception) and that, with the exception of Murphy, I have never seen a ceramic vessel from one of the late-period sites that could definitely be assigned to an early or middle Mississippian period occupation. Resolution of the question of continuity in or disruption of earlier settlement patterns in the Pemiscot Bayou locality should shed significant light on the vacant-quarter hypothesis. Specific methods for accomplishing this task are outlined in Chapter 9.

S. Williams (1980) lumped Campbell, along with McCoy and Holland, in his late-period Armorel phase (see Chapter 2), a group to which Price and Price (1990) added Cagle Lake and Murphy. Williams (1990: 178) views the "Armorel phase towns . . . [as] vibrant cultural centers at one end of the Markala trade routes. They were very much going concerns when de Soto and his Spanish vanguard arrived: up and down the St. Francis River were dozens of thriving towns and villages, grouped into separate demi-Chiefdoms. They met de Soto, and he was theirs, forever." Williams doesn't tell us how he knows that the various groups living along the St. Francis River arranged themselves politically into chiefdoms, nor does he tell us what he means by "de Soto . . . was theirs," but he clearly recognizes the importance of the Pemiscot Bayou sites in the prehistory of the central Mississippi River valley.

The question of whether the de Soto expedition ever reached any of the Armorel-phase settlements is probably unanswerable.[1] In fact, there is no incontrovertible evidence that any inhabitant of Campbell or any other Armorel-phase site ever saw a Spaniard. Evidence of contact with the Spanish has been found on sites in the greater St. Francis drainage basin (see D. F. Morse 1990: 82), including Campbell and Brooks, but the items could have been traded in from elsewhere long after the de Soto expedition had vacated the region. Thus I find it difficult

---

1. One skeleton of a Euro-American apparently was recovered from Middle Nodena in Mississippi County, Arkansas (D. F. Morse 1989), though the ethnic affiliation is unknown.

to support Morse's contentions that (a) Campbell "probably was the frontier trading site visited by Garcilaso de la Vega's informants in 1541 when they traded beans and European items for salt and copper" and that (b) "[b]ecause of the emphasis on indirect European trading, Campbell may well have moved south where it became the site of the Arkansas post, Osotouy, in 1686" (1990: 82). These contentions, unfortunately, are well beyond those that the available data allow.

The Database and Its Biases

Despite the obvious significance of the Pemiscot Bayou sites to developing a better understanding of the late prehistory of the central Mississippi River valley, we are faced with an equally obvious and, unfortunately, serious problem—the unreliability of data generated through analysis of materials from the sites. Too few archaeologists working in the region have confronted this problem head on, relying instead primarily on cursory examination of small collections. All 11 late Pemiscot Bayou sites have, at one time or another, been surface collected by individuals who either reported the results of the collection or sent the material to the University of Missouri for storage. As with any suite of materials that forms the nucleus of an archaeological study, not all site assemblages are equal in terms of size or classes of material represented. Hence coverage of the sites is, by extension, uneven in terms of topics covered. For example, although analyses of burial treatment and skeletal remains are important components of the examination of the Pemiscot Bayou sites, the size of the data sets ranges from no skeletons and no intact grave vessels from several sites to 218 skeletons and over 250 associated vessels from Campbell. The quality of the data sets also varies considerably. For example, skeletal-element recovery was, for the most part, excellent at Campbell—in part because of the condition of the material in the ground (easily recoverable) and in part because of the training of the excavator (Leo Anderson). In short, Anderson took his time and excavated carefully. Available skeletal series from other sites, however, in addition to being much smaller than that from Campbell, are spotty in terms of elements present. This resulted in some cases from careless excavation and in others from moist soil conditions. For example, skeletons at Murphy were excavated by a trained crew, but the field notes make it clear that high levels of soil moisture had destroyed a great majority of the bones.

The database was also conditioned by the goals and objectives of many different researchers, some of whom were working under duress to salvage materials that were in imminent danger of being destroyed. Thus they often did not have the luxury of opening large areas or even of excavating at a slower pace. At McCoy, for example, 48 burials were mapped prior to land leveling, but the field crew did not have time to carefully excavate them and to remove any vessels or other inclusions that were in association. Skeletal material was also recovered at Dorrah and Cagle Lake, but again time constraints precluded excavation of associated grave goods. At Murphy a mortuary mound and related structure were excavated, as were the skeletons associated with the mound and the structure, but the crew did not excavate any houses. Knowledge of late Mississippian period houses in the Pemiscot Bayou locality comes from Cagle Lake and Denton Mounds, where 1 house at each site was excavated, and from McCoy, where 38 house outlines were mapped and 22 were measured.

In summary, the database for the late Mississippian period occupation of the Pemiscot Bayou locality is diverse and is applicable to a broad spectrum of topics of archaeological interest. On the downside, there is a distinct lack of *redundant* data for several important topics. Therefore, it needs to be made clear what the features are of each data set used and what the biases are that condition the reliability of each set—a point repeated throughout this volume.

Quite apart from the issue of sampling bias is another type of bias, this one introduced during analysis of the materials. Previous attempts to understand the archaeological record of Pemiscot Bayou, like the record of many localities, have been based on comparing broad similarities and differences among assemblages so that spatial-temporal units (phases) could be constructed to encompass supposed like assemblages and thus separate them from ones that appeared to be qualitatively and, in some cases, quantitatively different. But in reality the phases have masked substantial variation in the archaeological record, thereby reducing our ability to pinpoint, let alone understand, subtle differences among assemblages—differences that might be related to time, space, function, or myriad other dimensions.

Part of the confusion over time and space—when certain traits arose, how widespread they were, and when they died out—is attributable in part to the complexity of the archaeological record, but archaeologists themselves have exacerbated the problem. Instead of keeping separate the issues of artifact style, form, and function and then applying those dimensions against both time and space, they have conflated the dimensions, in the process shifting analysis and subsequent discussion, inadvertently or otherwise, to how similar or dissimilar one set of artifacts is to or from another. The result has been the construction of a plethora of normative constructs—phases and ceramic types—that have the end result of masking the very thing we want to know about: variation.

But, one might ask, isn't difference variation? By stating that two objects are dissimilar, aren't we in actuality pinpointing variation? The answer to this question is a resounding *no*. Noting that two things are dissimilar tells us nothing about the ways in which they are dissimilar or about *how* dissimilar they are. Archaeologists have attempted to sort through this problem by splitting and resplitting categories of artifacts, such as ceramic vessels and sherds, into finer and finer subdivisions, but such exercises usually have as their central goal only chronological and spatial ordering. In other words, the ceramic "types" that are the result of the sorting exercise hopefully can be used to date the artifact assemblages of which they are a part and to link assemblages across space. This use of ceramic types is entirely appropriate, as long as the types perform up to expectation. And, in fact, extremely high marks can be given to several well-known ceramic types created for late Mississippian period vessels because they are meaningful in terms of the time units they represent. For example, Nodena red-and-white is a type that occurs with considerable frequency on sites in southeastern Missouri and northeastern Arkansas. It is an excellent late-period marker—a pedigree established through chronological controls that fix it as a post–A.D. 1350 type. I seriously doubt that any amount of future excavation will change its temporal position.

But the type Nodena red-and-white, along with other chronologically useful ceramic types that occur in the central Mississippi Valley, is not particularly useful for examining dimensions of technology or function, since neither technological nor functional dimensions were included in the type descriptions. All that matters from the standpoint of the type description is that a vessel is painted red and white. Yet, from the standpoint of technology, considerable variation exists among Nodena red-and-white vessels from widely spaced geographic locales (Dunnell and Jackson 1992), demonstrating that the vessels were made locally as opposed to being trade items that originated in a few central locales. When a sherd is cataloged simply as "Nodena red-and-white," variation in paste composition or in minerals used to create the white paint is ignored. In like manner, Nodena red-and-white is a decorative dimension that occurs on a wide variety of vessel forms (e.g., Hathcock 1988: 96–101), though in most cases variation is compressed by using catchall terms such as *bottle, jar,* and *bowl.* These terms, however, tell us little or nothing about how a particular vessel was used—a point addressed in Chapter 2. Unfortunately, when attempts are made to get around these problems, the resulting constructs—types based on combinations of technological, formal, *and* stylistic dimensions—are unwieldy creations. They are also extremely asymmetrical, meaning that the definitional emphasis for one type might be on decoration and function and for another type on paste composition and decoration. This problem will rear its ugly head in Chapter 9 when I examine efforts to create spatial subdivisions among contemporary components in the greater St. Francis drainage basin.

The case can be made, and often is, that types are not formulated to be end-alls; if other information is needed, such as information on vessel form or paste composition, the items placed in a particular type can be reexamined in light of the new research problems. Although in theory materials *can* be reexamined, they rarely are. What usually happens—and the central Mississippi River valley is a case in point—is that the materials are lumped into types, the type frequencies from a site are published, and the materials are never looked at again. The types, however, live on and are adopted by other researchers, who continue to pigeonhole materials that appear to be reasonably close to the original type descriptions. Perhaps the types are modified a bit through time as variants are discovered that do not fit the type norms, and perhaps some attempts are made to control for temporal and spatial variation, but the usual by-products of such exercises—either new types or varieties of existing types—are still aggregates of many different kinds of dimensions, such as how a vessel was made, what its form is, and how it was decorated.

I gave serious thought during analysis to abandoning established ceramic types and developing a series of classes that would address technology, decoration, form, and function separately. I abandoned the idea for the simple reason that it was beyond the scope of the project. My main goal in producing this volume was to make available the information that exists on the Pemiscot Bayou sites—information that I hope other researchers will use. At this point, where emphasis is on chronological ordering, it was deemed best to present the data in terms used by the majority of archaeologists working in the central Mississippi River valley. However, we are only delaying the inevitable. To understand changes made in prehistoric material classes such as ceramic vessels, we will have to set aside the type concept and focus on minute variation at the technological, formal, and functional levels. In effect, such progress has been made (e.g., Dunnell and Feathers 1991; Dunnell and Jackson 1992; Feathers 1989, 1990; Feathers and Scott 1989; Million 1975, 1980; O'Brien and Holland 1990, 1992; Steponaitis 1983), though decoration still receives the majority of archaeological attention.

In the following chapter Greg Fox and I examine how archaeologists have gone about creating ceramic types and how they have used those types to order sets of materials chronologically and spatially. The discussion is a distillation of dozens of local archaeological sequences and a composite of nomenclature that has evolved over the past four decades. We slice through the nomenclature and focus on the essential aspects of what is at best a very confusing situation.

2

SORTING ARTIFACTS IN SPACE AND TIME

Michael J. O'Brien and Gregory L. Fox

 Archaeologists are forever sorting artifacts into groups based on shared characteristics of the objects being studied. The assumption underlying many of these exercises is that things that appear similar were made by the same group of people or by related groups. Thus the conclusion is, at least intuitively, that items similar in appearance should have been made in locales near each other and at roughly the same time. If this assumption is true, then the objects can be used archaeologically to control for space and time, that is, to link assemblages that were both contemporary and located fairly close together. Archaeologists have introduced many caveats into these assumptions, especially caveats warning of pitfalls introduced by not keeping various analytical dimensions separate, such as style and function (e.g., Dunnell 1978; O'Brien and Holland 1990, 1992). As long as we maintain analytical focus on *stylistic* features of the archaeological record, our efforts are really no different from those of biologists, who use coincidence of homologous anatomical features—those that result from genea- logical closeness—to link related groups of plants or animals. On the other hand, when focus is shifted to *functional* features as markers of temporal and spatial relations, the results will often prove spurious, as is discussed in Chapter 9.

 In this chapter we examine the results of archaeological attempts to categorize Mississippian-period material remains from southeastern Missouri in terms of space and time. We preface the discussion with a look at some of the various "index fossils" that have been used to draw temporal and spatial boundaries around the archaeological sites. These "index fossils" consist primarily, though by no means exclusively, of decorated ceramic vessels or fragments from those vessels. What we will find is that the basic approach to slicing up the archaeological record in terms of space and time has remained fairly constant over nearly the past half century, but the resulting slices have changed considerably in terms of size as well as nomenclature. We will also find that often little agreement exists over how best to describe the index fossils used as the basis for partitioning the archaeological record.

Typological Systems for Ceramic Materials

Phillips et al. (1951) created the first comprehensive ceramic typological system for the central Mississippi River valley—a system that with some modifications (especially Phillips 1970) still forms the basis for how sherds and vessels from archaeological sites in the region are categorized. The authors envisioned ceramic types as continua in which individual ceramic vessels might vary within a single potter's work but with variation tending to cluster fairly tightly about a norm (Phillips et al. 1951: 62). Further, the authors were of the opinion that popular ceramic "styles" were tied to active population centers and that styles varied between the centers, subject to ethnographic and geographic factors in proportion to the distances between the centers. Phillips et al. (1951: 63) note that "the most carefully defined types always overlap" and as such are *"created units of the ceramic continuum"* (emphasis in original). The frequently implied goal of their typological framework was to identify variation that made sense archaeologically—variation that allowed distinct time-space contexts to be distinguished.

Phillips et al. (1951: 69) described 20 ceramic types for the Mississippian period in the Mississippi Valley.[1] Despite much debate in the 1950s and 1960s over the relative merits of type-variety classification schemes versus simple type classification (Ford 1954, 1961; Phillips 1958; R. E. Smith et al. 1960; Wheat et al. 1958), the Phillips et al. (1951) types were standards until publication of Phillips's *Archaeological Survey in the Lower Yazoo Basin, Mississippi, 1949–1955* in 1970, when the type-variety system came into vogue. In that study Phillips expanded the original 20 types into a system of over 40 types and 88 varieties in an attempt to refine the existing ceramic categorization system. Types, according to Phillips, should be established primarily on the basis of paste (e.g., clay-tempered, coarse-shell-tempered, fine-shell-tempered), surface treatment (e.g., plain-surface, cord-

---

1. The original 20 Mississippian-period ceramic types formulated by Phillips et al. (1951: 69) are (with capitalization of modifiers removed and punctuation marks added): Neeley's Ferry plain, Parkin punctated, Barton incised, Ranch incised, Vernon Paul appliquéd, Fortune noded, Bell plain, Kent incised, Rhodes incised, Walls engraved, Hull engraved, Old Town red, Carson red-on-buff, Nodena red-and-white, Avenue polychrome, Hollywood white-filmed, Wallace incised, Owens punctated, Leland incised, and Arcola incised.

marked), and design (e.g., incised, stamped). A secondary set of dimensions—modes of form and modes of decoration—is used to establish varieties within types. Phillips's opinion was that types are related to widespread regional expression of cultural and historical relations. Further, he viewed varieties and modes within a ceramic type as reflecting specific areal and temporal variations in the norm of the type (Phillips 1970: 25). Like most typologists, Phillips (1970: 25) did not view his system as complete but instead suggested that any typological system requires ongoing refinement until such time as it has reached the end of its usefulness.

Problems in Using the Typological Systems

Unfortunately, Phillips's system is not now the dynamic entity he envisioned but rather has become stagnant, with little if any effort expended to refine those "narrow intervals on the sliding scale of time and area" (Phillips 1970: 25). Both the Phillips et al. (1951) typology and the Phillips (1970) type-variety system exhibit overlap among and between types. As Phillips (1970: 26) states, "Intergrading [of types] is inevitable; it is in fact their very nature. As data accumulate and the sorting criteria become more explicit, two varieties juxtaposed in time or space naturally become more sortable." For example, based on their work at Campbell, Chapman and Anderson (1955) created three new (they termed them "provisional") types, one of which was Campbell punctated. Prior to their work, punctated sherds and vessels were placed in the type Parkin punctated, created by Phillips et al. (1951). Chapman and Anderson noted that in their surface-collected and excavated assemblages from Campbell there were numerous bottles and bottle sherds that had several rows of punctations restricted to the vessel neck (Figure 2.1b) as opposed to being spread over the body of the vessel (Figure 2.1a). As Phillips suggested, new data allowed creation of a new type—one that appeared to Chapman and Anderson to have spatial and chronological significance. As is shown in later chapters, Campbell punctated appears to be an excellent late Mississippian period marker, regardless of whether it is viewed as a type (as we do here) or as a mode (as Phillips [1970: 62] does). Either way, the result is the same.

But the archaeological record is replete with cases that are not so clear-cut—a fact not lost on Phillips (1970: 26), who, just having made the happy claim that new data allow troublesome types to become sortable, continued in a more pessimistic vein: "[J]ust about that time we begin to discern an intermediate category and the problem of sortability is with us once again." The following example bears out the truth in Phillips's statement and also helps to point out some of the differences between the type system of Phillips et al. (1951) and the type-variety system Phillips later developed (1970). Here we examine how to type vessels that have swirled designs on their exteriors.

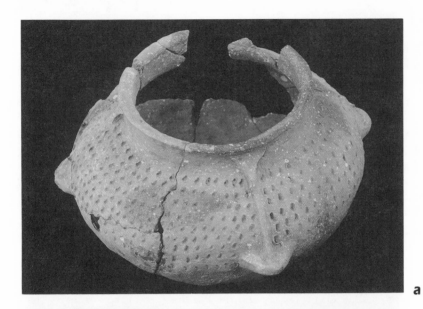

a

b

Figure 2.1. Punctated-vessel types: a, Parkin punctated, first described by Phillips et al. (1951); b, Campbell punctated, first described by Chapman and Anderson (1955) based on their work at Campbell. Vessel 2.1a (4 inches high) is from Berry, and 2.1b (6¼ inches high) is from Campbell, burial 98. Both in the University of Missouri–Columbia (hereafter MU) collection.

There is a type, labeled "Rhodes incised" by Phillips et al. (1951: 127), that includes jars, bowls, and bottles that exhibit spiraled designs incised into their exteriors. Often the lines are quite wide and deep and originate from the midpoint of the vessel, spiraling out to the base and neck. Phillips (1970: 157), on the other hand, established two varieties of Rhodes incised on the basis of paste composition, vessel form, and apparently the length of time a vessel had hardened prior to incising. Jars tempered with large shell particles and containing deeper and wider incisions were placed in the variety Rhodes; bottles tempered with finely crushed shell and exhibiting designs executed in what Phillips (1970: 157) termed a "drier" technique were placed in the variety Horn Lake. Phillips's rationale for creating the two varieties encapsulates his entire approach to categorizing ceramic material:

> As pointed out in the original description cited above [Phillips et al. 1951], the Rhodes treatment also occurs on bottles and other vessel forms having a fine, shell-tempered paste comparable to the *Bell* variety of Bell Plain. This poses the classificatory problem that always arises when specific decorative treatments normally associated with certain vessel shapes and wares appear on other shapes and wares. In many cases such transfers appear to be adventitious and can be ignored; in others they may be sufficiently recurrent to suggest a possibility of areal or chronological significance. When the circumstances do not clearly indicate which, it is perhaps safer to set up the new combination as a separate variety. Such is the *raison d'être* for a *Horn Lake* variety of Rhodes Incised. (Phillips 1970: 157)

Under his sorting criteria, Phillips (1970: 157) states that vessels of the Horn Lake variety exhibit "[c]losely spaced trailed incision[s] similar to that of Rhodes [variety] but executed in a 'drier' technique." Using Phillips's criteria, the vessel in Figure 2.2b would be placed in the Rhodes variety, and the vessel illustrated in Figure 2.2a would be placed in the Horn Lake variety—except for the fact that its design is engraved and not incised. What do we do with it now?

Although they never say so, Phillips et al. had an answer for this possibility: Place the vessel in the type Walls engraved (Phillips et al. 1951: fig. 110)—a catchall category for a host of vessel forms that carry engraved motifs. But what would Phillips do with it? The answer here is not as clear-cut. Phillips (1970) took the type name *Walls* and to it appended two variety names, *Walls* and *Hull*, the latter having previously been a type name devised by Phillips et al. (1951) to encompass fish-scale-like designs on the interiors of bowls tempered with finely crushed shell. Phillips (1970), in co-opting the name, kept with it the criterion that it was limited to bowl interiors. However, even though Phillips (1970) uses the term Walls *engraved* variety Hull (note the emphasis on the word *engraved),* he says that one sorting criterion is "[f]ine dry paste incision or engraving" (p. 170).

a

b

Figure 2.2. Vessels showing two methods of inscribing swirled designs: a, engraving; b, incising. The two vessels illustrate some of the problems in using existing typological systems. The engraved vessel is commonly referred to as Walls engraved (e.g., Phillips et al. 1951) and the incised vessel as Rhodes incised. Phillips (1970), however, identified an alternate method of design application, "dry-paste incising," which he distinguished from well-executed engraving. Using this distinction, the engraved vessel shown here might be termed dry-paste incising. Another alternative—the one we use here—is to refer to both vessels as Rhodes engraved/incised. Vessel 2.2a (6 inches high) is from Murphy, burial 75, and vessel 2.2b (3⅝ inches high) is from Pemiscot County (no site listed). MU collection.

In other words, the design on the bowl interior can be engraved or incised, even though the type name carries the word *engraved*. What does Phillips mean by "dry paste incision," a technique he referred to when discussing the sorting criteria for Rhodes incised variety Horn Lake (see above)? Our understanding is that engraving is done after a vessel is fired, whereas incising is done before a vessel is fired. In his general discussion of Walls engraved (p. 169), he sets up a direct distinction between the two techniques: "A number of sherds have recently turned up at Lake George (21-N-1) [Mississippi] with crude cross-hatched dry-paste incision treatment (it could hardly be called engraving)." Apparently Phillips is distinguishing between engraving and dry-paste incision on the basis of how well executed the design is, which makes it difficult if not impossible to duplicate his results. If he lumps engraving and dry-paste incising together, which he does for Walls engraved variety Hull, then it appears that at least here the actual design is more important to Phillips than are nuances between methods of application.

Hathcock's (1988: 36–37) solution to the problem is to place all engraved bottles in the type Walls engraved—a solution that seems to us as appropriate as any other. If the design is incised (Hathcock does not distinguish between "dry" and "wet" incising), he places it in the type Rhodes incised, adding a notation for those examples that carry added designs (swastikas or steps) that otherwise would place the vessels in Walls engraved (we discuss compound types in a later section). Our solution at this point is to ignore whether the design was incised or engraved and to place vessels with swirls on their exteriors in a type called *Rhodes incised/engraved* and to refer to individual specimens either as Rhodes engraved or Rhodes incised. It may turn out eventually that the engraved bottles (all Rhodes bottles in our samples are engraved) are earlier or later than the incised jars, but we presently have no evidence to suggest that such is the case. As an aside, Phillips (1970) followed this practice with a number of types, such as the early to middle Mississippian period type O'Byam incised, which S. Williams (1954) earlier had subdivided into O'Byam incised and O'Byam engraved.

Paste Types

The key to understanding the myriad types and varieties proposed for ceramic material from the central Mississippi River valley lies in understanding the difference between two terms introduced in the previous section, *fine paste* and *coarse paste*, which generally (though not exclusively) are shorthand notations used to refer to the degree to which the shell used as temper in vessel paste was pulverized. *Fine paste* refers to a paste temper made from finely crushed shell (sometimes to the point of powder); *coarse paste* refers to a paste temper made from larger, readily visible pieces of shell. The distinction is important because many types in both the Phillips et al. (1951) and the Phillips (1970) systems are constructed around paste type. Phillips (1970), especially, used paste types as grounds for establishing two varieties from a previously existing type.

In Phillips's typological system, coarse-paste materials are placed in the type Mississippi plain; fine-paste materials are placed in the type Bell plain. The two temper-based types are subjective at best because neither *coarse* nor *fine* is defined, nor is there room for the categorization of mixed-temper materials, though these are common occurrences in southeastern Missouri assemblages (see Teltser 1988; J. R. Williams 1967, 1968, 1972). Phillips created two varieties for Mississippi plain—Neeley's Ferry and Mississippi—to incorporate materials from southeastern Missouri, basing the subdivision solely on geographic location as opposed to distinguishing characteristics. The subdivision, in our opinion, is unwarranted. Fortunately, Phillips's two varieties are not commonly used, and archaeologists have reverted to using the type name *Neeley's Ferry plain*—first described by J. B. Griffin for Walker and Adams (1946) at the Matthews site in New Madrid County, Missouri, and used by Phillips et al. (1951) in their study.

The consequence of maintaining Neeley's Ferry plain as an analytical unit is that all coarse-paste, undecorated body sherds are lumped into a single type. The sherds could have come from a vessel that, if complete, would have been typed as Barton incised, Matthews incised, Manly punctated, Beckwith incised, Campbell punctated, or any one of numerous other types, but since the plain sherd was separated from the decorated portion of the vessel through breakage, it is labeled as Neeley's Ferry plain. The result is that Neeley's Ferry plain becomes a default category—more of a ware than a type—and corresponding frequencies of the type tend to dominate ceramic assemblages. The same holds true for undecorated sherds that have finely crushed shell as temper, which are placed in the Bell type. To make matters worse, Bell plain, defined by Phillips et al. (1951: 122) as a shell-tempered type (though Phillips [1970: 60] admits that other materials might also be present), has also been extended to include clay-tempered specimens that exhibit the other characteristics of Bell plain (e.g., smooth finish both interior and exterior, polishing marks visible). For example, J. R. Williams (1972: 123) states that "Bell Plain is often clay tempered in southeast Missouri." Williams, in fact, is one of the few investigators who actually presents sherd categories other than the established type names. Throughout the land-leveling reports Williams (1967, 1968, 1972) consistently used the type name *Bell plain* to refer exclusively to materials that are shell tempered. He used the term *Bell plain, clay-tempered* to refer to fine-paste materials tempered with clay instead of shell. Future studies will have to address the problem of mixed pastes and devise a quantitative means of assessing the variation in paste that surely has functional implications (begun in Dunnell and Feathers 1991; O'Brien and Holland 1990, 1992; O'Brien et al. 1994). That analysis is well beyond the scope of this book, though we can add that many of the sherds and vessels we have examined from the Pemiscot Bayou sites are tempered with combinations of shell and clay.

Late Mississippian Period Ceramic Types

Throughout the book, we discuss, in large part for chronological purposes, the occurrences of ceramic types in the Pemiscot Bayou assemblages. To clarify what we mean when we use a particular type name, we include below short descriptions of 18 of the 20 types (Neeley's Ferry plain and Bell plain are described above) that are found with some regularity in the late Mississippian period assemblages. Following in the tradition of Phillips (1970), drawings of most of the types (we exclude Varney red-slipped, Old Town red-slipped, and Hollywood white-slipped, since the slip covers the entire surface of the sherd and thus would not be distinguishable in the drawings) are placed adjacent to the descriptions for reference. Ranges in variation of the types are shown in chapters 5 through 7 and, for the slipped types, in the color plates.

Where possible, we rely primarily on Phillips et al. (1951) and Phillips (1970) for type descriptions, but the reader should note that we are interested only in the parts of the descriptions that address vessel-surface modifications (e.g., slipping, incising, punctating), since methods of surface modification on the whole appear to be the most chronologically useful dimensions. In the case of the incised, engraved, appliquéd, noded, and punctated types, we view the surface modifications as stylistic elements, that is, features that are not tied to vessel function. However, in the case of the slipped types, especially Varney red-slipped and Old Town red-slipped (which we combine into a single type termed red-slipped), we cannot rule out that slipping, especially when applied to the interior of a vessel, reduced permeability, therefore making the slip a functional as opposed to a stylistic feature. In fact, Dunnell and Feathers (1991) make an excellent case for slipping starting out as a functional trait and then, when vessel technology reached a level that slipping was no longer necessary to reduce permeability, becoming a completely stylistic (nonfunctional) trait.

The reader should also note that although we tend to limit discussion to type descriptions provided by Phillips et al. (1951) and Phillips (1970), other treatments of central Mississippi River valley ceramics exist, some of more recent publication date. Most of these, however, accomplish little except to refine in minor ways the established type descriptions. Among the three of them, Phillips, Ford, and Griffin probably saw more ceramic material—both sherds and complete vessels—than any two dozen archaeologists put together. Hence they were able to discuss variation in the types (and in Phillips's case, variation between and among varieties) they established and to speak intelligently about chronological placement, spatial extent, and stylistic connections with other types. It should be emphasized that with reference to chronological placement of types, few radiometric dates are available for specimens from the central Mississippi River valley. We address this vexing problem in more detail in Chapter 9.

Slipped Types[2]

Old Town red-slipped First described by Phillips et al. (1951: 129–32), who used the name *Old Town red*. They viewed the type as Neeley's Ferry plain or Bell plain with a red slip applied to the interior and/or exterior of the vessel walls. They note:

> Logically, there should be two divisions [one for coarse-paste examples and one for fine-paste examples]. We originally set it up that way, but they [the categories] broke down under sorting difficulties, the reason being that Old Town Red even when directly associated with Neeley's Ferry is inclined to have a somewhat finer paste. Since the differentiation of Neeley's Ferry and Bell turned out to be culturally significant [see Chapter 9 of this volume for an opposing view], it is to be hoped that some means will be found to distinguish their associated red and painted wares also. This may be possible when we have more information on shape.

Here Phillips et al. (1951) point out in the clearest words possible the problems involved in making subjective appraisals of the size of shell particles. The problem persists whether the vessel surface is plain or red slipped; hence the difficulty in sorting between Neeley's Ferry plain and Bell plain carries over when the vessel is coated with a red slip. Curiously, S. Williams (1954: 209) states that Phillips et al. (1951) defined Old Town red "as having a fine paste resembling Bell Plain, but it is noted that a variant with a coarser paste was finally included." This is not true. Phillips et al. (1951), as noted above, used the type name for both paste types. S. Williams (1954: 209) attempted to separate the two by placing fine-paste specimens in the type Old Town red-filmed and coarse-paste specimens in the type Varney red-filmed (see below).

Varney red-slipped First proposed by S. Williams (1954: 209–10), who used the name *Varney red-filmed*, as a solution to the sorting problem mentioned by Phillips et al. (1951). However, he restricted the type designation to "[l]arge simple curved-sided bowls, shallow or deep. . . . This is the shape often called the 'salt pan.' Another common shape is the large jar with a recurved rim" (S. Williams

---

2. We do not make the distinction in this volume between slip and paint. Although there will eventually be good reasons to do so, it would add too much confusion to an already difficult situation to do so here. One problem is the lack of standardized terminology. For example, is the term *slip* restricted to an undercoating intended to have paint applied over it? Does *slip* refer exclusively to a clay-and-water mixture to which pigment has been added? Are slips applied in the prefiring stage and paint applied after firing? At this point we prefer to simply use the term *slip* as part of a modifier that also contains a color (including red, white, and black).

1954: 209). Phillips (1970: 167) went a step further, restricting Varney red to "saltpans" only, "[o]n the theory that saltpans warrant special treatment." He placed coarse-paste jars with red slipping in the type Old Town red variety St. Francis and created the type Old Town red variety Beaverdam to encompass all fine-paste examples, regardless of vessel shape. For the sake of simplicity, not to mention consistency, we disregard these types and simply refer to specimens as "red-slipped."

Carson red-on-buff First proposed by Phillips et al. (1951: 132–33) to include Neeley's Ferry plain vessels that exhibit a buff-colored paste and broad bands of heavy red slip. Designs include swastika-like spirals, vertical panels, and a stepped motif; Phillips et al. (1951: 133–34) note that these designs correspond to those on Rhodes incised (swastikas), Walls engraved (swastikas and steps), and Kent incised (vertical panels). Phillips (1970: 63) subdivides the type into two varieties based on vessel form. As far as we are able to tell, all examples from the Pemiscot Bayou sites are bottles (including head pots), which correspond to Phillips's variety Carson.

Nodena red-and-white First proposed by Phillips et al. (1951: 133–34) to include Neeley's Ferry plain vessels that exhibit a buff-colored paste and red and white slip applied to separate areas of vessel exteriors. Designs are similar in most instances to those occurring in Carson red-on-buff. Phillips et al. (1951: 132) mention the possibility that Carson red-on-buff appeared prior to Nodena red-and-white, since the former not only is less common than the latter in sherd assemblages but also is rare in the south-

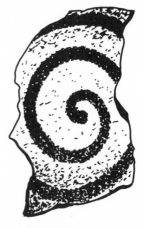

ern part of the lower Mississippi Valley: "These facts lend some support to the hypothesis that painting was moving down the Mississippi, and that red on buff was the earlier style" (Phillips et al. 1951: 132). Phillips (1970) established four varieties based on vessel form and design. One variety, Douglas, consists of gourd-shaped bowls that are red slipped on the interior and white slipped on the exterior. One such bowl sherd (though probably not from a gourd-shaped bowl) was recovered from Dorrah. Chapman (1980: 291) shortened the type name to Nodena red, pointing out that on some examples from southeastern Missouri the red slip was placed over the preexisting white slip (but see Dunnell and Jackson 1992 and Chapter 9, this volume). He also mentions that the designs occurring on Nodena red-and-white and Carson red-on-buff may be different, though he does not elaborate on the differences. For our purposes, regardless of the location of the red slip relative to the white slip, if a specimen exhibited both, we placed it in Nodena red-and-white.

Hollywood white-slipped First proposed by Phillips et al. (1951: 134), who used the name *Hollywood white-filmed* to include (apparently) both Neeley's Ferry plain and Bell plain vessels that exhibit white slipping on the exterior and sometimes on the interior. They note the problem in deciding whether a sherd with white slip on the exterior surface is from a Hollywood white-slipped vessel or from the white portion of a Nodena red-and-white vessel. We classified sherds as Hollywood white-slipped only if the white slip occurred either (a) on both surfaces or (b) on one surface and the other surface was unslipped, recognizing the possibility that a sherd may have come from a vessel that also contained red slipping on portions of the interior and/or exterior.

Incised Types

Barton incised First described by Phillips et al. (1951: 114–19) to account for vessels with a Neeley's Ferry plain paste and groups of carelessly executed incised lines that extend from the vessel lip down to the beginning of the shoulder or onto the shoulder, with the groups of lines often converging to form alternating triangles. Several types defined for the central Mississippi Valley are identified by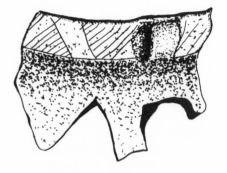
the occurrence of vertical parallel lines (e.g., Campbell incised and Kent incised) and have led to a confusing situation. Phillips (1970), for example, described six varieties of Barton incised. We restrict use of the type to occurrences of either parallel lines within incised triangles or groups of incised lines that form triangles (see Campbell incised and Kent incised).

Campbell incised First proposed by Chapman and Anderson (1955) to account for jars found at the Campbell site that exhibit narrow, usually vertical, parallel lines extending from the lip or near the lip to the shoulder. As discussed above, the type Barton incised, as originally defined, was a catchall category for vessels exhibiting linear incisions placed either vertically or diagonally, usually

on, but not restricted to, the neck area. Phillips (1970: 45) created variety Campbell to encompass vessels with parallel lines restricted to the neck and variety Kent for vessels with lines on the shoulder and body. We follow Phillips's criteria, though we treat Campbell incised and Kent incised (see below) as types, as opposed to varieties.

Kent incised First proposed by Phillips et al. (1951: 126–29) to accommodate Neeley's Ferry plain vessels that exhibit "[v]ertical incised lines extending from lower rim area to base, sometimes from lip. Character of line similar to that described for Barton Incised" (pp. 126–27). Phillips (1970: 46), as noted above, reduced Kent incised to the status of a variety of Barton incised. We treat it here as a type. Our criterion for distinguishing among specimens of Barton incised, Campbell incised, and Kent incised is the placement and arrangement of the vertical lines. If they are not enclosed within a triangle and if they extend down over the edge of the shoulder, then they are classified as Kent incised.

Ranch incised First proposed by Phillips et al. (1951: 119–20) to account for Neeley's Ferry plain vessels that had their exteriors covered or nearly covered with "groups of parallel, curved incised lines . . . that intersect one another to give an imbricated design somewhat like the appearance of fish scales" (p. 119). Phillips et al. (1951: 129) proposed the type Hull engraved seemingly to accommodate fine-paste specimens that have the imbricate design of Ranch incised. We found no such examples in the Pemiscot Bayou assemblages. Phillips (1970: 156) advocates abandoning Ranch incised as a type since, as he correctly points out, the fish-scale motif can occur on the bodies of vessels that exhibit Barton-type incising on the neck. He suggests (p. 156) that the "motif be handled as a mode in the various type contexts in which it occurs." We cannot argue with the fact that the incised diagonal lines characteristic of the type Barton incised do occasionally occur as rim treatment on vessels that also contain the fish-scale motif. This phenomenon again points out the problem of using ceramic types as currently constructed. We retain the type here, recognizing the problems of so doing.

Mound Place incised A tentative type first proposed by Phillips et al. (1951: 127–29) and later supported by S. Williams (1954: 224) to encompass coarse- and fine-paste bowls that exhibit two or more parallel lines placed horizontally around the exterior rim. Occasionally "the lines dip down on each side of the vessel in concentric festoons. Sometimes these festoons occur beneath semi-circular lugs. . . . The technique of decoration varies from a moderately broad incision comparable to that of Barton Incised to

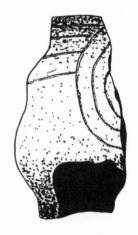

fine engraving comparable to that of Walls or Hull Engraved" (Phillips et al. 1951: 147). Phillips (1970: 135) created two varieties of Mound Place incised, Mound Place and Chickasawba, the former consisting of vessels with two or more parallel horizontal lines on bowl rims and the latter consisting of vessels in which the lines either dip down under rim-riding effigies or loop around to form festoons. He notes (p. 136) that "Mound Place Incised in Southeast Missouri is apparently of, or closely related to, this Chickasawba variety," named after the large Mississippian-period site near Blytheville (not Blythedale, as stated by Phillips [1970: 136]), Arkansas, a few miles south of the Missouri state line.

Wallace incised First proposed by Phillips et al. (1951: 134–36) to accommodate Neeley's Ferry plain vessels that they felt have the primary distinguishing feature of being thin-walled, rather than plain-surfaced, and that exhibit shallow, U-shaped incised lines. Usually the designs below the vessel rims are curvilinear arrangements of concentric circular elements; rims often contain line-filled

triangles similar to those on Barton incised vessels. To differentiate among rim sherds, we used a cutoff of 3 mm for the line width: If the incised lines were wider than 3 mm, they were placed in Wallace incised; if narrower than 3 mm, they were placed in Barton incised. The only other type exhibiting wide, curvilinear elements on the body is Rhodes incised (see below), though sherds of that type are easily distinguishable.

Rhodes incised First proposed by Phillips et al. (1951: 127) to encompass Neeley's Ferry plain (occasionally Bell plain) jars and bottles that contain "wide, deep, generally U-shaped curvilinear incisions, closely spaced. Incisions vary in width from ca. 2 to 3 mm. Spaces between the lines are sometimes narrower than the incisions themselves but are usually somewhat wider. . . . Whorls and festoons cover the body and occasionally

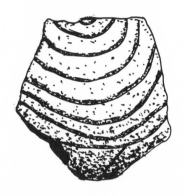

the rim. This design, as observed on whole pots, characteristically spirals from a nuclear swastika or triskele repeated four times on the vessel." The swirled design characteristic of Rhodes incised is so distinctive that sherds of that type can easily be distinguished from sherds of Wallace incised. As mentioned earlier, we include in the type all examples with a swirl design, regardless of whether the design was incised or engraved.

Engraved Type

Walls engraved A catchall category first proposed by Phillips et al. (1951: 127–29) to account for Bell plain vessels that contain fine-lined engraving in a wide variety of designs. The most common design consists of curvilinear bands of cross-hatching that form various figures, such as the feathered serpent and "Southern Cult" motifs, which include the long-nosed god and the weeping eye. Phillips (1970) proposes two varieties—

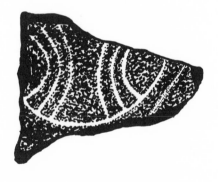

Walls and Hull—based on design location (bottle exteriors for Walls; bowl interiors for Hull [see earlier discussion]).

Punctated Types

Parkin punctated First proposed by
Phillips et al. (1951: 110–14) to account
for vessels of Neeley's Ferry plain that
have their exteriors covered or nearly covered with punctations. In most cases the
punctations, made through a variety of
means, cover the entire vessel, except for
perhaps the neck, but occasionally the
punctations occur only in zones outlined
by trailed lines. Phillips (1970) restricts
Parkin to vessels completely covered

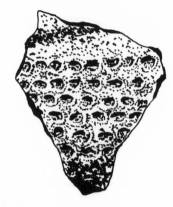

(neck and body) with punctations. He also subdivides the type into five varieties
based on how the punctations were produced and how neatly they are aligned.

Campbell punctated First proposed by
Chapman and Anderson (1955) to accommodate vessels found at the Campbell site that exhibit 2–5 rows of small
punctations around the bases of the necks
of bottles. Based on our inspection of the
Campbell burial-vessel assemblage, the
punctations, which on the whole are
better executed than those that charac-
terize Parkin punctated, occur exclusively on large, squat bottles with short

to medium-height necks. Phillips (1970) argues that since Campbell punctated
is a rim treatment that crosscuts other types, it should be treated as a mode. To
us, it appears to be one of the better late Mississippian period markers. It also
appears to be fairly restricted in geographic range—primarily the Pemiscot Bayou
locality—though more work needs to be done on this aspect of the type.

Noded Type

Fortune noded First proposed by Phillips et al. (1951: 120–22) to include Neeley's Ferry plain vessels that contain "hemispherical or conical nodes in rows, groups, or as an all-over treatment of the vessel body." In some cases the nodes begin at the base of the rim and extend down the body, with the rim being left plain except perhaps for a single row of nodes just below the lip. In some cases the rim contains incised designs, indistinguishable from those on Barton incised, or rows of punctations, similar to those

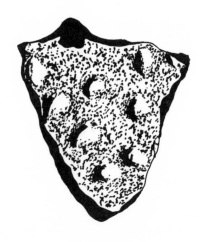

on Parkin punctated. Phillips (1970) notes that it is a rare type in the Mississippi Valley, a point that we would echo for the Pemiscot Bayou locality.

Appliquéd Types

Campbell appliquéd First proposed by Chapman and Anderson (1955) to account for vessels found at the Campbell site that exhibit slender vertical ribs of clay applied to vessel exteriors. They describe the decoration as "addition of appliqued handles vertically around the rim . . . grading into more stylized arcaded handles and characteristically so stylized that the appearance is a series of vertical applique strips. . . . Handles are made by the addition of

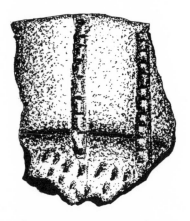

applied strips of clay luted to the rim wall" (p. 42). Phillips (1970) advocates calling Campbell appliquéd a rim treatment that crosscuts a number of established types. He suggests (p. 62) that the Campbell rim be restricted to those examples that exhibit notches on the appliquéd strips.

Vernon Paul appliquéd First proposed by Phillips et al. (1951: 120) to include vessels that exhibit wide, vertical ribs of clay applied to vessel exteriors, apparently only on jar bodies below the neck area (Phillips 1970: 167–68). The effect is the reverse of gadrooning, which in our sample is confined primarily to bottles. In addition to the location of the ribs, the method of molding the ribs to the body differs between Campbell appliquéd and

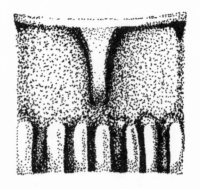

Vernon Paul appliquéd. In the latter, the edges of the ribs are smoothed into the vessel wall; in the former, the ribs, being much narrower, are simply glued to the wet body.

Compound Types

After perusing the type descriptions it should be obvious that major differences exist between the earlier Phillips et al. (1951) method of categorizing ceramic material and the method later employed by Phillips (1970). Each method—the type system and the type-variety system—recognizes variation in the materials being sorted, but each handles that variation differently. One justification Phillips cites for using the type-variety system is that it is expandable—as new "modes" are discovered, new varieties can be developed to encompass the variation. Nowhere is the difference between the two systems more distinct than in how they treat combinations of designs. Phillips et al. (1951: 116), through reference to Barton incised, are clear about how they handle such combinations: "Barton Incised occurs as a rim decoration in combination with several distinct types of body treatment. Sherds showing such combinations have been counted as Barton incised *on the principle that rim decoration determines the type*" (emphasis added). Phillips, on the other hand, would still use the rim as the type designator (Barton incised), but would treat different body decorations as varieties.

Most of the ceramic assemblages from the Pemiscot Bayou sites are composed of sherds as opposed to whole vessels. Most of the sherds are small enough that we do not have large sections of vessels present and thus do not see combinations of designs. Such pieces are sortable into one type or another, since we are blissfully ignorant of the compound treatments that once might have been present. For example, Figure 2.3 illustrates two vessels, one we would type as Campbell appliquéd (Figure 2.3a) and the other (Figure 2.3b) as Parkin punctated (for reasons discussed below). If we had only a rim section from the vessel shown in Figure 2.3b, however, we would type it as Campbell appliquéd, never knowing that the rim sherd was from a vessel with punctations covering the area below the neck-body juncture.

Figure 2.3. Two vessels with vertical appliquéd strips extending downward from the lip: a, Campbell appliquéd, first described by Chapman and Anderson (1955) based on their work at Campbell; b, Parkin punctated. Although both vessels have appliquéd strips, they are placed in different types based on the presence or absence of additional decoration. The examples demonstrate a logical weakness of the typological systems, namely, if only the neck portion of the Parkin punctated vessel existed, it would be typed as Campbell appliquéd, since we would have no way of knowing that the body portion carried punctations. More importantly, the examples demonstrate the additive nature of late Mississippian period decoration, which for the archaeologist creates hybrid types. The addition of appliquéd strips to the Parkin punctated vessel could, potentially, have chronological as well as spatial significance. Vessel 2.3a (4¼ inches high) is from Pemiscot County (no site listed), and vessel 2.3b (2⅜ inches high) is from Campbell backdirt. MU collection.

In cases where we have an intact vessel (or a large sherd) that exhibits the characteristics of two or more types, such as in the assemblages from Campbell and Murphy, we assign it to one type or another, depending on the amount of vessel surface covered by the individual design characteristics. For example, a jar with a Barton incised rim and a Ranch incised body would be placed in the latter type. In such instances we point out through footnotes or parenthetical notes which vessels are of "hybrid types." A desire to move away from this kind of subjectivity was behind Phillips's call for abandoning some of the established types such as Ranch incised and instead handling them as varieties. This might work well for the vessel shown in Figure 2.4b, which might be typed as Parkin variety Ranch, but what should we do with the vessel shown in Figure 2.4a, which is plain-surfaced above and below the "fish-scale" decoration? Does it become Neeley's Ferry plain variety Ranch? If it does, then should not a vessel that exhibits punctations over the body be typed as Neeley's Ferry plain variety Parkin? Following this line of thought, we could end up with two types—Neeley's Ferry plain and Bell plain—and an infinite number of varieties. Surely this is not what Phillips intended when he said that the type-variety system was expandable.

It is worth emphasizing again that our use of types to categorize the Pemiscot Bayou material is aimed primarily at chronological ordering. At this point in our knowledge of the archaeological record of the locality, it makes little or no difference which system—types or types and varieties—is used. For example, Campbell appliquéd, devised by Chapman and Anderson (1955) after examining materials from the Campbell site, is a useful late Mississippian period marker. It has several things going for it: (a) it is easily recognized, (b) it (apparently) occurs over a fairly restricted area, and (c) it (apparently) lasted for only a short time. Phillips's (1970: 62) statement notwithstanding, Campbell appliquéd is just as good a type as any other in existence and probably much better. The point is this: We do not care whether Campbell appliquéd remains a type or whether it is changed to Type X variety Campbell. All we care about is that rims with appliquéd strips can be identified and sorted in space and time. Future analysis can be aimed at examining all vessels and sherds that contain appliquéd strips to determine what the variation is within that class of artifact and how it sorts out spatially and chronologically.

Vessel Form

Many of the types named by Phillips et al. (1951) and the varieties labeled by Phillips (1970) include descriptions of vessel form, such as bowl, bottle, and jar. Curiously, these terms are never defined, our supposition being that the authors figured that the average reader would know what was meant by each term. And in many cases everyone would agree, based on common experience, that a particular vessel is either a bowl or a jar. However, there are also many examples

Figure 2.4. Examples of the type Ranch incised: a, fish-scale design used alone; b, fish-scale design used in conjunction with zoned punctations (Parkin punctated or Barton incised), creating a hybrid type (top vessel is $8\frac{1}{4}$ inches high; bottom vessel is 5 inches high). Provenience for both vessels is Pemiscot County (no sites listed). MU collection.

from late Mississippian period sites in the central Mississippi Valley that do not conveniently fall under one vessel form or another. Hathcock (1988: 54) sums it up well: "Somewhere between the 'tall-necked' jar and the 'short-necked' bottle there is a dividing line. The exact location of this division can be a matter of opinion or an opening for debate." In our "opinion," Hathcock's (1988: 48) use of change in diameter as a distinguishing characteristic between bowls and jars is appropriate: "The bowl becomes a jar when the mouth of the vessel recedes to a smaller diameter than the widest measurement of the body." But don't the mouths of bottles also recede? Hathcock (1988: 48) concedes overlap between jars and bottles: "Some jars with longer necks could easily become classified as bottles." Because of the enormous variation in design and size of late Mississippian period bottles and jars, we find it difficult to derive an acceptable method for distinguishing between these two forms. More out of exasperation than inspiration, we use the following criterion: If a vessel has an orifice diameter of 10 cm or more, it is a jar; if the diameter is under 10 cm, the vessel is a bottle. The only vessels that are exceptions are miniatures, which we deal with on a case-by-case basis.

Obviously one way out of the dilemma of assigning ceramic vessels to "native" form categories (native with respect to modern American culture) is to create categories based on actual vessel measurements. We might have opted for such an approach if we had had a large sample of complete vessels. Anderson's excavated vessels from Campbell (Chapter 6) would have presented such an opportunity, especially with regard to bottles, but for the majority of the vessels all we have are photographs taken just prior to their sale (Price and Price 1979). Where possible, in our discussions we present metric data, but the sample is inadequate to create form classes that have sufficient representation. Sherds are of some help, but one cannot, for example, determine the height of a bottle neck from a bottle-rim sherd. We decided our best option was to use the "native" categories and to document the variation through photographs and line drawings of as many intact vessels as possible.

Vessel form does not equate necessarily with vessel function, though many of the terms used to describe Mississippian vessel forms have either an implicit function or in some cases (e.g., water bottle) an explicit function connected to them. One of the most-used formal-functional terms is *saltpan,* a form category used by Phillips et al. (1951) and by Phillips (1970) to refer to the shallow, large-diameter vessels ostensibly used as solar evaporators to derive salt from saline water. Those vessels, usually red slipped, are included here in the bowl category. They occur with great frequency in the earlier Mississippian sites such as Kersey and the early component at Murphy, but by A.D. 1350 they had declined greatly in frequency. And lest it be forgotten that vessels can serve different functions during their use-lives, we include Figure 2.5, which shows two Carson red-on-buff containers. The vessel in Figure 2.5b began life as a bottle, almost identical in

a

b

Figure 2.5. Carson red-on-buff vessels: a, unmodified bottle ($9^7/_8$ inches high); b, bottle modified into a bowl ($4^1/_4$ inches high). Provenience for both vessels is Pemiscot County (no sites listed). MU collection.

Figure 2.6. Vernon Paul appliquéd–Bell plain compound jar and bottle. This specimen is from Denton Mounds and is similar to vessels that have been found at Campbell (Chapter 6). Hathcock collection.

shape (and design) to the vessel in Figure 2.5a, but, probably after the neck broke and the vessel could no longer serve as a bottle, it was reshaped into a bowl.

One category of vessels—those of compound form—deserves special mention. Such vessels are rare, but on occasion Mississippian potters decided to create freakish vessels that combine, for example, a bottomless miniature Vernon Paul appliquéd jar with an arcaded neck sitting on top of a large Bell plain bottle (Figure 2.6) or a Kent incised miniature jar—complete with handles—acting as the neck of a large jar (Hathcock 1988: 78). For purposes of tabulation, we list such vessels by one form or the other but also point out that the vessel is of a compound form.

Archaeological Phases[3]

Given the problems inherent in the existing ceramic typological schemes for the central Mississippi Valley, one should not be too surprised to find similar problems in the larger taxonomic units—phases—used to organize sites and

3. The basis for this discussion is found in Fox 1992.

components in space and time. Southeastern Missouri, northeastern Arkansas, and northwestern Tennessee—an area that we will refer to below as the tristate region—have enjoyed their share of phases and similar units over the years, with phase designations changing with each new crop of archaeologists. Fortunately, the situation appears to have stabilized somewhat over the last few years, though this lull shows signs of being impermanent (e.g., G. P. Smith 1990).

A phase, according to Willey and Phillips (1958: 22), who redefined an older term coined by McKern (1939), is "an archaeological unit possessing traits sufficiently characteristic to distinguish it from all other units similarly conceived, whether of the same or other cultures or civilizations, spatially limited to the order of magnitude of a locality or region and chronologically limited to a brief period of time." Willey and Phillips (1958: 22) acknowledge that it is virtually impossible to standardize the amount of time and space that a phase occupies because of the enormous variation in the conditions entering into its formulation. They emphasize (1958: 23–24) that a phase has "no appropriate scale independent of the cultural situation in which it is applied. . . . [P]hases may have very considerable and highly variable spatial and temporal dimensions." In other words, phase A might be designed to include archaeological materials from a 200-year span of time and from an area of 300 km^2. Phase B, on the other hand, might include materials from a 100-year span of time and from an area of 100 km^2.

Willey and Phillips (1958: 22) label the phase as the "practical and intelligible unit of archaeological study." Phases are constructed from similar components, or what are thought to be temporally limited, culturally significant assemblages identified within sites. Components are defined on the basis of their artifactual contents and represent culturally homogeneous stratigraphic units within single sites. Artifacts are analyzed on the individual and assemblage level and the results compared to the results of similar analyses of other assemblages in a region. The person doing the comparison examines the assemblages from the standpoint of how similar or dissimilar each is to the others and assigns them to phases. We would agree with Willey and Phillips (1958: 22) that phases are "practical and [at some basic level] intelligible" units. Just as the term *Nodena red-and-white* immediately tells the reader that the author is discussing a late Mississippian period vessel or sherd from the central Mississippi Valley, the term *Nodena phase* gives the reader some information about space and time. Thus, as a preliminary form of shorthand notation, there is nothing inherently wrong with using phases as basic units of regional synthesis. But unfortunately, phases take on lives of their own and far exceed their very limited capabilities. We forget that phases are nothing more than intuitive categories comprising intuitive categories (e.g., ceramic types). In short, phases are the results of inductive (often casual) pattern-recognition procedures.

To date, all phases defined for the Mississippian period in the tristate region have been based primarily, though not exclusively, on the presence (or, in some cases, the absence) of ceramic types in excavations and surface collections. In strict terms, ceramic types used as defining criteria of phases should be exclusive to a particular phase and should not overlap among phases. However, with the exception of assemblages from short-term, single-component sites, archaeological data rarely reflect such exclusivity. Change, in terms of artifact style, can be a gradual process, resulting in considerable variation within a component or phase, the effect of which is the blurring of the boundaries of units, often to the point where individual units overlap considerably. Differences between units are consequently diminished, making it difficult for an investigator to reliably include data within any one unit. Archaeological seriation, of course, is built around the concept of increasing and declining percentages of one style relative to others, but phase construction is not. For example, no phase could logically be formulated using a criterion such as "50% of an assemblage from phase A will be Nodena red-and-white." Some quantitative criteria can be used, such as "Phase A will include more Nodena red-and-white than Parkin punctated," and as we discuss below, phases in the tristate region have been examined from this angle. However, as we demonstrate, the cumulative-percentage graphs that result from such examinations are confusing. When nonstylistic features are used as phase definitions, leading to statements such as "Phase B contains 25–50% Neeley's Ferry plain," the results can be worse than confusing. This conflation of style and function is examined in considerable depth in Chapter 9.

In summary, the development of Mississippian phases in southeastern Missouri has not followed the slow, deliberate procedure, subject to corrections and maximum constructive criticism, that Willey and Phillips (1958) envisioned. Rather, phases have been proposed and adopted on the basis of limited excavations (mostly heretofore unpublished) and small surface collections. Since neither in theory nor in practice are there rules for determining exactly how similar components must be in order for them to be considered as belonging to the same phase, two outcomes can occur, depending on the predilection of individual archaeologists. Splitters will proliferate the number of phases, and lumpers will tend to keep the number small, often reluctantly assigning a component to an existing phase even though the component's artifact assemblage does not really match the phase's criteria. Both results have been common occurrences in studies of the archaeological record from southeastern Missouri. We examine a few of the phases below in terms of how they were established and what they actually do in terms of ordering data from the Pemiscot Bayou sites both spatially and temporally.

The Pemiscot Bayou Phase

S. Williams (1954) formulated the Pemiscot Bayou phase to incorporate components from Pemiscot County that did not contain some of the materials he designated as hallmarks of the Cairo Lowland phase, which was defined on the basis of his excavations at Crosno in Mississippi County, Missouri, and surface collections of sites well to the north of the Pemiscot Bayou locality: "The Pemiscot Bayou phase is partially defined by negative traits. It lacks the three characteristic Cairo Lowland series [Kimmswick, Wickliffe, and O'Byam] but does possess a new type—Parkin Punctate. The sites of this phase are not as well laid-out although the largest mound [Murphy] of the area falls into this phase. No walled or ditched villages have definitely been assigned to this phase" (S. Williams 1954: 275).

From the mid-1950s to the mid-1960s few archaeological investigations were undertaken in southeastern Missouri, and Williams's phase designation was accepted as formulated, as were his other three southeastern Missouri phases (Cairo Lowland, Malden Plain, and Nodena [discussed below]). However, highway salvage work during the mid-1960s added substantial information on Mississippian-period occupation in the region. Based on two years of work at Kersey, Marshall (1965) identified three components—Kersey 1, dating to the Late Woodland period; Kersey 2, dating to the early Mississippian period; and Kersey 3, dating to the middle portion of the Mississippian period. He assigned Kersey 3 to the Pemiscot Bayou phase and expanded the list of hallmarks:

> The Kersey 3 component fits the general description of the Pemiscot Bayou phase and is characterized by Parkin Punctated, Barton Incised, Bell Plain, Old Town Red, Neeley's Ferry Plain pottery types, small constricted mouth deep bowls, water bottles with high cylindrical necks, notched rim applique and occasional beveling of the inner rims of vessels, ground and polished chipped beveled-edge gouges or adzes, and the absence of salt pan and Wickliffe ware. Also present is the placement of pottery vessels with some of the dead, extended, supine, primary, and horizontal and vertical bundle burials intruded in a mound and triangular and Nodena type projectile points. (Marshall 1965: 76–77)

Clearly, Williams's (1954) surface collection from Kersey did not contain some of the artifact types Marshall later assigned to the Pemiscot Bayou phase. But did Marshall's addition of those types clear up the definition of the Pemiscot Bayou phase, or did it add to the confusion? For example, Neeley's Ferry plain, Bell plain, Old Town red ceramics, and Nodena points are all found at sites attributed to other Mississippian-period phases, so they are not particularly useful markers for any phase. In fact, Nodena points (willow-leaf-shaped points) are one of the hallmarks of the Nodena phase, and polished adzes have been found in late Mississippian period contexts at Murphy (Chapter 5) and Denton Mounds (Chapter 7). The interment types that Marshall attributes to the Pemiscot Bayou phase also are found throughout the Woodland and Mississippian sequences in southeastern Missouri.

Writing several years later, Phillips (1970: 929) presented the following view of the Pemiscot Bayou phase:

> This is one of our weakest Mississippian formulations as Williams would freely admit. It was prompted by the difficulty of assigning a small group of components in the Little River Lowland (north, i.e., above the Missouri line) to the Cairo Lowland phase. The components in question are practically without any of the more specific Cairo Lowland markers (O'Byam Incised, Kimmswick Fabric Impressed, and Wickcliffe [*sic*] Thick). . . . Some of these Pemiscot Bayou components, especially Persimmon [Grove] (8-Q-4) and the type site Kinfolk Ridge (8-R-2), differ also in having elements such as Parkin Punctated and various unclassified shell-tempered incised, punctated, and noded types that are not present in Cairo Lowland. The source of these features seems to be in the south, from which one might infer that Pemiscot Bayou is simply intermediate culturally, as it is geographically, between the Cairo Lowland and Nodena phases. The difficulty with this simple explanation is that there are perfectly good Nodena components in the same locality, e.g. Holland (8-Q-5), Campbell (8-Q-7), and Chute (8-R-3 [McCoy]) that are ceramically quite distinct from the Pemiscot Bayou sites. If the difference cannot be explained on the basis of geography, it must be chronological with a strong probability that Pemiscot Bayou is earlier than Nodena.

This citation is important because it illustrates the manner in which many of the phases were defined. Williams's (1954) classification and Phillips's (1970) subsequent evaluation of those phases make it clear that all phases were defined using the Cairo Lowland phase as the model or archetype for Mississippian-period occupation in southeastern Missouri. Consequently, what occurred was the intuitive comparison of excavated and surface-collected assemblages with materials recovered from excavations at Crosno. Thus there are different kinds of samples (excavated and surface collected) and different sizes of samples being compared. In addition, although both Williams (1954) and Phillips (1970) used a spatial-temporal method to order materials, homogeneity within diverse geographic regions was not as important as the overall degree of fit between the Crosno assemblage and assemblages from other sites.

Crosno, like many of the large sites in southeastern Missouri, appears to have been occupied, perhaps continuously, from at least A.D. 800 to sometime around A.D. 1250. Despite the length of occupation and the depth of deposits in some areas of the site (well over a meter), there are few if any stratigraphic differences that make sense chronologically, which is in large part attributable to the fact that Mississippian people consistently used trash to construct platform mounds, thereby creating deposits that are more homogeneous (e.g., Dunnell n.d.). In fact, Brainerd-Robinson similarity coefficients (see discussion in Chapter 3) of 23 analytical units from Crosno average an incredibly high 186, with a very tight range around the mean (Fox 1992). We know that throughout the Mississippian period ceramics in the Cairo Lowland changed in several significant ways, but the deposits, because of severe mixing, reflect homogeneity. This is a sure indication that Crosno is not a particularly useful site to employ as the basis of phase designations.

The Nodena Phase

Nodena was first suggested as a phase by S. Williams, in a paper read at the 1954 meeting of the Southeastern Archaeological Conference (Phillips 1970: 933), based on his examination of James K. Hampson's extensive collection of pottery from the Upper Nodena Plantation in Mississippi County, Arkansas. In terms of what it attempts to provide, the phase is no better or worse than most in the central Mississippi Valley, a statement supported by Phillips (1970: 934–35): "Nodena is no more in need of exact definition than are three-fourths of the other phases." Nineteen years after Phillips published that comment, D. F. Morse (1989: 97) notes that "[t]he Nodena phase has never been adequately defined and this paper is no exception to previous treatments." Ironically, Morse's statement appears in the summary volume on Nodena. He cogently points out (D. F. Morse 1989: 109) the major problem with not only the Nodena phase but all central Mississippi Valley phases: "Cairo Lowland, Nodena, Parkin, Walls and many other phases are essentially geographical constructs of Mississippian culture." In other words, time has been deleted from the equation, and as a result we are left with a map full of phases that not only are floating in time but also have overlapping boundaries. This situation is expressed graphically in Figure 2.7, which shows the locations of five middle- to late-Mississippian phases in the central Mississippi Valley.

The spatial boundaries of the Nodena phase as currently defined (e.g., D. F. Morse 1990; Morse and Morse 1983; Phillips 1970; G. P. Smith 1990) extend from southern Pemiscot County, Missouri, on the north to just above Memphis on the south and from the Mississippi River on the east to Pemiscot Bayou and the lower half of the Little River on the west (see Chapter 4 for maps of the Pemiscot Bayou–Little River region). Phillips (1970) includes several sites in northwestern Tennessee in the Nodena phase; Morse and Morse (1983) place them in an unnamed phase. Morse and Morse (1983: 284–90) state that Nodena sites occur in three geographical clusters. A small cluster of sites with Nodena components, including Campbell and Chickasawba, occurs in southeastern Missouri and northeastern Arkansas. A second cluster occurs in Mississippi County, Arkansas, and includes Upper and Middle Nodena, Shawnee Village, Notgrass, and the well-known Pecan Point, which by 1911 had produced nine head pots. A third cluster occurs in Crittenden County, Arkansas, and includes Banks and Bradley, the latter having produced Spanish material (Moore 1911).

As opposed to the Pemiscot Bayou phase, several pottery types appear to be good markers for the Nodena phase, which D. F. Morse (1989: 111) places between

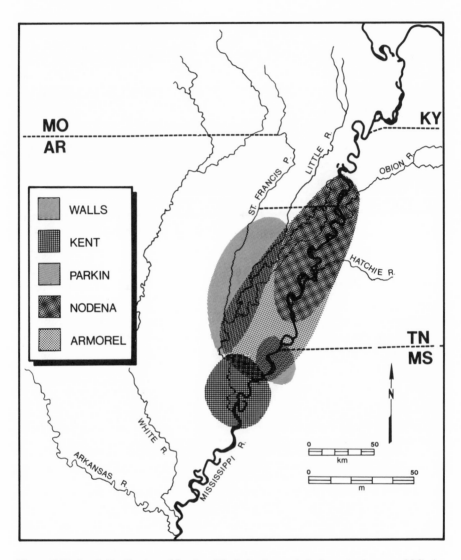

Figure 2.7. Areal distribution of five late Mississippian period phases in the central Mississippi River valley (from Holland 1991).

A.D. 1400 and 1650. For example, Nodena red-and-white is such a candidate, but it occurs with such low frequency on sites in the greater St. Francis drainage basin that it is rarely recovered in surface collections. Compounding the problem is the small size of most surface collections. Several types of appliquéd and incised ceramics are also good markers, but again, they occur but rarely in many sherd assemblages. Given the low frequency of occurrence of many of the types that postdate A.D. 1400, standard practice is to examine percentages of occurrence for the types that do exist in abundance, with the goal of placing sites with similar percentages of various types in the same phase. In fairness, there is validity to this concept, at least in theory. Potters in closely spaced communities could, at any one time, decorate their pots in similar fashion. Ceramic types formed on the basis of decoration would demonstrate this connectedness. But we have no way of knowing what this connectedness means (one group might have been making the pots and trading them, for all we know). We could also propose that at any one time the proportions of similar pottery decoration within the ceramic assemblages of two neighboring groups should be similar. In other words, if at time 1 community A produced 30% Parkin punctated vessels, 10% Nodena red-and-white vessels, and 60% Vernon Paul appliquéd vessels, then neighboring community B might do the same. If such were the case, then we would have some grounds for assigning the sites to the same phase, regardless of whether we knew why the assemblages were identical. At this point all we are interested in is time and space.

To determine the degree of similarity among supposed Nodena sites, Phillips (1970: fig. 448) graphed cumulative ceramic percentages for three Nodena-phase sites in northeastern Arkansas, which we reproduce in Figure 2.8. Phillips used 24 types in his graphs,[4] including Mississippi plain (Neeley's Ferry plain) and Bell plain. Importantly, of those two types only rim sherds were used, whereas body sherds of the other types were included. As Phillips (1970: 935) notes, "The results . . . are not very impressive. Notgrass and Upper Nodena are closely related—this I know from comparing the sherds—but there is something clearly wrong with one sample or the other, resulting in a complete reversal in the proportions of Mississippi Plain, *var. Neeley's Ferry,* and Bell Plain." In most Nodena-phase samples, Phillips explains, Neeley's Ferry plain sherds outnumber Bell plain sherds by a ratio of approximately 4:3, whereas in the Upper Nodena sample Bell plain outnumbers Neeley's Ferry plain by approximately 3:1. Phillips suggests that this irregularity may result from a bias introduced by pothunters. At the same time, Carson Lake deviates from the other two sites graphed in its higher percentages of Neeley's Ferry plain, Parkin punctated, and Barton incised and in its lower percentage of Bell plain. This discrepancy may result from Carson Lake having been surface collected less frequently than Notgrass or Upper Nodena, or from its being older than the other two, or both. Since the most highly decorated pots are often found at later sites, Carson Lake may have undergone less collecting simply because collectors knew it was an older site. As Phillips (1970: 935) wryly notes, "One fine head pot will attract more sounding rods than a carload of early Mississippian plain vessels." On the other hand, if it is an older site, why was it ever placed in the Nodena phase, unless the phase has enough time depth that wholesale ceramic changes occurred during the life of the phase? If this is the case, then it does not sound as if the Nodena phase is a very useful concept.

4. Phillips (1970) used a standardized set of ceramic types for all his cumulative graphs; in Figure 2.8 we deleted several types that contributed no specimens to the Nodena-phase distributions.

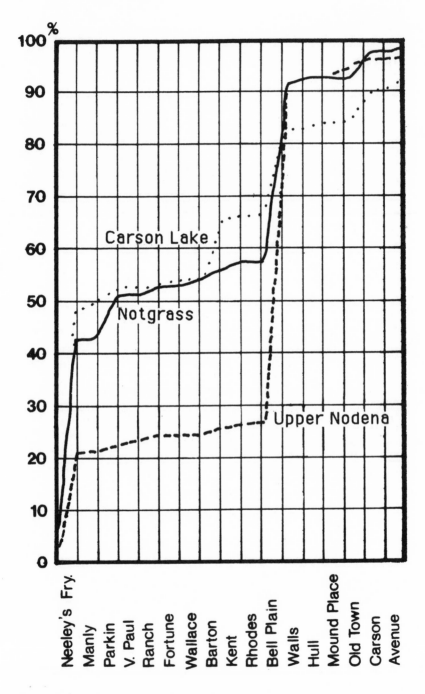

Figure 2.8. Cumulative graph showing ceramic type percentages in surface collections from Upper Nodena, Notgrass, and Carson Lake (after Phillips 1970).

The Armorel Phase

Recently, S. Williams (1980) proposed Armorel as a phase and placed 3 late Pemiscot Bayou sites—Campbell, Holland, and McCoy—and 17 Arkansas and Tennessee sites in it. Named after the late Nodena site of Armorel in Mississippi County, Arkansas, the phase "represents the latest aboriginal culture unit in the region just prior to significant decimation and dispersal by strong European contact" (S. Williams 1980: 105). Williams views the Armorel phase as being contemporaneous with the late portions of the Walls, Kent, and Nodena phases (Figure 2.7), but the sites Williams considers as part of the Armorel phase (Figure 2.9) overlap with portions of the geographic extent of the Walls, Kent, Parkin, and Nodena phases. This type of construction is counter to standard archaeological practice, where contemporaneous phases do not overlap geographically. Williams (1980) suggests a date of ca. A.D. 1500–1700 for the Armorel phase and identifies a number of phase markers:

> *Ceramics:* Late Mississippi types and modes: Well executed Bell Plain, late Parkin Punctate, Campbell Applique, Fortune Noded; arcaded handles, "jar-necked" bottles and other composites (see Chapman and Anderson 1955; Moore 1910, 1911; also Hathcock 1976; White 1976 for Field Museum collection).
> *Lithics:* Snub-nosed scrapers—large and small (thumb nail); Nodena (willow leaf) projectile points; "pipe" drills; basalt groundstone adzes; catlinite, especially Siouan disk pipes. (S. Williams 1980: 105–6)

The phase also encompasses what S. Williams (1980) designates the "Markala horizon," the traits of which are nonrepoussé copper eagles (Moore 1911: plate 10; Hamilton et al. 1974: 165–68) and square, engraved-shell buttons. Spanish trade goods in the form of Clarksdale bells and other metal objects have been found at a few sites (e.g., Campbell and Brooks in Pemiscot County [chapters 6 and 7] and Parkin [Klinger 1977b], Rhodes [Moore 1911], Bradley [Moore 1911], and Clay Hill [John House, pers. comm. to S. Williams as cited in S. Williams 1980: 106] in Arkansas). Although we believe the Armorel phase is a difficult concept to defend, primarily because of the use of artifacts that also appear in other phases, Williams correctly identified a number of what we believe to be excellent markers from the late fifteenth and sixteenth centuries, including catlinite disk pipes, shell buttons, jar-necked bottles, and Campbell appliquéd vessels.

The Campbell Phase

G. P. Smith (1990: 163–64) recently proposed adding the Campbell phase to the ever-increasing list of nomenclature for southeastern Missouri, noting that the

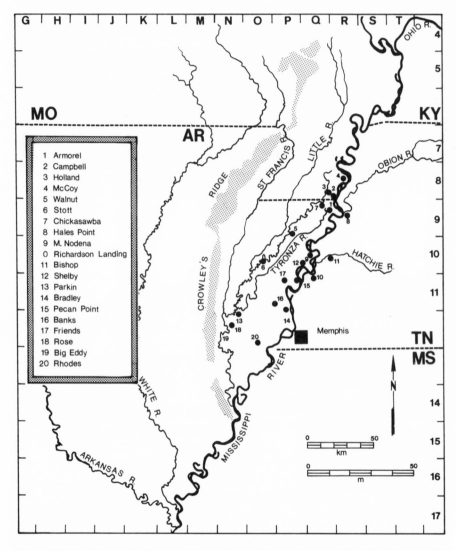

Figure 2.9. Distribution of Armorel-phase sites. Grid coordinates are those used by the Lower Mississippi River Valley Survey (after S. Williams 1980).

Campbell phase is one of the better-known phases in the region. Since this was the first mention of such a phase, it is difficult to see how Smith determined it was one of the better-known phases. Smith (1990: 164) provides an extensive list of characteristic attributes for the Campbell phase:

> The ceramic complex shows a continuity of the trends developing in Pemiscot Bayou, with the addition of a wide variety of decorated types, most of them apparently introduced from the south. The decorated types include Nodena Red

and White, Kent Incised, Barton Incised, Rhodes Incised, Ranch Incised, Fortune Noded, Walls Engraved, Campbell Punctate, Matthews Incised on Neeley's Ferry paste, Hollywood White Filmed, and Carson Red on Buff. Vessel forms include low- to flared-rimmed jars; water bottles with large globular bodies and relatively small cylindrical necks; water bottles with globular bodies and flared necks, often with flared annular bases; flared-wall and subhemispherical bowls; rim effigy bowls including tail-riding effigies; effigy water bottles; and head effigy vessels. While quite similar to the Nodena ceramic complex, that of the Campbell phase is distinguishable by its higher frequency of Parkin Punctated, Old Town Red, and Campbell Punctate, much lower frequency of Kent and Barton Incised, and distinctive bottle forms.

The lithic assemblage includes Nodena points, snub-nosed end scrapers, bipointed perforators, ground-stone celts, chipped and polished adzes and chisels, and ground-stone discoidals. Bone artifacts include bone pins, split bird-bone awls, antler tine flakers, and possible arrow points. Shell items include disk beads, conch columella beads, and mushroom shaped earplugs.

The inclusiveness of the attribute list results in a broadly defined phase that has little temporal or spatial integrity. For example, Nodena points are markers for the Nodena phase, mushroom-shaped earplugs have been found in middle Mississippian period sites, disk beads are found in the Late Woodland period throughout eastern North America, and Barton incised is a feature of the earlier Pemiscot Bayou phase (S. Williams 1954; see also Phillips 1970). Along with the Campbell site, Smith (1990: 164) places McCoy, Holland, and Cagle Lake in the Campbell phase, but he presents no statistical rationale for their assignment. Although we have no problem in placing the sites late in the Mississippian sequence, based on the presence of appliquéd and punctated sherds, we see little reason to assign them to a new phase.

Beyond Phases

The late-period archaeology of southeastern Missouri and northeastern Arkansas is a confusing amalgam of phases, ceramic traits, and horizon markers concocted by archaeologists to pigeonhole excavated and surface-collected remains. New phases have grown out of older constructs as archaeologists have concluded that the older phase designations have outlived their usefulness. However, these reformulations have not left us the legacy that Willey and Phillips (1958) envisioned. What archaeologists have done is to use ceramic types, which were formulated for seriation studies (some of which work well), as index fossils for various phases (R. C. Dunnell, pers. comm. 1993). In some cases, the presence of a particular ceramic type (those with limited spatial-temporal range) will be used to mark a phase, and in other cases a percentage contribution made by a type (e.g., Neeley's Ferry plain) to an assemblage will be used. We examine this issue in

Chapter 3. What we demonstrate is that, unremarkably, some of the existing ceramic types—but only those based on decorative dimensions—can be used not only to examine similarities between site assemblages but also to help order the sites chronologically. None of the analyses we present in Chapter 3 are novel; the only remarkable thing about them is that they have never been used to examine Mississippian-period sites in the central Mississippi River valley.

3

ASSEMBLAGE SIMILARITIES AND DISSIMILARITIES

Michael J. O'Brien and Gregory L. Fox

The principal objective of the analysis of the Pemiscot Bayou assemblages is to document the range of variation in select aspects of the archaeological record. As we discussed earlier, noting similarities and differences among assemblages is not the same as documenting variation, though from several standpoints, such as generating overviews of assemblages and developing chronological control, comparisons of features such as percentages of ceramic types in different assemblages can yield useful information. We propose that the late Mississippian period Pemiscot Bayou sites share enough similarities that they form a sensible unit of study—in effect, they form a coherent starting point from which to explore the topic of variation in Mississippian assemblages in general. Our primary objective in this chapter is to examine the degree of interrelatedness among the Pemiscot Bayou assemblages in terms of content, with emphasis on the co-occurrence of ceramic types, and to contrast those assemblages against other Mississippian-period sites from adjacent regions. Importantly, we examine the degree of similarity and dissimilarity among site assemblages quantitatively instead of subjectively deciding that two or more assemblages are enough alike to justify constructing a new phase.

Despite the fact that numerous complete vessels have been excavated from some of the sites discussed here, we restrict our samples to sherds. As we discuss in chapters 5 through 7, the University of Missouri houses numerous complete vessels from Murphy, Berry, and especially Campbell, and these could have been used to augment the sherd assemblages. The Berry and Campbell samples could have been further increased by using photographs of vessels in private collections, especially that of Leo Anderson (Price and Price 1979), but we excluded them because of the paucity or lack of complete vessels from the other sites. Whether such conservatism is warranted might be questionable, but, as we point out below, there are enough potential biases to worry about at this preliminary stage without the possibility of adding another. We should also make clear that, because of sample size, not all sherd assemblages from all late Mississippian period Pemiscot Bayou sites were used in all analyses. For example, the surface collection from Berry housed at the University of Missouri contains only nine sherds, and thus it was excluded from Brainerd-Robinson correlation matrices (discussed below).

We want to make it very clear from the outset that the sample sizes we are dealing with are, for the most part, small. As is intuitively obvious, small samples bias our views of a site's ceramic assemblage—for example, they probably will not contain representatives of all ceramic types present at a site. Also, a sample's size can accentuate biases that already exist in that sample as a result of the methods used to collect the sample. One of our colleagues strongly recommended that we delete portions of the analysis presented below on the grounds that the samples are inadequate. We could not agree more that the sample sizes in some instances weaken the empirical rigor that we had hoped to bring to this study, and in the end we did delete some of the original presentation. On the other hand, we believe strongly that the kinds of analytical methods we are advocating will in the end prove extremely valuable for identifying similarities and sorting out differences among the late-period assemblages, and thus we encourage other archaeologists to use them. We also believe that the data at hand, though preliminary, are suggestive of interpretable temporal and spatial orderings of the assemblages, and we hope the discussion will lead to the generation of larger samples by other archaeologists working in the central Mississippi River valley.

Methods

We use two methods to examine similarity/dissimilarity—the Brainerd-Robinson index for similarity and multidimensional scaling for dissimilarity. Both are commonly applied to archaeological problems, though even some archaeologists have difficulty explaining exactly why they use one or the other. Neither is difficult to use, though interpretation of results is often anything but straightforward. Since some readers might be unfamiliar with Brainerd-Robinson indexing and multidimensional scaling, and since the results play important roles in the discussion, we offer the following brief discussion of the basics of each method.

Brainerd-Robinson

Several statistics can be used to examine interassemblage similarity, two of the most commonly used being the Brainerd-Robinson *(BR)* index and the Pearson's *r* statistic. For reasons discussed below, we selected the former. Brainerd-Robinson produces coefficients of similarity based on the proportion of an assemblage that is represented by each set of diagnostic materials examined. The formula looks complicated, but it is not:

$$BR = 200 - \sum_{i=1}^{N} |p_{iA} - p_{iB}|$$

The formula says simply to take the percentage of class *i* (or, in our case, pottery type *i*) in assemblage A and subtract from it the percentage of the same class (or type) in assemblage B. The vertical bars tell us to take the absolute value of the difference (convert a negative percentage to a positive percentage). Then, sum the percentages, which gives us a coefficient of *dissimilarity,* and then subtract that number from 200 to convert the product into a *similarity* coefficient. The method provides a pair-wise similarity coefficient ranging from 0 (no similarity) to 200 (identical in every respect). Consequently, a small cumulative difference between assemblages A and B will produce a high coefficient, and a large difference will produce a low coefficient.

The *BR* coefficient of similarity is generally employed to chronologically order assemblages, though it has also been used to interpret cultural relations among archaeological components (e.g., Connolly 1986). Since Pearson's *r* statistic is commonly used in archaeological analysis, and some readers might question why we chose Brainerd-Robinson over it, we provide Cowgill's (1990: 513) clear explanation of why *BR* is preferred over Pearson's *r* to examine similarities between pairs of collections:

> The task of comparing collections of artifacts is quite different. A very common way to do this is to begin by characterizing each collection by sorting the objects into groups by means of some appropriate system of classification and then computing the percent of the total collection constituted by objects assigned to each type. . . . It is then perfectly possible to pose the question "Is there a nearly linear relation between the percentages of types in collection A and the percentages of types in collection B?" That is, if we draw a scattergram that measures percentages of types in collection A along one axis and percentages of types in the other collection along the perpendicular axis, can we find a sloping straight line that comes close to all the points? Pearson's *r* is a logically correct answer to this question.

The trouble is, the question as posed is significantly different from what we usually have in mind in asking how similar the assemblages are to one another. Thus, while *r* answers a question, it is one that bears a rather remote relation to the question we meant to ask. If we start with the idea that what we mean by high similarity between collections is that they both have very similar proportions of the relevant types, and what we mean by low similarity is that the proportions of the types differ considerably in the two collections, then the Brainerd-Robinson coefficient, *BR,* is a more natural statistic. As defined by Robinson (1951) (see also Brainerd 1951; Doran and Hodson 1975: 139; and Shennan 1988: 208), it is related to the total of the absolute differences in type percentages between the two collections being compared. . . . As it stands, it is a "distance" coefficient. That is, it is zero for a pair of collections with identical percents of everything and it reaches a maximum of 200 for collections that have no types at all in common. It is customary to convert it into a similarity coefficient by subtracting the sum from 200. . . . This makes *BR* equal 200 for identical collections and zero for totally different collections.

Multidimensional Scaling

As with the analysis of interassemblage *similarity,* several methods are also available to analyze *dissimilarities* among assemblages, including nonmetric multidimensional scaling *(MDS).* The basic function of the analytical method is to place points (here assemblages) in *n*-dimensional space, the value of *n* being one less than the number of cases (assemblages) under investigation. The statistic is "nonmetric" because it works on the rank-ordering of the dissimilarities between cases instead of on the values themselves (for example, sherd frequencies or vessel-rim diameters). Because we would never be able to understand, say, a 10-dimensional rank-ordering of dissimilarities, the method sequentially reduces the number of dimensions by one, each time attempting to preserve the best-fit rank-ordering of the cases. In other words, it tries to minimize the distortion that invariably arises as the number of dimensions is reduced. Importantly, at each dimension, dissimilarities between or among cases can be viewed in terms of distance: The closer together two points are, the more similar they are; the farther away the points are, the more dissimilar they are. But how can the human brain decipher a hyperspace? Even if *MDS* reduces 10 dimensions to 5 dimensions, that's 2 more than we can conceptualize readily. And so we let the method decrease the number of dimensions, each time attempting to preserve, as much as possible, the relational distance between points. The method lets us know how successful each attempt to preserve the distances is by giving us what are known as "stress values." Inspection of general trends in these values gives us some indication of the adequacy of the final solution. Theoretically, the more dimensions in which the points and their relative positions can be viewed, the better the conclusions that can be drawn. Realistically, this usually amounts to either 2 or 3 dimensions. Below, our purposes are served by viewing the assemblages in 2 dimensions, but later, when we examine the Pemiscot Bayou sites by themselves, we will use 3 dimensions.

Sampling Biases

Although Brainerd-Robinson indexing and multidimensional scaling provide less arbitrary means of examining relations among components than does intuition, the results obtained from using these methods are only as good as the data used in the analysis. The Pemiscot Bayou data comprise surface-collected and excavated materials gathered by several individuals, over several years, employing several different field techniques. Numerous biases can affect an analytical output, including those related to collection strategy, sample size, sample source, and the length of time over which materials were deposited. As we discuss below, it appears that at least some site collections are indeed biased in several interrelated ways. To illustrate these effects, we examine several ceramic assemblages from Campbell, the type site for G. P. Smith's (1990) late-period Campbell phase and an important component of S. Williams's (1980) Armorel phase as well as the Nodena phase (e.g., D. F. Morse 1990; Morse and Morse 1983; Phillips 1970).[1]

Our use of multiple assemblages from a single site is based on the assumption that, everything being equal, the highest coefficients of similarity should occur within a single site, especially one predicted to have been occupied for only a short time, before they would occur between assemblages from different sites. If they do not, why not? Conversely, we would expect multiple collections from a large site that had been occupied over an extended period of time to exhibit lower coefficients of similarity since collectors and excavators would be more likely to sample different components than they would on a smaller site that had been occupied for a shorter period of time. If the coefficients are highly *similar*, we would again have to ask why. Campbell, based on what we know of the site

---

1. For the comparison of the Campbell assemblages, as well as for the broad comparison of southeastern Missouri assemblages discussed later in this chapter, we use data provided by Fox (1992), who in his analysis used 25 ceramic types. He reduced the 20 ceramic types described in Chapter 1 (counting Old Town red-slipped and Varney red-slipped as separate types) to 16 types by combining Campbell punctated, Campbell incised, Campbell appliquéd, and Vernon Paul appliquéd into a single group labeled "Campbell" and by combining Old Town red-slipped and Varney red-slipped into a category labeled "red-slipped." (For subsequent analyses we separate the Campbell series and Vernon Paul appliquéd but continue to lump red-slipped sherds into 1 type [see Chapter 2].) To these 16 types he added 9 other types that occur in the southeastern Missouri assemblages and usually are thought of as early to late Mississippian period types: Matthews incised, O'Byam incised/engraved, Winterville incised, Manly punctated, Wickliffe (all surface treatments), Kimmswick (both plain-surface and fabric-impressed), Crosno/Cahokia cordmarked, Sikeston negative-painted, and Angel negative-painted.

(Chapter 6), was occupied over a very short period of time and thus should yield high correlation coefficients between various collections. As indicated in Chapter 1, an extremely small amount of material predating the late Mississippian period occupation has occasionally been recovered from Campbell (e.g., Chapman and Anderson [1955] found a Mulberry Creek cordmarked sherd and a Baytown plain sherd on the surface), but the vast majority of items appear to date late in the Mississippian sequence. As we demonstrate below, the fact that a site was occupied over a short duration does not necessarily imply that collections will be similar.

We used three sets of data in our analysis of the Campbell assemblages: surface-collected and excavated materials reported by Chapman and Anderson (1955), intact vessels from burials (reported in Chapter 6), and surface-collected materials reported by S. Williams (1954). For comparative purposes, an excavated assemblage from Parkin (northeastern Arkansas [Klinger 1977b]), which S. Williams (1980) labels an Armorel-phase site, was added. Our rationale for using Parkin was based primarily on its large sample size and on the fact that although Williams (1980) labels it an Armorel-phase site, most other archaeologists place it in the Parkin phase, a phase contemporary with Nodena and Armorel along the middle reaches of the St. Francis River. We hasten to point out that we do not expect Campbell and Parkin, given the considerable geographical distance between them (roughly 130 km), to score particularly close in terms of similarity coefficients. We do, however, hope to show that there was (and still is) little reason to place them in the same phase.

The first step in the analysis was to derive overall similarity coefficients for the 10 samples used. Brainerd-Robinson coefficients are presented in Table 3.1 (sherd frequencies can be found in Fox [1992]). The *BR* coefficients range from a high of 183 (fill above burials 15 and 16 at Campbell compared with fill above burial 17) to a low of 54 (S. Williams's [1954] surface collection compared with excavated materials from Parkin [Klinger 1977b]). The burial fills (1–4 in Table 3.1) are fairly homogeneous (low *BR* coefficient is 150), as are the two test-pit fills (5 and 6 in Table 3.1—*BR* coefficient of 155) and Chapman and Anderson's (1955) and Williams's (1954) surface collections (7 and 8, respectively, in Table 3.1—*BR* coefficient of 158). Conversely, the Campbell mortuary assemblage (9 in Table 3.1) is not similar to either of the surface collections (*BR* coefficients of 84 [between the mortuary assemblage and Williams's collection] and 90 [between the mortuary assemblage and Chapman and Anderson's collection]). Two samples from Campbell have coefficients above 155 when compared with the excavated assemblage from Parkin (Klinger 1977b); the remaining coefficients between Campbell and Parkin assemblages range from a high of 142 to a low of 54. These coefficients raise a number of interesting questions concerning both the cohesiveness of the Armorel phase as defined by Williams (1980) and the occupation sequence at

Table 3.1
Similarity Matrix of Brainerd-Robinson Coefficients for
Nine Ceramic Assemblages from Campbell and One from Parkin

2:	169								
3:	178	183							
4:	163	150	161						
5:	162	147	158	177					
6:	171	175	181	155	155				
7:	126	105	118	129	126	103			
8:	107	96	103	131	140	106	158		
9:	152	180	169	142	136	164	90	84	
10:	140	156	142	109	106	135	80	54	160
	1	2	3	4	5	6	7	8	9

Source: Campbell data, except where noted, from Chapman and Anderson 1955.

Note: 1—fill above burials 10B, 11, and 12; 2—fill above burials 15 and 16; 3—fill above burial 17; 4—test-trench fill west of and above burial 18; 5—west test pit; 6—northwest test pit; 7—Chapman and Anderson's surface collection; 8—S. Williams's (1954) surface collection; 9—whole vessels from Campbell burials (Holland 1991); 10—excavated (1966) sample from Parkin (Klinger 1977b).

Campbell and Parkin, but our interest here is really on the possible effects that particular biases might have on the coefficients.

To better understand the nature of the dissimilarities among the Campbell and Parkin assemblages, we subjected the data to nonmetric multidimensional scaling, the two-dimensional results of which are presented in Figure 3.1. Of interest is the representation of the two surface collections (7 and 8) as outliers to the main grouping of ceramic samples from Campbell. The Parkin site (10) also is an outlier to the group, and its closest neighbor in the main cluster is the Campbell mortuary assemblage (9). This supports the interpretation made on the basis of the similarity matrix (Table 3.1) that the Parkin ceramic assemblage is more similar to the Campbell mortuary assemblage than it is to any of the other assemblages from Campbell. But why are so many of the Campbell assemblages so unlike one another, particularly the two surface collections relative to the excavated assemblages? One might suppose, intuitively, that surface collections, even grab samples, will perform better in terms of representing what actually occurs at a site than will spatially restricted excavated samples, but such a proposition needs to be examined empirically. We examine below three potential sources of bias in the collections.

Collection-Method Bias

Chapman and Anderson (1955) acknowledge that a bias exists in at least one of their assemblages from Campbell. Relative to their surface collection, they state

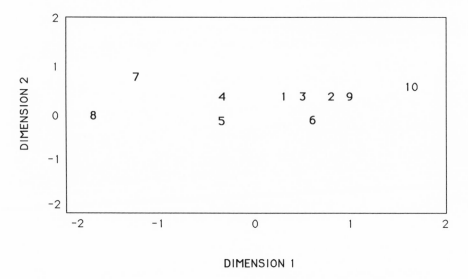

Figure 3.1. Results of multidimensional scaling (two dimensions) of two surface-collected (7 and 8) and seven excavated (1–6 and 9) ceramic assemblages from Campbell and one excavated assemblage from Parkin (10) (after Fox 1992). See Table 3.1 for key to specific proveniences.

(p. 29), "This is a selective sample in that not all sherds, but only those that were rimsherds or that had some decoration or special shape characteristic were picked up. Plain body sherds got in the collection *by chance rather than purposefully*" (emphasis added). If this statement applied *only* to their surface collection, we might intuitively expect *BR* coefficients among the different Campbell assemblages to increase dramatically after removal of sherds of Neeley's Ferry plain and Bell plain from all assemblages, in effect smoothing out differences based on changing collection strategy. But, interestingly, just the opposite occurs (Table 3.2). After removal of the two types, *BR* coefficients for assemblages from burial fill (1–4 in Table 3.2) tend to retain some semblance of similarity, but coefficients between those assemblages and others from Campbell are low, as are all coefficients between Campbell assemblages and the Parkin assemblage (10 in Table 3.2). Multidimensional scaling of the data (Figure 3.2) illustrates the scattered nature of the multiple assemblages when Neeley's Ferry plain and Bell plain have been removed.

What could be causing the lowering of *BR* coefficients once the plainwares have been removed? We believe the answer goes well beyond the collection or noncollection of plainwares and is tied directly to the manner in which *all* ceramic materials were collected. Some of the bias was introduced because different investigators made the collections, but even Chapman and Anderson apparently did not maintain any type of systematic control over what they did

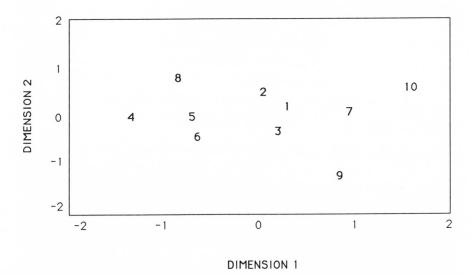

Figure 3.2. Results of multidimensional scaling (two dimensions) of two surface-collected (7 and 8) and seven excavated (1–6 and 9) ceramic assemblages from Campbell and one excavated assemblage from Parkin (10), with Neeley's Ferry plain and Bell plain sherds removed (after Fox 1992). See Table 3.1 for key to specific proveniences.

Table 3.2
**Similarity Matrix of Brainerd-Robinson Coefficients for
Nine Ceramic Assemblages from Campbell and One from Parkin,
without Neeley's Ferry Plain and Bell Plain**

2:	153								
3:	152	133							
4:	73	80	67						
5:	98	105	92	125					
6:	91	80	133	100	133				
7:	106	120	108	12	37	42			
8:	73	120	67	104	109	104	62		
9:	43	24	90	22	43	61	83	12	
10:	106	86	69	3	28	3	92	16	34
	1	2	3	4	5	6	7	8	9

Source: Campbell data, except where noted, from Chapman and Anderson 1955.

Note: 1—fill above burials 10B, 11, and 12; 2—fill above burials 15 and 16; 3—fill above burial 17; 4—test-trench fill west of and above burial 18; 5—west test pit; 6—northwest test pit; 7—Chapman and Anderson's surface collection; 8—S. Williams's (1954) surface collection; 9—whole vessels from Campbell burials (Holland 1991); 10—excavated (1966) sample from Parkin (Klinger 1977b).

or did not collect. Table 3.3 lists sherd frequencies and percentages by type in the Williams collection and in the Chapman-Anderson collection. Note the sizable differences between the two. With regard to the plainwares, Neeley's Ferry plain accounts for 73% of Williams's collection but only 19% of the Chapman-Anderson collection. On the other hand, Bell plain makes up 39% of the latter but only 21% of the former—a difference of almost two to one. As an aside, it should be noted that, whether intentional or not, Chapman and Anderson *did* collect numerous plain-surface body sherds.

But even after removing the plainware sherds, we are left with a significant difference between the two collections. In fact, the Williams collection is reduced to 21 sherds spread across 4 types (ignoring the 2 "other" sherds). The Chapman-Anderson collection, however, still contains 535 sherds spread across 12 types (ignoring the 54 "other" sherds). We are willing to grant that some disparity between Williams's surface collection and all other Campbell samples is attributable to the fact that the Campbell-series types (incised, appliquéd, and punctated) were not in use when Williams completed his study in 1954. Looking at the sheer number of incised, punctated, and appliquéd sherds in the Chapman-Anderson collection, however, one cannot help but wonder about the near absence of decorated sherds in Williams's collection, which was made at roughly the same

Table 3.3
Frequency and Percentage of Sherds in
Two Surface Collections from Campbell, by Type

Type	S. Williams Collection		Chapman-Anderson Collection	
	Number	%	Number	%
Neeley's Ferry plain	282	73	274	19
Bell plain	83	21	550	39
Nodena red-and-white	3	1	0	0
Ranch incised	7	2	51	4
Kent incised	2	1	15	1
Parkin punctated	7	2	107	8
Red-slipped	0	0	61	6
Vernon Paul appliquéd	0	0	11	<1
Walls engraved	0	0	5	<1
Hollywood white-slipped	0	0	3	<1
Carson red-on-buff	0	0	1	<1
Mulberry Creek cordmarked	0	0	1	<1
Campbell appliquéd	0	0	228	16
Campbell incised	0	0	31	2
Campbell punctated	0	0	21	1
Other	2	<1	54	4
Total	386	~100	1,413	~100

time as that by Chapman and Anderson. How can their collection contain 239 appliquéd sherds (combining, for the moment, Campbell appliquéd and Vernon Paul appliquéd, since Williams probably would have used the latter type), or 17% of their entire collection, and Williams's collection contain none? Chapman and Anderson also collected 61 red-slipped sherds (6% of their collection) to Williams's 0, 128 punctated sherds (9%) to Williams's 7 (2%), and 97 incised sherds (7%) to Williams's 9 (3%). The only nonplainware type more prevalent in Williams's collection is Nodena red-and-white (3 sherds to 0).

Collector bias at Campbell is not only evident between collectors but also in how the same collector or team of collectors operated over time, a fact noted by Chapman and Anderson (1955: 98): "[S]urface collections were selected on the basis of decoration and rimsherd fragments in most instances, whereas the collections from the excavation were less selective in nature." The context of the quote is their discussion of the reversal in percentages of Bell plain and Neeley's Ferry plain noted between the surface collection and various excavated assemblages. But they also suggest that perhaps the differences are chronological: "[T]here is another possibility, and that is that the site was inhabited over a fairly long period of time and that the samples in the fill, being mainly below the surface level, represent an earlier phase when Neeley's Ferry Plain predominated." However, we now know enough about Campbell in terms of the placement of burials and the time span reflected (discussed in Chapter 5) to reject a long occupational history. We believe the differences among the assemblages are attributable to (a) intercollector bias, (b) different recovery strategies employed at various times, and (c) sample-size bias, which we discuss below.

Sample-Size Bias

When sample sizes vary over an extreme range, as they do among the Campbell samples as well as among the sites discussed later in the chapter, not only can type percentages fluctuate widely, but the number of types present can do likewise. However, one cannot automatically conclude that larger samples are any more reliable than smaller ones in estimating the *nature* of the population from which the sample was drawn, since recovery methods and techniques obviously can play a significant role in effecting the result. One method of controlling for sizable disparity in sample size is to standardize the samples by subtracting the mean from each case and dividing the difference by the standard deviation of the sample. Given the low frequencies of most types, however, along with the fact that the Brainerd-Robinson index is based on percentage differences, we did not standardize the samples. Table 3.4 shows the size of the contributions made to the Campbell and Parkin samples by the types Neeley's Ferry plain and Bell plain. In effect, the percentages of those two types dwarf the percentages of the other types, on average contributing 85% of the sherds to an assemblage. Removing the combined effects of the two types allows the other types greater representation, a point related to sample diversity (discussed later).

Typological Bias

For lack of a better term, we call the last kind of bias discussed here *typological bias,* or bias that results from using sherds as opposed to complete vessels. As discussed in Chapter 2, one problem with using the central Mississippi River valley ceramic types as currently defined is the inability to distinguish between plain-surface sherds that came from undecorated vessels and plain-surface sherds that came from undecorated portions of decorated vessels. Hence, the types Neeley's Ferry plain and Bell plain, being default categories, will always be overrepresented in sherd collections. This phenomenon is evident in Table 3.4. Note that the complete vessels exhibit the lowest percentage of the types Neeley's

Table 3.4
Total Ceramic Assemblages and Percentages Represented by Plainware Types in Campbell and Parkin Samples

	Assemblage	Total Ceramic Assemblage	Neeley's Ferry Plain and Bell Plain	Plainware Percentage
1.	Fill above burials 10B, 11, and 12	59	48	81
2.	Fill above burials 15 and 16	60	55	92
3.	Fill above burial 17	33	30	91
4.	Fill west and above burial 18	16	14	87
5.	West test pit	39	31	88
6.	Northwest test pit	19	16	84
7.	Chapman and Anderson surface collection	1,068	824	77
8.	S. Williams surface collection	379	365	96
9.	Mortuary vessels[a]	190	133	70
10.	Parkin site	1,956	1,581	81

[a] The number of mortuary vessels derived from Anderson's excavations differs from the 164 listed by Fox (1992: appendix 1), who was using Holland's (1991) count. The actual number of Campbell vessels (see Chapter 6) is 254, 190 of which are of known type (no type information exists for the others). This is the figure used above. However, the percentage of plainwares shown above (70%) is almost identical to the 72% listed by Fox (1992: table 19). *BR* coefficients shown in Tables 3.1 and 3.2 which have been adjusted from those presented in Fox 1992, changed very little.

Ferry plain and Bell plain (70%) of all 10 assemblages, for the simple reason that their completeness allows these types to be recognized. Whereas plain-surface body sherds from a Campbell appliquéd vessel might be typed as Neeley's Ferry plain or Bell plain, an intact Campbell appliquéd vessel would never be typed as Neeley's Ferry plain or Bell plain. This is another reason that the Campbell-Parkin assemblage coefficients were run the second time without Neeley's Ferry plain or Bell plain types.

Sample Diversity

Problems related to sample size and sample comparability confound our ability to document variation in the archaeological record—whether our interest in variation is related to time and space or to other analytical dimensions such as technology and function. Sampling problems come in different shapes and forms, but the one that is of particular interest here concerns the issue of representativeness, that is, how representative is an excavated or surface-collected sample of the population of artifacts from which it was drawn? The collections discussed in this volume were not the result of any probabilistically structured sampling program but rather were, for the most part, uncontrolled, "grab-bag" samples. Some of the excavated materials came from units over which there existed some degree of vertical and horizontal control, but other excavated samples were recovered from road-grader cuts or from backfill that resulted from the excavation of burials. Given the varying degrees of control exercised in the field, it is difficult in any a priori sense to assess the statistical representativeness of the samples.

Another area of concern is sample size. For example, do small collections underrepresent the frequency of certain ceramic types? Or, in like fashion, do small collections completely lack certain ceramic types that actually occur at a site, albeit in low frequencies? How large do collections have to be before we can feel fairly confident that most types present at a site are represented in the collection? In other words, how large does a sample have to be before we start getting redundant information? These are difficult questions to answer without knowing the nature of the sites. Are the deposits shallow or deep? Are materials from chronologically earlier components completely buried under later deposits? At issue is richness—how many classes or types of things are represented in a sample? For our immediate purposes this question translates into: How many ceramic types are represented in an assemblage? And can we use either percentage of occurrence or presence/absence of the different types to examine intersite variation? We have examined some of these issues relative to intrasite variation; now we extend discussion to examination of a range of Mississippian-period sites from southeastern Missouri.

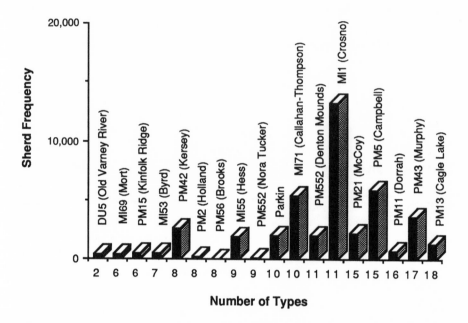

Figure 3.3. Ceramic type richness plotted against sherd frequency for 17 Mississippian-period sites in southeastern Missouri and 1 in northeastern Arkansas (Parkin) (after Fox 1992). Sources of assemblage composition are as follows: Parkin (Klinger 1977b), Callahan-Thompson and Hess (Lewis 1982), Crosno and Old Varney River (S. Williams 1954), Mort and Byrd (J. R. Williams 1968), Kersey (Marshall 1965); all other assemblages (regardless of whether they were previously reported) were (re)sorted in 1992.

Figure 3.3 illustrates the relation between sample size and richness (the number of types[2] represented) of 18 excavated and/or surface-collected assemblages from southeastern Missouri—5 from Mississippi County, 11 from Pemiscot County, 1 from Dunklin County (the Old Varney River site), and 1 from northeastern Arkansas (Parkin). We used all surface-collected material housed at the University of Missouri and, when available, augmented the samples with excavated material. Berry, because of the small sample size, was again deleted from analysis.

Intuitively, we might predict that as sample size increases so too does the richness of an assemblage. If we were to look only at the four leftmost sites in Figure 3.3, we might believe that such was the case. But notice what happens when we add Kersey, Holland, and Brooks to the sample. The Kersey assemblage is by far the largest of the three, but all three contain the same number of named types. Moving farther to the right, Nora Tucker, the second-smallest assemblage,

2. For this exercise we use only established types, such as Bell plain or Nodena red-and-white. In Chapter 7 we describe the odd sherds that cannot be accommodated by the normally used type names, but they are not included here.

contains 9 types. Crosno, represented by what is by far the largest of the assemblages, ties with the much smaller assemblage from Denton Mounds with 11 types and is completely outdistanced by assemblages from 5 other Pemiscot County sites. Dorrah and Cagle Lake, both of which are in the bottom half of the assemblages in terms of size, are ranked 3 and 1, respectively, in terms of the number of types present.

The simple message here is that as sample size increases, the number of classes in the assemblages does not necessarily increase either proportionately or logarithmically. Why do the smaller assemblages from Pemiscot County perform so well in terms of number of types? Is it strictly because of chance, or could it be a result of collector bias? It undoubtedly is not due to chance and perhaps is controlled to a small degree by collector bias, but there is another reason for the high ranking of the smaller assemblages—one tied directly to the periods during which the sites were occupied. During the late Mississippian period, a wide range of decorative methods (incising, engraving, slipping) and motifs became popular, and hence the number of types devised by archaeologists to encompass this variation is high. For example, Walls incised, Ranch incised, Rhodes incised, Carson red-on-buff, Nodena red-and-white, and Hollywood white-slipped were late types that are not found on sites dating to before ca. a.d. 1350. Plain-surface vessels (Neeley's Ferry plain and Bell plain) were still common constituents of assemblages, but more and more vessel surfaces were being modified. Consequently, the number of types present in the Pemiscot Bayou assemblages—where sites contain late Mississippian period components—is generally greater than in the Mississippi County assemblages—where sites were occupied during the early and middle Mississippian periods, when a higher percentage of vessel surfaces were left undecorated. The same is true for the earlier sites of Old Varney River and Kersey.

Richness—here, the number of types present in an assemblage—is only one half of a statistical measure that examines not only the number of categories (types) but also how evenly divided objects are relative to the number of categories (evenness). In other words, do some types have many more sherds than others, or is the distribution much more even? This measure is called *diversity*, and it can be used to examine intersite differences and similarities. We know from earlier discussion that Neeley's Ferry plain and Bell plain contribute heavily to collections from Parkin and Campbell, a trend evident in all southeastern Missouri collections. But this contribution, as large as it is, does little to affect the diversity measure of some assemblages. Using base-10 logarithms, we calculated a Shannon Index of Diversity for many of the assemblages discussed above. The higher the index value, the greater the diversity in the assemblage. Five late-Mississippian Pemiscot County sites—the four "richest" sites shown in Figure 3.3 plus Holland—came out as having the greatest diversity values. In other words, not only do four of the Pemiscot Bayou sites contain the most ceramic types, but they also contain inherent differences relative to the other sites in terms of how evenly sherds are distributed among the types. This is our first indication that there are grounds for examining at least some of the Pemiscot Bayou sites as a larger analytical unit.

The Pemiscot Bayou Assemblages

Although the Pemiscot Bayou assemblages for the most part score high on the diversity index, this tells us little or nothing about their similarities and dissimilarities, either among themselves or relative to other Mississippian assemblages from southeastern Missouri. Two questions still remain to be answered. First, are the Pemiscot Bayou assemblages different enough from other Mississippian assemblages—differences that are a result of time and/or space—to warrant grouping them? Second, what are the degrees of similarity between and among only the Pemiscot Bayou sites? To examine these topics we can construct additional Brainerd-Robinson matrices and multidimensional-scaling plots.

We examine the first question by using 15 assemblages: 1 from northeastern Arkansas (Parkin, listed in Figure 3.3) and 14 from southeastern Missouri (those remaining in Figure 3.3 minus Brooks, Kinfolk Ridge, and Nora Tucker). We do not show here the *BR* coefficients obtained when Neeley's Ferry plain and Bell plain sherds are left in the assemblages (see Fox 1992: table 20), but Figure 3.4 presents the two-dimensional results of multidimensional scaling. The exercise yields a fairly continuous spiraled pattern of site distribution, which we might have accepted as representing a temporal continuum from early (left) to late (right) except for the cluster of sites at the left end, which contains among others Crosno, Parkin, and Dorrah. Crosno (site 1) was a much earlier site than Dorrah (site 14) and probably Parkin (site 12) (Parkin persisted at least up into the sixteenth century [P. A. Morse 1981], whereas Crosno was abandoned much earlier). Size itself appears to have little to do with the grouping, since Crosno is by far the largest assemblage (see Figure 3.3) and Dorrah is one of the smallest, though this does not imply that the great disparity in sample sizes did not affect the results (see below).

At present, we have no ready interpretation of the pattern that was produced, though we note that a few expected site associations are evident, such as that between Old Varney River (site 13) and Kersey (site 10), both of which contain high percentages of red-slipped sherds. In hopes of achieving a more interpretable pattern, we ran the plot in three dimensions, but those results (not shown) were also uninterpretable. The Shepard plots associated with both the two-dimensional and the three-dimensional scalings were, to say the least, messy, which probably indicated that we had reached a degenerate solution as the statistic tried in vain to minimize stress. Our first thought was that sample-size disparity was indeed a problem, and in hopes of achieving a better solution we removed sherds of Neeley's Ferry plain and Bell plain from the samples. The drawback to this approach,

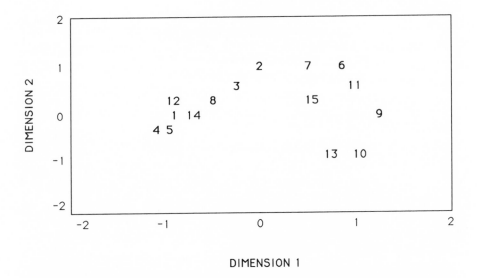

Figure 3.4. Results of multidimensional scaling (2 dimensions) of excavated ceramic assemblages from 14 Mississippian-period sites in southeastern Missouri and 1 in northeastern Arkansas (Parkin) (after Fox 1992). Key to sites: 1, Crosno; 2, Callahan-Thompson; 3, Hess; 4, Mort; 5, Byrd; 6, McCoy; 7, Cagle Lake; 8, Denton Mounds; 9, Holland; 10, Kersey; 11, Campbell; 12, Parkin; 13, Old Varney River; 14, Dorrah; 15, Murphy (1–5 are in Mississippi County, 12 is in Cross County, Arkansas, 13 is in Dunklin County, and all others are in Pemiscot County).

which, given the results below, appears minor, is that it creates a direct bias against assemblages from time periods (or geographic areas) when (where) vessel decoration occurred less frequently than it did in others.

Table 3.5 lists the *BR* coefficients from the 15 sites after removal of Neeley's Ferry plain and Bell plain. Coefficients range from a low of 2 to a high of 191. Table 3.6 lists the 9 highest-ranked pairs of sites (*BR* coefficients of over 140). Note that 8 of those 9 rankings are between Pemiscot Bayou sites or between a Pemiscot Bayou site and Old Varney River, which makes it into the group because of its high percentage of red-slipped sherds. Interestingly, only one coefficient above 140 includes sites from Mississippi County, that being a *BR* coefficient of 149 between assemblages from Crosno (site 1) and Byrd (site 5). In other words, the Pemiscot Bayou sites on the whole *appear* to have more in common among themselves than either they do with the Mississippi County sites or the Mississippi County sites do with each other.

Despite their lower *BR* coefficients relative to those for the Pemiscot Bayou sites, once Neeley's Ferry plain and Bell plain sherds are removed, the Mississippi County sites group in a more definable cluster (Figure 3.5) than they did when the plain-surface sherds were included. All five Mississippi County sites are to the

Table 3.5
Similarity Matrix of Brainerd-Robinson Coefficients for
15 Mississippian-Period Sites, without Neeley's Ferry Plain and Bell Plain

	1	2	3	4	5	6	7	8	9	10	11	12	13	14
2:	116													
3:	71	137												
4:	13	76	74											
5:	149	85	103	25										
6:	3	17	41	7	37									
7:	3	16	57	9	44	151								
8:	2	12	72	6	43	104	92							
9:	7	19	76	6	48	53	71	84						
10:	8	16	78	9	49	38	56	73	175					
11:	2	15	72	6	43	113	105	165	110	91				
12:	2	8	4	4	4	112	121	30	15	5	80			
13:	2	10	72	6	43	37	55	73	175	191	47	4		
14:	45	55	80	6	72	83	111	56	54	40	80	84	40	
15:	4	19	77	9	44	93	100	119	154	142	91	28	141	61

Note: 1—Crosno (S. Williams 1954); 2—Callahan-Thompson (Lewis 1982); 3—Hess (Lewis 1982); 4—Mort (J. R. Williams 1968); 5—Byrd (J. R. Williams 1968); 6—McCoy (J. R. Williams 1968); 7—Cagle Lake (J. R. Williams 1972); 8—Denton Mounds (J. R. Williams 1972); 9—Holland (Marshall 1965); 10—Kersey (Marshall 1965); 11—Campbell (UM Museum collections); 12—Parkin (Klinger 1977b); 13—Old Varney River (S. Williams 1954); 14—Dorrah (UM Museum collections); 15—Murphy (UM Museum collections).

Table 3.6
Nine Highest-Ranking Brainerd-Robinson Coefficients of
Similarity for 15 Mississippian-Period Sites

Site	Site	*BR* Coefficient
Old Varney River	Kersey	191
Kersey	Holland	175
Old Varney River	Holland	175
Campbell	Denton Mounds	165
Murphy	Holland	154
Cagle Lake	McCoy	151
Crosno	Byrd	149
Murphy	Kersey	142
Murphy	Old Varney River	141

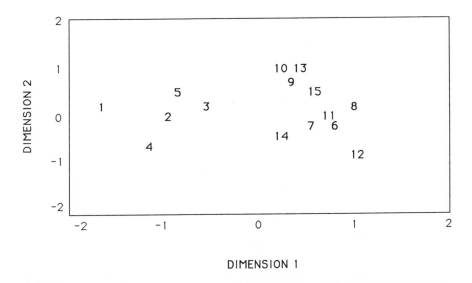

Figure 3.5. Results of multidimensional scaling (2 dimensions) of excavated ceramic assemblages from 14 Mississippian-period sites in southeastern Missouri and 1 in northeastern Arkansas (Parkin), with Neeley's Ferry plain and Bell plain sherds removed (after Fox 1992). Note the separation between the five Mississippi County sites on the left and the more southern (and for the most part later) sites on the right. Compare the distribution seen in Figure 3.4. Key to sites: 1, Crosno; 2, Callahan-Thompson; 3, Hess; 4, Mort; 5, Byrd; 6, McCoy; 7, Cagle Lake; 8, Denton Mounds; 9, Holland; 10, Kersey; 11, Campbell; 12, Parkin; 13, Old Varney River; 14, Dorrah; 15, Murphy (1–5 are in Mississippi County, 12 is in Cross County, Arkansas, 13 is in Dunklin County, and all others are in Pemiscot County).

left of the centerline and well away from the Pemiscot Bayou–Parkin–Old Varney River group. The association of the five Mississippi County sites is based on fairly high representation of Manly punctated, Wickliffe, and O'Byam incised/engraved and a low representation of red-slipped and other types. The Pemiscot Bayou sites form a cluster to the right of the centerline, along with Old Varney River (13) and Parkin (12). Sites often cited in the literature as being very late—Campbell (11), Cagle Lake (7), and McCoy (6)—cluster together, as do Old Varney River, Holland (9), and Kersey (10). The three late sites exhibit significant percentages of the ceramic types Barton incised, Campbell appliquéd/incised/punctated, and Parkin punctated, while Old Varney River, Holland, and Kersey do not. One feature those three sites have in common is a significant percentage of red-slipped ceramics. The site intermediate between the two clusters, Murphy (15), contains smaller percentages of the late ceramic types than do the four late sites, as well as a significant percentage of red-slipped sherds. Parkin, a supposed component of the Armorel phase (S. Williams 1980), lies well away from Campbell, another Armorel component. Dorrah (14) and Denton Mounds (8) lie outside the cluster comprising McCoy, Campbell, and Cagle Lake.

We now turn attention to another matter: How similar are the collections from the Pemiscot Bayou sites? To answer this question, we again use Brainerd-Robinson and multidimensional scaling, this time increasing the sample of sites from Pemiscot County to 11. We included in the sample 10 of the 11 Pemiscot County sites shown in Figure 3.3[3] plus Wardell (23PM28), a presumably early and middle Mississippian period site in northern Pemiscot County (Figure 1.5). We use two sets of data in the analysis: (1) surface-collected items only and (2) combined surface-collected and (for 6 sites) excavated samples. As shown in Table 3.7, which lists the frequencies of surface-collected ceramic types by site (see chapters 5 and 7), the samples from several of the sites are relatively small. We have again deleted Neeley's Ferry plain and Bell plain from the analysis and, unlike in the previous analyses, have subdivided the Campbell series into appliquéd, punctated, and incised. *BR* coefficients are listed in Table 3.8. For the sake of convenience, the highest coefficients are listed in Table 3.9 in descending order.

Coefficients range from a high of 185, between Wardell and Kersey, to lows of 18 between Dorrah and Kersey, 19 between Dorrah and Wardell, and 20 between Wardell and McCoy. In fact, Wardell and Kersey, except for their high coefficient of 185, never exhibit a coefficient above 90 with any other site except Denton Mounds. Wardell and Denton Mounds have a *BR* coefficient of 179, and Kersey and Denton Mounds have a coefficient of 178. The next highest coefficient between Denton Mounds and any other site is 115, which it reaches with Brooks. The relation among Kersey, Wardell, and Denton Mounds is shown graphically on the right side of Figure 3.6. Lines in Figure 3.6 connect sites that have *BR* coefficients of 134 or above, which was the minimum coefficient that allowed every site to be connected with another site (between Dorrah and Campbell). Single arrows point to the site with which the site at the tail end of the arrow scores highest; double arrows indicate that two sites score highest with each other. In other words, Denton Mounds scores equally (actually within 1 point, which we counted as a tie) with both Kersey and Wardell, but the highest coefficients of similarity exhibited by Kersey and Wardell are with each other.

The left side of Figure 3.6 shows the relations among the 8 remaining sites at a *BR* coefficient of 134 or higher. McCoy and Kinfolk Ridge have the highest coefficient, 179, followed by Murphy and Kinfolk Ridge at 160 and Cagle Lake and Brooks at 159. The lowest link, at 134, is between Campbell and Dorrah. Murphy and Cagle Lake have the most connections above *BR* 134, with 3 each, including a mutual connection of 151.

How do we interpret the *BR* coefficients? Are we seeing time represented in the diagram, with the Kersey–Wardell–Denton Mounds group being the earliest sites, followed by Cagle Lake, Brooks, Holland, then by Murphy, Kinfolk Ridge,

---

3. We inadvertently deleted Nora Tucker from analysis and did not discover the deletion until the manuscript was completed.

Table 3.7
Frequencies of Decorated Sherds by Ceramic Type in
Surface-Collected Assemblages from 11 Pemiscot County Sites

Site	Ceramic Type							
	Barton	Red	Parkin	C. appliquéd	C. incised	C. punctated	Ranch	Nodena
Holland	4	4	2	2			1	
Campbell		61	107	228	31	21	51	
Dorrah	8	7	49	23	5	4	1	
Cagle Lake	17	47	43	4		1		
Kinfolk R.		11	38					
McCoy	3	15	65	6		3	1	1
Wardell		13						1
Kersey		37						
Murphy		4	6					
Brooks	3	8	4	2				
Denton Mds.	1	8						

	Carson	Hollywood	Kent	Walls	Wallace	Rhodes	M. Place	Fortune
Holland								
Campbell	1	3	15					
Dorrah		1	2	2	1		3	
Cagle Lake		1		2			1	1
Kinfolk R.				5				
McCoy		1	1			1		1
Wardell								
Kersey								
Murphy								
Brooks		1						
Denton Mds.								

McCoy, and finally by Dorrah and Campbell? That does not appear unreasonable, except for the placement of Denton Mounds, which, as we discuss below and in Chapter 7, contains burial vessels of Campbell appliquéd, copper-covered wooden ear plugs, and numerous other presumed late Mississippian period vessels. Perhaps Denton Mounds was occupied over a fairly long period of time, and the surface collection is biased in favor of the early end of the occupation. Or perhaps sample size is biasing the results. We return to the problem of the placement of Denton Mounds below, but for now we will keep it in the group with Wardell and Kersey.

One significant feature evident in Figure 3.6 is, with one exception, the reduction in linking coefficients that occurs to the right of McCoy. Except for the link between Cagle Lake and Holland, with a coefficient of 137, the lowest coefficient to the left of McCoy is 148. The remaining coefficients are in the 150

Table 3.8
**Similarity Matrix of Brainerd-Robinson Coefficients for
11 Surface-Collected Ceramic Assemblages from Pemiscot County,
without Neeley's Ferry Plain and Bell Plain**

	Holland	Campbell	Dorrah	Cagle L.	Kinfolk R.	McCoy	Wardell	Kersey	Murphy	Brooks
Campbell	101									
Dorrah	94	**134**								
Cagle Lake	**137**	75	119							
Kinfolk Ridge	96	66	110	123						
McCoy	81	88	**140**	127	**164**					
Wardell	63	25	19	80	41	20				
Kersey	62	24	18	79	40	30	**185**			
Murphy	128	66	108	**151**	**160**	**158**	81	80		
Brooks	**148**	88	98	**159**	86	93	89	88	124	
Denton Mds	84	24	32	101	40	36	**179**	**178**	80	115

Note: Coefficients equal to or higher than 134, the lowest score at which every site is linked to at least one other site (Dorrah and Campbell), are in bold.

Table 3.9
**Nine Highest-Ranking Brainerd-Robinson Coefficients of Similarity for
11 Surface-Collected Ceramic Assemblages from Pemiscot County**

Site	Site	BR Coefficient
Wardell	Kersey	185
Wardell	Denton Mounds	179
Denton Mounds	Kersey	178
Kinfolk Ridge	McCoy	164
Kinfolk Ridge	Murphy	160
Cagle Lake	Brooks	159
Murphy	McCoy	158
Cagle Lake	Murphy	151
Holland	Brooks	148
Dorrah	McCoy	140
Cagle Lake	Holland	137
Dorrah	Campbell	134

range or above. Are the low coefficients between McCoy and Dorrah and between Dorrah and Campbell a reflection of time, or are they the result of sample bias? In other words, did the initial occupation of Campbell occur after—perhaps well after—occupation of Dorrah began, which itself began well after the founding of McCoy? Dorrah connects to Murphy and Kinfolk Ridge, McCoy's nearest *BR*

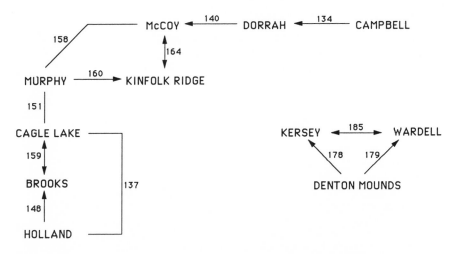

Figure 3.6. Diagram showing Brainerd-Robinson coefficients based on surface-collected ceramic samples for pairs of Pemiscot County sites. Lines connect sites that have *BR* coefficients of 134 or above, which was the minimum coefficient that allowed every site to be connected with another site. Single arrows point to the site that the site at the tail end of the arrow scores highest with; double arrows indicate that the two sites score highest with each other.

neighbors, with coefficients of 108 and 110, respectively, well below its 140 coefficient with McCoy. It connects with Cagle Lake, Brooks, and Holland at coefficients ranging from 94 to 119, similar to its coefficients with Murphy and Kinfolk Ridge. There is, then, a precipitous drop in coefficients to the 18 to 32 range when Dorrah is compared with the Kersey–Wardell–Denton Mounds group. The second highest coefficient involving Campbell—a tie at 88 between McCoy and Brooks—is 46 points lower than its coefficient with Dorrah.

The key to understanding the distribution of *BR* coefficients shown in Figure 3.6 might lie in linking the Kersey–Wardell–Denton Mounds group (Kersey group for short) with the sites in the other part of the diagram. Interestingly enough, when we rank order the remaining *BR* coefficients for each of the 3 sites in the Kersey group (the top two coefficients for each site being with the other two sites in the group), they show amazing resemblance to each other in terms of the sites represented. The third- through sixth-place coefficients for each site are shown in Table 3.10. Note that the same 4 sites are represented in each column—Brooks heads all 3 lists, followed by Murphy in 2 lists. Cagle Lake is ranked second under Denton Mounds and third under both Wardell and Kersey, within a point of each other in both columns; Holland is third under Denton Mounds and fourth under both Wardell and Kersey. Although Murphy is ranked fourth under Denton Mounds, it is only 4 points behind Holland, whereas under Wardell and Kersey, the fourth-ranked site—Holland in both cases—is no closer than 17 points to the third-ranked site—Cagle Lake in both cases. We earlier noted the high correlation between Murphy and Cagle Lake (151) and between Cagle Lake and Brooks (159). Given the data just presented (Table 3.10), we thus should expect a relatively high similarity coefficient between Brooks and Murphy, and it turns out that their *BR* coefficient is fairly high, at 124.

Table 3.10
Rank-Order of Third- through Sixth-Place Brainerd-Robinson Coefficients for Wardell, Kersey, and Denton Mounds

Wardell	Kersey	Denton Mounds
Brooks (89)	Brooks (88)	Brooks (115)
Murphy (81)	Murphy (80)	Cagle Lake (101)
Cagle Lake (80)	Cagle Lake (79)	Holland (84)
Holland (63)	Holland (62)	Murphy (80)

Campbell appears, at least in this analysis, to be the latest site chronologically. We emphasize the words *in this analysis.* In reverse chronological order would come Dorrah, McCoy, Kinfolk Ridge, and Murphy, followed by Cagle Lake, Brooks, and Holland, and then the oldest sites, Wardell, Kersey, and Denton Mounds. But this linear scenario does not take into account the ties exhibited by the midrange coefficients shown in Table 3.8 between Wardell, Kersey, and Denton Mounds on one hand and Brooks, Murphy, Cagle Lake, and Holland on the other. We thus suspect that the *BR* coefficients might not be reflecting only time but rather time *and* space. Interestingly, the group of sites composed of Murphy, McCoy, and Kinfolk Ridge lies in the extreme eastern third of Pemiscot County (Figure 1.5). That they score their highest similarity coefficients with each other might have as much to do with geographic location as with time of occupation.

What about geographic proximity as a potential reason for the similarity among the Kersey–Wardell–Denton Mounds group? The distance involved between any of the two sites suggests that proximity cannot be used to explain the high *BR* coefficients. We might alternatively suggest chronological clustering, though this would indeed be surprising given the lateness of the excavated materials from Denton Mounds (Chapter 7). Could an underrepresentation of late ceramic types on the surface contribute to the early placement of Denton Mounds? J. R. Williams (1972: 94) states that "[s]urface material was collected from Area I at the site, but little was found due to the lack of rain and the fact that the field had been recently plowed." Only 51 sherds were collected, 42 of which were Neeley's Ferry plain and Bell plain (Chapter 7). This is hardly what one would call an acceptable sample.

As shown in Table 3.7, from which the Neeley's Ferry plain and Bell plain samples have been removed, 8 of the 9 remaining sherds were red-slipped, and 1 was Barton incised. The dominance of the small surface collection by red-slipped sherds guarantees that it will correlate highly with other assemblages also dominated by red-slipped sherds, such as Wardell and Kersey. The surface collections from Wardell and Kersey, on the other hand, are much larger, and hence we should have a better chance of seeing types that occur with lower frequency than does the red-slipped type. Although Table 3.7 lists only 14 "decorated" sherds from Wardell (13 red-slipped and 1 Nodena red-and-white), the surface collection made by S. Williams (1954: 185) was large—513 sherds (the remainder were Neeley's Ferry plain [Williams uses the type name *Mississippi plain*] and "unidentified incised"). The Kersey surface collection, also made by S. Williams (1954: 186–87) contained 99 sherds he assigned to the Mississippian period, 58 of which were plain-surface and 4 of which were either Matthews incised or unidentified brush-marked (neither of which are considered here). This leaves the 37 red-slipped sherds listed in Table 3.7. Kersey also contained 715 Woodland-period sherds, the dominant type of which was Mulberry Creek cordmarked (clay-tempered). Although a few Woodland-period sherds show up here and there in the other Pemiscot Bayou site assemblages, indicating minor use of the locales prior to ca. A.D. 900, Kersey apparently dominated the Late Woodland landscape in the Pemiscot Bayou locality. The site clearly received a sizable occupation during the period before and perhaps for a few centuries after A.D. 900, but its major occupation predated the occupations of most if not all the other Pemiscot Bayou sites.

Returning to the surface assemblage from Denton Mounds and the question of bias, exactly how biased is the sample? We can answer this question by examining the combined surface-collected *and* excavated assemblages generated by J. R. Williams (1968), which are presented, along with combined surface-collected and excavated totals from other sites, in Table 3.11. For Denton Mounds, the table lists material from 7 types as opposed to the 2 in the surface collection (Table 3.7). Differences between the surface-collected and excavated assemblages go well beyond the matter of richness. In the surface collection, the 8 red-slipped sherds represent 89% of the small assemblage. In the combined collections, however, red-slipped sherds make up only 36%, while Campbell appliquéd sherds, which do not occur in the surface collection, make up 41% and constitute the dominant type.

If the Denton Mounds surface collection severely underrepresents ceramic types that occur at the site, including the type with the highest frequency, what about the other 5 sites for which we have excavated materials? Do the surface collections from those sites underrepresent types known to occur? Comparing types listed in Table 3.7 (surface-collected material) with types listed in Table 3.11 (surface-collected and excavated material) demonstrates that in all cases the number of types

Table 3.11

Frequencies of Decorated Sherds by Ceramic Type in Excavated and Surface-Collected Assemblages from 11 Pemiscot County Sites

Site	Ceramic Type							
	Barton	Red	Parkin	C. appliquéd	C. incised	C. punctated	Ranch	Nodena
Holland	4	4	2	2	1			
Campbell	80	960	267	713	22	20	61	4
Dorrah	8	7	49	23	5	4	1	
Cagle Lake	35	63	93	17	4	3	3	1
Kinfolk R.		11	38					
McCoy	19	129	337	145	12	15	9	1
Wardell		13						1
Kersey	1	1,367						
Murphy	14	589	71	93	16	11	3	
Brooks	3	8	4	2				

	Carson	Hollywood	Kent	Walls	Wallace	Rhodes	M. Place	Fortune
Holland								
Campbell	5	7	37	13		15		1
Dorrah		1	2	2	1		3	
Cagle Lake		1	2	2		1	3	1
Kinfolk R.				5				
McCoy		1	1	4		5	4	1
Wardell								
Kersey								23
Murphy				2		5	7	1
Brooks	1							
Denton Mds.						10		

differs, often significantly. The most extreme case is the Murphy combined assemblage, which contains sherds of 11 types, only 2 of which are represented in the small surface collection. In addition, although red-slipped sherds occur in the Murphy surface collection, they only contribute 40% of the total. In the combined sample, however, they far outweigh any other type at the site (73% [589/812]). Surface collections from Campbell and Cagle Lake underrepresent the number of known types by 5 each, but the sherd frequencies within those types are small and do not greatly affect the similarity coefficients. The same is true for McCoy, which is underrepresented by 3 types. Kersey picks up 2 types in the excavated assemblage, but these serve to lower the percentage of red-slipped sherds only from 100% to 98%. Denton Mounds, however, is the site most affected, not necessarily in terms of the number of underrepresented decorated types (5 of 7) in the surface collection but rather, as noted above, from the standpoint of the sheer *numbers* of sherds of types not in the surface collection. To control for the biases, we can compute a new *BR* matrix using both surface-collected and excavated sherds. The resulting matrix is shown in Table 3.12.

Table 3.12
Similarity Matrix of Brainerd-Robinson Coefficients for
11 Surface-Collected and Excavated Ceramic Assemblages from
Pemiscot County, without Neeley's Ferry Plain and Bell Plain

	Holland	Campbell	Dorrah	Cagle L.	Kinfolk R.	McCoy	Wardell	Kersey	Murphy	Brooks
Campbell	129									
Dorrah	102	99								
Cagle Lake	142	115	142							
Kinfolk Ridge	77	78	115	129						
McCoy	109	119	166	152	139					
Wardell	65	90	15	59	40	39				
Kersey	65	90	15	59	40	39	184			
Murphy	111	135	65	99	59	90	154	148		
Brooks	138	143	96	148	85	110	89	89	131	
Denton Mds	123	161	88	94	55	106	79	73	121	112

Note: Coefficients equal to or higher than 139, the lowest score at which every site is linked to at least one other site [Kinfolk Ridge and McCoy], are in bold (also shown in bold is the coefficient between Holland and Brooks [138], since it essentially ties with Kinfolk Ridge–McCoy).

The *BR* coefficients are plotted in Figure 3.7 using the same format as in Figure 3.6, that is, plotting all coefficients above the coefficient at which all sites are shown connected to at least one other site—in this case 139, between Kinfolk Ridge and McCoy (we also link Holland and Brooks at 138, since it essentially ties with Kinfolk Ridge–McCoy). Now, Murphy takes the place of Denton Mounds as an early site, along with Kersey and Wardell. Denton Mounds, instead of showing up as an early site, connects strongly with Campbell, with a coefficient of 161. Instead of linking to Dorrah, as before, Campbell is now linked directly to Brooks. Kinfolk Ridge, McCoy, and Dorrah still exhibit strong ties, as do Brooks and Cagle Lake. Interestingly, the two highest-ranking of the coefficients not shown in Figure 3.7 are between Murphy and Campbell (135) and between Murphy and Brooks (131). As discussed in Chapter 5, Murphy contains a late component similar to those at Campbell and Brooks, causing it to link to those sites, though the sizable contribution of sherds from its large early component causes it to exhibit stronger links with Kersey and Wardell.

Based on the combined surface-collected and excavated assemblages, the chronological positioning of the sites would include Campbell and Denton

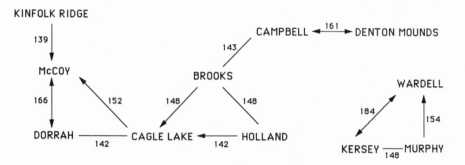

Figure 3.7. Diagram showing Brainerd-Robinson coefficients based on surface-collected and excavated ceramic samples for pairs of Pemiscot County sites. Lines connect sites that have *BR* coefficients of 139 or above, which was the minimum coefficient that allowed every site to be connected with another site. Single arrows point to the site that the site at the tail end of the arrow scores highest with; double arrows indicate that the two sites score highest with each other.

Mounds on the late end and Kersey and Wardell on the early end. The six-site grouping of Brooks, Holland, Cagle Lake, McCoy, Kinfolk Ridge, and Dorrah is somewhere in the middle. Murphy is an early site that also contains a late component. Again, we cannot emphasize too strongly that the Pemiscot Bayou sites were not occupied sequentially. What the similarity coefficients show is how similar one assemblage is to another, which we assume is based in large part on their chronological positions relative to each other. But certainly several sites, or most of the sites for that matter, could have been occupied simultaneously. What the linkages show is when certain sites were occupied in a relative sense, as is shown in the *hypothetical* situation depicted in Figure 3.8. It is well beyond the available data to indicate exactly when or for how long each site was occupied. For those types of determinations we need absolute dates, which, except for a single radiocarbon date from Denton Mounds, are not available.

To this point we have focused on the similarity of the Pemiscot Bayou sites, but we can also ask how *dissimilar* the sites are. To develop that line of evidence we can use multidimensional scaling, which we employed earlier to examine dissimilarities among the larger group of assemblages. Recall that when sherds of Neeley's Ferry plain and Bell plain were removed, the sites from Mississippi County, Missouri, separated themselves from the Pemiscot Bayou sites (Figure 3.5). In examining the dissimilarities among the Pemiscot Bayou sites, we shift from a two-dimensional plot to a three-dimensional plot in order to bring out subtle differences that would otherwise be compressed. Figure 3.9 illustrates

A.D. 900   A.D. 1540

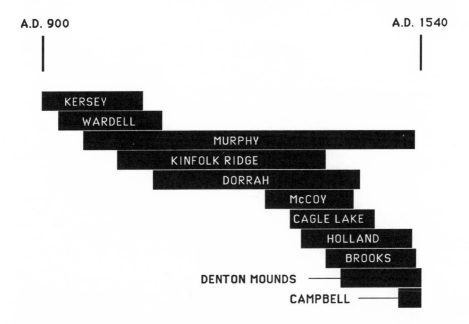

Figure 3.8. Hypothetical chronological arrangement of 11 Pemiscot County sites, showing inferred relative lengths of site occupation.

the multidimensional scaling in three dimensions, using the combined surface-collected and, when possible, excavated assemblages (data from Table 3.11).[4]

Several features are evident in the site positionings. First, Denton Mounds and Brooks contain almost identical coefficients in all three dimensions and are mapped essentially as a single site (A). Second, with the exception of Campbell (J) and Cagle Lake (H), all sites lie between -0.27 and 0.38 of the zero line on the Y-axis. Campbell has a Y-axis value of -1.95 and Cagle Lake 1.35, a one-dimensional "distance" of 3.30. It is difficult to assess exactly why Campbell exhibits such an anomalous coefficient, unless it is due to the high frequency of sherds of Barton incised relative to the rest of the assemblages or to a combination of a high frequency of Barton incised in conjunction with high frequencies of other types, such as Campbell appliquéd.[5] On the X-axis, Campbell aligns itself along the zero line with Brooks, Denton Mounds, Holland (E), Murphy (F), and Kersey (D).

4. For those readers who are interested in the technical side of multidimensional scaling, we ran the plot in both 2 and 3 dimensions. In 2 dimensions the Systat MDS program ran 35 iterations, with a final stress of 0.078. In 3 dimensions it ran 49 iterations, with a final stress of 0.023—a much superior solution to the scaling. The Shepard diagram from the 3-dimensional plot showed an almost straight line of points, whereas the 2-dimensional Shepard diagram did not.

5. Curiously, only 1 of the 190 burial vessels of known type from Leo Anderson's work at Campbell is of Barton incised (Chapter 6).

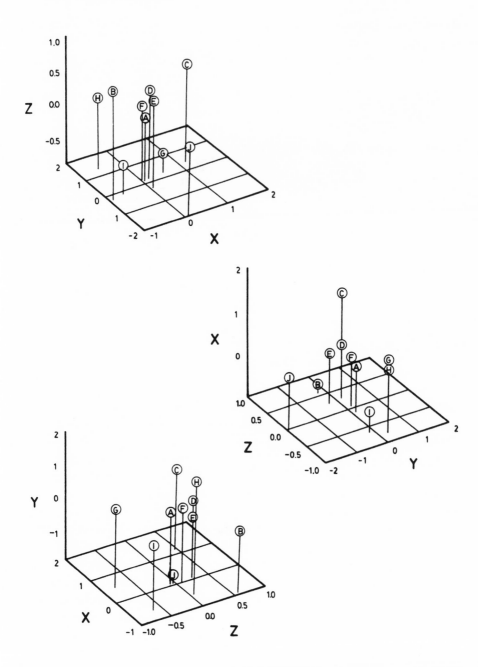

Figure 3.9. Results of multidimensional scaling (3 dimensions) of surface-collected and excavated ceramic assemblages from 11 Pemiscot County sites, with Neeley's Ferry plain and Bell plain sherds removed. Key to sites: A, Denton Mounds and Brooks; B, McCoy; C, Dorrah; D, Kersey; E, Holland; F, Murphy; G, Wardell; H, Cagle Lake; I, Kinfolk Ridge; J, Campbell.

McCoy (B) and Dorrah (C) assume the extreme outlier positions at -0.91 and 1.16, respectively. On the Z-axis, differences among the assemblages are at their maximum, which we thought might be a reflection of the widely fluctuating variance in within-type frequencies across the ceramic types. To ensure that sample size was not contributing to the differences, we standardized the ceramic type frequencies and reran the multidimensional scaling. No site changed position on any axis more than 0.13.

It is clear from the multidimensional scaling that extreme differences exist among the assemblages in terms of composition. Despite the high Brainerd-Robinson coefficients exhibited by different pairs of sites, the assemblages still contain significant differences. For example, using the combined surface-collected and excavated assemblages, Campbell and Denton Mounds have a *BR* coefficient of 161, and in the multidimensional scaling they equate extremely well along the X- and Z-axes. But along the Y-axis they are very different, as Campbell is from all other sites. One baffling feature of the multidimensional scaling results concerns the positioning of the Brooks and Denton Mounds assemblages. With a *BR* coefficient of 112, we would have expected considerable separation between them in three dimensions.

Discussion

Considerable variation exists in the Mississippian-period archaeological record of southeastern Missouri—variation that, once isolated, can be measured and plotted spatially and temporally. We have attempted here to present only a broad overview of how sites in Pemiscot County are similar and dissimilar in ceramic content, using that information to examine how the sites fit in time. We again state that the analysis leaves several important questions unanswered—partly a product of the manner in which the materials were collected and the small sizes of the samples. Despite the biases that are undoubtedly affecting the samples, statistical comparisons of assemblages presented here indicate that past attempts to partition the archaeological record have, in fact, masked the variation necessary to develop an explanatory framework of the Mississippian-period occupation of the region. We will return to this important topic in Chapter 9, when we examine how the late Mississippian period Pemiscot Bayou sites fit into a regional framework of phases, some of which were introduced in Chapter 2. Of more immediate importance is taking the information presented in this chapter and using it as a backdrop for our examination of the specific late-period sites and their assemblages in chapters 5 through 7. Thus far we have used only sherds from surface and excavated contexts to examine similarities and dissimilarities among the Pemiscot Bayou sites. In later chapters we will focus on complete vessels and other burial-related items. The sherds have allowed us to make some tentative statements about the relatedness of the assemblages, but in many ways they distort the temporal positioning of the major site occupations. They also seriously under-represent the extraordinary range of objects that the sites have produced.

What about the validity of the phases that have been proposed for southeastern Missouri, especially as they relate to the Pemiscot County sites? Are they valid? Do they identify temporal variation in any meaningful manner? We leave it to the judgment of the reader to answer these questions for himself or herself, although in defense of the phases we note that they probably are no worse than others that have been proposed. Archaeologists before us (e.g., Marshall 1965; S. Williams 1954) certainly recognized considerable time depth in the archaeological record of the Pemiscot Bayou locality, and they recognized some differences between that record and the one from the Cairo Lowland. Our analysis further bears out some of the geographically related differences. For example, we would argue that the multidimensional-scaling plot shown in Figure 3.5 is in large part a reflection of geographical distance. The plot is reproduced in Figure 3.10 with the late-period sites—Parkin, Campbell, Brooks, McCoy, Dorrah, Holland, and Denton Mounds—removed. The two early sites—Kersey (10) and Old Varney River (13)—and Murphy (15), because of its obvious Late Woodland and early Mississippian period components (Chapter 5), have been left, as have the five sites from Mississippi County, Missouri (1–5). We doubt the division between the Mississippi County site group and the Pemiscot County–Dunklin County site group can be explained in any way other than in terms of space. S. Williams recognized this and established the Pemiscot Bayou phase to distinguish early and middle Mississippian period materials in Pemiscot County from those in the Cairo Lowland.

But even if we can partition sets of archaeological assemblages into gross spatial-temporal units, we still have not really begun to address the interesting questions concerning *how* different the assemblages are or what the variation among objects within any particular artifact class means. Identifying a site assemblage as belonging to the Nodena phase is no different than saying a particular bifacially flaked stone piece is a Nodena point. Each term imparts some knowledge in terms of time and space, but it most assuredly masks underlying variation that the assemblage or stone piece exhibits relative to all other assemblages or stone pieces placed in the same normative category. Archaeological phases for southeastern Missouri were developed implicitly from the essentialist concept of the archetype, and they reflect the typological notion that variation is measured only as distance from a true and real type. For example, S. Williams's (1954) development of the original four Mississippian phases reflects that typological paradigm, wherein all classification is based on the excavated assemblage from Crosno and on assemblages from sites assumed to be related to it. Continued reference to the phases without a critical examination of the underlying nature of the remains used to construct the phases constitutes an acceptance of the typologi-

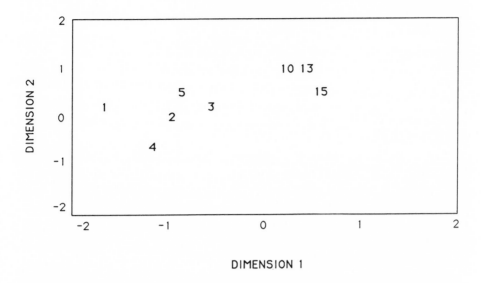

Figure 3.10. Results of multidimensional scaling (2 dimensions) of surface-collected and excavated ceramic assemblages from two Pemiscot County sites, one Dunklin County site, and five Mississippi County sites, with Neeley's Ferry plain and Bell plain sherds removed. All sites contain large early and probably middle Mississippian period components. Note the clustering of Mississippi County sites on the left and the grouping of Pemiscot County–Dunklin County sites on the right. Key to sites (using same numbering system as in Figures 3.4 and 3.5): 1, Crosno; 2, Callahan-Thompson; 3, Hess; 4, Mort; 5, Byrd; 10, Kersey; 13, Old Varney River; 15, Murphy (1–5 are in Mississippi County, 10 and 15 are in Pemiscot County, and 13 is in Dunklin County).

cal system as a "reality." Consequently, current and future students of the region's prehistory, lacking firsthand knowledge of those early excavations and the nature of the assemblages, can be misled by continuing pronouncement of statistically unsubstantiated interpretations and explanations.

How do we resolve this dilemma and present a logical interpretation of the Mississippian-period archaeological record? Perhaps the obvious place to start is by abandoning the phase concept and instituting a reexamination of the actual materials that have been excavated and surface collected from the sites in the Pemiscot Bayou locality. Although we are interested in similarities among sites, we are more concerned at this stage with documenting certain kinds of variation in the archaeological records of the sites along and near Pemiscot Bayou and with determining the spatial extent of that variation.

4

THE PHYSICAL ENVIRONMENT
Michael J. O'Brien

Understanding the archaeological record of any locale necessitates at the very least more than a passing knowledge of its environmental history. Physical-environmental variables, including climate, vegetation, and erosion, not only influenced the behaviors of prehistoric human groups in terms of where they lived and what they ate but also influenced and continue to influence the preservation and exposure of archaeological remains. For example, in active floodplain settings such as the Mississippi River valley, remains deposited on a natural levee or point bar can be buried by subsequent flooding or removed entirely through channel erosion. Since not all geomorphological features currently evident across a floodplain were created simultaneously, the ages of archaeological materials found on any given landform, unless the materials were redeposited, date to a time period subsequent to the formation date of the landform. Knowing the ages of archaeological materials allows us to derive a minimum date for the landform, but the date might be too late by several thousand years. Even when landscape sequences have been identified correctly, as they have been in parts of the Mississippi Valley, erroneous estimates of landform age can seriously impede our understanding of how past human groups used the environment.

The landscape history of southeast Missouri—itself only one chapter in the long evolutionary history of the lower Mississippi Valley—must be one of the most complex on the continent. Perhaps no other part of the continent has witnessed such a degree of modification throughout the Quaternary—modification brought on by climate, river-flow volume, and type and amount of sediment load. The Mississippi Embayment, from which the Mississippi River valley was derived, began forming at least by Cretaceous time (Autin et al. 1991: 547), but it is the last 20,000 years—encompassing the tail end of the last glaciation and the subsequent postglacial period—that is of particular interest here.

The lower Mississippi Valley begins roughly at Cape Girardeau, Missouri, and extends south to the Gulf of Mexico, a distance of some 780 km (Figure 4.1). Valley width ranges from about 40 to 200 km, and floodplain elevations vary from 84 m at the confluence of the Mississippi and Ohio rivers to sea level downstream of New Orleans. Along with its major tributaries—the Ohio, the Missouri, the Red, and the Arkansas—the Mississippi River drains about 3,200,000 km^2 (Autin et al. 1991: 547).

The upper and lower portions of the Mississippi Valley are a study in contrasts. Driving south along Interstate 55 below Cape Girardeau, one cannot help but notice the abrupt drop in elevation and a landscape that has suddenly been transformed from rolling hills and limestone outcrops into what at first glance appears to be a flat, almost topographically featureless plain (Figure 4.2). Continuing south, one might reach the conclusion that one part of the modern alluvial valley is boringly like another—flat for about as far as the eye can see. But the valley is deceiving, for the apparent lack of features betrays an exceedingly complex aggradational and depositional history that is still not completely understood. Recent action by the Mississippi River in some places has eradicated evidence of ancient landforms; in others it has buried the evidence under tens of meters of alluvium.

Thus the casual observer might be surprised to learn that during the waning stages of the Pleistocene the Mississippi River was located 100–130 km west of its current position, draining what are termed the Western Lowlands, located between the Ozark Escarpment to the west and Crowley's Ridge to the east (Figure 4.3). The Eastern Lowlands, a series of named lowlands that encompass all of the alluvial valley east from Crowley's Ridge to the uplands of Kentucky and Tennessee, were actually formed primarily by the downcutting of the ancestral Ohio River. About 16,500 years ago, the Mississippi broke through Crowley's Ridge between Bell City and Oran, Missouri, considerably reduced its flow in the earlier course, and began to flow southward across the older braided surfaces of the Ohio, which had by then moved eastward. About 9,600 years ago, the Mississippi broke through a gap near Thebes, Illinois, moved south and eastward, and captured the Ohio near Cairo, Illinois.

The casual observer would not see the current floodplain for what it is—a dizzying array of ancient valley trains, pieces of which are often barely perceptible, and former river channels that are testament to an incredibly complex history of landscape development. The complexity inherent in the geomorphological history of the alluvial valley plays a significant role in how we examine and interpret the archaeological record. Because of the dynamic nature of the river systems, which included hundreds of small tributary streams and bayous that filled relict channels

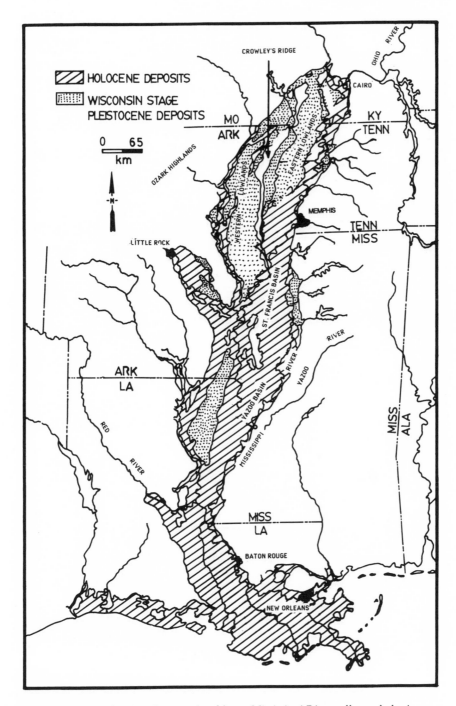

Figure 4.1. Map showing the central and lower Mississippi River valley and physiographic features mentioned in the text.

Figure 4.2. Photograph of the extreme northern end of the Mississippi Embayment, looking south from the Commerce Hills along Interstate 55. The topography of the river valley remains essentially flat from this point south to the Gulf of Mexico.

of the Mississippi and Ohio rivers, the land that was available for hunting, habitation, and eventually farming constantly changed. As streams migrated across the landscape, they left behind meander scars that became oxbow lakes and then, in many instances, swamps. Natural levees, formed by overflow deposits during flooding episodes, created more swampland as they began to block the flow of small drainages.

In faster-moving streams, coarse materials such as sand were deposited as point bars, which, after stream channels shifted position, formed well-drained topographic features in an otherwise wet environment. All of these features offered something to prehistoric groups in the region—swamps and rivers in which to hunt and fish for aquatic animals and sandbars and levees upon which to live. Knowledge of how the landscape changed through time provides clues not only as to where prehistoric remains might be found but also as to where they might not be found. For example, few archaeological remains dating before the time of Christ have been found in eastern Pemiscot County, not because the area was uninhabited but because the processes associated with an active floodplain have either removed or buried them. The Archaic (pre–ca. 1000 B.C.) and Early Woodland (1000–300 B.C.) remains that are found occur on topographic highs that have escaped removal by channel erosion or burial by overbank deposits.

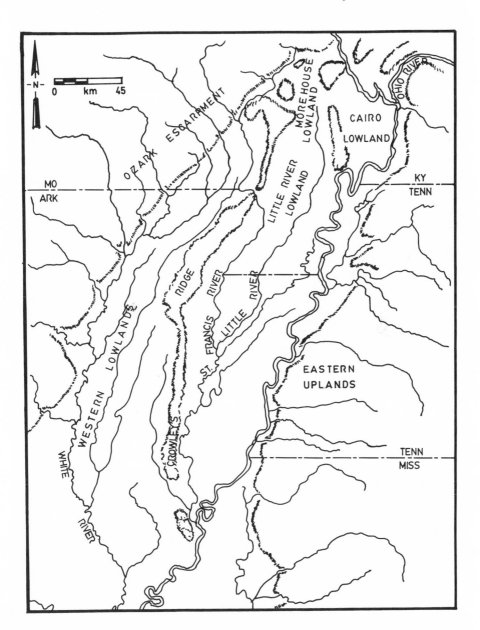

Figure 4.3. Detailed map of the northern end of the central Mississippi River valley showing locations of physiographic features mentioned in the text. Base map after Morse and Morse (1983).

The Little River Lowland

The Pemiscot Bayou sites are located in the heart of the Little River Lowland (Figure 4.3), a physiographic region composed of remnants of the braided-stream and meandering-stream regimes of the ancestral Mississippi and Ohio rivers as well as more modern features associated with the Little River and its tributaries. Modern topographic distinctions between the Little River Lowland and the Morehouse Lowland to the north are negligible; however, braided-stream courses of the ancestral Mississippi in the Little River Lowland are not as noticeable as they are farther north, indicating significant erosion or burial by deposition of recent alluvium. Fisk (1944: 26) bounds the Little River Lowland on the south with the abandoned St. Francis segment of the Mississippi meander belt. Saucier (e.g., 1981: fig. 1) includes the Little River Lowland in the St. Francis Basin.

The geomorphological history of the Little River Lowland, like the history of much of the lower Mississippi Valley, is the story of two different fluvial regimes—the braided stream and the meander-belt stream—each leaving dissimilar evidence of its history across the landscape. Understanding the evolution of the alluvial landscape is based on understanding the factors that condition the formation of landscape features and knowing specifically when certain features formed. The problem is compounded, however, by processes that have obscured and in many cases obliterated evidence of previous features. The great depth at which some features are buried precludes our knowing much about them other than information that can be gleaned from corings. When discussing the evolution of the alluvial valley, one must keep firmly in mind that some of what we are seeing is the result of the last few hundred years of alluviation, especially in the meander belt.

Harold Fisk, in his monumental *Geological investigation of the alluvial valley of the lower Mississippi River* (1944), attempted to provide a history of the valley by mapping all features from just north of Cairo, Illinois, south to the Gulf of Mexico and by explaining their origins and chronological placements. No comparable study of the alluvial valley at that level of detail has since been attempted, nor is such a study likely to be undertaken again. In short, despite an additional 50 years of work since Fisk undertook his study, "[i]t is still not possible to do what he implied could be done" (Saucier 1981: 8). One of the things that Fisk produced was a series of large, multicolored maps showing abandoned channels and courses and other features, with different colors and shading techniques used to place each feature chronologically. Although his maps are both aesthetically pleasing and in many cases accurate portrayals of the locations of previous channels of the Mississippi and Ohio rivers, his channel reconstructions are speculative and in many cases incorrect, and his chronological positioning of the channels, both in terms of absolute time and relative time, is totally inaccurate (Autin et al. 1991; Saucier 1981).

However, these problems have not kept archaeologists (e.g., Phillips et al. 1951; Scully 1953; S. Williams 1954) from attempting to correlate prehistoric sites with specific channels. Fisk based his sequence of events on sea-level changes throughout the Pleistocene: When sea levels fell during periods of continental glaciation, the ancestral Ohio and Mississippi rivers began cycles of deep entrenchment, during which time they cleaned the alluvial valley of all earlier sediments; when sea levels rose, the rivers filled the valley with new sediments. Saucier (1981: 10), on the other hand, points out that the Ohio-Mississippi system "responded to changes in sea level no farther north than the latitude of Baton Rouge, Louisiana." Although the valley north of that latitude experienced aggradation and degradation, the magnitudes of each were smaller than what Fisk imagined, and, instead of responding to sea-level change, the rivers were responding to changes in water volume and sediment load linked to glacial advances and retreats in headwater regions (Saucier 1981: 10). Mapping of the alluvial valley more recently has refined (actually replaced) Fisk's chronology and sequence of events. The new chronological sequence is best explained in terms of the two stream regimes responsible for creating the alluvial valley.

Braided Streams

Braided streams characteristically are complex features composed of master channels and an interlocking series of gathering channels and dispersal channels (Figure 4.4). Bars form in the master channel and its gathering and dispersal channels; these bars eventually block the flow of water and lead to creation of new channels. In general, braided-stream systems are highly dissected networks that, because of the constant cutting of new channels, lose their integrity. Extensive evidence of braided-stream courses is found in the Western Lowlands (Royall et al. 1991; Saucier 1974; Smith and Saucier 1971)—the result of the ancestral Mississippi River—and in the Morehouse–Little River Lowland—the result of both the ancestral Ohio and Mississippi rivers. Valley trains containing the braided courses are composed of outwash derived from midcontinental glaciers that formed at different intervals during the Pleistocene (Autin et al. 1991; Saucier 1974; Teller 1987, 1990). The oldest exposed valley-train surface in the Western Lowlands is located east of the extreme southwest edge of Crowley's Ridge and probably dates back in excess of 120,000 years (Autin et al. 1991; Rutledge et al. 1985).

The older exposed valley-train deposits in the Eastern Lowlands are (a) a narrow strip along the base of the northern half of Crowley's Ridge and (b) Sikeston Ridge—a discontinuous projection southward from just east of the Bell City–Oran Gap in Crowley's Ridge to New Madrid, Missouri. Formed as a result of glacial outwash, the deposits were once continuous from the point where the Ohio River exited the Illinois uplands (the current position of the Cache River in Illinois) southwestward to its then junction with the Mississippi River in southern

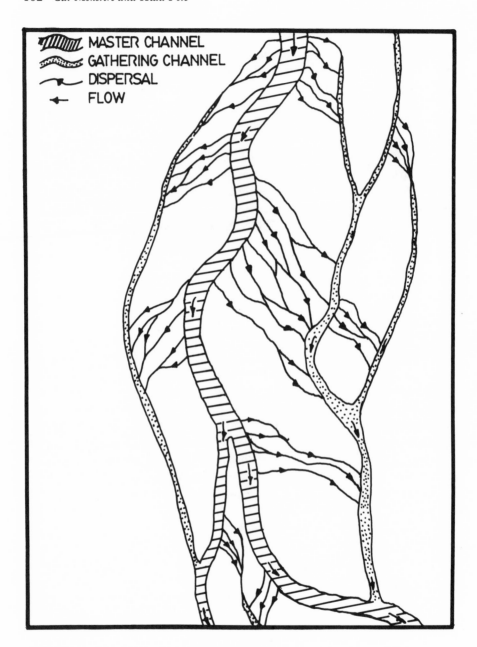

Figure 4.4. Channel features associated with a braided-stream regime (after Fisk 1944). Gathering streams take in water diverted from the master channel through dispersal channels and funnel it back into the master channel downstream.

Arkansas. Toward the end of the Pleistocene, when the Mississippi abandoned its Western Lowlands course and began draining to the east of Crowley's Ridge, the Ohio alluvial fan was bisected by south-flowing Mississippi River channels and buried under Mississippi outwash.

At least two northeast-southwest-trending braided surfaces connected with the displaced Mississippi River are exposed in the Morehouse and Little River lowlands. The more western of the two, the Malden Plain, extends in an arc shape from the base of Crowley's Ridge at Dexter, Missouri, to near Levesque, Arkansas, a distance of approximately 175 km. Primary drainage of the surface today is provided by the St. Francis River. The eastern braided surface extends from the northern wall of the alluvial valley, through the Bell City–Oran Gap, to Marked Tree, Arkansas, a distance of approximately 170 km. When the Mississippi River shifted its course east of Crowley's Ridge and began to drain the Morehouse and Little River lowlands, it created its own outwash fan and braided drainage pattern, in the process reworking earlier sediments and eradicating previous northeast-southwest-trending Ohio channels. After the Mississippi changed course again and moved into the channel occupied by the Ohio River (discussed below), underfit streams such as the Little River developed to drain the abandoned braided-stream surface in a due-south pattern. But as Saucier (1964: 6 [unnumbered]) notes, "The establishment of the [Mississippi] river in its present meander belt did not mean the end of Mississippi River sedimentation in the [area east of Crowley's Ridge], however. For long periods of time, the Little River system served as an outlet for [Mississippi River] floodwaters that entered the upper end. . . . Its well-developed natural levees and other meander belt features attest to its role in carrying sediment-laden floodwaters of the Mississippi River."

The radiocarbon chronology of sediments from corings in Powers Fort Swale near the base of the Ozark Escarpment in Butler County, Missouri, establishes the most recent shift in fluvial competence and capacity that occurred in the Western Lowlands as the Mississippi River began to flow permanently east of Crowley's Ridge (Royall et al. 1991). Continuous to intermittent braided-stream flow in the Western Lowlands occurred about 18,000 years ago, characterized by accumulations of medium-size sands. A major decrease in fluvial competence and capacity about 16,300 years ago may have resulted from partial diversion of meltwater through the Bell City–Oran Gap. After that time, meltwater flow became progressively sporadic, with the Western Lowlands serving as an "ephemeral sluiceway, particularly between about 14,500 and 11,500 yr B.P. In Powers Fort Swale, the last deposition of fine sand layers by 11,500 yr B.P. marks the termination of glacial meltwater flow through the Western Lowlands, after which full meltwater flow was funneled east of Crowley's Ridge" (Royall et al. 1991: 167–68).

Royall et al. (1991: 168) present a plausible set of factors that could have led to the diversion of the Mississippi River through Crowley's Ridge:

> We speculate that an initial, partial shift eastward in flow . . . [corresponded] with the first pulse of increased meltwater discharge associated with the full-glacial/late-glacial climatic transition and the initial phase of deglaciation along the southern and southwestern margins of the Laurentide Ice Sheet . . . characterized by a fluctuating series of minor glacial readvances, alternating with episodes of ice wastage and ephemeral ponding of glacial meltwater in extensive proglacial lakes. Catastrophic release of this meltwater . . . provided the mechanism in the Central Mississippi Alluvial Valley for flood overtopping and incision of the Bell City–Oran Gap.

The second great diversion event occurred when the Mississippi River breached the Commerce Hills near Thebes, Illinois, and captured the Ohio River south of Cairo, Illinois. Several minimum ages of this last movement east by the Mississippi are available, based on radiocarbon chronology of sediments: 8,810 years ago from the Old Field site, located in the Bell City–Oran Gap (King and Allen 1977); 9,050 years ago from Big Lake, Arkansas (Guccione 1987; Guccione et al. 1988; Scott and Aasen 1987); and 8,530 years ago from Pemiscot Bayou just south of the Missouri-Arkansas line (Guccione 1987; Guccione et al. 1988; Scott and Aasen 1987). Saucier (1981: 16) states "emphatically that at no time in the last 9000 years have the Mississippi and Ohio rivers flowed in separate channels farther south than a point only 16 km south of Cairo, Illinois."

The shift in channel location from the Bell City–Oran Gap to the Thebes Gap probably was caused by several interrelated events. Fisk (1944: 25, 41) states that a minor north-flowing stream drained the Commerce Hills during a portion of the glacial cycle and that perhaps faulting and erosion of the southern margin of the Commerce Hills by the Ohio River when it occupied the Cache River channel caused a sag in the escarpment of the Eastern Lowlands. Entrenchment by the stream to reach grade with the Mississippi River, along with later aggradation, also to reach grade with the Mississippi River, caused the tributary to become subject to backwater flooding by the Mississippi. Continued erosion during periods of overflow finally eroded the valley to a relief position where more normal flow could exit through the gap.[1] The shorter course through the gap provided a gradient advantage over that provided by the Bell City–Oran Gap, leading to increased erosion in Thebes Gap and the shift of all or most of the flow east. Royall et al. (1991: 169), while not denying Fisk's scenario of a prolonged period of erosion by the Ohio River and valley development by the north-flowing stream, cite another, more direct cause of the diversion through Thebes Gap: "We speculate that the catastrophic release of water from the Emerson high stage of proglacial Lake Agassiz (which covered 350,000 km^2) down the

---

1. M. J. Guccione (pers. comm. 1992) has cores from other tributaries that substantiate backwater flooding of the Commerce Hills.

Mississippi Alluvial Valley at about 9500 yr B.P. (Teller, 1987, 1990) was responsible for cutting the new meltwater channel at Thebes Gap."

When Fisk published his work (1944), he placed the last major glaciation at about 25,000–30,000 years ago,[2] a date that is today placed at 18,000 years ago (Saucier 1981: 9). Given that Fisk erred somewhat liberally in his placement of the last glacial maximum, it is difficult to determine why he erred so conservatively in his dating of the braided-stream surfaces of the ancestral Ohio and Mississippi rivers. He dated the earliest visible surface in the Western Lowlands at 6,000 years ago and the youngest at 3,000 years ago. Fisk's chronology for the Morehouse and Little River lowlands, accordingly, was also much too recent. Instead of the 2,000–6,000-year-old braided surfaces he envisioned, we know today that they are between 9,000 and 18,000 years old. Fisk (1944: table 3) clearly was of the opinion that while the Ohio River was developing a meandering pattern in the entrenched valley to the east, the Mississippi River was maintaining a braided, aggrading pattern in the Morehouse and Little River lowlands—a pattern that would, he believed, last until 2,000 years ago, when the Mississippi broke through Thebes Gap and entered the Ohio River meander belt. The importance to archaeologists of understanding these discrepancies should be clear. Instead of a young surface that could not possibly contain Paleoindian, Early Archaic, or Middle Archaic remains, the entire Western Lowlands (except along modern stream valleys) and the Malden Plain–Sikeston Ridge outwash surface were stable long before humans entered North America. All of the Morehouse Lowland and all of the Little River Lowland west of the meander-belt region (again, discounting modern stream valleys) were stable by the beginning of the Early Archaic period (9,000 years ago).

Meander-Belt Streams

After the Mississippi River began flowing through Thebes Gap, the combined Mississippi-Ohio River (hereafter referred to as the Mississippi River) converted to a meandering regime, the result of disequilibrium between sediment load and discharge brought about by a change in sediment type from coarse glacially derived sands and gravels to a mixed load (Saucier 1964, 1968, 1970). The exceedingly complex history of the Mississippi River meander belt is a result of 9,000 years of channel migrations across the floodplain, where older channels were abandoned during periods of flooding, newer channels cut off older ones, and new levees were built up over previous levees and channels. Many of the features associated with the meandering system were not associated with the braided

2. Fisk changed his mind repeatedly over the time of maximum glaciation (see Fisk and McFarlan 1955; Saucier 1981).

system. Six of these contributed to the late prehistoric period landscape of the Pemiscot Bayou locality, and they are defined here (Figure 4.5).[3]

Natural levees are low ridges of sediments that form along both sides of streams as a result of overflow episodes. As streams flood, the greatest amounts of sedimentary material are deposited closest to the streams, and as a result levees grow asymmetrically. Water velocity correlates inversely with distance from the stream channel and hence deposits the coarser particles closer to its channel than the finer particles such as silts and clays. In locales where a river has formed closely spaced loops, levees coalesce to form large continuous features, often 3–6 m high and up to several kilometers wide. *Abandoned courses* are long segments of a stream that were cut off when it changed its course across the floodplain. The abandoned course is filled with sediments both from overbank deposits that spill over from the new course and from smaller streams that enter the older course. *Abandoned channels,* also referred to as clay plugs, are partially or completely filled segments of stream channels formed when a stream shortens its course. Abandonment can result from either truncation across the narrow neck of a meander belt (neck cutoff) or a shift in course to a point-bar swale (see below) during flood stage and abandonment of the outer portion of the loop (chute cutoff). Soon after formation, abandoned channels are open-water (oxbow) lakes, but they can subsequently become choked by vegetation and/or sediments and turn into swamps and mucks. Abandoned channels of the Mississippi River characteristically contain greater quantities of sand than do those of smaller streams.

Backswamps are formed by overflow that becomes trapped either between natural levee ridges on separate meander belts or between levees and uplands or older terrace ridges. Backswamp areas are characterized by very low relief and complicated drainage patterns in which channels alternate as tributaries and distributaries at different times during the annual flood cycle. Backswamp sediments tend to be high in silts and clays. *Point bars* consist of sediments deposited on the insides of stream bends opposite the side of active erosion. During periods of high water levels, sands and silts continue to accumulate on top of earlier deposits; during periods of receding water levels, finer particles—silts and clays— are deposited at lower levels on the point bar. Through time, as a stream continues its outward erosion, it leaves behind an arc-shaped series of sand ridges and intervening swales. *Crevasse channels* (not shown in Figure 4.5) start out as small drainage channels located on the backslope side of a levee. As a result of continued overflow, they grow to form major break points through the levee. Crevasse channels continue to be enlarged as they siphon water, especially during periods of flooding, from the main channel.

Fisk's (1944) chronology for the meander-belt region was divided into 20 stages based on reconstructed histories (derived from inspection of aerial photographs)

---

3. Based on Saucier 1964.

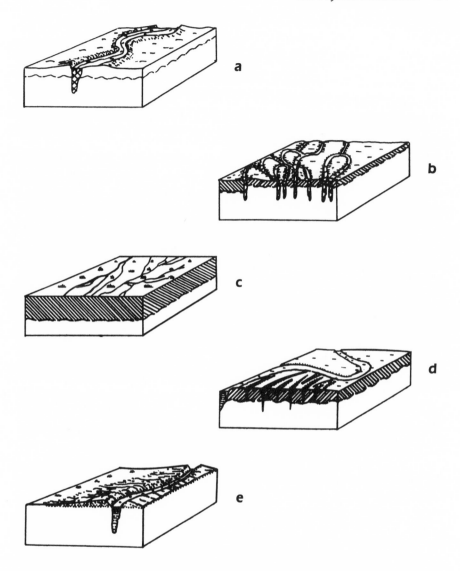

Figure 4.5. Physiographic features associated with a meandering stream: a, abandoned course; b, abandoned channel; c, backswamp; d, point bar; e, natural levee (after Saucier 1964).

of floodplain accretion and channel migration. Stages 1 to 17 covered approximately 100 years each, an interval based on known rates of channel migration since 1765, the end of stage 17. The problem with the chronology is that it begins much too late (Saucier 1981: 15) and is based on the erroneous assumption that the river maintained a cycle of sediment load and water volume parallel to that calculated for periods after 1765. Based on work conducted subsequent to that of Fisk, Saucier (1981: 15) dates the oldest discrete meander belt in the alluvial valley at 7,500–9,000 years old. Its only exposures occur in the northern and northeastern parts of the Yazoo Basin, which occupies the floodplain on the eastern bank of the Mississippi River from Memphis, Tennessee, to Vicksburg, Mississippi. The youngest discrete meander belt, located between Vicksburg and the mouth of the Red River in eastern Louisiana, was first occupied about 2,800 years ago. Absolute dating of intervening meander belts and channels would be difficult (though not impossible, given a large suite of radiocarbon dates), since, as Saucier (1981: 15) points out, there simply is no way of knowing, without a large suite of dates, how long any particular channel within a meander belt was occupied or, for that matter, how long a meander belt was occupied.

Climatic and Vegetational Changes

In a subsequent section of this chapter I will take an in-depth look at the best available information on the composition and density of the late Mississippian period forests in the Pemiscot Bayou portion of the Little River Lowland. This information is derived from General Land Office (GLO) survey notes from the first half of the nineteenth century. Although the forest descriptions postdate the period of archaeological concern by several centuries, considerable confidence can be placed (within limits) both in the accuracy of the information and in its relevance to the earlier period. Here, however, my concern is more with general trends in climate and vegetative response, using pollen as a guide to understanding climatic change in the Little River Lowland. Climatic changes that were responsible in part for the evolution of the drainage regimes in the Mississippi Valley also effected large-scale changes in both the composition and distribution of plant communities across the landscape. Understanding the response of plant communities to these climatic/geomorphological changes is crucial to understanding the evolution of the floodplain during the Holocene and how and why human groups residing in the area responded as they did.

The pattern of vegetation today in the Little River Lowland and adjacent regions gives little hint to the patterns in existence throughout the last 10,000 years. Changes in vegetational patterns—which can range from minor shifts in composition of plant communities to wholesale replacements of communities—can result directly from climatic shifts, but often the changes are more indirectly influenced by climate. If the reasons given earlier for the Mississippi River breakthroughs at Bell City–Oran and Thebes are correct, that is, increased stream flow tied to glacial melting and glacial-lake discharge, then plant communities certainly were affected. After diversion of the river through the Bell City–Oran Gap, communities that had become established on the valley-train deposits of the ancestral Ohio River east of Crowley's Ridge would have been radically altered by the newly forming braided-stream system of the Mississippi River. Later, the replacement communities that formed on the outwash surfaces of the braided Mississippi system would have been altered as glacial-water overflow caused the Mississippi River to breach the Commerce Hills and abandon the outwash surface.

Unfortunately, our knowledge of these changes is extremely limited. Most of what we know comes from pollen profiles, which were derived from examining frequency distributions of recognizable types of pollen extracted from sedimentary cores taken in natural pollen traps such as sinks or bogs where pollen has been preserved. The problem has always been, however, that, because climatic conditions can vary among regions, pollen profiles and other lines of paleoclimatic evidence from one region may have little bearing on the actual conditions that existed in another area. Thus, without numerous data points spread more or less evenly across a region as large as the midwestern and southeastern United States, interpretations are subject to local conditions. The larger the sample, the better the interpretations, though even within an area as large as the Mississippi Valley, ten times the number of profiles currently available would still only allow us to construct a baseline approximation of climate and vegetation. The problem is exacerbated in the alluvial valley because of the extraordinary and often rapid changes to the landscape caused by river-related activities. The constantly changing landscape created new habitats for plant communities, but within a short period of time it could also destroy those habitats, in the process creating new habitats for different plant communities. Hence, a pollen profile, though exhibiting temporal shifts in frequency of different kinds of pollen, might represent a very localized phenomenon that only at the grossest level would be duplicated elsewhere. Such profiles are extremely useful for analysis of particular locales, but the trends they exhibit might be so fine grained that they distort regional trends.

In extremely abbreviated form, the Midwest, including the Western, Morehouse, and Little River lowlands, experienced the following sequence of events, with varying degrees of results depending on location. During the final Pleistocene glaciation, when ice lobes pushed southward into northeastern Iowa and central Illinois, a wide band of coniferous forests stretched eastward from the Great Plains to the Atlantic coast (Wright 1971). In some areas these forests were composed almost entirely of spruce, while in other areas, such as southern Illinois, they were mixtures of spruce, oak, and herbaceous openings (Wright 1981). In still other areas, such as portions of south-central Missouri, forests contained mixtures of coniferous and deciduous trees (Frest and Fay 1980). When late-Pleistocene temperatures rose, the conifers died and were replaced by closed-canopy deciduous forests composed primarily of mesic (wet-tolerant) taxa such as oak, hickory, ash, and elm. Concurrently, about 11,000 years ago, dry westerly winds began flowing across the Midwest with increasing frequency (Webb and Bryson 1972), and grasses began moving into the central Midwest from the Plains (Wright 1976). By 9,500 years ago, grasses were well established in northeastern and central Missouri (Bernabo and Webb 1977). Grasses probably controlled drying upland flats, while forests migrated downslope to relatively moist positions along stream courses (Warren 1982b: 72).

During this prolonged dry spell, referred to as the Atlantic, or Hypsithermal, climatic episode, westerly winds increasingly dominated weather patterns, leading to severe moisture stress in some portions of the Midwest by about 7,000 years ago. Prairies continued to expand, and in some regions previously forested areas experienced increased erosion (Ahler 1973; Butzer 1977) and perhaps eolian deposition (O'Brien et al. 1989; Porter and Guccione n.d.; Saucier 1978). Stream discharge decreased in parts of Missouri and Illinois (Hill 1975; Klippel et al. 1978). Animal size (Purdue 1980) and range (e.g., McMillan and Klippel 1981) changed as well among at least some mammals.

These trends were reversed about 5,000 years ago as westerly winds diminished in strength and effective moisture increased, though in many areas the moisture levels never approximated those of pre-Hypsithermal times. This relatively moist interval lasted until about 2,800 years ago and witnessed the return of some forests to positions lost previously to the grasses. There then followed an 1,100-year-long period of (at least in some areas) decreased precipitation—the Sub-Atlantic climatic episode—which was never as pronounced as the Hypsithermal. The Sub-Atlantic was followed by several short periods of warm conditions (dry in some areas, moist in others) and then a much cooler period, the Neo-Boreal, or "Little Ice Age."

Several sites in the Eastern and Western lowlands have produced pollen profiles for the late Pleistocene and the Holocene, four of which are discussed here: the Old Field site in the Morehouse Lowland (King and Allen 1977), Big Lake and Pemiscot Bayou in the Little River Lowland (Guccione 1987; Guccione et al. 1988; Porter and Guccione n.d.; Scott and Aasen 1987), and Powers Fort Swale in the Western Lowlands (Royall et al. 1991). Two of them—Powers Fort Swale and Old Field—provide supporting evidence of broad trends in Holocene climate that have been observed in other areas of the Midwest. The other two are important not only for documenting the developmental history of the Little River Lowland but also for examining the evolution of an alluvial-ridge and backswamp system in the Mississippi River meander belt.

The Powers Fort Swale pollen profile documents the transition from late-Pleistocene/early-Holocene communities to more modern communities, especially the shift from boreal forest dominated by spruce *(Picea)*, pine *(Pinus)*, and fir *(Abies)* to the mixed conifer–northern deciduous forests dominated by oak *(Quercus)*, hickory *(Carya)*, hornbeam *(Carpinus)*, and maple *(Acer)* that occurred between 14,500 and 9,500 years ago. Buttonbush *(Cephalanthus occidentalis)*, which today commonly occurs along lake and stream margins in temperate regions, became established by 14,500 years ago, indicating climatic warming. Royall et al. (1991: 168) state that between 9,500 and 4,500 years ago cool-temperate deciduous taxa either were eliminated from the Powers Fort Swale area or were greatly reduced in frequency. They were replaced by warm-temperate trees such as bald cypress *(Taxodium)* and sweet gum *(Liquidambar)*. Oak, ash *(Fraxinus)*, and hickory increased in frequency, along with open-mudflat taxa such as goosefoot *(Chenopodium)* and ragweed *(Ambrosia)*. Significant numbers of pollen grains of several kinds of grasses were interpreted as representing early- and mid-Holocene cane thickets along the nonforested edges of the swale. Pollen assemblages less than 4,500 years old were similar to the modern pollen spectrum. Oak decreased by nearly 40%, and swamp-forest trees such as bald cypress, willow *(Silax)*, ash, elm, and sycamore *(Platanus)* increased. This pattern follows the general trend noticed in other parts of the Midwest (see Delcourt et al. 1986) of increased precipitation following the Hypsithermal. As Royall et al. (1991: 168) note, "Higher available moisture permitted the re-establishment of mesic tree species on well-drained levees and relict bars of braided-stream terraces; the increased area of standing water favored populations of hydric trees in bottomland swamps and slackwater swales (Robertson and others, 1978)."

The Old Field pollen sequence indicates that between 9,000 and 8,700 years ago, the Morehouse Lowland contained a mixture of bottomland forest, possibly canebrake, and open-water/swamp communities (King and Allen 1977: 319). By 8,700 years ago, the open-water/swamp community declined, and the herb and grass communities expanded. As the water level in Old Field dropped, bottomland swamp forests migrated to lower, wetter areas, greatly reducing their areal extent. By 8,000 years ago, grasses and ragweed increased significantly in frequency, a result of expansion of their habitat by the lowering of the water table. As King and Allen (1977: 319) point out, the Morehouse Lowland has so little relief that lowering the water table by only 1.5 m increases the surface area above fluctuating seasonal water by *at least 10 times*. By 6,500 years ago grasses declined abruptly, and taxa such as ash and willow reappeared. In response to an increase in effective precipitation, by 5,000 years ago swamp size increased and the bottomland arboreal vegetation renewed its development.

The pollen profile from Big Lake (Guccione et al. 1988)—a meander-belt locale—parallels trends seen in the previously discussed profiles. Zone A, dating ca. 9,050–6,450 years ago, contained pollen representative of a well-developed, bottomland arboreal community with herbaceous communities. The zone contained relatively high frequencies of oak and hickory and lower but significant frequencies of sweet gum and pine, indicative of relatively dry environments. Zone B, which began about 6,450 years ago and ended before 3,500 years ago, was transitional between the well-developed arboreal community in Zone A and the open-water and wetland communities in Zone C. Significant percentages of several plants in Zone C, most notably ragweed and sumpweed *(Iva)*, indicate a rise either in precipitation or in the water table, which inundated much of the surrounding bottomland that previously had supported arboreal vegetation. Zone D, which began sometime after 3,500 years ago, showed a dramatic increase in percentage of arboreal pollen (especially that of oak) over that in Zone 3. Pine and elm were present in the lower two-thirds of the column, suggesting a drier arboreal habitat than that evident in Zone C. Pollen from willow and chenopodium increased toward the upper portion of the zone, indicating a slightly wetter environment.

The Pemiscot Bayou core (Scott and Aasen 1987) fairly well mirrors that from Big Lake, showing dominance by open-water/swamp habitat from about 4,700 to 2,400 years ago. One important distinction is the cyclic change in streamside taxa (e.g., willow and mud-flat grasses) as the local environment changed from natural levee to backswamp, to natural levee, and finally to channel fill.

In summary, pollen profiles from Powers Fort Swale and Old Field yield complementary data documenting the change in the Western Lowlands and Morehouse Lowland from wet, cool conditions toward the end of the Pleistocene to drier conditions at the beginning of the Holocene, to hotter and drier conditions during the mid-Holocene, and finally to more mesic conditions. Apparently the driest conditions, at least in the Morehouse Lowland, existed between 8,700 and 6,500 years ago (King and Allen 1977: 320). The profiles from Big Lake and Pemiscot Bayou substantiate the relatively moist conditions that dominated the Midwest during the late Holocene. They also indicate that, at least in the meander-belt region of the alluvial valley, the xeric conditions evident over much of the Midwest during the Hypsithermal might not have been as drastic. Sedimentation rates calculated for Big Lake were decidedly lower during the Hypsithermal (Guccione et al. 1988: table V) than during the late Holocene, signifying reduced stream flow or the underdevelopment of the Little River (M. J. Guccione, pers. comm., 1992), but the area still had enough moisture to support a backswamp arboreal community. It was not until later that nonarboreal taxa began to dominate the pollen profile from Big Lake, but this apparently had more to do with extensive levee development (sedimentation rates rose significantly during the period) and hence habitat alteration than with reduced moisture and conversion of open-water areas to dry land.

I again feel compelled to note that despite the general correlation between these pollen profiles and climate and vegetation data from elsewhere in the Midwest, many of the trends evident in the profiles may be more reflective of local developments than of larger, more global events. It must be remembered that changes in climate precede major changes in vegetational patterns and that changes in the latter, even when panregional, are time-transgressive.

The Pemiscot Bayou Locality

Pemiscot Bayou is a sluggish stream that currently heads about 12 km southwest of Hayti, Missouri, and meanders in a southwesterly direction to its junction with the St. Francis River north of Marked Tree, Arkansas. Technically, the name *Pemiscot Bayou* applies to that portion of the course north of Big Lake, Arkansas, with the name *Left Hand Chute of Little River* applied to the portion to the south. However, the course is continuous and occupies a meander belt of an older stream that Fisk (1944: 26) termed "larger than any draining the region today," based on the sizes of the meander ridges. Fisk (1944: plate 22, sheet 3) shows Pemiscot Bayou occupying a Mississippi River cutoff chute (labeled "13" on his map) that extended south from Portage Open Bay, itself a cutoff chute (labeled "14" on his map). He shows Portage Open Bay as meandering south, then west, then southwest across the slightly earlier Pemiscot Bayou meander belt and then turning east to meet the Mississippi River. Aerial photographs taken in 1959 by the United States Soil Conservation Service (SCS) show meander scars of the old channel of Pemiscot Bayou from its modern point of origin (2 mi north of Steele, Missouri) north to Hayti and pieces of 2 distinct channels north of Hayti. But it is difficult to make a case for which pieces go with which channel.

Saucier (1970: 2851) suggests a recent date for the formation of Pemiscot Bayou, perhaps as recent as 1,000–1,500 years ago. He also suggests that Pemiscot Bayou–Left Hand Chute of the Little River formed as a crevasse channel through the west levee of one of the meander channels of the Mississippi River. As the meandering river developed a difference in elevation of 4–6 m or more between its natural-levee crests and adjacent floodplain areas, it formed a crevasse channel through the levee to achieve a slightly steeper gradient (Saucier 1970: 2851). The new stream developed its own natural levees and began to dam water back along the Right Hand Chute of the Little River and the St. Francis River, which were flowing as underfit streams in relict braided-stream channels. Continued levee building and impoundment led to the formation of what are commonly referred to as the St. Francis Sunk Lands (Guccione and Hehr 1991; Saucier 1970: 2851). The majority of the sunk lands are in present-day Arkansas, but the northern reaches of one sunken area—Big Lake—extend up the Right Hand Chute of the Little River into southern Dunklin County, Missouri.

Prior to the construction of large drainage ditches in the late nineteenth century, the Little River was the major interior drainage feature of Pemiscot County. It meandered its way across the northeastern quarter of the county, running southwest across the braided-stream surface to a point south of Kennett where it met, and then flowed south along the edge of, the Malden Plain valley-train deposit. Starting in 1875 (Brown 1971: 40) and continuing into the twentieth century, massive amounts of earth were moved to provide an integrated system of drainage for the county as part of a larger effort to provide drainage for all of southeastern Missouri. Water in the northwestern portion of the county, which was previously drained by the Little River, is now channeled west to large northeast-southwest-trending ditches that extend from near Cape Girardeau in the north to Big Lake, Arkansas, in the south (Figure 4.6). Drainage in the central portion of the county is provided by feeder ditches that empty into the canalized Elk Chute, a tributary of the Little River that heads west of Hayti, and drainage in the southeastern portion of the county is provided by numerous ditches that flow into Pemiscot Bayou.

Figure 4.6. Photograph (looking south) of one of the large ditches draining the Little River Lowland.

The preditch drainage pattern for the 1,248 km² of Pemiscot County was controlled entirely by the topography induced by the activities of the Mississippi River. Elevations in the county are highest in the northeast corner and lowest in the southwest corner. The difference in elevation insured that in the preditch era the majority of the drainage pattern was to the southwest. The elevational difference, however, is so slight that it is not surprising that the county was swampy historically. In fact, Pemiscot County has the least amount of relief of any county in Missouri, with an average change in elevation per 2.5 km² of less than 1.5 m (Brown 1971). The most prominent floodplain features,

such as they are, are the natural levees associated with the braided-stream surface
and the recent natural levees and point bars associated with the meander belt.
Personal recollections of longtime residents indicate that as late as 1940 much of
the county was wet for up to three months out of the year as a result of flooding
by sluggish streams such as Elk Chute and the Little River (see below).

The Late Holocene Landscape

The distribution of significant Holocene landscape features in and to the west of
the Pemiscot Bayou locality is shown in Figures 4.7–4.9. Shown are features
mapped by Saucier (1964) during his analysis of the geomorphic history of the St.
Francis Basin. As opposed to Fisk (1944), Saucier did not attempt to match up
channel remnants, nor did he date the channels. As noted previously, there
presently are few data on either paleocourse location or chronology that allow for
such precision. What Saucier's maps clearly show is the distribution of sediments
deposited by the earlier braided courses of the Mississippi River and by the later
meandering courses. Coarse, glacially derived valley-train deposits laid down by
the braided Mississippi River are visible across Dunklin County (Figures 4.7 and
4.8) and the western one-third to one-half of Pemiscot County (Figure 4.8). To
the east and southeast (Figure 4.9) they either (a) are overlain in a few areas by
point-bar deposits associated with the meander belt of the Mississippi River or
(b) have been removed completely in most areas by the meandering course and
replaced with point-bar deposits. Natural-levee deposits occur across the entire
younger surface and for several kilometers west, out onto the valley-train deposits.
To the west of the Mississippi River meander-belt system are point-bar deposits
laid down during the Holocene by the Little River channel complex as it
meandered southwest across the older surface.

In simplified terms, the evolution of the Pemiscot County landscape was tied
to the eastern movement of the Mississippi River. As the river changed from a
braided stream to a meandering stream, and as it continued moving its meander
courses farther east, it left behind a levee-and-point-bar landscape that developed
a fairly stable suite of plant communities that persisted up to the time of
nineteenth-century logging and drainage for agricultural development. As the
landforms stabilized, soils evident today began to form, and their distributions
give some approximation of the type of ground cover under which they formed
and the type of geomorphic position on which they formed (e.g., on levees versus
in meander cutoffs). It is reasonable to assume that the time-transgressive development of the Mississippi River floodplain was paralleled in terms of occupation
by prehistoric groups. In other words, we might expect to find the earliest evidence
of human occupation on valley-train deposits, with progressively later occupations
both on the valley train and on meander-belt surfaces. Hence, additional information on the late Holocene landscape in the Pemiscot Bayou locality can be derived

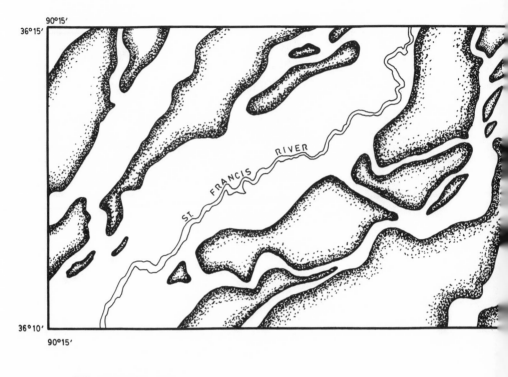

90°15'

36°15'

ST. FRANCIS RIVER

36°10'

90°15'

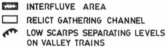

INTERFLUVE AREA
RELICT GATHERING CHANNEL
LOW SCARPS SEPARATING LEVELS
ON VALLEY TRAINS

from maps of modern soil distributions, GLO records, and archaeological-survey records.

Archaeological-Site Locations

The temporal distribution of archaeological sites reported to the Archaeological Survey of Missouri is shown in Figure 4.10. Sites dating from before the time of Christ are woefully underrepresented. The only Archaic-period (pre–1000 B.C.) site is located along the eastern margin of Grey Horse Lake in the northwestern corner of Pemiscot County. However, Archaic remains are known to occur at numerous locations along the crests of older natural levees along the Little River and Portage Open Bay (Whittaker 1993). Sites dating between 1000 B.C. and the birth of Christ are also underrepresented; the only reported site containing Early Woodland sand-tempered pottery is located on the surface of the valley train between Elk Chute and the Little River. Sites dating from roughly A.D. 1–1000 occur primarily along the Little River and Portage Open Bay, with only 5 of the 27 sites located in the meander

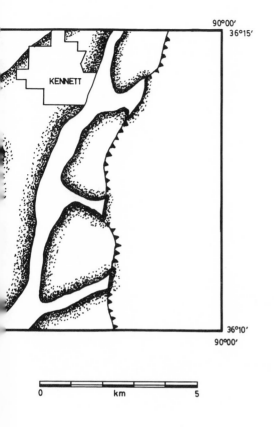

Figure 4.7. Distribution of alluvial deposits on the Malden Plain. The scarp area east and southeast of Kennett, Missouri, is the edge of the Malden Plain. The St. Francis River follows an earlier channel cut through the valley-train deposit (after Saucier 1964).

belt. Early and middle Mississippian period (A.D. 1000–1350) sites are located in all topographic settings, especially on the natural levees along Portage Open Bay, along the banks of the Little River and Elk Chute, and on higher ridges in the meander belt. In contrast to locations of earlier sites, early and middle Mississippian period sites occur across the meander belt with considerable frequency (29 of 67 sites). By ca. A.D. 1350, the situation had changed completely. The number of known sites after that date declines from 67 to 12, and population aggregated in the extreme southern and southeastern parts of the county.

The distribution of prehistoric remains, unless it is strongly influenced by sampling bias, indicates either that pre-Christian-era groups avoided the meander-belt portion of Pemiscot County or that the remains were removed or buried by riverine processes. My guess, untested at the moment, is that Archaic and Early Woodland groups made continuous use of the meander-belt landscape but archaeological materials from that era will be found only on the crests of older point bars and levees that escaped subsequent destruction. The small number of Late Woodland sites in the meander belt, though probably in part an artifact of

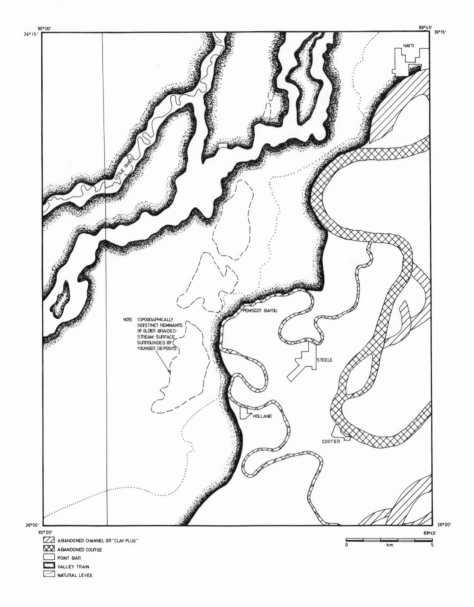

Figure 4.8. Distribution of alluvial deposits in southeastern Dunklin County and southwestern Pemiscot County. The Little River and its tributaries cut through the valley-train deposits during the Holocene, creating a low-lying area that General Land Office surveyors called "Little River Swamp." Notice how former courses of the meandering Mississippi River eroded the eastern edge of the older valley-train deposits. Pemiscot Bayou, perhaps a crevasse channel of the Mississippi River, filled one of the abandoned courses (after Saucier 1964).

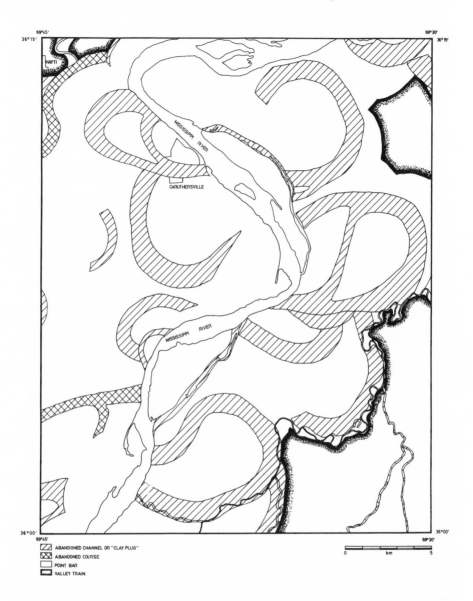

Figure 4.9. Distribution of alluvial deposits in southeastern Pemiscot County. Note the occurrence of valley-train deposits around Hayti (upper left corner) and corresponding deposits across the Mississippi River in Tennessee (after Saucier 1964).

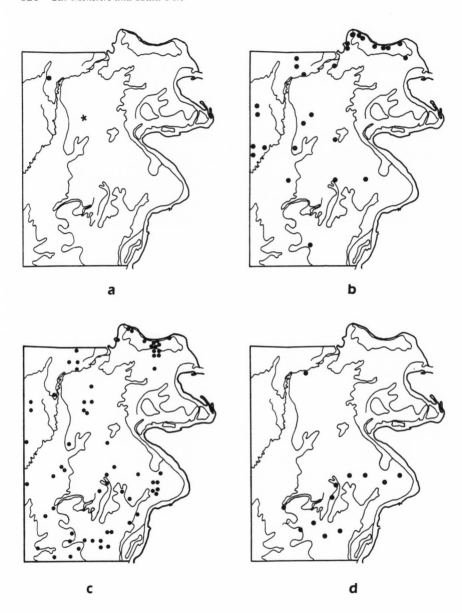

Figure 4.10. Distribution of known archaeological sites in Pemiscot County by time period: a, Archaic period; b, Baytown period; c, early Mississippian period; d, late Mississippian period.

sampling bias, might also reflect the continuing erosional/depositional influence of the Mississippi River in eastern Pemiscot County. The greater number of early and middle Mississippian period sites indicates that by 1,000 years ago much of the county was no longer under constant reworking by the Mississippi River, and thus meander-belt levees and point bars had stabilized and were available for occupation. By that time even the landscape as far east as Caruthersville (Figure 1.4) had stabilized to the point that a major community (the Murphy site [Chapter 5]) had developed.

Topographic Biases

Efforts to better understand the use of the late Holocene landscape by prehistoric groups would benefit greatly from a finer-grained understanding of the distribution of landforms stable enough to support human occupation. Unfortunately, knowledge of such distribution is woefully incomplete, due in part to the absence of small-scale topographic maps sensitive to the microrelief. United States Geological Survey (USGS) topographic maps are produced using a 5-ft contour interval, which shows some of the larger features, but field inspection has demonstrated that in many cases the interval fails to delineate extensive ridges and other important topographic features. In other cases the contours of natural features blend in with those of the myriad drainage ditches that cross the region, precluding attempts to plot even some of the larger floodplain features. The modern relief that has resulted from land leveling confounds our ability to reconstruct the late Holocene topography. But even with widespread cutting and filling, literally thousands of small topographic highs still dot the landscape, most of which are small remnants of natural levees that have been bisected any number of times by stream-course changes and erosion. Although these features are low compared to some of the older levee remnants on the valley-train deposits, many of them were probably above water except during periods of exceptional flooding.

Soil Associations and Topographic Expressions

Perhaps the most useful indicators of relief in the county are SCS field maps made in the 1960s (Brown 1971), which plot the locations of distinct soil-mapping units. Individual soils are the products of a host of variables such as type of parent material, climate, time, and vegetation. They also are affected by processes such as leaching of soluble salts and carbonates, oxidation and reduction, translocation of silicate clays, and weathering. Soils in Pemiscot County are young, their mineralogical composition is almost identical to that of their parent materials, and climate has had little influence on their formation (Brown 1971: 34, 38). The most important factor in their formation is the type of alluvial material available, itself an indicator of past fluvial processes and topographic position. Sedimentary deposits, depending on whether they are from backwater areas, swamps, valley trains, point bars/swales, or natural levees, contain different amounts of sand, silt, and clay. The soils that subsequently are formed from the deposits likewise carry roughly the same percentages (all things being equal). The distribution of soils thus provides a line of evidence with which to examine both the distribution of landforms and the processes that created the features.

Five major soil associations—landscapes that have distinctive proportional patterns of soils (Brown 1971: 2)—occur in Pemiscot County (Figure 4.11). The Wardell-Sharkey association, covering about 6% of the county, consists of level to gently undulating, poorly drained soils on low natural levees west of the Little River drainage system. The association comprises two major soils—Wardell and Sharkey—the distribution of which configures the surface of the late-Pleistocene–early-Holocene valley-train deposit. Sharkey soils are primarily clay or clay loam; they developed in low, slack-water areas such as abandoned distribution channels associated with the braided Mississippi system. Wardell soils make up about 75% of the association and consist of loam or sandy clay loam over a loam to clay subsoil. Soil-mapping units in the Wardell-Sharkey association trend north-south, parallel to the direction of flow of the braided Mississippi River system. Native vegetation supported by soils in the Wardell-Sharkey association includes oak, gum, and cypress.

The Sharkey association consists of level and nearly level, poorly drained soils on the broad slack-water area of the Little River floodplain. The association, which occupies about 34% of the county, extends in a 10–12-km-wide band across the upper half of the county in a northeast-southwest direction. The primary soil in the association is Sharkey silty clay loam, which extends in large unbroken tracts across the Little River and Elk Chute floodplains. This soil is replaced in places by what the SCS (Brown 1971: 48 [unnumbered]) refers to as Sharkey sandy loam, overwash—a soil that formed on the crests of former Little River natural levees. Native vegetation includes cypress and water-tolerant species of oak and gum.

The Dundee association, which occupies about 16% of the county, consists of level to very gently undulating, somewhat poorly drained soils that exist unbroken along Portage Open Bay and as a discontinuous northeast-southwest-trending band along the eastern margin of the valley-train deposit. They developed in moderately fine-textured alluvium, with a surface layer of silty clay loam or sandy loam. I surmise, because of topographic position and type of vegetation supported, that the Dundee association contains the oldest soils in the county. Several areas of Dundee association soils correlate with positions mapped by Saucier (1964) as relatively early valley-train deposits that occur on later deposits of a similar nature. It is likely that most if not all of the Dundee soils were formed from late-Pleistocene–early-Holocene braided-stream sediments. Activities associated with the Little River system to the west and the Mississippi River meander-belt system to the east have reduced the surficial extent of the Dundee association to that shown in Figure 4.11. Another indication of the age of the Dundee soils is the dark color

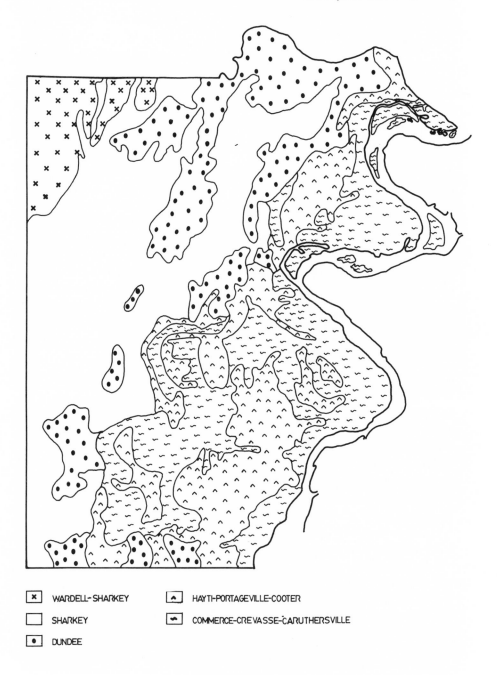

WARDELL-SHARKEY
SHARKEY
DUNDEE
HAYTI-PORTAGEVILLE-COOTER
COMMERCE-CREVASSE-CARUTHERSVILLE

Figure 4.11. Distribution of soil associations in Pemiscot County. Note that valley-train soils (Wardell-Sharkey) are easily distinguished from meander-belt soils (Hayti-Portageville-Cooter) at the association level (after Brown 1971).

and high organic content of the Tiptonville and Reelfoot soils that occur on the rims of high natural levees along Portage Open Bay. As suggested by the SCS (Brown 1971: 14, 17), these soils, which have well-developed B horizons, probably formed under grass cover, perhaps influenced by organic materials deposited during occupation of the levees by prehistoric groups. The soils also support oak and hickory.

The Hayti-Portageville-Cooter association covers about 16% of the county and consists of undulating to depressional, very poorly drained to moderately well drained soils on areas that currently flood and on those that flooded prior to levee construction. The soil association extends from Portage Open Bay south into Arkansas and occupies positions along the western edge of the meander belt or, in the case of the largest continuous expanse, farther out in the floodplain. Two major soils—Hayti and Portageville—make up about 75% of the association. Hayti soils are dark sandy loam or silty clay, and they formed on point-bar ridges. Portageville soils are very dark calcareous clay or silty clay loam that formed in point-bar swales or in deep depressions left by former lakes. Two minor soils— Crevasse and Cooter—replace the other two soils in several locations. In many areas the alternating bands of Hayti and Portageville soils (Figure 4.12) give a fairly accurate picture of the formation of point-bar deposits by the Mississippi as it migrated across the landscape. Native vegetation supported by soils in the association includes cypress and other water-tolerant taxa.

The Commerce-Crevasse-Caruthersville association occupies about 25% of the county and consists of nearly level or, in some cases, gently undulating, poorly drained to excessively drained soils on natural levees. It occupies a 3–6-km-wide band adjacent to the Mississippi River and also occurs on areas bordering Pemiscot Bayou and similar overflow channels on the floodplain. All three major soils in the association are moderately well drained to well drained and for the most part contain slightly coarser to much coarser sediments than occur in soils in the Hayti-Portageville-Cooter association. Preclearing vegetation consisted of willow, cottonwood, elm, and related species.

Nineteenth-Century Physiographic Features

General Land Office surveyors mapped Pemiscot County between 1821 and 1860, during which time township plats were constantly updated and filed with the surveyor of the public lands. Surveyors' notes and the resulting plats present an excellent overview not only of physiographic features in the region but also of vegetation (discussed below). The length of time involved in completing the survey of Pemiscot County is attributable in large part to the conditions faced by the survey parties. It probably is fair to say that few if any areas of the United States posed as many problems as southeastern Missouri. Forests were dense (see below), understory was thick, and in many areas water stood almost year-round. In short, the region was a swamp in the true sense of the word. For example,

Figure 4.12. Distribution of soil series in section 32 of T17N R12E, Pemiscot County (after Brown 1971).

surveyors of T17N R11E, located in the southern half of the county (Figure 1.4), noted the height of overflow evident along each section line, probably in the form of high-water marks on trees and height of debris in trees. Every section-line description carries a notation of overflow, which ranged in depth from 1 to 7 ft. That particular township was surveyed in late winter 1855, and apparently surveyors encountered little standing water except for Pemiscot Bayou.

Figure 4.13 shows the locations of major water courses, swamps, and lakes noted during GLO surveys of Pemiscot County between 1821 and 1860. The majority of lakes marked on the plats occupy landscape positions within the old meander belt, though this gives the false impression that with the exception of that area labeled "Little River Swamp," the braided surface to the west was dry. The map is a composite of finished township plats (completed in several different years) submitted to the Office of the Surveyor of the Public Lands in the States of Illinois and Missouri (St. Louis). Some features are discontinuous between townships, indicating that ponded areas noted by one set of surveyors were not noted by subsequent survey parties. This suggests strongly that the landscape was drier in some years (as well as in some months) than it was in others.

The most striking evidence of changing conditions is shown in Figures 4.14 and 4.15. Figure 4.14 is a plat of township T17N R12E, surveyed in the first quarter of 1841. "Pemisco Lake" encompasses almost all of the township and extends into four other townships, an area of approximately 120 km². By the time the next plat for T17N R12E was produced—in late 1854/early 1855—the body of water had been reduced to several lakes (Figure 4.15), including one labeled "Big Lake or Lake Pemiscot" and one labeled "Pemiscot Bayou." The latter was not actually an active channel of Pemiscot Bayou but rather a slough (known as Cagle Lake [see below]) that connected with Pemiscot Bayou during periods of flooding.

The disparity between the plats points out not only the changing conditions of the landscape but also the problem of determining for any given period of time what land was submerged and what land was out of water. A reasonable guess is that all portions of Pemiscot County, especially those in the southern half, were susceptible to flooding. Increased flow in the Mississippi River as a result of meltwater runoff in the upper third of the Mississippi Basin, together with periods of heavy spring rain, probably inundated hundreds of square kilometers of Pemiscot County at fairly regular intervals. The duration of flooding is impossible to calculate, though I suspect some areas of the county drained extremely slowly. The distribution of clayey soils indicates that many of the swales produced by the meandering Mississippi River were wet year-round.

To the west, on the braided-stream surface, the landscape was a combination of swampland and open-water lakes. Figure 4.13 shows the extent of the Pemiscot County portion of what is labeled on the plat maps as "Little River Swamp" as well as the eastern portion of an unnamed lake known historically as Grey Horse Lake. However, the plat maps for T19–21, R10E (not shown here) show lands east of the edge of the Malden Plain as being part of what is labeled as "Lake Nic-Cormy or the East Swamp." No eastern boundary of the swamp is shown on the plats, and one is left with the impression that the entire braided surface from the edge of the Malden Plain east to the Little River was a swamp. The main channel of the Little River and Grey Horse Lake must have contained water deep enough to prohibit cypress growth and thus allow the margins of open water to be mapped. The Malden Plain was subject to flooding from the St. Francis River (Figure 4.16), especially as it backed water up numerous sloughs such as the Varney River. The sloughs were former braided-stream channels of the Mississippi River.

Of particular interest here, given their proximity to the archaeological sites upon which we will focus attention later, are four Pemiscot County lakes east and

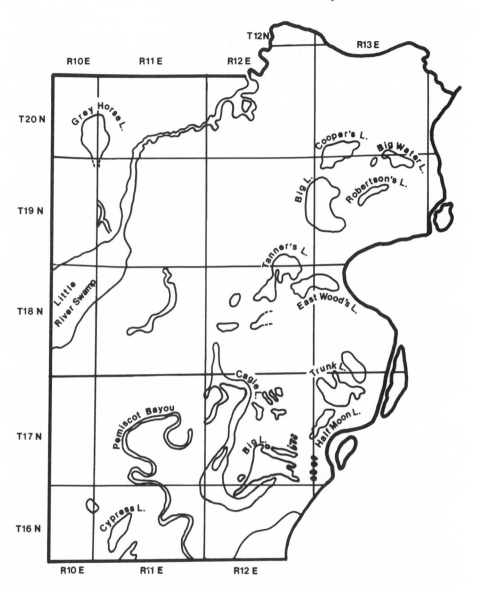

Figure 4.13. Locations of water courses, lakes, and swamps in Pemiscot County as shown on General Land Office plats. This is a generalized map of impoundments and wetlands drawn by the Soil Conservation Service; compare with Figure 4.17 (after Brown 1971).

northeast of Pemiscot Bayou (Figure 4.13). The largest of these is Cagle Lake (unnamed on the GLO plats), a 30-km-long course that follows an old meander of the Mississippi River. At one time the upper end of Cagle Lake probably was part of Pemiscot Bayou (see Brown 1971: fig. 15), but for the most part the lake has been confined during historical times to portions of Fisk's (1944: plate 22,

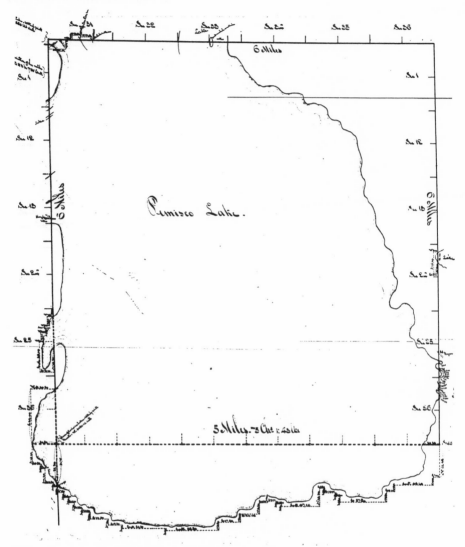

Figure 4.14. General Land Office plat of T17N R12E completed in 1841. No interior section lines could be surveyed because of the presence of "Pemisco Lake." Notice that the surveyors chained around the southern edge of the lake.

sheet 3) Mississippi River stage 3. North of Cooter, the channel that Fisk depicts as number 3 divided around small remnants of levees that were connected with his stages 1 and 2, leaving them as topographic highs (see Figure 4.8; also noted on Saucier's [1964] Hayti quadrangle). When Cagle Lake later formed, these remnants were island highs. The average width of the lake was less than 1 km; elevations suggest its depth was about 2 m or less.

Big Lake (not to be confused with the Big Lake in Mississippi County, Arkansas, referred to previously) lay just to the east of Cagle Lake and, as mentioned above,

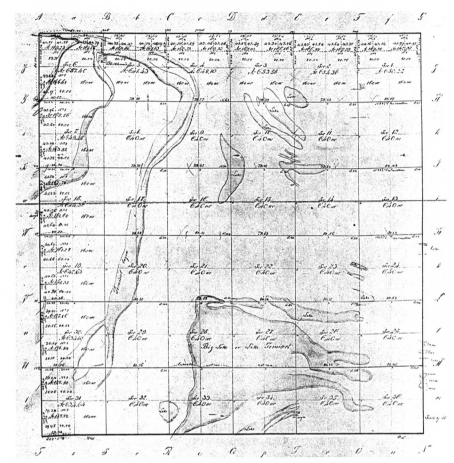

Figure 4.15. General Land Office plat of T17N R12E completed in 1854–1855. "Lake Pemisco" has disappeared, leaving smaller impoundments. It probably was not a rare occurrence in the Pemiscot Bayou region to have standing bodies of water one year measuring several miles across and then to have them shrink down to pond size the next year.

fluctuated widely in size. The troughs, or swales, along the eastern margin of the lake and to the north of the lake shown in Figure 4.15 are silt-and-clay-lined depressions that formed opposite a meander bend in an ancient channel of the Mississippi, what Fisk (1944: plate 22, sheet 3) refers to as stages G–J. Half Moon Lake lay just to the northeast of Big Lake and late in historical times was about 3 km long and 1 km wide. Its position conformed to a piece of Fisk's (1944: plate 22, sheet 3) stage 15. As an aside, Fisk's relative sequence of stages appears reasonable here. He shows the stage 16 Mississippi River as having truncated a meander of its earlier stage (15), which, after it was cut off by natural levees associated with stage 16, became Half Moon Lake. Trunk Lake, 2 km north of

Figure 4.16. Photograph of the St. Francis River showing formation of sediment-choked channels. I suspect that this view is typical of what Pemiscot Bayou looked like in the nineteenth century prior to timber clearing.

Half Moon Lake, was approximately of the same size as the latter and conformed to a portion of Fisk's (1944: plate 22, sheet 3) stage 9.

Nineteenth-Century Vegetation

The modern Mississippi Alluvial Valley in general conforms to the area delimited by Kuchler (1954) as the Southern Floodplain Forest, a mix of deciduous trees that are moisture sensitive. Guccione et al. (1988: 67) subdivide the valley into three communities—swamp forest, hardwood bottoms, and ridge bottoms (natural levees and low terraces)—each of which is present in the Little River Lowland. Swamp forests, where water stands year-round except during periods of prolonged drought, are dominated by bald cypress and tupelo *(Nyssa)*. Hardwood bottoms, which are subject to frequent flooding and prolonged periods of inundation during late winter and spring, are dominated by sweet gum, maple, oak, and elm. Ridge bottoms, which flood infrequently and drain rapidly, are dominated by hardwood-bottom taxa and by hickory.

Although there is every reason to suspect that the taxa currently present in the region reflect to a large degree those present before the area was cleared during the late nineteenth century, forest density has changed dramatically. Because the

GLO surveys were conducted prior to timber clearing and land drainage, the records offer us the opportunity to examine large, undisturbed tracts of timber. Although the GLO records contain biases (Potzger et al. 1956; Wood 1976), they provide the best available information on presettlement vegetation patterns (Warren 1982a). Records list the common names, diameters, and locations of trees encountered along section lines as surveyors chained their way north-south and east-west and of "bearing trees," which were blazed to enable relocation of section and quarter-section corners. The records also provide descriptions of understory.

When the GLO surveys of Pemiscot were carried out, the entire county, except for areas of deep water, was heavily forested. Several expanses labeled "prairie" on the GLO plats lay in Dunklin County, west of the Little River swamp, though these were probably dry because of their higher elevations. Trees mentioned most often in the GLO survey notes for Pemiscot County include cottonwood (*Populus* sp.), sweet gum *(Liquidambar styraciflua),* willow (*Silax* sp.), ash (*Fraxinus* sp.), and elm (*Ulmus* sp.). To understand the composition and density of the forests, individual trees mentioned by the surveyors were plotted for three townships: T17N R11E, T17N R12E, and T18N R12E. For forest-compositional data, both "line trees" and "bearing trees" were used. When setting section corners and quarter-section corners, surveyors actually recorded distances and bearings to two trees, but to simplify analysis I only employed the closer of the two here. To compute forest density (discussed in more detail below), only bearing trees were used.

Forest Composition

Table 4.1 presents frequencies of trees by type for each of the three townships examined. Figure 4.17 shows the distribution of eight selected taxa using only the nearest bearing tree for each section and quarter-section corner. Several points need to be made about the distributions. First, the number of trees varies from township to township. T18N R12E contains the fewest number of trees in the sample, 148, and T17N R12E contains the most, 544. However, the southeast quarter of T18N R12E apparently never had the interior section lines run (or if they were run, the records have been lost); thus, I have no data for 9 sections. If we assume that forest composition was uniform across the township, we can estimate the total, including those in the unsurveyed sections, at 197 trees, which is close to the total for T17N R11E. As pointed out below, however, forest composition was anything but uniform.

In each of the three townships, cottonwood was the dominant taxon, ranging from 28% to 36% of the total sample of trees. Willow, ash, and sweet gum essentially tied for second place. However, the ranks of taxa, with the exception of cottonwood, vary among townships (Table 4.2). For example, ash, willow, and sweet gum each rank once in second place and then trade places to rank once in third place in different townships. Elm and maple (*Acer* sp.) rank fourth and fifth,

Table 4.1
Frequencies of Trees in Three Pemiscot County Townships

Taxon	Township			Total
	17N R11E	17N R12E	18N R12E	
Box Elder	12	16	1	29
Cottonwood	62	179	54	295
Pin Oak	8	5	8	21
Cow Oak	1	0	0	1
Sycamore	13	26	5	44
Willow	10	72	18	100
Ash	33	59	10	102
Hackberry	10	12	1	23
Sweet Gum	29	50	24	103
Hickory	6	3	0	9
Elm	23	27	14	64
Locust	0	20	1	21
Maple	13	12	8	33
Cypress	1	51	1	53
Mulberry	2	1	0	3
Sassafras	1	1	0	2
Black Walnut	0	2	1	3
Pecan	0	4	2	6
Persimmon	0	3	0	3
Hickory	0	1	0	1
Total	224	544	148	916

Source: Data from General Land Office surveys.

respectively, in two townships but do not make the list of top-five-ranked taxa in T17N R12E. Cypress is the fourth-ranked taxon in T17N R12E, occurring in the sample 51 times (almost 10%), but the other two townships have only single representatives. T17N R12E also contains an overabundance of locust (*Gleditsia* sp.) trees, with 20 of the 21 locust specimens in the pooled sample. Box elder *(Acer negundo)* and hackberry *(Celtis occidentalis)* occur primarily in T17N R11E and T17N R12E, with only one tree of each occurring in T18N R12E.

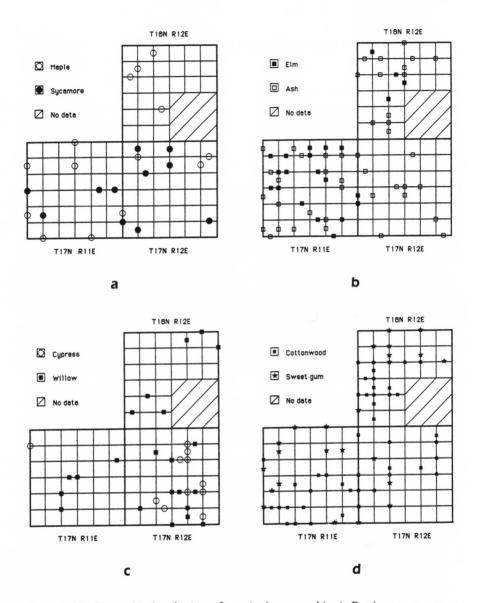

Figure 4.17. Geographic distributions of trees in three townships in Pemiscot county, as recorded by General Land Office surveyors: a, maple and sycamore; b, elm and ash; c, cypress and willow; d, cottonwood and sweet gum.

Table 4.2
Rank-Order of Five Dominant Taxa in Three Pemiscot County Townships

Rank	Township		
	T17N R11E	T17N R12E	T18N R12E
1	Cottonwood	Cottonwood	Cottonwood
2	Ash	Willow	Sweet gum
3	Sweet gum	Ash	Willow
4	Elm	Cypress	Elm
5	Maple	Sweet gum	Maple

The differences in composition are attributable in large part to the amount of seasonal moisture in the various townships, itself attributable in part to differences in topographic relief. Topography in general increases from the southwestern corner to the northeastern corner of Pemiscot County; hence, relief in T18N R12E is greater than in T17N R11E. Relief in T17N R12E is extremely low, which allowed seasonal impoundment of large bodies of water such as Big Lake (Lake Pemisco[t]). The survey records for T17N R12E document the problems encountered by the surveyors who mapped the township. They encountered so much standing water in the winter of 1854–1855 that their witness trees often were no closer than about 300 ft to section and quarter-section corners. This wide spacing of trees in areas of standing water leads one to suspect that some of the impoundments were permanent as opposed to occasional and that the depth of water was sufficient to preclude the growth even of cypress. The significant percentages of willow, locust, and cypress—all mesophytic (water-tolerant) taxa—in T17N R12E are consistent with a swampy environment. On the other hand, T18N R12E contains the fewest trees in the sample but contains twice as many pin oaks *(Quercus palustris)* as either of the other two townships. This is consistent with the expectations for higher, drier areas.

Several taxa deserve special mention, either because of their low frequency of occurrence or because of problems with nomenclature. The reader will notice that I list in Table 4.1 the taxon "pin oak" *(Q. palustris)*. However, this specific taxon never was listed as such in the GLO survey notes. The various surveyors listed other oak types, including black oak, "cow oak," Spanish oak, and in many cases simply "oak." I agree with Asch and Sidell (1992: 182) that black oak *(Q. velutina)*, an inhabitant of dry uplands, is ecologically out of place in a floodplain setting. On the other hand, the pin oak is the most common Mississippi River floodplain oak (Klein et al. 1975). I therefore changed black oak to pin oak. Asch and Sidell (1992: 183) also note that Michaux (1819) mentions "swamp Spanish oak" as an alternative designation for pin oak (see also Little 1953: 345). Thus I changed the single Spanish oak in the sample to pin oak. I left the designation "cow oak" *(Q. prinus)*, which sometimes is referred to as a swamp chestnut oak or basket oak.

The infrequent occurrence of black walnut is not particularly surprising for a swampy area, and were it not for a reference made by Chapman and Anderson (1955: 11) in their preliminary report on the Campbell site, I would have assumed that it was nothing more than a minor constituent of the swamp forest. However, they relate that Ellis Barger, who was born in 1878 in a house on the Campbell site (T16N R12E), recalled that when Cagle (Franklin) Lake was drained in the early twentieth century, a vast quantity of black-walnut logs and stumps were found on the lake bed. Barger used the occurrence of black walnut as evidence that Cagle Lake was formed during the New Madrid earthquake and aftershocks of 1811–1812, since the taxon is not particularly tolerant of standing water. Barger's claim is difficult to evaluate. It is possible that prolonged periods of relatively low water across Pemiscot County could have led to the proliferation of walnut trees, which were subsequently drowned by prolonged periods of standing water. On the other hand, he might have made an erroneous identification.

In general, the distribution of taxa evident across the Pemiscot Bayou locality corresponds to those described by Shelford (1963), Lewis (1974), and others for floodplain environments in adjacent regions of the Mississippi River valley. Classificatory schemes that order floodplain taxa into plant communities (e.g., Lewis 1974 and Shelford 1963) all note the importance of small elevational differences, which in the meander-belt region of the Mississippi Valley may be on the order of 10 ft or less. Lewis (1974), for example, based on GLO records, identifies 5 tree-bearing communities for Mississippi County, Missouri: cypress deep swamp, willow and/or cottonwood water-edge brush, sweet gum–elm–cypress seasonal swamp, sweet gum–elm–cane ridge forest, and cottonwood-sycamore natural-levee forest. Although these communities contain taxa that can, in some cases, grow in more than one environment, on average they tend to occur in more or less restricted slope positions.

Tree Size

The General Land Office records give us compositional data not only on presettlement floodplain forests but also on the sizes of the trees in the forests, measured as diameter at breast height. The largest trees on average are the pin oaks, with a mean diameter (20 specimens) of 39 inches. Cypress exhibit the largest range in diameter, from 6 inches (immature) to 95 inches (the mean for 51 specimens in T17N R12E was 21 inches, as was the standard deviation—a figure more than 3 times that for any other taxon). Five of the 51 specimens in T17N R12E were over 60 inches in diameter, which equates to trees with circumferences in excess of 15 ft. These are not unusual dimensions for cypress in the Mississippi Valley, as evidenced by modern specimens ringing the margins of Reelfoot Lake in extreme western Tennessee. Lewis (1974: 26) mentions that a GLO surveyor noted a cypress stump in Mississippi County that had a circumference of 55 ft, which yields a diameter of 17.5 ft.

Cottonwoods, the most prolific taxon in each of the 3 townships examined, varied in diameter from 7 to 40 inches. It might be expected that the diameters vary with tree density, with the largest trees in areas of low overall density (see below). This holds true for cottonwoods in T17N R12E, which have a mean diameter of 18 inches and a low standard deviation of almost 6. However, the largest mean diameter for cottonwoods (25 inches, s.d. = 9) occurred in T17N R11E, which had the second highest overall tree density. The intermediate mean diameter (20 inches, s.d. = 7) occurred in T18N 12E, which had the lowest density of the sample.

Understory

Trees were not the only flora mentioned by GLO surveyors. After surveying a section line, surveyors would mention the types of understory encountered, or, if the understory inhibited their progress along a line, they would mark the precise points at which they entered and left the understory. The most frequently mentioned understory taxa in GLO notes are cane (*Arundinaria gigantea*) and "green brier" (greenbriar [*Smilax* sp.]), with occasional mention of spice bush (*Lindera benzoin*). In places the surveyors noted several miles of thick cane, which slowed their progress considerably. Cane was noted along section lines in each of the three townships analyzed and appears to have had no slope preference. Without exception it bordered all the lakes encountered, being especially thick in T17N R12E. Historical accounts of nineteenth-century canebrakes are prolific and attest to the difficulty humans had in penetrating them. Flint (1832: 53), for example, noted, "A man could not make three miles a day through a thick cane brake. It is the chosen resort of bears and panthers, which break it down, and make their way into it, as a retreat from man." Original cane stands often attained heights of 20–30 ft (Brackenridge 1962; Nuttall 1905).

Floral Resources

Several taxa listed in the GLO survey notes are known to have been used by Native Americans and probably by early Euro-Americans as well. The more commonly mentioned taxa include maple, elm, ash, mulberry, hazelnut, walnut, hickory, black oak, hawthorn, coffeetree, locust, grape, and hackberry. It is difficult to derive estimates of fruit, sap, and nut yields for the area examined because of (a) the effects of cyclicity: mast resources (e.g., acorns, hickory nuts) tend to be plentiful for a 2–3-year period then to go through a nonproductive period, and (b) the imprecision of the estimates of tree density. Regardless, the resources would have been a strong magnet for myriad avian and mammalian fauna as well as for the humans who hunted them.

Forest Density

General Land Office records can also be used to calculate forest density, which is an inverse function of distance between trees. Trees included in section-line descriptions are unsuitable as data points because of sampling bias; however, the nonrandom bearing trees, tied as they are to evenly spaced section and quarter-section corners, are suitable. Several methods of density calculation are used in the ecological literature, the most common being that of Cottam and Curtis (1956; see also Cottam 1949). Their method involves the use of bearing trees recorded by GLO surveyors for each section corner and each quarter-section corner; to simplify calculations, I used only the bearing tree that was closer to the corner. Distance-to-corner was calculated for each point, township by township. Then, the values, by township, were averaged and the resulting values used as radii of circles to calculate the "average" area covered by a tree within each township. These values could then be used to figure trees/acre or trees/mi^2. The number of sample trees varied by township (111 in T17N R11E, 83 in T17N R12E, and 63 in T18N R12E) mainly because of surveyors' inability to penetrate several swampy areas. I deleted 19 points in T17N R12E because of the extreme distances involved between trees and posts when the latter were set in lakes. Although the calculations are not affected directly by missing data points, the results are only approximations of the actual tree density in each township. Also, although only one value per township is given, densities were not homogeneous across the townships.

Density values range from 44 stems/acre (28,160 stems/mi^2) in T18N R12E to 54 stems/acre (34,560 stems/mi^2) in T17N R11E, to 70 stems/acre (44,800 stems/mi^2) in T17N R12E. In other words, the township with the highest elevation and the least amount of standing water exhibits the lowest density; the "wettest" township exhibits the highest density. If one stops and thinks about these values, one should be struck immediately by the denseness of the presettlement forests along Pemiscot Bayou. Added to the dense overstory were innumerable small-diameter trees (less than 6 inches) and thick, sometimes impenetrable, stands of cane and other understory taxa, creating a daunting environment that even into the late nineteenth century was sparsely populated.

Site Location and Environmental Variation

Numerous studies have been undertaken of Mississippian-period site location in the central Mississippi River valley, especially site location relative to soil fertility and topography (e.g., Guccione et al. 1988; Lafferty 1984, 1987; Lewis 1974; P. A. Morse 1981; D. F. Morse 1989; Morse and Morse 1983). All of these studies have found that, not unexpectedly, sites tend to be located on natural levees, which would have afforded protection against flooding. Sites in the Pemiscot Bayou locale were no exception. Although few of the sites have been mapped in detail, inspection of site locations relative to USGS topographic maps and SCS soils maps indicates that the crests of natural levees were preferred features upon which to locate communities. Examination of site locations relative to soil mapping units, bodies of water, and presettlement vegetation, however, allow us a more in-depth picture of the environments in the vicinity of the late Mississippian period communities.

All the Mississippian-period sites discussed in this volume lay within a mile of a water source marked on the GLO survey plats. Wardell, the most northern of the group, was on the north bank of the Little River. Two sites—Holland and Denton Mounds—were adjacent to Pemiscot Bayou; four others—Berry, Campbell, Brooks, and Dorrah—were adjacent to a low area that was labeled "Pemiscot Bayou" on the GLO plats but that in actuality was a slough (a filled-in meander scar of the Mississippi River) that connected with Pemiscot Bayou at its northern end (Figure 4.13). Kersey was a mile north of the slough. Murphy was at the northern end of Trunk Lake, Kinfolk Ridge was at the southern edge of the lake, and McCoy was a mile east of the lake. Dorrah was a half-mile west of Half Moon Lake. Recall, however, from earlier discussion that the sizes of the permanent impoundments changed from year to year. There is no way to tell exactly where the lake edges were when the sites were first occupied. However, in 1841, when Lake Pemiscot covered almost all of T17N R12E and the southern portion of T18N R12E, Kersey and Dorrah were completely inundated. Interestingly, the only two known late Mississippian period sites located in T17N R12E—Cagle Lake and Dorrah—occur either along the eastern edge (Cagle Lake) or near the northern edge (Dorrah) of the township. The lack of sites in the interior of the township may be a reflection of the inhospitable nature of the dense canebrakes and cypress swamp.

With two exceptions, all sites are located on Commerce or Hayti soils, usually large expanses of Commerce silt loam that are proximal to Hayti silty clay loam. These excessively drained to poorly drained soils cap natural levees throughout the meander-belt portion of Pemiscot County and today are among the most agriculturally productive soils in the county. McCoy is located on Caruthersville very fine sandy loam, and Denton Mounds is located on Dundee silt loam; both mapping units occur primarily on old natural levees. Seven sites—Berry, Brooks, Holland, Campbell, Denton Mounds, Murphy, and Kinfolk Ridge—are marked on the SCS mapping sheets as "middens" (dark, organic stains that resulted from human habitation). All are located on extremely large expanses of Commerce silt loam or, in the case of Denton Mounds, a large expanse of Dundee silt loam.

Summary

It is difficult to overemphasize the role of the physical environment in shaping the prehistoric settlement of the Pemiscot Bayou locality. The dynamic nature of the meander-belt regime of the Mississippi River throughout the Holocene sequentially created landforms then eradicated or modified them as the channel migrated across the low-relief landscape, in the process leaving new landforms behind. But to focus exclusively on the meander-belt history of the region is to bypass an important era in the central Mississippi Valley—one that created the landscape that the meander-belt regime inherited. Although the late Mississippian period sites discussed here were located well within the meander-belt portion of the valley, there is every reason to believe that the older, valley-train surface to the west, with its wet prairies and braided streams, was an important part of the environment for the occupants of the Pemiscot Bayou sites.

And yet it was the meander-belt region to which adaptations by late Mississippian period peoples were directed. Communities were located, apparently, where topographic relief—what little there was—offered dry land for at least part of the year and some protection from periodic flooding. Dense forests of cottonwood, sycamore, elm, and cypress offered an abundant supply of fuel and building materials and served as a haven for myriad species of birds, reptiles, amphibians, and mammals. Edible plant resources were available within short distances of any of the communities, as was water. Assuming late-Mississippian groups were agricultural (discussed later), arable land was abundant, provided the land could be cleared—the forest canopy would have been too thick to allow sunlight through without clearing—and the crops not destroyed by flooding. Periodic firing by Mississippian peoples could have helped retard undergrowth, though it is difficult to imagine, given the amount of standing water that must have been present, that this would have been very effective.

In conclusion, it is difficult to envision a more productive environment than the Pemiscot Bayou locality during the late Mississippian period. The incredibly rich and diverse biomass of a hardwood swamp must have served as a magnet to human groups that had the technology to adapt to it. Archaeological-survey data indicate that sometime after the birth of Christ prehistoric groups began exploiting the natural resources of southern Pemiscot County on a more or less continual basis. Archaeological materials dating ca. A.D. 900 and later are prolific, especially in the extreme southern and southeastern portions of the county (Figure 4.10). I assume that the peoples who left the remains were ancestral to those who occupied the region after A.D. 1400. However, the number of post–A.D. 1400 sites declined, and the reasons for this decline are unclear. This phenomenon could be due to sampling error, to an actual decline in the number of people occupying the region, or to a rearrangement in how people distributed themselves across the landscape. Whatever the reason, it probably was not tied to changes in the physical environment, which if anything was becoming more stable. Certainly by ca. A.D. 1400 the Mississippi River had migrated eastward to more or less its approximate current position, leaving behind a landscape that had begun to stabilize in terms of its landforms and bodies of water. Site locations along Pemiscot Bayou indicate that that stream maintained a more or less stable position up through the end of the nineteenth century. The relative shallowness and apparent stability of archaeological deposits on the tops of natural-levee remnants indicate that although episodes of sedimentation, and probably of erosion, occurred after the materials were deposited, the episodes were not severe enough to destroy the remains or to bury them at considerable depths. The precise nature of those remains—the material evidence of the adjustments made by late-Mississippian groups to the hardwood swamps along Pemiscot Bayou—is the subject of the remainder of this volume.

5

LATE MISSISSIPPIAN PERIOD ANTECEDENTS: MURPHY AND KERSEY

Michael J. O'Brien and Richard A. Marshall

It is difficult to understand the late Mississippian period prehistory of the Pemiscot Bayou locality without understanding something of its earlier prehistory, especially that of the period A.D. 900–1350. As Figure 4.10 shows, remains from this period have been found across southern Pemiscot County. We obviously are looking at a biased sample of sites, since no systematic survey of the region has been undertaken, but even so the number of locations is striking in comparison to the number of late-period sites. At least by A.D. 900—a date based solely on cross-correlation of ceramic material with dated contexts elsewhere—dozens of localities were being used by Mississippian groups. Although there is currently little information on either the activities carried out at many of those sites or the length of time a group used any particular locality, we can be fairly confident that some sites served residential functions, and probably over fairly long periods of time. We base this proposition on the fact that the Archaeological Survey of Missouri (ASM) files contain numerous references to sites that at one time contained mounds and that produced large quantities of shell-tempered pottery. Determination of which sites to include in the early Mississippian period site-distribution map (Figure 4.10) was based on these ceramic materials. If the material reported on an ASM site consisted solely of the types Neeley's Ferry plain, Bell plain, or red-slipped, the site was placed in the early Mississippian period.

Fortunately, fairly large scale excavations were carried out at two southern Pemiscot County sites that contained components dating pre–A.D. 1350. Both produced human skeletal material, large amounts of ceramic sherds, and some intact vessels. Kersey is the earlier of the two (see Chapter 3), though the exact time span during which the site was occupied is open to question. Murphy contains an earlier Mississippian-period component as well as a late-Mississippian component. The most interesting aspect of the two sites concerns the burial programs represented. When information from Kersey and Murphy is added to that from Campbell (Chapter 6) and Denton Mounds (Chapter 7), what emerges is an impressive picture of mortuary practices among Mississippian Pemiscot Bayou groups that span the period ca. A.D. 900–1540.

Murphy

Between November 23 and 25, 1954, and again between March 30 and April 8, 1955, Carl H. Chapman and his associates at the University of Missouri recovered a large number of skeletons and associated grave goods from a Mississippian-period site in Pemiscot County that was undergoing extensive land leveling. What appeared prior to examination to be a small mound containing burials within it and around its perimeter was actually a complex deposit of mound fill, crematory basin, burned structure, and human bone. Several methods of burial treatment were identified, including vertical and horizontal bundling, cremation, and extension. Based on ceramic design and vessel form, we determined that the area was used from at least ca. A.D. 1200 until sometime in the sixteenth century.

The burial-related deposits were part of Murphy, also referred to as the Caruthersville Mound site, located approximately 3 km southwest of Caruthersville (Figure 1.4). The alternate name of the site refers to the 10-m-high earthen mound that represents the highest point in Pemiscot County (Figure 5.1). A description provided early in the twentieth century (Houck 1908: 54) noted that the mound was "the largest existing mound in the state. This immense monument of prehistoric times is 400 feet long, 250 feet wide, and 35 feet high, with an approach from the south end leading up to the top of the mound. On the north end it is 15 feet higher than at the south end. Upon this mound a residence has been erected [long since razed]. The sides [of the mound] apparently were covered with burnt clay three or four inches thick, with split cane originally laid between the layers."[1]

The site is listed on the National Register of Historic Places and has been subjected to intensive artifact collection for at least the last 50 years. Despite the size of the artifact scatter (at least 20 ha) and the presence of perhaps the largest prehistoric earthen structure in existence in the state, the site has received little

1. Houck 1908 also includes a photograph of the mound.

Figure 5.1. View (looking northeast) of the Murphy mound taken in 1954.

attention from archaeologists other than during the 1954–1955 excavations, and even those investigations received only a small note in the *Missouri Archaeological Society Newsletter* (Chapman 1957).

The maps, notes, and other field records that formed the basis of the analysis presented here are of variable quality—a result of time constraints and degree of expertise but also simply a product of the times. Despite certain inadequacies, however, the records allowed us to locate burials, vessels, and other features relative to each other, and enough cross sections and plan maps of excavated units existed to enable us to understand the sequence of mound construction and mortuary activities. Bone preservation in the field ranged from excellent in a few cases to poor in most cases. Field records clearly indicate that in many instances the state of preservation was such that the bones could not be removed from the ground. Burial drawings, however, are remarkably clear, as are burial descriptions. In all but a few cases, extensive photographic coverage allowed us to verify the field notes regarding burial position and orientation.

Excavated Areas

A newspaper clipping found in the Chapman archives (newspaper name and exact date unknown) states that word of impending site destruction reached Chapman prior to Thanksgiving 1954. The landowner, C. E. Murphy, was leveling a high area southeast of the large mound on his property when he exhumed pieces of five skeletons. He discontinued operations, and a member of the state archaeological society notified Chapman, who, with his wife, Eleanor, and their two sons, spent the Thanksgiving holidays exposing and removing the five skeletons. On March 8 of the following year Chapman and two of his university associates, Richard Marshall and Robert Bray, together with students and other volunteers (including Leo Anderson), began a 10-day investigation that resulted in an area of approximately 2,597 ft[2] being excavated.[2]

In 1954 a datum stake labeled "0-north, 0-west" was established at an unspecified distance south and east of the large mound; based on the field map and excavation photographs, we judge the stake to have been approximately 200 ft southeast of the edge of the mound, just at the southern edge of the small rise (Figure 5.2). An additional stake—0-north, 30-west—was placed due west of the primary datum, and two more stakes—40-north, 30-west and 50-north, 30-west—were placed north of that (Figures 5.2 and 5.3). These stakes were later used as alidade stations but unfortunately were never used as coordinates of a central grid. Rather, excavation was by area, with designations assigned somewhat arbitrarily. Units within areas were placed opportunistically, during both field periods, over exposed skeletons. Excavation units established in 1954 (areas B–D and F–H in Figure 5.2) were placed over the five skeletons uncovered initially; in 1955 areas adjacent to the earlier units were opened and given separate letter designations (I for units adjacent to earlier units F–G and K for units adjacent to earlier units B–D). In addition, areas J, L, P, and S were opened on other areas of the mound (Figure 5.2). Individual 5-ft units within areas I–L, P, and S were labeled by their position relative to an imaginary "center line" (sometimes north–south, sometimes east–west) that ran through each area. Unit designations are shown in Figure 5.2; the large letters designate the areas, the small letters designate right or left of the "center line," and the numbers represent the distance from the zero square. When we attempted to position excavation areas relative to one another, we used original alidade readings shot from the three stakes along the 30-west line and from excavation-unit corners. Since a continuous grid was not employed when the site was excavated, the alidade-derived distance measures were all that was available. Our best guess is that the positioning could be off by a maximum of 2 to 3 feet between the northeast corner of area B and the southwest corner of area J (Figure 5.2).

Depth of excavation varied from unit to unit, depending on the nature of the deposit and the depth of the skeletal material. In some areas land-leveling activities had exposed material, and it was removed without excavation. In other areas mound fill and crematory-related deposits were excavated to a depth of several feet. Of particular concern during analysis was deriving an understanding

---

2. Excavation measurements used in this chapter are in feet and inches, following the system used by Chapman and associates in the field.

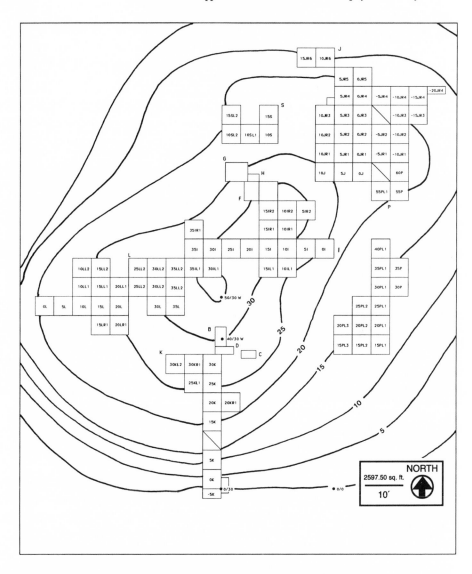

Figure 5.2. Contour map (plotted from elevation points shot in 1955) of the excavated portion of Murphy showing locations of excavation areas (capital letters) and unit designations. Number-letter combinations indicate distance and direction of unit from imaginary centerline established for each excavation area. For example, unit 25KL1 is 25 ft left of the centerline established for Area K.

Figure 5.3. View (looking north) of the excavated portion of Murphy.

of how much dirt had been removed in 1954, prior to Murphy's cessation of leveling activities, and how much was removed during the 1955 excavation. Photographs show that tractor-pulled blades were used to remove overburden during the excavation and that these activities lowered the rise in which the burials were located. Statements in the press clipping indicated that the mound was once 12 feet high, though this figure is greatly exaggerated. We suspect the mound was actually a levee deposit that provided a topographic high relative to the flat surrounding terrain. As discussed below, at least part of the feature indeed was a man-made mound, probably erected on top of the levee remnant.

Field notes indicate that excavators quickly recognized various landmarks such as different-colored sedimentary layers, which could be followed from area to area across the excavated locale, and that they used those markers to determine how deep to excavate. For example, units in Area S were excavated to a depth of only 12 inches, probably because of the absence of visible soil landmarks and because of the fact that many of the burials in Area J, to the east of Area S, were within the upper foot of deposit. The field notes, especially the cross sections, indicate that in many excavation units the base of the archaeological deposit was not reached.

Units were excavated in vertical slices of varying depth, the two most common being 6 inches and 12 inches. None of the deposit was screened; artifacts were recovered as seen during troweling or shovel scraping and were bagged by level.

Thousands of sherds, lithic items, and other artifacts were recovered, including small beads, but large numbers were obviously missed. Faunal remains are mentioned on the field forms, but few were collected because of the softness of the bone (few human-skeletal remains were collected either [Chapter 8]).

The Excavations

The contour map shown in Figure 5.2 is derived from alidade readings taken in 1955 on elevations of (a) excavation-unit corners, (b) various points between excavation areas, and (c) skeletal parts and ceramic vessels. Elevations of a few points outside the excavated areas also were added, though the number of off-mound points is too small to be of much use. Not all unit-corner elevations were shot, nor were all skeletons and vessels. Where depths below datum of vessels and skeletons were recorded, the depth below ground of the object (if recorded in the field notes or discernible from photographs) was subtracted from the crosshair reading to calibrate the ground elevation. In March 1955 the highest point of the mound was approximately 35 inches above the surrounding terrain. Based on our best guess, up to 36 inches of soil was bladed from the mound prior to the time when the elevation readings were taken. Photographs indicate that this removal was fairly uniform across the mound surface; hence the contour map probably reflects relative heights fairly accurately.

Unit profiles, especially those along the western face of the north–south trench in Area K (units 0K to 25K [Figure 5.4]), clearly show that the excavation did not reach the bottom of the mound. Those profiles also document the complexity of mound construction. The profile illustrated in Figure 5.4 (simplified slightly from the field drawings) shows several levels of mound-related sediments, including a deeper, light gray clay overlain by a level of dark gray clay. The lower, lighter clay level was the earliest mound-construction level encountered across the site. Chisel plowing in spring 1991 documented that the subsoil in the offmound areas was a mottled yellow-brown clay-silt distinct from the consistently noted light gray clay across the excavation area. The band of light gray clay is not continuous across the profile shown in Figure 5.4; rather, it dips toward the center of the profile. The reasons for this are unclear.

The overlying layer of dark gray clay is also discontinuous, a result of two large prehistoric pits that were excavated at different times into the mound. The pit in units 15K and 20K (feature 1) was excavated directly through the dark gray clay surface, as evidenced by the presence of overlying deposits. The pit in unit 5K (feature 2) was excavated through the later sediments, a process that removed any traces of them that would have shown up in the profile. Both pits were filled with burned earth, charcoal, ash, and tiny bone fragments. The southern end of the earlier pit was covered with a layer of light gray clay, which was overlain by a thin layer of burned clay, ash, and charcoal that continued and thickened considerably

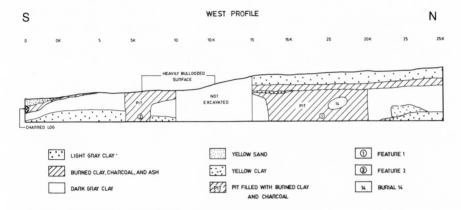

Figure 5.4. West profile of trench excavated in Area K at Murphy, showing roughly the southern half of the crematory mound and associated fill (northern 15 ft of profile deleted from figure).

upslope. A thin layer of yellow sandy clay overlay the burned-material layer in the northernmost six feet of the profile. A similar band of yellow sandy clay occurred in the unit 0K profile, where it intersected another burned-material layer that rested on the layer of dark gray clay. Recent (post-mound-construction) sediments have been deposited over the burned-clay layer. A right-angle profile of unit 25KI1 documents the presence of another large pit (feature 3) overlain by the burned-clay-and-charcoal layer and light gray clay layer evident in the long profile.

Figure 5.5 shows the west profiles of units 35IL1 and 35I. The profiles were constructed from field notes, which gave the depths and orientations of various mound-related sedimentary layers, and were checked against field photographs. The profile differs significantly from the one to the south (Figure 5.4). Not seen in the southern profile is a layer of fired clay at least a foot thick. The surface of the fired layer stretches horizontally across the profile from north to south and then dips down at the southern edge of unit 35I and continues to dip to the south across that unit. The fired layer seals a small basin (feature 4) that had been excavated into underlying sediments. The fired-clay layer is overlain by (a) a layer of compact ash and chunks of burned clay and burned bone; (b) a layer of yellow sandy clay; and (c) a layer of ash and bone. That sequence is overlain by layers of (a) light gray clay; (b) yellow sandy clay; (c) charred wood and cane; and (d) light gray clay.

The lower burned-clay layer and associated ash and burned bone were apparently connected with the cremation of bodies in and around the basin evident in the unit 35IL1 profile (Figure 5.5). Excavation of units east of the profiled units followed the crematory basin and associated fill. The basin floor began to rise along

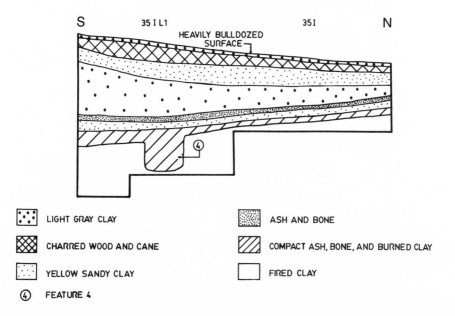

S   35 I L1   35 I   N

HEAVILY BULLDOZED
SURFACE

	LIGHT GRAY CLAY		ASH AND BONE
	CHARRED WOOD AND CANE		COMPACT ASH, BONE, AND BURNED CLAY
	YELLOW SANDY CLAY		FIRED CLAY
④	FEATURE 4		

Figure 5.5. West profile of units 35IL1 and 35I at Murphy, showing crematory basin and depositional levels above.

the western edge of unit 20I, with the thickness of the burned-clay layer thinning significantly. The upper edge of the basin, detectable by the presence of the thinning compact ash-and-bone layer above the also thinning burned-clay layer, was found along the eastern edge of that unit (Figure 5.6). Four dense concentrations of burned bone and charcoal were noticed in the burned-ash layer and were subsequently recognized as pits (features 4–7) that continued down through the hard-packed burned-clay floor of the crematory basin (Figure 5.6).

Excavation of unit 20I and adjacent units to the east and southeast (Figure 5.6) revealed a series of post molds representing one or more structures (feature 15). Our guess is that the post molds represent a single ovoid structure, the entrance to which was on the northwest corner. Two recurvate lines of posts formed a protective entryway. The structure definitely predated the crematorium pit, since the compact ash-and-bone layer that overlay the crematorium basin to the west continued upslope to the east, covering the post molds in unit 20I. Post molds to the east of the eastern edge of unit 20I were not covered by the ash-and-bone layer. Four large post molds (features 8–11) and two small post molds occurred within the structure; the function of the original posts is unknown. Three pits containing cremated bone (features 12–14) were found within the structure boundary; we presume, on the basis of similarity of fill between these pits and those in the crematorium pit, that features 12–14 postdate the pulling of the posts connected with the structure.

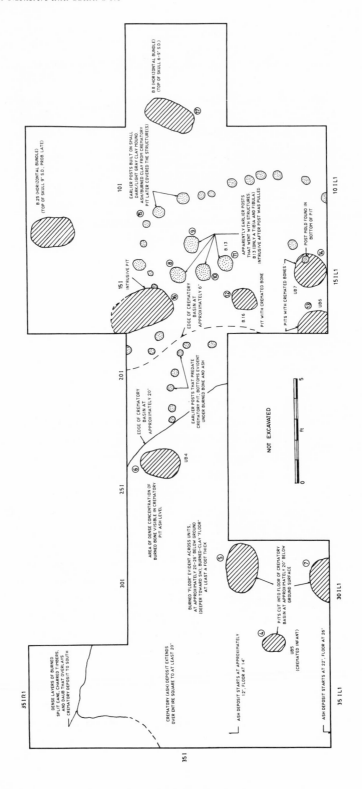

Another bit of stratigraphic evidence came from the south wall of unit 15IL1. Feature 13 was excavated not only through the dark gray layer seen in other profiles but also through a layer of yellow sandy clay that overlay the gray layer. Field notes state that excavators saw evidence of basket loading in the gray layer. The profile documents a series of alternating bands of different-colored clays and layers of burned clay and compact ash. All of the bands, along with the surface of the dark gray core, which showed evidence of basket loading, tilted sharply to the north. Importantly, profiles of all walls in units 10IR2 and 5IR2 revealed only a homogeneous gray sandy clay. Therefore, the banding evident in the west wall of unit 15IR1 must have run diagonally across the square from the northwest corner to the southeast corner. The sediments evident to the north and east were deposited up against the tilted layers, which presumably were the result of erosion off the original mound (see below). Excavations in areas J and L yielded homogeneous gray sandy-clay deposits similar to those in units 10IR2 and 5IR1.

Construction and Use Sequence

Stratigraphic evidence suggests that several specific episodes of activity can be defined. We emphasize that because of the noncontiguous area excavated and the variation in completeness of the field records, we cannot precisely correlate every construction/use layer across the locale.

Stage 1: Initial Construction of the Mound and Crematory Basin

In areas I and K excavators encountered initial mound-construction deposits consisting of a dark gray clay that in several places exhibited evidence of basket loading. The recorded size of the original mound is speculative, though its prehistoric dimensions were considerably less than those shown by the 1955 contour lines (Figure 5.2). The deposit of dark gray clay occurred in the north–south trench in Area K and throughout the eastern half of Area I. The slope of the deposit at the southern end of the Area K trench indicates that the trench almost reached the southern edge of the mound; the slanted surface of the deposit in the west wall of unit 15IR1 suggests that the unit encountered the northern edge of the original mound. Based on that information, we calculate that the mound would have measured approximately 70–80 ft north–south. As noted above, unit 15IR1 cut across the mound face at an angle, which indicates that the mound outline could have been elliptical, probably conforming to the levee remnant. We

Figure 5.6. Plan of Area I units, showing crematory basin to west (left) and later structure to east (right) at Murphy.

can give no estimate of the east–west dimensions, though the mound must have extended through the western end of Area L (Figure 5.2).

The mound was apparently constructed as a ramp up to a crematorium basin at its summit. Figure 5.5 shows the west wall of Unit 35IL1 as constructed from the detailed notes for that unit. The lowest zone is described as a hard-fired layer of clay that extended at least a foot below the crematorium floor. We assume that repeated and prolonged fires in the basin baked the underlying sediments. Above the basin floor was a layer of compact ash, burned bone, and loose burned clay—a result of repeated firings. A layer of yellow sandy clay and another layer of ash and bone lay above that zone. The layers above that point relate to a later period of mound construction, after the basin was abandoned.

The exact size of the basin is unknown, though we know that it was at least 20–25 ft across. Figure 5.6 shows the eastern edge of the basin, just inside the western edge of unit 15I. The basin floor was 14 inches deeper 5 ft to the west, where it flattened out as it continued west across the excavated area. The floor also started to rise in the northern half of unit 35I and continued to rise across unit 35IR1. The southern edge of the basin was north of Area K and did not occur in the Area K profile (Figure 5.4). Several pits, most of which contained partially cremated bone, occurred across the excavated portion of the basin. The tops of the pits were either encountered at the interface of the compact ash layer and the crematorium-basin floor or, in the case of feature 6, actually in the compact ash layer. Three other pits containing ash deposits and partially cremated bone, features 12–14, occurred just to the west of the basin in primary-mound deposits. To the south, feature 1 in the north–south profile through Area K (Figure 5.4) contained an identical deposit.

Stage 2: Abandonment of the Crematory Basin and Additional Mound Construction

At some point the crematory basin was abandoned, and the area containing the basin was filled with a light gray clay (Figure 5.5). This was followed by the deposition of a layer of yellow sandy clay (Figure 5.5). Apparently these layers were deposited only over the crematory basin, since neither was evident in the Area K profile or in the eastern third of Area I.

Stage 3: Construction and Abandonment of Structure 1

During or subsequent to Stage 2, Structure 1 was erected on the mound (Figure 5.6), just east of the crematorium basin. The post molds that held the posts forming the southwestern portion of the entryway extended through the new fill and down into the crematorium-basin floor. The ovoid structure was approximately 30 ft long (north–south) by 20 ft wide. The proposed entryway on the northeast corner was approximately 3–4 ft wide. Wall posts ranged in diameter from 2.5 to 7.5 inches, with an average of about 5 inches. The four interior posts concentrated in the northeast quadrant of the structure (Figure 5.6) averaged 10 inches in diameter.

At some point the posts associated with Structure 1 were pulled and several post molds (e.g., burial 13 in feature 11) were partially filled with skeletal elements. The structure may have been burned, as evidenced by the occurrence in several excavated areas of large portions of burned posts and other possible construction elements in the upper levels of mound-related sediments. For example, units 35IR1, 35I, and 35IL1 contained a several-inch-thick layer of charred wood and cane that mantled the underlying layer of yellow sandy clay (Figure 5.5). What we suspect to be the same layer extended south along the entire Area K profile (Figure 5.4), except where it had been removed by the bulldozer. Feature 2 (Figure 5.4) was filled with this deposit.

Stage 4: Final Mound Construction

At some point after deposition of the charred-wood layer, the entire mound was raised by the addition of layers of light gray clay and yellow sand/sandy clay. It is unclear from the field notes exactly how the units relate one to another across the mound. For example, we suspect that one excavator used the term *yellow sand* to refer to a unit identified by another excavator as *yellow sandy clay*. Additionally, bulldozing removed traces of these deposits in areas critical to our ability to tie units together. For example, mechanical earth removal was especially severe in units in and around the structure, to the point that the tops of the post molds were just below the surface. Hence in the profile of the west wall of unit 15IR1, the tilted strata ended at ground level, as opposed to continuing up over the mound. In that area a layer of light gray clay was the uppermost depositional unit, perhaps the same layer seen as the uppermost layer in units 35I and 35IL1 and in the Area K profile.

Dating the Construction Phases

Attempts to use excavated ceramic materials to date construction phases of the mound and associated post-mold structure and crematory basin were futile. For the most part, excavation units were excavated in 6–9-inch levels, though in several instances 12-inch levels were used. Only in a few instances were depositional units (e.g., mound-fill layers) excavated separately. Catalog numbers were assigned to a variety of provenience types (e.g., burial-pit fill), but our analysis of sherds from these contexts yielded no information that was useful chronologically. Individual pits contained a wide spectrum of Mississippi Valley ceramic types that crosscut the projected time of site use. These ranged from earlier materials— mineral- and clay-tempered sherds—to supposed late types such as Campbell punctated.

Using pit fill to establish chronological control is difficult enough under ideal conditions, that is, in situations where extreme care has been exercised in removing the fill. At Murphy, prehistoric pits were excavated into older, occupation-related deposits, confusing the situation further. Thus it appeared our only hope of dating the construction phases was to use grave associations, specifically ceramic vessels, to date the burials and then to link types of burial to specific time periods. For example, it appeared reasonable to assume that the cremated individuals were the earliest interments, based on our reconstruction of the mound sequence. Based on overwhelming evidence from Campbell (Chapter 6), late-period burials were extended. But do the data from Murphy support this sequence? We examine the evidence below.

The Burials

Ninety-one burials are reported here, though the minimum number of individuals represented by all skeletal material is probably higher. Excavators labeled 75 burials and often mentioned on the forms material that was recognized in the field as human bone but left unnumbered. We added 14 burial numbers (UB designation) based on the excavation notes, tending to ignore an isolated bone or two found near an already-numbered burial. Chapman's notes state that a Walls engraved vessel was found with each of burials 11A and 11B. The field notes and maps mention neither the burials nor the vessels, though the latter are in the University of Missouri collection. No skeletal material from either burial is in the collection, and we suspect it was graded away prior to the excavation. Our guess is that Murphy had salvaged the vessels and given them to Chapman. We include the two burials in the total of 91.

Spatial Patterning

Figures 5.7–5.10 show the locations of all burials by burial number and type of interment (discussed below). Area J had the most burials of any area as well as the highest number per excavated square footage of the larger areas. The remainder of the burials were divided fairly evenly among the other areas, with the exception of Area S, which contained none. Area L, labeled "pot field" on the field forms, contained 10 intact vessels with no bones in association (Figure 5.11). The vessels appeared to be in primary context when excavated; our guess is that the bones had deteriorated to such an extent that they were unrecognizable in the field. In general the human remains found in Area L were in extremely poor condition.

Table 5.1 summarizes the burials by area and type of interment. The 10 cremations were divided into 7 from Area I and 3 from Area K—locales containing the crematory basin. Thirteen of the 14 extended burials occurred in an arc on the eastern periphery of the mound, in areas F, J, and P. One extended burial occurred in Area L (Figure 5.12c). If we are correct in our assumption that excavation unit

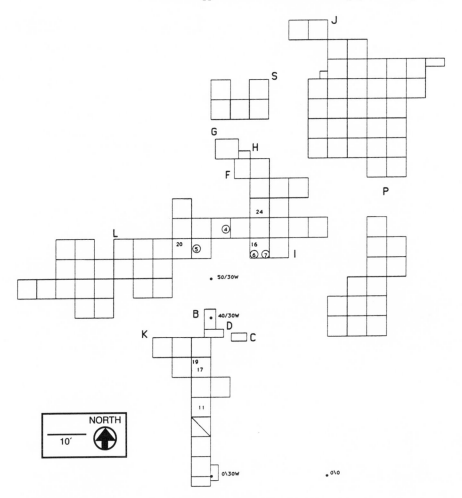

Figure 5.7. Locations of cremated burials at Murphy. Numbers in circles refer to burials that were not numbered in the field.

15IR1 caught the northern edge of the mound (Figure 5.2), then all burials in Area J lay completely off the structure. The same apparently was true for burials in areas F and P. Horizontal bundle burials (Figure 5.12a, b), the most numerous type of burial found (30 of 75 burials of identified type), were found in every excavation area except H and K. Vertical bundle burials occurred only in areas J, K, and P. Area P contained an infant buried in an urn (Figure 5.11b), and partial remains of two individuals were found in post molds, one in Area H and one in Area I. One flexed burial was recovered at Murphy, from Area P.

Some spatial patterning is evident in the distribution of burials by interment type (Figures 5.7–5.10), though care should be exercised in interpreting the pattern because of the small number of burials of known type of interment—75, divided among the 4 primary types (horizontal bundle, vertical bundle, extended,

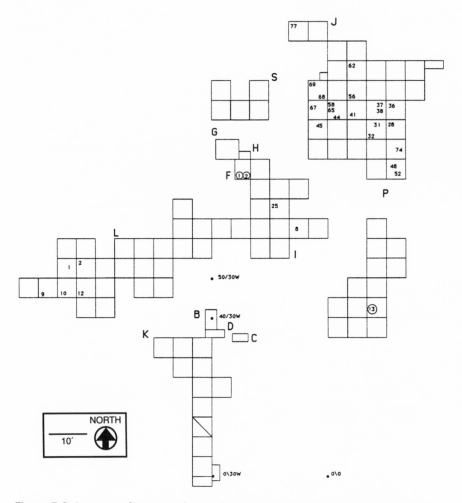

Figure 5.8. Locations of horizontal bundle burials at Murphy. Numbers in circles refer to burials that were not numbered in the field.

and cremation), plus one each of urn, post mold, and flexed. The most notable patterning is evident in the distribution of cremations, which occurred only in areas I and K—areas in and around the crematory basin. Horizontal bundles occurred off the mound to the east (Area L), north (Areas F and I), and northeast (Area J and the northernmost two units in Area P). Vertical bundles occurred exclusively in Area J and the northernmost two units in Area P, with the exception of a single interment in the Area K portion of the mound. In Area J, which contained the densest concentration of burials, no segregation of vertical from horizontal bundles is evident. Extended burials in that area were, with two exceptions, located north and northeast of the bundle burials.

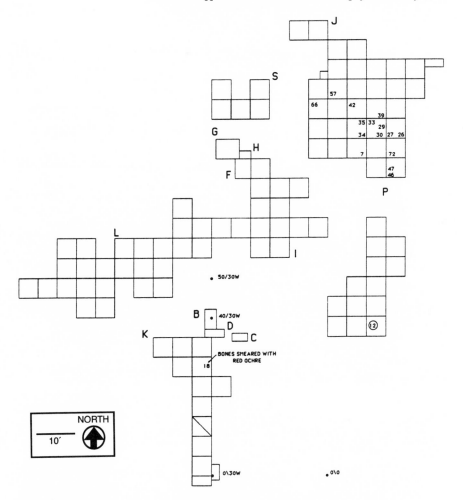

Figure 5.9. Locations of vertical bundle burials at Murphy. Numbers in circles refer to burials that were not numbered in the field.

Burial Inclusions

Appendix 1 lists each burial, the type of interment if known, and burial inclusions, if any. Table 5.2 lists the number of vessels of each ceramic type (if known) from the burial sample (see examples in Figures 5.13–5.17). If our chronological sequence is correct—cremations being the earliest, followed by bundled burials and then by extended burials—the vessels included as offerings should mirror the sequence. The problem, as we have emphasized, is that few independent checks on chronological ordering exist for southeastern Missouri. All available data indicate Campbell punctated and Walls engraved are late types, but it would be

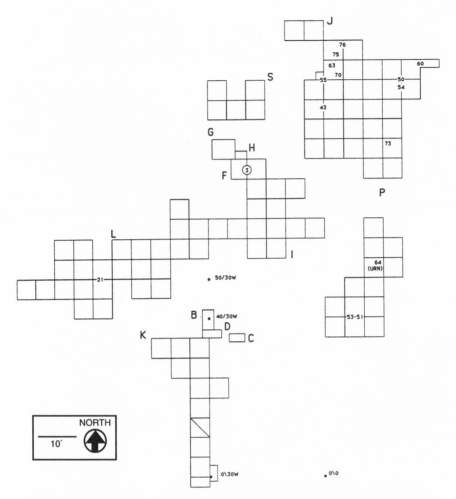

Figure 5.10. Locations of extended burials at Murphy. Burial 64 (Area P) is an urn interment but is included with extended burials. Numbers in circles refer to burials that were not numbered in the field.

helpful to know exactly when the types first appeared in the ceramic sequence. On the other hand, the types Neeley's Ferry plain and Bell plain, as currently employed, cannot be used to internally differentiate post–A.D. 900 deposits.

Eight of the 10 cremated bodies were interred with nothing. However, the other two cremations—burials 17 and 19—contained numerous items, placing them among the "richest" burials unearthed at Murphy. Both were located in the large crematory basin. Burial 17 contained 2 drilled shell beads, a pipe bowl exhibiting a human face, and a miniature straight-neck bottle with an exterior

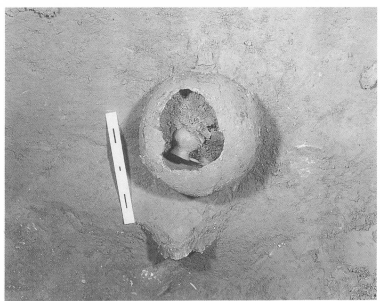

Figure 5.11. Vessels from Murphy burials: a, view (looking north) of "pot cluster" (a grouping of pots with no associated bone) in Area L; b, urn containing child's skeleton (burial 64) and conjoined-bottle vessel.

Table 5.1
Number of Burials by Area and Type of Treatment at Murphy

Type of Treatment	Burial Area							
	F	H	I	J	K	L	P	Unknown
Extended	1			9		1	3	
Horiz Bundle	2		2	17		5	4	
Vert Bundle				12	1		4	
Cremation			7		3			
Flexed							1	
Urn							1	
Other		1[a]	1[a]					
Unknown				6	3	3	2	2
Total	3	1	10	44	7	9	15	2

[a] Burial in a post hole.

orange slip and a black overslip applied in stripes. The bottle is 1 of 2 polychrome vessels found at Murphy. Neither exhibits the classic zonation of slips characteristic of Avenue polychrome (but see Dunnell and Jackson 1992), and we do not assign the pieces to any other established type. Burial 19 contained a small Fortune noded jar, a vessel of unknown type and form, and a fragment of a fine-paste, orange-slipped bottle exhibiting bird wings modeled in relief (Figure 5.13b). In summary, the ceramic inclusions with the 2 cremations do little to help place the cremations in absolute time. Polychrome vessels occur rarely in Pemiscot Bayou assemblages, and although Fortune noded does appear at other sites, it is always a minority type. It may have been a ceramic type that began fairly early in the St. Francis River–Pemiscot Bayou region, perhaps about A.D. 1300, and lasted for several centuries. Avenue polychrome is a type that occurs in the lower portion of the central Mississippi Valley, especially along the lower reaches of the Arkansas River. As described by Phillips et al. (1951) and by Phillips (1970 [see Ford 1961]), Avenue polychrome usually consists of either broad panels or interlocking meanders of red and white paint separated by a thin line of black paint. It is an extremely late type, probably lasting in some areas into the seventeenth century. We assume the polychrome vessels from Murphy are late, but this is an untested assumption.

Horizontal bundle burials were found in association with a wide variety of ceramic types and forms. Burial UB1 contained a cat-monster-effigy bowl, burial 2 contained a miniature Walls jar engraved with a variety of motifs (Figures 5.13f and 5.18), burial 41 contained a miniature bottle with red and orange slips, burial 44 contained a flaring-neck bottle with stepped ("cloud" motif) incisions around the rim, burial 59 contained a small jar with appliquéd medallions on the exterior,

a

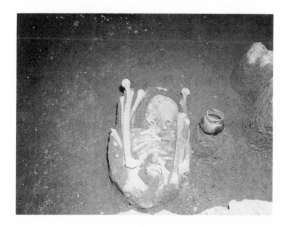

b

c

Figure 5.12. Burials from Murphy: a, horizontal and vertical bundle burials in Area J (looking west); b, horizontal bundle burial (25); c, extended burial (21) with elbow pipe and bottle.

Figure 5.13. Vessels from Murphy burials: a, "pot cluster" (Neeley's Ferry plain; $3^5/_8$ inches high); b, burial 19 (untyped; $2^7/_8$ inches high); c, "pot cluster" (Manly punctated; $4^5/_8$ inches high); d, burial 61 (Neeley's Ferry plain; 6 inches high); e, "pot cluster" (Barton incised–Fortune noded; $3^1/_2$ inches high); f, burial 2 (Walls engraved; $3^3/_4$ inches high). All from MU collection.

Figure 5.14. Neeley's Ferry plain bowls from Murphy burials: a, burial 8 (3½ inches high); b, burial 61 (3⅜ inches high); c, burial 8 (3 inches high); d, "pot cluster" (3 inches high). All from MU collection.

and burial 77 contained a turtle-effigy bottle (Figure 5.16f) and a Parkin punctated jar. None of these vessels are easy to place in time. Vessels almost identical to the turtle-effigy bottle, the cat-monster bowl, and the Parkin punctated jar occur in the Campbell and Berry burial-vessel assemblages, but the other forms are not represented. In terms of workmanship, the appliquéd vessel is nothing like those placed in the type Campbell appliquéd but instead resembles a rather crude approach to applying strips of clay to a vessel exterior. The bottle with the incised stepped design might be typed by some archaeologists as Walls, though the design is represented only on one small portion of the neck.[3] Parkin is a type that is not

3. Unfortunately, the vessel was apparently never returned from the field; the only documentation is a crude sketch by Chapman.

Figure 5.15. Everted-neck bottles from Murphy burials (a, c, and d—Bell plain; b, e, and f—Neeley's Ferry plain): a, burial UB3 (5$\frac{1}{2}$ inches high); b, "pot cluster" (5$\frac{1}{4}$ inches high); c, burial 49 (5$\frac{3}{8}$ inches high); d, burial 44 (5$\frac{7}{8}$ inches high); e, burial 12 (5$\frac{3}{8}$ inches high); f, burial 50 (5$\frac{3}{4}$ inches high). All from MU collection.

Figure 5.16. Bottles from Murphy burials (a–d, f—Bell plain; e—Walls engraved): a, "pot cluster" (8⅞ inches high); b, burial 10 (7⅛ inches high); c, burial 51 (6½ inches high); d, burial 25 (6⅜ inches high); e, burial 11B (7¼ inches high); f, burial 77 (3½ inches high). All from MU collection.

Figure 5.17. Vessels from Murphy burials: a, "pot cluster" (Bell plain; 3 inches high); b, burial 64 (Neeley's Ferry plain; 11¼ inches high).

Table 5.2
Number and Percentage of Intact Ceramic Vessels Recovered from Murphy

Ceramic Type[a]	Form[b]		
	Bottle	Bowl	Jar
Neeley's Ferry plain	5 (19%)	7 (54%)	4 (44%)
Bell plain	11 (42%)	2 (15%)	0 (0%)
Campbell punctated	1 (4%)	0 (0%)	0 (0%)
Fortune noded	0 (0%)	1 (8%)	2 (22%)
Vernon Paul appliquéd	0 (0%)	1 (8%)	0 (0%)
Walls engraved	3 (11%)	0 (0%)	1 (11%)
Red-slipped	1 (4%)	2 (15%)	0 (0%)
Rhodes incised	2 (8%)	0 (0%)	0 (0%)
Parkin punctated	0 (0%)	0 (0%)	1 (11%)
Manly punctated	0 (0%)	0 (0%)	1 (11%)
Polychrome	3 (11%)	0 (0%)	0 (0%)

[a] One "hybrid" type—a Campbell punctated–Campbell appliquéd jar—is included in the Campbell punctated category; another "hybrid" type—a Vernon Paul–red-slipped bowl—is included in the Vernon Paul category.

[b] Includes vessels from the "pot cluster."

well tied down chronologically, though it certainly appears to date post–A.D. 1350. The weeping-eye motif (Figure 5.13f) is another late-period marker, usually occurring on well-made bottles typed as Walls engraved. Its appearance on a small, crudely made jar may place the piece in the early half of the late period. In fact, our impression is that three of the vessels described here—the bottle with the cloud motif, the appliquéd jar, and the weeping-eye jar—are like prototypes of decorative things to come. They resemble the more elaborate expressions seen on the Campbell vessels without the completeness and well-executed appearance of designs on the Campbell forms.

The majority of vertical bundle burials had no inclusions. The ones that did, with two exceptions, had nothing that is of chronological interest. Burial 66 contained a Nodena point, which we assume was a purposeful inclusion as opposed to being incorporated accidentally with the pit fill. Its presence should place the burial post–A.D. 1350. Burial 18 is unique because the bones associated with it were stained heavily with red ochre. Whether such staining is chronologically significant remains to be demonstrated, though we do note that very few skeletons from Campbell are stained and none as heavily as burial 18 from Murphy.

Figure 5.18. Design on Walls engraved vessel from Murphy burial 2 (see Figure 5.13f).

Good evidence exists to place at least some of the extended burials late in the Mississippian sequence. Burials 55 (Figure 5.19) and 75 (Figure 5.20) contained well-executed Rhodes engraved bottles (Figure 5.21), and burial 70 contained a Campbell punctated–Campbell appliquéd jar. Rhodes engraved is a late ceramic type in the central Mississippi valley, existing up into the sixteenth century, and Campbell punctated and Campbell appliquéd were probably contemporary with Rhodes engraved. At Campbell, Rhodes is a minor constituent of the late-period record, but the other two types are major constituents (Chapter 6). Burial 75 also contained a large bowl with stepped (cloud motif) cutouts around the rim and two copper-covered wooden disks (Figure 5.22) that, based on their location on the parietal bone, we suspect were parts of a hairpiece. The cloud motif occurs on the Walls engraved bottle from burial 11A (the original location of which is unknown) (Figure 5.23) and on the bottle from burial 44 (see above). In addition to the Rhodes engraved bottle, burial 55 contained 4 well-made and well-polished (through use) adzes (Figure 5.24) placed at the proximal end of the femur. These pieces, made from light tan chert, are unequaled in workmanship among other adzes from the region we have seen, with the exception of the 4 adzes from Denton Mounds (Chapter 7).

Based on stratigraphic evidence and on burial inclusions, the burial sequence mentioned earlier—cremations being the earliest and extended burials the latest—appears reasonable. The locations of the cremations in and around the crematory basin, especially the presence of cremations under sealed layers of ash

Figure 5.19. Burial 55 (looking southeast) at Murphy, with a Rhodes engraved bottle at the crossed feet and four chert adzes (two not visible below the others) on the proximal end of the right femur.

and later fill, tie the cremations and the basin together. Stratigraphic evidence clearly indicates that the post structure on the mound postdates the basin. While its purpose is unknown, it may have been related to the processing of skeletons for subsequent burial. The abundance of bundled burials found around the northern perimeter of the mound indicates that bodies were being processed somewhere in the vicinity. Ceramic evidence does not negate the proposition that bundled burials were intermediate chronologically between cremations and extended burials. Vessel forms and ceramic types present during this intermediate stage include cat-monster and turtle effigies and Parkin punctated, all of which occur at Campbell. Several design motifs evident during the very late portion of the Mississippian record are present—for example, the two Walls engraved bottles mentioned earlier along with two others, one from burial 11B (Figure 5.25) and one from burial 22 (Figure 5.26), but as discussed above those on vessels associated with bundled burials appear to be incipient expressions as opposed to the well-developed expressions seen on late pieces from sites such as Campbell. Vessels associated with extended burials, however, such as the Rhodes engraved bottles with burials 55 and 75, cannot be distinguished from Rhodes vessels from sites such as Campbell and Berry.

Figure 5.20. Burial 75 (foreground) and burial 76 at Murphy, with a Rhodes engraved bottle and stepped bowl associated with the stratigraphically lower burial 75. The badly decomposed skull of burial 75 (next to ruler) had two copper-covered wooden disks on the parietal.

Figure 5.21. Rhodes engraved bottle from Murphy burial 75 ($7\frac{1}{8}$ inches high).

Figure 5.22. Two copper-covered wooden disks (each ca. $1\frac{1}{2}$ inches in diameter) on the parietal of Murphy burial 75 (see Figure 5.20).

Figure 5.23. Walls bottle and design from Murphy burial 11A (5¼ inches high).

Figure 5.24. Four chert adzes found with Murphy burial 55 (specimen on the left is $4\frac{1}{2}$ inches long) (see Figure 5.19).

The vessels from the "pot field" in Area L (10 vessels were excavated, but 3 are missing from the University of Missouri collections) are a mix of types, including a Bell plain bowl with a bear- or bat-effigy rim rider (Figure 5.14c), a miniature Manly punctated jar (Figure 5.13c), and a miniature Fortune noded jar with a Barton incised design on the neck (Figure 5.13e). There is no way of estimating when the vessels were placed in the ground.

Table 5.3 tallies the number of burials by type of interment, the number of artifact classes present for each type of interment, and the number of vessels present at Murphy. For example, there were 14 extended burials, 5 of which contained no grave goods, 6 of which contained only 1 class of item, and 3 of which contained 2 classes of items. Continuing across the row, 4 burials that contained ceramic vessels contained a single vessel each, and 4 contained 2 vessels each. Artifact classes used are ceramic vessel, ceramic pipe, lithic item (adze or arrow point), shell bead, copper ornament, and ceramic disk.

Nine of the 14 extended burials contained at least 1 burial inclusion; 3 of the 9 contained items in 2 artifact classes. Four of the 8 extended burials that produced ceramic vessels had 2 vessels each, and 4 had 1 vessel each. Among the bundle burials, only 15 of 47 bodies were interred with grave goods, and no burial contained more than one class of material. Seven bundle burials contained single vessels, 3 contained 2 vessels each, and 2 contained 3 vessels each. The dropoff in percentage of burials with grave goods from extended to bundled is significant at the $p = .05$ level, which to us indicates a difference in burial treatment that includes more than physical preparation of the body. Another aspect of the

Figure 5.25. Walls bottle and design from Murphy burial 11B ($4^5/_8$ inches high).

Figure 5.26. Walls bottle and design from Murphy burial 22 (5¼ inches high).

mortuary program that is significant at the $p = .05$ level is the difference between horizontal and vertical bundle burials. Only 2 of 17 vertical bundle burials contained grave associations, while 13 of 30 horizontal burials did. The single urn burial contained conjoined bottles placed in with the infant (Figures 5.11b and 5.27). If our estimate of timing is correct, the bundle burials were intermediate chronologically between the (early) cremations and the (late) extended burials. Is there a temporal difference between the horizontal bundles and the vertical bundles, or, on the other hand, were they contemporary disposal methods, the choice of one over the other resting on social factors? We admit the data are rather skimpy, but we see no evidence, stratigraphic or otherwise, to suggest that the two types of disposal were temporally distinct. In other words, we believe they were contemporary.

Table 5.3
Frequencies of Burials by Type of Interment,
Number of Artifact Classes Represented by Burial Inclusions,
and Number of Ceramic Vessels per Burial at Murphy

Interment Type	Number of Classes				Number of Vessels		
	0	1	2	3	1	2	3
Extended	5	6	3	0	4	4	0
Vertical Bundle	15	2	0	0	1	0	0
Horizontal Bundle	17	13	0	0	6	3	2
Cremation	8	1	0	1	1	0	1
Urn	0	1	0	0	0	1	0
Post Hole	1	0	0	0	0	0	0
Flexed	0	1	0	0	1	0	0
Unknown	7	8	0	0	3	2	0

Kersey

Kersey, also referred to as Canady (e.g., S. Williams 1954), was excavated over two seasons, 1964 and 1965, with crews directed by Marshall. The results of the earlier excavation were summarized in a limited-distribution report for the Missouri State Highway Department (Marshall 1965); the results of the second season's work were drafted in manuscript form (Marshall n.d.) but were never published. The reports, each of which summarizes only the work accomplished the previous season, were never integrated into a comprehensive study of the archaeological remains. This is unfortunate, especially given the depth of the deposits in certain areas of the site and hence the opportunity to examine artifact

Figure 5.27. Conjoined bottles from Murphy burial 64 (3¼ inches high) (see Figure 5.11).

variation through time. Our modest objective here is to summarize the excavations, especially those in mound 1, which produced 72 human burials and 2 mortuary-related structures. We also briefly discuss some of the material classes present, but the staggering amount of material from the site precludes in-depth examination.

Kersey was excavated because a sizable portion of it lay in the right-of-way for expansion of U.S. Highway 61, which later became the northbound lane of Interstate 55. The only topographic features on the site were two low mounds along the east side of U.S. 61, both of which had been damaged by ditching. In addition, deep plowing had disturbed the upper foot or so of the archaeological deposits, and the then owner of the site reported in 1964 that several other mounds (and/or small levee remnants) had been leveled during cultivation (Marshall 1965: 44). Earlier, S. Williams (1954: 186) had reported that several mounds, including a "burial mound," were still visible, but he gave no exact number. The two mounds in existence in 1964–1965 became the focus of excavation, but several adjacent areas were opened to determine the site limits and depth of deposits.

No reliable estimate can be made of the area containing archaeological materials, but our guess is that the area was extensive. In 1964 Marshall excavated a 40-ft-long, 18-inch-wide trench nearly 400 ft north of mound 1 and still recovered artifacts to a depth of 2 ft. Although we have no precise distance between mounds 1 and 2, the latter apparently lay several hundred feet to the south of the former. The area between the mounds contained material, as did the area west of U.S. 61. Even taking the conservative tack that the extent of material was only 800–1,000 ft on a side, we can derive a lower estimate of around 14 acres.

The majority of work during both seasons was focused on mound 1, a 15-inch-high, oblong-shaped rise that repeated plowing and erosion had elongated along the north–south axis (Figure 5.28) to the point where the original dimensions are indeterminable. An area of 287.5 ft^2 was opened in 1964 and expanded the following season to 1,687.5 ft^2. Excavators could easily detect the interface between the mound fill and the underlying sediments: "At the base of the mound there was a marked contrast in the ability of the soil to retain moisture. The [underlying] occupational zone remained moist throughout the time that the pro- files were exposed. The mound fill . . . soon dried and became hard, suggesting a difference in the compaction and content of the two soils" (Marshall 1965: 48). Mound fill varied from 1 ft on the margins of the mound to 18 inches near the center. Artifact-bearing sediments beneath the mound extended to depths of up to 4 ft; where the sediments were cut by pits, artifacts were found at much deeper depths.

The stratigraphic sequence evident in the mound 1 profiles was confusing at best (Figure 5.29). Marshall (n.d.) subdivided the pre-mound deposit into four zones based on differences in color and texture. Stippling in Figure 5.29 represents artifact-free sand that underlay the cultural deposits. Above that was a light brown, very sandy soil that contained few artifacts; above that layer were two artifact-rich deposits that in places could be distinguished by differences in soil color. Marshall (n.d.: 112–13) states that the majority of pits and post molds extended downward from the uppermost occupation zone, but the profiles presented in Figure 5.29 indicate the disturbances in all zones. The large pit shown in Figure 5.30 was of unknown function. The base of the pit was found at 8 ft below modern ground surface.

It is impossible to detect stratigraphic changes in ceramic type frequencies in the non-mound sediments. All levels, within and outside the pits, contain clay-tempered as well as shell-tempered ceramics. In one excavation unit a particular level might contain a high percentage of Neeley's Ferry plain relative to clay-tempered Baytown plain or clay-tempered Mulberry Creek cordmarked, but an adjacent unit will exhibit just the opposite proportions. The most commonly occurring ceramic type is Mulberry Creek cordmarked, which accounts for about 57% of the excavated ceramic assemblage, followed by shell-tempered red-slipped (14%), Neeley's Ferry plain (12%), Baytown plain (8%), Bell plain (3%), and a host of other clay-tempered types. Sand-tempered Barnes cordmarked

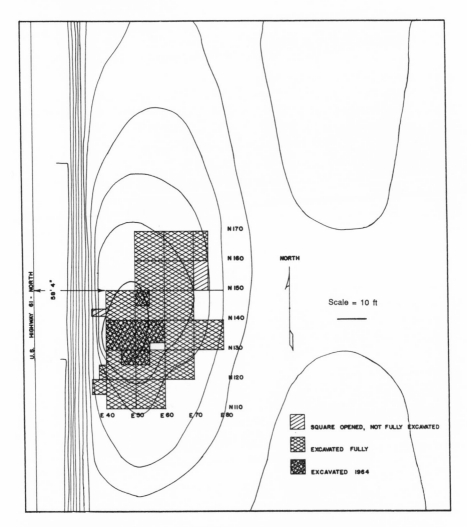

Figure 5.28. Plan of excavation of mound 1 at Kersey, 1964 and 1965. Contour interval is 3 inches (from Marshall n.d.).

is present, but it makes up less than 1% of the assemblage. Marshall (n.d.) states that the landowner remembered a Fortune noded vessel coming from one of the leveled mounds, but this report was unverified. The only late Mississippian period sherds unearthed during excavation were a few sherds of Parkin punctated and 1 shell-tempered sherd that had an appliquéd strip on the exterior surface.

Burial-Related Features

Mound 1 contained 72 human burials and 1 dog burial; a few additional burials might have been present in unexcavated portions of the mound (Figures 5.31 and

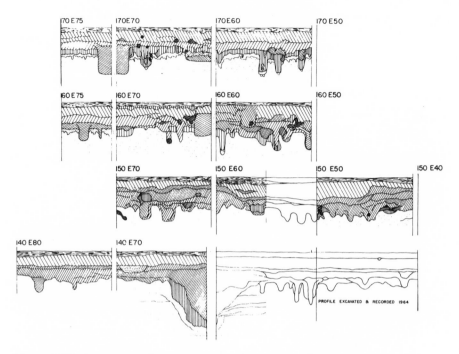

Figure 5.29. East–west profiles through mound 1 at Kersey (from Marshall n.d.).

5.32). As at Murphy, several types of burials were found—articulated in pits, cremations, and bundles—and at different levels throughout the mound. The sequence of events presented here follows, for the most part, that appearing in Marshall (n.d.: table 14), though we made some modifications based on inspection of photographs. Complicating the reconstruction is the fact that burial numbers were duplicated the second season instead of continuing the number sequence. To clarify the situation, we use a burial-number prefix of either 64 or 65 to distinguish burials. Also, the poor condition of the vast majority of the bones in curation at the University of Missouri–Columbia precluded any analysis. Hence, we use Marshall's designations of age and sex.

Burial-Stage 1

The initial interments were made in the artifact-bearing zones underlying the mound. Seven skeletons of infants in tightly flexed positions—burials 64-16, 65-23, 65-25, 65-26, 65-27, 65-28, and 65-30—were found in small pits that had been cut from various levels in the pre-mound cultural deposits. None contained burial inclusions. On the basis of stratigraphic positioning, Marshall (n.d.: table 14) separated the seven burials into two groups, one of three and the

a

b

Figure 5.30. Large pit feature in mound 1 at Kersey: a, pit as it appeared in plan and profile; b, pit in profile. Note the slumping of the 1964 balk and prehistoric slumping of white sand into the pit.

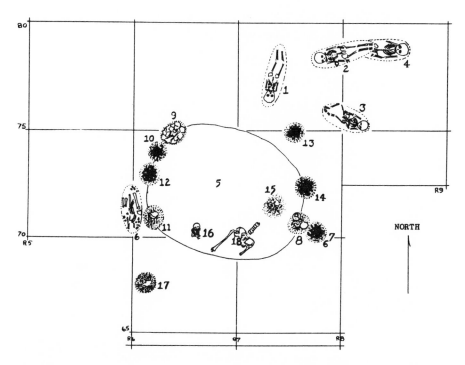

Figure 5.31. Plan of 1964 excavation of mound 1 at Kersey showing locations of burials. Burial 5 contained the remains of 20 individuals in 10 bundles apparently placed in a charnel house (see Figure 5.34 for detailed drawing). Burials 7, 10, and 12–14 were cremations; burials 6, 8, 9, 11, 15, and 17 were bundled (from Marshall 1965).

other of four, assigning one group to the chronologically earlier Baytown "Kersey phase" and the other to the early Mississippian "Hayti phase." The deeper burials were found at depths of more than 2 ft below ground level; the others were found at between 18 and 24 inches. We do not follow Marshall's original subdivision here because although the skeletons were found at different levels, there is no indication of the stratigraphic position of the pit orifices. Some pits could well have been deeper than others but could have been cut from a higher level than earlier but more shallow pits. Field notes and profile drawings, however, suggest that all seven pits originated in the pre-mound sediments as opposed to being excavated through mound deposits.

Burial-Stage 2

Near the top of the pre-mound deposits (exact position unknown), a small, oval structure of upright posts was erected to encircle 22 bodies, 20 of which (lumped together as burial 5 by Marshall [64-5 here]) were bundled (Figures 5.33 and 5.34). The structure was approximately 8 x 6 ft and was outlined by a wall trench

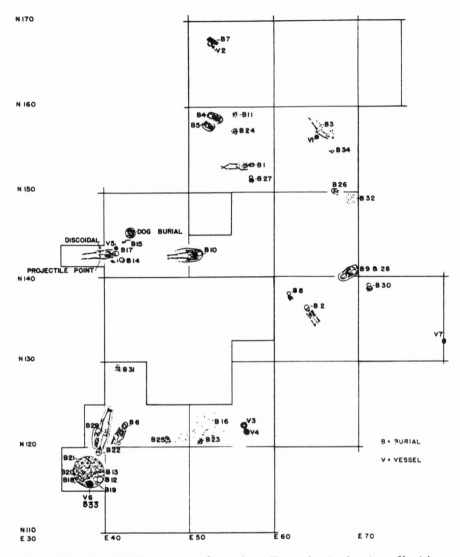

Figure 5.32. Plan of 1965 excavation of mound 1 at Kersey showing locations of burials. The large vacant area in the middle of the plan was excavated in 1964 (see Figure 5.31).

containing the post molds. Marshall (1965, n.d.) labels the structure "charnel house 1." The 10 bundles containing the 20 individuals (6 of the 10 bundles contained 2 individuals each, 2 contained 3 individuals each, and 2 contained a single individual each) were "very rectangular . . . strongly suggesting that placement was in a rectangular container of some perishable material" (Marshall 1965: 51). The skeletons "showed clearly that the bodies had been 'processed' to remove the flesh from the bones and the skeletons disarticulated for placement into the containers. . . . [T]his was clearly demonstrated . . . in Burial 18, which had had the lower portion of the leg removed but the femur was still articulated with the acetabulum." Burial 64-18 was not termed a bundle burial by Marshall, though its positioning with respect to the bundle burials led Marshall (1965) to assume it was contemporary (but see below). Burial 64-15, that of an infant, "probably [a] bundle" (Marshall 1965: 53), was on the floor of the "charnel house," beneath the large group of bundles. With respect to burial 64-18, a photograph and a line drawing presented by Marshall (1965: figs. 12 and 13) indicate that burial 64-18 was intrusive into burial 64-5. The figures are reproduced here as Figures 5.33 and 5.34 (a few post molds shown in the photograph do not appear in the drawing because they later were deemed to be unrelated to the structure). Note that the distal end of the burial 64-18 femur clearly protrudes beyond the line of post molds. On the drawing the femur lies between two post molds; in the photograph it clearly lies over at least half a post mold. Thus we strongly suspect that the burial dates to a subsequent time.

Marshall (n.d.: table 14) also includes burials 65-9, 65-22, and 65-29 in stage 2. Burial 65-9, of an adult placed in the supine position, was above burial 65-28. The legs and hands were missing; the right arm lay under the pelvis. Burial 65-22 was also of an adult placed in the supine position. Burial 65-29 was of an adult that had been bundled; the burial pit intruded into the pit containing burial 65-22. The three skeletons lay at depths below surface of 6–24 inches, but it is difficult to figure out the depths of the pit orifices. Marshall (n.d.: table 14) assigned all stage 2 burials to the Hayti phase.

Burial-Stage 3

After the posts associated with the "charnel house" were pulled, according to Marshall (n.d.: table 14), seven additional burials—64-7 and 64-9 through 64-14—were placed around the perimeter of the bundle burials. Two of the burials—64-9 and 64-11—were of bundled children placed in pits; the others were cremated remains that had been placed in pits. Burial 64-8 contained two tall-necked bottles, one red-slipped and the other Neeley's Ferry plain. All seven pits originated from the surface containing the rectangular bundles; intrusion of some of the pits into post molds associated with the "charnel house" clearly indicates that the stage 3 burials postdate the oval structure. The integrity of the 10 bundled burials, that is, their lack of disarray, suggests that after the oval structure was dismantled they were protected, perhaps being encased in boxes. Marshall (n.d.: table 14) assigns burial-stage 3 to the end of the Hayti phase.

Burial-Stage 4

Stage 4 began with the addition of soil over the existing burials to form a low mound. The mound was probably never over a few feet high, with the highest

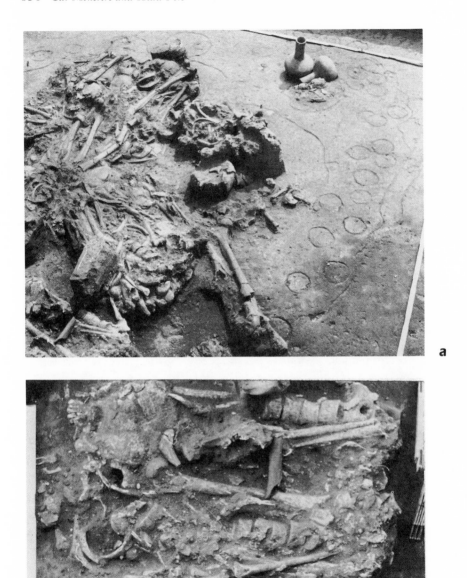

a

b

Figure 5.33. Bundled bones (burial 5) recovered from mound 1 at Kersey in 1964: a, view (looking northeast) across the southern end of the charnel-house floor; b, view of bundles 8 and 9. Note that several skeletal elements, such as portions of the vertebral column, are still in articulated position, suggesting that although the bodies were processed prior to interment, the processing did not completely remove all ligaments (from Marshall 1965).

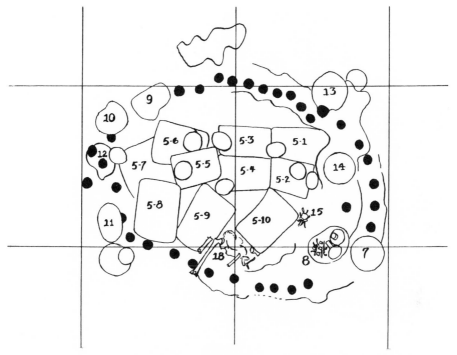

Figure 5.34. Plan view (north at top) of area of mound 1 at Kersey excavated in 1964 showing bundled burials (labeled burial 5 by Marshall [1965]) surrounded by post molds. Burial 5—a collective group of 10 bundled units of human bone representing 22 individuals—along with burials 15 and 18, were found within a row of post molds that had been set in a wall trench. The other burials apparently intruded into the charnel house (from Marshall 1965).

point over the 10 bundle burials that had been enclosed by the posts. At this juncture it becomes impossible to clearly delineate individual burial episodes, though, as is suggested below, one episode might have been as late as ca. A.D. 1400. The post-mound-construction burial regime contained both extended burials of adults and children and bundled burials of adults and children. The crest of the mound contained four extended skeletons of children (burials 64-1 through 64-4 [Figure 5.35]), one of which (burial 64-2) contained a miniature jar with a single loop handle. Marshall (1965) states that at least two of the bodies probably were wrapped prior to interment. Excavators found 3 other burials within 2 ft of the 10 bundle burials associated with burial-stage 2: burial 64-8, an infant bundle burial containing 2 bottles; 64-6, an adult bundle burial; and 64-17, a vertical bundle burial of an adult. As was typical of many of the vertical bundle burials from Murphy, the skull was placed on top of the vertically oriented long bones.

a

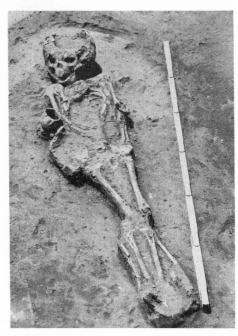

Figure 5.35. Burials of juveniles recovered from mound 1 at Kersey in 1964: a, burial 3; b, burial 2, with a Bell plain jar located next to right arm. See Figure 5.31 for locations (from Marshall 1965).

b

Out away from the crest of the mound were numerous other burials of adults and children (all burial numbers preceded by 65): extended adults (2, 3, 6, 10, and 17), bundled adults (4, 5, 7, and 15), adults of unknown burial treatment (14, 16, and 34), an extended adolescent (1), bundled children (8, 11, and 31), and a flexed infant (24). Several items were found next to Burial 65-17 and may have been included with it: a vessel of unknown type and form, a small discoidal, a drilled bear tooth, and the base of a small triangular point. Burial 65-3 contained a small, Neeley's Ferry plain double-handle jar placed at the left elbow; burial 65-7 contained a vessel of unknown type and form placed near the skull; and burial 65-16 contained 2 vessels, one a Neeley's Ferry plain bottle with a very short neck and the other a Bell plain bottle with the neck broken off. The most elaborate vessel found at Kersey is a Neeley's Ferry plain bowl with a human-head rim rider that exhibits a top knot and what appear to be ear spools. The vessel came from unit N130, E80 but was not found with human remains.

The most interesting set of burials occurred in unit N110, E40 (Figure 5.36), where the remains of six bundled adults and a child's mandible were found in a pit that measured 33 inches in diameter and about that deep. Marshall (n.d.: 33) states that the six skeletons occurred in pairs, with burials 65-12 and 65-13 on top, burials 65-18 and 65-19 below them, and burials 65-20 and 65-21 on the bottom. He also states that there was no particular orientation to the bones. A Neeley's Ferry plain bowl containing the child's mandible (burial 65-33) was found next to the skull of burial 65-19, though Marshall suggests that it had originally been placed next to burial 65-12. Marshall (n.d.: table 8) states that five of the six skulls exhibited occipital flattening, but he does not list the sexes of the individuals. Reanalysis indicated that the five occipitally flattened skulls were from females and that the undeformed skull was from a male. As discussed in Chapter 6, occipitally deformed skulls found at Campbell are overwhelmingly from females. Does this indicate that the Kersey skeletons are likewise late? Perhaps, although none of the Campbell skeletons with occipital flattening were bundled, and the majority contained associated vessels.

The dog burial (Figure 5.37), the only one documented from a Pemiscot Bayou site, apparently was unassociated with any human burial. The animal had been placed into a small pit with its muzzle between the forepaws and its tail between the hind legs. Marshall (n.d.: 76) suggests that the dog had been wrapped prior to burial. Marshall (n.d.: table 14) assigned the dog burial as well as the human burials in stage 4 to the Hayti phase and possibly some to the Pemiscot Bayou phase, but he also questioned whether the burials that exhibited occipitally flattened skulls might belong in the Nodena phase.

a

b

Figure 5.36. Mass bundle burials recovered from mound 1 at Kersey in 1965: a, view (looking east) of skulls of burials 12 and 13 with Bell plain bowl; b, disarticulated long bones and partially articulated vertebral column overlying artificially flattened cranium of burial 18 (from Marshall n.d.).

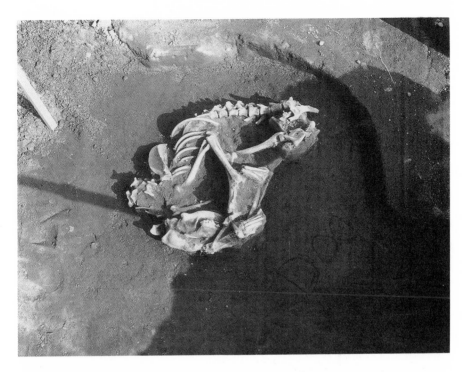

Figure 5.37. Dog burial recovered from Kersey in 1965. The dog was placed in a pit on its right side with its head to the north and facing west. The muzzle was placed between the fore-paws and the tail between the hind legs. See Figure 5.32 for location (from Marshall n.d.).

Other Excavated Areas

Fifteen 25-ft^2 units were opened on mound 2, a 15–21-inch-high rise located several hundred feet south of mound 1. As shown in Figure 5.38, the contours defining the rise indicate the presence of two mounds, though informants told Marshall that a farmhouse had stood on the rise and that the low area between the higher-elevation areas was a driveway. The excavation units produced fewer artifacts than did the units in mound 1, leading Marshall to suspect that the mound was near the southern limits of the occupation area. The same pottery types that characterized the ceramic assemblage from the excavations on mound 1 were duplicated on mound 2, though no Parkin punctated or appliquéd sherds were recovered. Paralleling the lower artifact counts in the mound-2 units was the lower frequency of pits, both beneath and within the mound. Three burials were found, all in pits that were cut into mound fill. Burial 1 was of a semiflexed adult, with the body placed on its right side. Burial 2 was of an adult, possibly bundled, and burial 3 was of an adult placed in a flexed position. None of the burials contained grave inclusions.

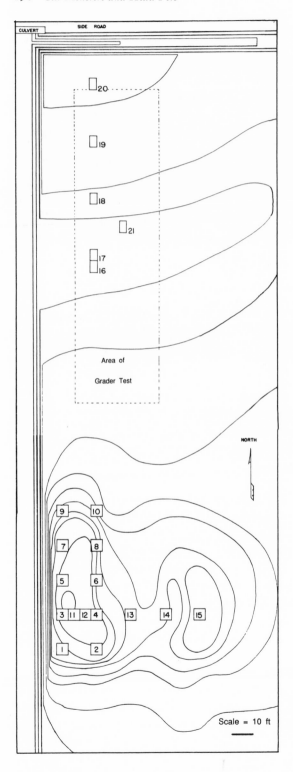

Figure 5.38. Plan of 1965 excavation of mound 2 at Kersey. Contour interval is 6 inches (after Marshall n.d.).

Excavators tested several other areas, including a slight depression between mounds 1 and 2 that was thought to be a palisade ditch. Grading and hand excavation revealed no subsurface features. Another area was examined through the use of a road grader, this one located north of mound 1, where artifact-bearing deposits were known to be several feet thick (see earlier discussion). After excavators removed 10 inches of topsoil, they encountered a pattern of 45 irregularly spaced post molds. The post molds averaged 6–7 inches in diameter and enclosed an area 48 ft north–south by 10–12 ft east–west (Figure 5.39). Inside the lines of posts was a layer of clean yellow sand that reached a maximum thickness of 4 inches; on that surface were several charred timbers, one 8 ft long. As Marshall (n.d.: 146) notes, the size and shape of the structure is unlike that of Mississippian houses, most of which are in the neighborhood of 12–18 ft on a side. No function can be assigned the structure.

Summary

Excavations conducted at Kersey in 1964 and 1965 produced a number of interesting pieces of information that provide some glimpses into early Mississippian life in the Pemiscot Bayou locality. First, excavations in mounds produced a mortuary sequence that was not unlike that at Murphy. Either late during the Late Woodland period or sometime during the early portion of the Mississippian period, burials were placed in pits excavated into artifact-bearing deposits at Kersey. Unfortunately, we have no knowledge regarding the distribution of bodies, so questions about mortuary practices remain unanswered. For example, during that early period, was the area of the community in which mound 1 was eventually placed a designated cemetery area, or were burials placed at random throughout the community?

All infants were found in tightly flexed positions. Later, adults as well as at least one infant were buried in the same general area, but, if the assignment of burials to stages is correct, the majority of interments were bundles placed within an enclosed structure. Later still, after removal of the posts that formed the enclosure, bodies were cremated and the bones placed in small pits around where the posts had been. Importantly, it appears that the bundle burials had been left in place after removal of the posts, since the small pits containing the cremated remains cut through some post molds but not through the bundle burials. In the case of two children, at least, the bodies were left uncremated and buried as bundles.

The last burial stage included extended as well as bundle burials of both adults and children. One burial episode involved the interment of six females, five of whom exhibited occipital flattening. Whether or not they were interred at one time is open to speculation, but (a) the fact that no other skeletons from Kersey

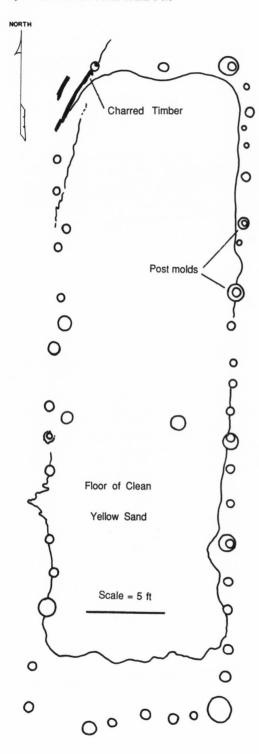

NORTH

Charred Timber

Post molds

Floor of Clean

Yellow Sand

Scale = 5 ft

Figure 5.39. Post-mold pattern in relation to sand layer and charred timber excavated at Kersey (after Marshall n.d.).

Figure 5.40. Vessels from Kersey burials: a, burial 8 (8$^1/_8$ inches high); b, unit N130, E80 (2$^1/_4$ inches high); c, unit N110, E50 (6$^1/_4$inches high); d, unknown provenience (4$^1/_4$ inches high). All from MU collection.

exhibit cranial deformation (at least as far as can be ascertained from the fragmented bone in the University of Missouri–Columbia collections), (b) the fact that they appeared late in the stratigraphic sequence from mound 1, and (c) the fact that the late-period Campbell site produced numerous examples of skulls with occipital flattening all suggest that the six bundle burials might date ca. A.D. 1400 or later.

Burial inclusions were rare at Kersey, which is not the case at the late-period sites that have produced skeletal series (e.g., Campbell [Chapter 6] and Denton Mounds [Chapter 7]). The ceramic vessels that were found are plain-surface jars, bowls, and bottles and a red-slipped bottle (Figure 5.40). The three bottles have either short or tall necks, but the distinguishing characteristics are the straight shape of the neck, the small diameter of the neck, and the flat or slightly dimpled base. Later, bottle-neck diameters expanded to several times those on the Kersey vessels, the necks flared, and annular ring bases became common.

6

CAMPBELL

Michael J. O'Brien and Thomas D. Holland

Campbell, one of the most often referenced late Mississippian period sites in the central Mississippi River valley, is located along the southern shoreline of the former Cagle Lake, approximately a mile east of the town of Cooter (Figures 1.4 and 1.5). Phillips et al. (1951), in their landmark survey of the lower Mississippi alluvial valley, made note of Campbell, which they called Cooter (site 8-Q-7), and a few years later S. Williams (1954) collected almost 400 sherds from the site for use in his dissertation work. Based on his surface collection from the site, together with materials excavated by Leo Anderson (see below), Williams (1954; see also Phillips 1970) placed the Campbell site in the late Mississippian period Nodena phase. Later, Williams (1980) included the Campbell site in what he termed the Armorel phase—a very late Mississippian period manifestation. As pointed out in Chapter 2, both the Nodena phase and the Armorel phase are, at best, poorly defined.

Sporadic articles describing select items from Campbell appear in the archaeological literature (e.g., Klinger 1977a), and numerous references to the site appear regularly (e.g., Morse and Morse 1983; D. F. Morse 1990; Price and Price 1990; G. P. Smith 1990; S. Williams 1980, 1983, 1990). The presence of beautifully crafted vessels at Campbell was the lure for Leo Anderson (Figure 1.6a), an amateur collector who, along with his wife, Mary Ellen (Figure 1.6b, c), began in 1954 what would be the only systematic excavation of the site. During the first year of work another well-known avocational archaeologist, Dr. J. K. Hampson—best known for his excavations at the Upper and Middle Nodena sites in Arkansas—visited Anderson's excavation and rendered some on-site physical analysis of several of the skeletons. The Andersons were joined in 1954 by Carl and Eleanor

Chapman, who assisted in the excavation of 15 burials (Figures 1.6d and 1.7). The Anderson-Chapman collaboration resulted in an article in *The Missouri Archaeologist* (Chapman and Anderson 1955) that stood for many years as the final word on Campbell. But several inaccuracies appear in the article and have been perpetuated by archaeologists who accept Chapman and Anderson's report on faith.

In an effort to clear up some of the inaccuracies, Holland (1991) plotted the locations of all graves excavated by Anderson and completed a thorough examination of all available skeletal material. Between January 6, 1954, and February 6, 1968, Anderson uncovered at least 218 Mississippian skeletons, 144 of which were given to the Museum of Anthropology at the University of Missouri (see Cole 1965).[1] The remaining 74 (or possibly more) skeletons either never were removed from the ground or never made their way to the university. The Campbell skeletons represent the most complete prehistoric skeletal assemblage in the state of Missouri and one of the larger Mississippian-period skeletal collections from west of the Mississippi River. Several aspects of the mortuary program are discussed here, and analysis of the skeletal material appears in Chapter 8. Readers should consult Holland (1991) for details on the individual skeletons.

In addition to human remains, the Anderson collection at one time included almost 200 ceramic vessels and other artifacts found in association with the burials (Price and Price 1979, 1990). Some of the vessels were donated to the University of Missouri, but many of them were gifted to friends of the Andersons, to the Brown and Campbell families (the landowners), or to the Peabody Museum of Archaeology and Ethnology at Yale University. The majority, however, were displayed at Anderson's small museum in Van Buren, Missouri. Anderson's museum holdings were in turn sold as a unit to Big Springs Village, a private corporation, which subsequently sold many of the artifacts at public auction in New York and St. Louis (Price and Price 1990: 62). The documentation that remains consists of smudged photocopies of Anderson's field notes and an inventory of Anderson's collection prepared by Price and Price (1979) for Big Springs Village. The Price and Price inventory includes photographs and descriptions of most of the vessels that had been in Anderson's museum.

In addition to the vessels produced from Anderson's work, thousands of pots have been excavated at Campbell, including at least 24 head pots (J. Cherry, pers. comm., 1993). It is fair to say that the occurrence of elaborately decorated vessels and the presence of European glass and metal goods have created an aura around Campbell and elevated it to its status as one of the most well known sites in the central Mississippi Valley. To our knowledge, no other Pemiscot Bayou site has

---

1. The number of provenienced skeletons available for examination in 1990, however, was 138; of those, 132 were sufficiently intact to allow analysis (Holland 1991). In addition, UMC curates a number of skeletal parts labeled "23PM5" that otherwise lack any form of provenience; they may or may not be from Anderson's excavations.

produced as many European items as Campbell, and certainly no other site has produced as many vessels. We spent considerable time tracking down myriad leads on the whereabouts of Campbell material, and we interviewed people knowledgeable about various activities that took place on the site between 1955 and 1977. The whole story of what happened at this one extraordinary site has yet to be written, and perhaps will never be written, but at least we have a much better handle on the events and materials produced. The majority of items described and illustrated in this chapter were excavated by Anderson, but to document the wide range of material that has come from Campbell, especially with regard to ceramic vessels, we supplement the discussion with descriptions and photographs of materials from private collections.

Site Structure

It is difficult to distinguish fact from fiction in attempting to understand the spatial extent of archaeological materials at Campbell and where certain features were in relation to others. Based on the distribution of surface artifacts and on Anderson's limited excavation up to 1955, Chapman and Anderson (1955: 13) state that the occupied village probably did not exceed 40 acres and that the area containing surface material was roughly 400–500 yards north–south by 300–400 yards east–west. We do know that the site contained a single mound, though its dimensions vary considerably depending on which account one reads. Houck (1908: 56), in his survey of Missouri mounds, lists the earthen structure as being 150 ft long, 75 ft wide, and 15 ft high. Chapman and Anderson (1955: 13) cite Ellis Barger, the local informant referred to in Chapter 4, as saying the mound was considerably smaller in length and width and only 10 ft high. Barger specifically stated that no other mounds existed on the site. Morse and Morse (1983: 289) state that the mound

> was alleged to have covered a 5-m-deep (16 ft.) shaft grave with considerable artifact content, including a large catlinite disk pipe, a glass bead (Nueva Cadiz), several brass hawk bells, and such other items as fabrics and a wood effigy. Whether this intelligence is valid, there is no doubt that a considerable number of European artifacts existed at the site. Blue glass beads, iron tubular beads, and other fragments of iron had been discovered associate with graves at the site by Leo Anderson (Chapman and Anderson 1955).

Morse and Morse are correct that Anderson recovered European artifacts, but "(Chapman and Anderson 1955)" is a strange reference to insert after that statement, since in their discussion of the first 35 burials from Campbell, which were all that were covered in the 1955 report, Chapman and Anderson make no mention of European items.

The nature of the mound at Campbell is enigmatic, to say the least, and our efforts to verify some of the stories that have arisen concerning the mound and its contents have produced more questions than answers. Based on conversations with present landowner Tom Campbell and with people whom we consider to be reliable sources, we suspect the mound was actually a large levee remnant, as opposed to a man-made structure. A barn that had been built on top of the levee remnant was razed in about 1977, and the "mound" was excavated soon thereafter. Most of the informants independently corroborate portions of the Morse and Morse (1983) account, especially the depth at which some of the burials occurred and the items that were recovered. We are unsure of that portion of the account that refers to the shaft grave. There appears to be no doubt that a large burial pit had been excavated prehistorically and that numerous bodies were placed in the pit at various depths. It also appears that the pit had been excavated down through the mound; hence the great depth at which the skeletons were encountered. As discussed later, the burials excavated by Leo Anderson all occurred above a depth of 42 inches, which is close to what probably was the water table ca. A.D. 1500. Therefore, we surmise that the orifice of the deep burial pit was near the summit of the "mound." There is also a report that the outline of clay steps descending into the burial pit could be discerned in the sidewalls of the 1977 excavation, though we could not corroborate the story. The number of individuals buried in the pit is unknown, but apparently they were numerous. The only artifact from the mound area that we have seen mentioned by Morse and Morse (1983) is the catlinite disk pipe shown in Plate 1d.

The "Plaza" and Its "Shaman"

Chapman and Anderson (1955: 13), in a flight of whimsy, made a statement about the configuration of Campbell that was to have lasting consequences: "Due to the small amount of pottery fragments and other debris on the surface, plus the packed condition of the earth to a depth of one foot, there is reasonable basis for assuming that the area immediately east of the mound had been the plaza, devoid of structures, and the scene of Indian dances. A single burial was located in this area." Chapman and Anderson (1955: fig. 17) present a map of the site, which we reproduce as Figure 6.1, showing the relation of the plaza to the mound. Neither Chapman nor Anderson conducted anything approaching controlled, systematic excavations, nor did they make controlled surface collections. Neither do they present any data on the "packed condition of the earth." Thus we can find no "reasonable basis" for assuming the existence of a plaza. In fact, as we point out below, further excavation by Anderson demonstrated that burials were scattered all across the proposed plaza. We highlight this point because the myth of the plaza at Campbell permeates the literature (e.g., Price and Price 1990: 60; G. P. Smith 1990: 164).

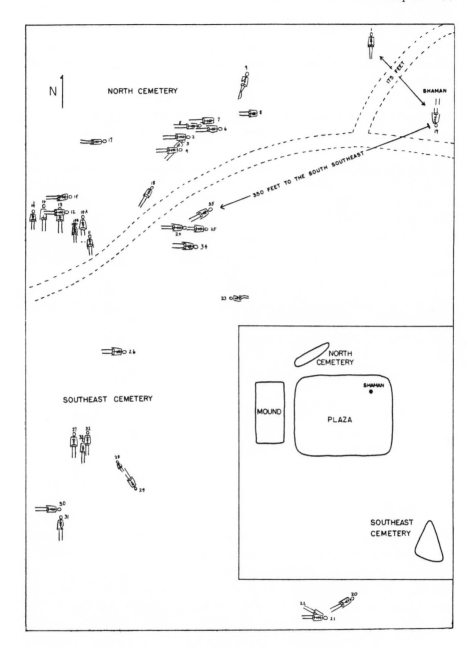

Figure 6.1. Chapman and Anderson's (1955: fig. 17) map of Campbell showing the locations of their north and southeast cemeteries and (inset) their relation to the mound and proposed plaza. Note that in their drawing the southeast cemetery was inadvertently moved to the southwest.

While we are pointing out mythical statements regarding Campbell and its content and spatial arrangement, we should point out perhaps the most famous story, that of the shaman burial. We note below how Anderson's nonsystematic excavation led to the belief that Campbell contained spatially isolated cemeteries, which led to the statement by Chapman and Anderson (1955) that a plaza separated the north and southeast cemeteries. Inspection of Figure 6.1 reveals that the "plaza" is not quite void of all remains, for in its northeast corner is a burial (19) labeled "shaman." As far as Chapman and Anderson knew in 1955, this was the only burial in the area. Its location, along with erroneous paleopathological information, led them to speculate that the burial was that of a shaman:

> Religious leaders, or keepers of the sacred fire, probably were present at Campbell, tending to the temple on the mound. Medicine men or shamans must also have been feared and respected in the community. The finding of a single unusual burial, distant from all the rest, and in the plaza area gives some idea of this aspect of village life. He was probably a medicine man or shaman. His body was deformed; the right upper arm shortened and the lower arm twisted. One of the lumbar vertebrae had slipped to one side causing a lateral twisting to the spine. The *Old Town Red* effigy bottle placed with the burial was unusual in itself. It appeared to be [a] dog effigy, with four legs and curved tail. Most unusual was the fact that the vessel had been ceremonially "killed". . . . Assuming that the man's deformity aided in establishing him as a shaman or medicine man, which was often the profession of cripples, the killing of his familiar object, the "red dog" vase, is understandable. Perhaps the "red dog" vase was feared as much as its owner, and upon the shaman's death, it was immolated to accompany him, but in such a manner that its spirit could not find its way back. Lending credence to this interpretation is the placement of this burial beneath the plaza or dancing ground, where the trampling of many feet in ceremonies for the good of the community would help negate any evil powers still inherent in the shaman and his familiar, and would so confuse his spirit helpers that they could not return to his remains. (Chapman and Anderson 1955: 116–18)

We know from Anderson's later excavations that many burials occurred in the "plaza" area, but the myth of the shaman still persists (e.g., G. P. Smith 1990: 164). In actuality, the individual was not "deformed," as Chapman and Anderson claim, though he was arthritic and may have suffered from a tuberculosis-like disease. The red-slipped dog effigy interred with the individual is shown in Plate 2d.

"Individual Cemeteries"

Anderson, in the sum of his excavations (discussed later), achieved nothing close to total recovery, but Chapman and Anderson (1955) delineated two cemeteries— one labeled "north" and the other "southeast" (Figure 6.1). This division appears to have been based on too little excavation—only 35 burials had been recovered at the time the report was written—and too much speculation. Further work by Anderson over the subsequent decade and a half not only filled in much of the area between the two cemeteries but also resulted in Anderson defining a third area, labeled in the field notes as "west of fence." When all the burials designated in Anderson's field notes are plotted (Figure 6.2), it is clear that the principal reason for the segregation of the north and southeast (labeled "south" in Figure 6.2) cemeteries was the location of a road (Route E). Burials not destroyed when the road was constructed at the very least would have been inaccessible to Anderson. Similarly, the vacant area between the north and west cemeteries probably reflects the presence of a fence row running along the section line between sections 7 and 8, which represents the modern property line between the Campbell and Brown farms.

Thus, the maintenance of separate north, southeast (south), and west cemeteries cannot be supported with the evidence at hand. As a consequence, the Campbell skeletal assemblage is considered to be from a single cemetery area of unknown size. Additional burials have been reported east of the Campbell house on property owned by the Coleman family (Cole 1965), under the Campbell house, and under the Brown house in the southwest corner of the site (Cole 1965; T. Campbell, pers. comm., 1990). Burials continue to turn up during cultivation.

The Excavations

Anderson's excavations were aimed almost exclusively at burials, though it is not altogether clear why Anderson chose to dig in the areas that he did, nor is it certain that he used a consistent survey technique through time and across space. Examination of his field notes (discussed below) sheds little light on his excavation strategy. Fortunately, the condition of the curated bones provides some insight into how they were recovered. Numerous skeletons display round punctures indicating that Anderson used a probe to detect the presence of bones (or, more likely, the presence of a ceramic vessel). Sounding rods, which continue to be the favorite tools of collectors in the region, typically are metal rods about a meter or a little more in length attached to wooden handles. Often, a ball bearing is welded onto the rod's tip to soften the impact of the probe when it strikes a ceramic vessel. Clean punctures in some of the Campbell bones indicate that the tip of Anderson's probe measured approximately 8 mm in diameter. Confirmation that Anderson used a probe is provided by photographs taken at the site in 1954 (Figure 6.3).

One potential bias in the recorded locations of burials is that not all skeletons are equally likely to be detected by a probe. Bundle burials, for example, might be less detectable (though one of the probed skeletons at Campbell was in a bundle). In addition, although no difference exists in the incidence of probe damage with regard to sex of individual, Holland (1991: table 5.3) demonstrates

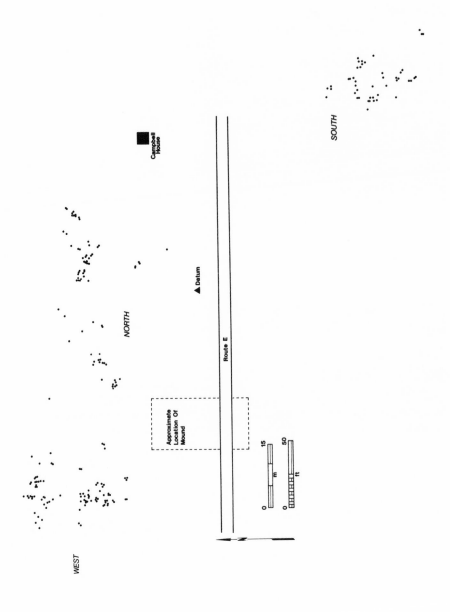

Figure 6.2. Distribution of 218 burials excavated by Leo Anderson at Campbell (from Holland 1991). See Figures 6.5–6.7 for burial numbers and orientations of skeletons.

Figure 6.3. Campbell burial 19, showing probe holes around the legs and sand-filled earthquake crack at the knees (from Chapman and Anderson 1955).

that infant and child skeletons, both of which occupy less space, were less likely to be struck by a probe than was a fully extended adult skeleton. Similarly, softer bones such as those associated with a child or with a more decomposed skeleton may not be equally detectable. There is some evidence to suggest that perhaps it was not always easy to tell when the probe had struck bone. Of the 58 skeletons showing probe holes, at least 37 (64%) have holes in two or more bones, while only 21 (36%) have probe damage on a single element. Conversely, few if any of the vessels in the Anderson Collection (Price and Price 1979) appear to have suffered any probe damage. Given the soil conditions in the months of December, January, and February—when Anderson did most of his work at Campbell—it was probably easier to identify ceramic vessels with a probe than it was to identify bone. This means that burials without ceramic offerings might have been less detectable. However, there appears to be no statistically significant relation between probing and the presence of vessels, since of 39 burials with no ceramic vessels in association, 12 (31%) definitely had been probed.

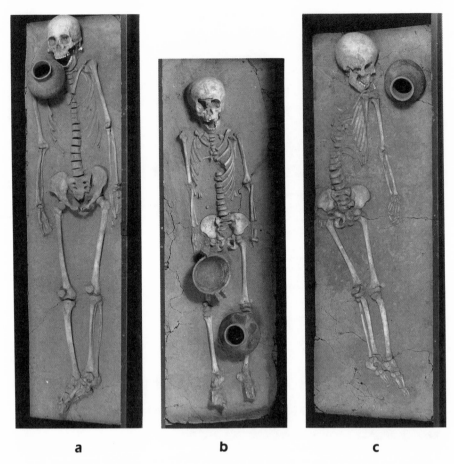

a   b   c

Figure 6.4. Skeletons and associated grave goods from Campbell removed in block sections by Leo Anderson: a, burial 48; b, burial 45; c, burial 51. Note the excellent state of preservation of the bone.

Since the majority of our analysis focuses so heavily on the work of one man—Leo Anderson—it is appropriate to ask what kind of an excavator he was. Did he excavate carefully, or did he pull skeletons and vessels from the ground with little notation of association? Did he keep records, and, if so, how detailed are the records? Fortunately, although Anderson excavated only after probing an area and hitting an object, he was quite deliberate in how he excavated a burial—as the condition and completeness of the skeletal remains attest (e.g., Figure 6.4). Most importantly, he assigned individual burial numbers to almost all skeletons (Figures 6.5–6.7); in a few instances he noted the occurrence of isolated bones but did not assign them unique numbers. Large block excavations certainly would have allowed him to see associations among burials much more easily than his method allowed, but he was in most cases able to sort out which bones went with which burial and which inclusions were associated with which skeleton.

Figure 6.5. Locations of Campbell burials in the northern area (after Holland 1991).

Figure 6.6. Locations of Campbell burials in the southern area (after Holland 1991).

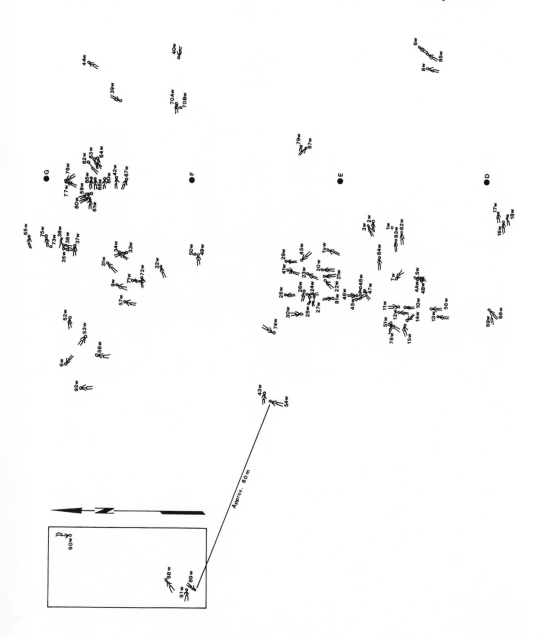

Figure 6.7. Locations of Campbell burials in the western area (after Holland 1991).

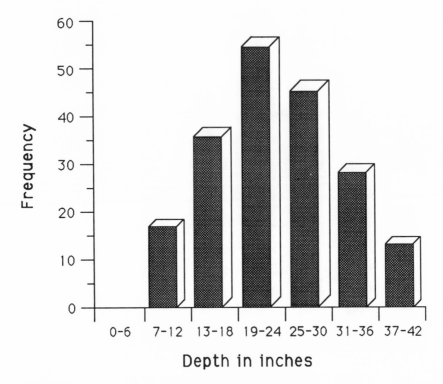

Figure 6.8. Number of burials by depth below ground surface at Campbell (data from Holland 1991).

The information we were able to glean from the field notes and the Chapman and Anderson (1955) report suggests that the burial pits were excavated through midden deposits, as opposed to being excavated in nonmidden areas. Under the best of circumstances we would be able to discern at what elevation individual burial pits began, but we often cannot derive such information. Chapman and Anderson (1955: 49) state that only 1 of the first 35 burials excavated had been disturbed by plowing and that the others lay at depths of 1–4.5 ft. If one or more of the original 35 burials lay at a depth of 4.5 ft, neither this depth nor any depth close to it was duplicated by the remainder of the burials subsequently removed by Anderson. The deepest of those burials occurred at 41 inches, with the great majority at depths of 32 inches or less (Figure 6.8). In some cases one burial pit lay above another, and in other cases one pit intruded into another. The situation must have been confusing. In a journal entry describing the excavation of burials 45W–50W, Anderson states, "After this mess, I'm yearning for single burials." A glance at his plan of the excavation (Figure 6.9) shows the reason for Anderson's yearning.

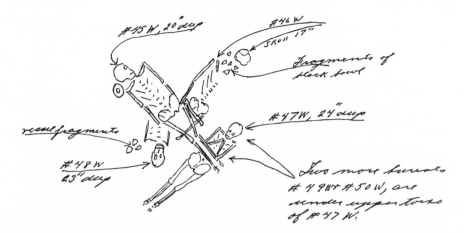

Figure 6.9. Burial plan from Leo Anderson's notes showing positioning of Campbell burials 45W–50W.

Anderson kept both a journal and a running set of field sheets that contained burial number, orientation, depths of bones and artifacts, and sketch maps. Some field notes were later edited and typed by Anderson. The maps are especially indispensable for reconstructing the burials. In Figures 6.10 and 6.11 we present, unedited by us, Anderson's notes for burial 28W—one of the six documented interments that contained metal. We later will refer back to the entry for its information on the archaeological context of burial 28W, but we include it here as an example of Anderson's attention to detail. In all fairness, not all journal entries are this detailed—burial 28W (which Holland [1991] subdivided into 28AW and 28BW) was atypically complicated—but the field sketch is typical.

In addition to the areas that were probed and then excavated to remove the skeletons and grave goods, two test pits (dimensions unknown, although one extended to a depth of at least 30 inches) were excavated west and northwest of burial 14 (Figure 6.1), and a "trench" (dimensions unknown) was opened west of burial 18 (Figure 6.1). Chapman and Anderson discuss the few artifacts from the units and note that one of the test pits hit the corner of a square or rectangular house that had a "puddled floor." The unit was not expanded to follow the house outline.

The Artifacts

Taken in the aggregate, the artifacts produced by the many years of Anderson's work at Campbell form the most comprehensive set of late Mississippian period materials from the Pemiscot Bayou locality. "Most comprehensive" does not imply

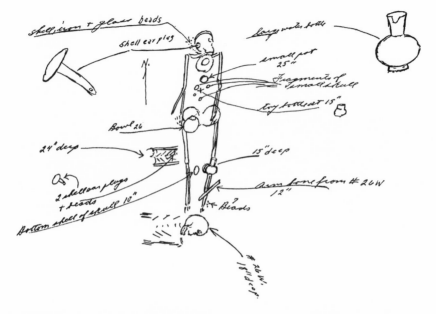

Figure 6.10. Page from Leo Anderson's notes for Campbell burial 28W showing positioning of skeleton and grave goods. Note the detail in the drawing, especially in terms of assigning various bones to different burials.

that the artifact assemblage is not without its biases. For example, no soil was screened from any of the excavations, nor were the surface materials collected systematically. We do believe, however, that Anderson was quite thorough in searching for small objects in the burial fill—an assessment based on the number of small bones (including hyoids) included in the skeletal sample. It also appears that all burial inclusions were labeled properly. Suffice it to say that Anderson's notes and the photographs of his material made by Price and Price (1979) are invaluable references to what objects were recovered from Campbell and where those objects were originally located.

The ceramic-vessel assemblage that resulted from Anderson's excavations is biased in another, and somewhat unusual, manner. We earlier noted that somewhere in the neighborhood of two dozen head pots have been recovered from Campbell, only one of which was found by Anderson. In fact, Anderson found few "exotic" vessels at Campbell compared to those that were removed in the 1970s. We first found it difficult to believe the sheer number of beautifully crafted pieces that Campbell has produced over the years, but, having seen the vessels and talked with people knowledgeable about activities that took place at the site, we have no reason *not* to believe it. The number of head pots found at Campbell over the years is testimony to the absolutely frenzied activities that took place at the site. Of course, we have no way of knowing how many burials on average one has to unearth

23-Pm-5   # 28 - W   1/28/58

These are the re-writt en notes on this burial. The reason for this is that
so many things that seemed unimportant while digging now help fill out the picture.

The bottom of this grave was about 30" deep (deep = from surface). Body extended,
on back, arms by side. Head N. and slightly on L. side. Top of skull 24" from surface.

Below 10" there was a bed of solid, pure ashes. Very little refuse mixed with
it, except a few sherds and numerous human bones, generally fragmentary. In this
grave fill was, among other things, an adult upper arm bone at depth of 12", lying
above lower legs of #28. This bone was later identified as belonging to Burial
#26-W, whose skull was just above toes of #28W, but was extended at right angles to
the W. At a depth of 10" (plow sole) the dark earth of the surface changed to pure
ash. Embedded in this ash was the back of a skull, cut away by the plow until only
a shallow bowl of bone remained. If this had been a burial, and at the time I
assumed it had been, the plow had removed all other traces! I did not attempt to
orient this burial exactly, but as the bowl of bone was oblong to N. & S. parallel
it would seem that this very shallow burial had been laid head to N. or S. parallel
to #28W. At a depth of 15" lay a small water bottle on its side. This was above the
left knee of #28 W. A few inches north of this vessel a shell disk bead was found
at this same level, and at a point directly above the abdomen of #28W, also at 15",
lay a small toy pot, on its side. Also encountered in the grave fill were numerous
bits of human bone. Fragments of skull were most numerous. One piece of mandible,
with teeth, came about 20" deep, about mid way. At depth of 24" some small bones,
shell beads, and two shell ear plugs were discovered on the W. side of the excavation.
The small bones came to a clean cut end at a point that would have been the child's
neck, which had been buried head to E. The child bones terminated at a point that
was 6" W. of the right femur of #28", although no change in soil colorization was
discernible where the grave of #28" had cut through the child burial. It continued
to be all nearly pure ashes. At depth of 26", just above the right hip lay a dark
bowl, tipped to the N. In the bowl, and under it were fragments of a small skull.
Also under the bowl was another shell ear plug, of same size and shape as those recovered from child burial. The bowl was not touching the bones of #28W by at least
2". At the left ankle of 28W were 7 shell disk beads. All were on the E. side of the
bone, somewhat scattered. Immediately S. of the chin, but not touching was a 10" high
flaring neck, annular base water bottle. About 6" S. of this water bottle lay a
toy pot similar to the one recovered earlier at 15" depth. This second toy pot was
also on side at depth of 25" and appeared to be in the grave fill and not associated
with "28". Two shell disk beads were found close to right elbow. These, by accident,
became mixed with beads from neck. Along the West side of the skull of #28W were
numerous shell beads, about 160. Among these beads were tiny specks of a bluish
substance that I first thought indicated copper, but among the shell beads were 3
blue beads of the same material, apparently glass trade beads. Also associated with
the shell beads were two whole and some fragments (of a rusty appearing material that
might be brass) of a rolled tubular type bead. The tiny bits of blue material was
soft, and could be crushed between thumb and finger. The rusty looking material has
a metallic feel. At each side of the skull, with the disk to the front, were two
large, heavy shell ear plugs, of the same type as those associated with the child.
All shell artifacts were in an excellent state of preservation. Grave goods definitely with #28W are the ear plugs, beads of shell, glass and metal at neck, shell
beads at right elbow and left ankle and the water bottle. The bowl might possibly
Have been associated with #28W, as it would be difficult to account for it otherwise.
The two toy pots and one shell bead in the grave fill could have been with the disturbed child burial. The small water bottle at 15" is harder to account for. The
evidence at hand indicates that of the 4 burials (assuming that the skull fragment
at 10" indicated a burial) the child was earliest, then #28W, after which came both
#26W and the shallow 10" burial, in unknown order.

Figure 6.11. Page from Leo Anderson's burial notes for Campbell describing his excavation of burial 28W.

to find a head pot, but we estimate that it might be on the order of 200–300. If we add some of the other unique vessels to the pool, it is not difficult to believe that relic collectors have gone through thousands of burials at that one site alone to recover just the number of head pots and other rare vessels on which we have information. The number of "ordinary" vessels that must have come from the feeding frenzy would itself be in the thousands.

Our discussion of artifacts from Campbell, particularly the ceramic vessels, centers around Anderson's materials since they carry intrasite provenience. Hence we can use them to gain some insight into the types and forms of containers placed with the dead. How well the observed patterns would hold up against a larger sample is impossible to gauge. In appropriate places we bring in discussions of other materials to document the tremendous variation in vessel design that late Mississippian period potters were able to effect.[2]

Surface Materials

The Campbell site has been surface collected an untold number of times, and collecting continues to the present. Collectors, as well as individuals purporting to represent professional archaeologists in Arkansas, routinely scour the site's surface. In only two instances, however, have the results of surface collecting been reported: in 1954, when S. Williams included the site in his dissertation, and in the following year, when the results of Anderson's nonsystematic surface collection were published (Chapman and Anderson 1955). The principal aim of Williams's (1954) work, the more narrowly defined of the two, was to obtain a ceramic series from Campbell in order to place the site within a cultural and temporal framework he was attempting to establish. To that end, he collected and classified 386 sherds into six types (Table 3.3). The collection was dominated by Neeley's Ferry plain (Williams used the type name *Mississippi plain*) sherds (73%), with Bell plain sherds accounting for approximately one-quarter of the collection. Nodena red-and-white, Ranch incised, Kent incised, and Parkin punctated provided only a fraction of the total, and two sherds were classified as unidentified punctated. Based on his surface collection and discussions with local collectors (including Anderson), Williams (1954) assigned Campbell to the Nodena phase.

In contrast to Williams's small sample, Anderson (Chapman and Anderson 1955) collected at least 1,413 ceramic sherds, including 985 rim sherds, that he and Chapman subsequently grouped into 12 previously described types and 3 proposed types in their table 2.3.[3] Unlike in Williams's collection, Bell plain is the dominant ceramic type, accounting for almost 39% of the collection and

---

2. Figure captions identify whether vessels under discussion are from Anderson's excavations.

3. As in Chapter 2, Old Town red and Varney red are combined into the type "red-slipped."

outnumbering Neeley's Ferry plain sherds by a ratio of 2:1. Perhaps the most striking feature of the ceramic signature is the large number of appliquéd sherds—a feature not found either at other sites in the Pemiscot Bayou locality (Chapter 7) or at Nodena sites in northeastern Arkansas. Williams recovered no appliquéd sherds, but Anderson recovered 239 appliquéd sherds. Instead of fitting the sherds into the appliquéd type commonly used by archaeologists then working in the central Mississippi Valley—Vernon Paul appliquéd—Chapman and Anderson looked at differences among sherds in width, location, and application of appliqué strips and devised a new type, Campbell appliquéd (Figures 6.12 and 6.13), to house 228 of the 239 sherds, placing the other 11 in the Vernon Paul appliquéd category (for differences between the 2 types, see Chapter 2). They also coined two additional types—Campbell incised (Figure 6.14) and Campbell punctated, the latter as a category for vessels that exhibited rows of small punctations on the lower portion of the neck and the former for vessels that exhibited vertical fine-line incising on the body. Other significant contributors to the surface assemblage were the established types Parkin punctated (Figure 6.15) and Ranch incised (Figure 6.16).

Other ceramic objects recovered from the surface include 48 pottery disks. Some of the disks have ground edges, some have perforations, and at least one was painted on one surface with hematite. Chapman and Anderson (1955) suggest that many of the disks may have been gaming pieces. Also recovered were 2 fragments of a pottery trowel and 4 Bell plain sherds with grooved surfaces.

The Anderson surface collection also contains numerous arrow points: 147 willow-leaf (Nodena), 186 triangular (Madison), 1 corner-notched (Scallorn), and 2 straight-stemmed. In addition, 225 willow-leaf "rejects" or "blanks" and 165 triangular "blanks" were recovered, along with 23 unidentified-biface and blank fragments (Table 6.1). Other bifaces include 5 specimens identified by Chapman and Anderson (1955) as knives, 22 "pipe drills," and 115 "snub-nosed scrapers." Woodworking activities are represented by 9 intact and 14 fragmented adzes, chisels, and gouges (Chapman and Anderson combined these into a single category). Sixty-three large chert artifacts were lumped into a core/chopper/hammerstone category. Groundstone and pecked-stone artifacts are represented by 2 diabase celts (probably used in woodworking), a red granite mortar with hematite residue (indicating its probable use for grinding pigment), 2 pitted hammerstones, 2 pumice abraders probably used for sharpening bone pins or awls, 9 discoidals or gaming stones, and numerous sandstone palette/whetstone fragments.

In addition to ceramic and lithic artifacts, several bone, antler, and shell artifacts were recovered from the surface (Table 6.1). Three bone-pin fragments, a bone punch, and a scapula fragment were collected. Chapman and Anderson (1955) suggest that the bone pins were hair ornaments. Two other bone artifacts—a split bird-leg bone and a fish-fin bone—were classified as awls. Nine antler artifacts

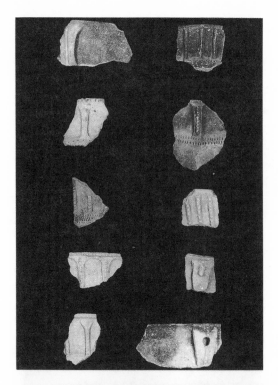

Figure 6.12. Sherds of Campbell appliquéd in the Chapman-Anderson surface collection from Campbell.

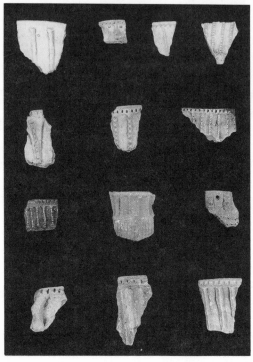

Figure 6.13. Sherds of Campbell appliquéd in the Chapman-Anderson surface collection from Campbell.

Figure 6.14. Sherds of Campbell incised in the Chapman-Anderson surface collection from Campbell.

Figure 6.15. Sherds of Parkin punctated in the Chapman-Anderson surface collection from Campbell.

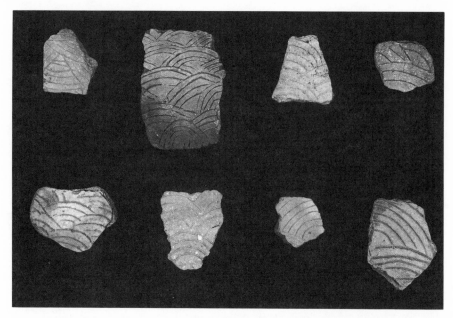

Figure 6.16. Sherds of Ranch incised in the Chapman-Anderson surface collection from Campbell.

Table 6.1
Nonceramic Artifacts in the Chapman-Anderson Surface Collection from Campbell

Artifact	Number	Artifact	Number
Biface		Ground/pecked stone	
Willow-leaf (intact)	147	Celt	2
Willow-leaf (fragment/blank)	225	Mortar	1
Triangular (intact)	186	Hammerstone	2
Triangular (fragment/blank)	165	Abrader (pumice)	2
Stemmed arrow point	3	Discoidal/gaming stone	9
Knife	5	Bone/Antler/Shell	
Pipe drill	22	Bone pin	3
Snub-nosed scraper	115	Bone punch	1
Core/chopper/hammerstone	63	Scapula (hoe?)	1
Adze/chisel/gouge (intact)	9	Awl	2
Adze/chisel/gouge (fragment)	14	Antler tip	9
Unidentified	23	Shell bead (mussel)	8
		Shell bead (conch)	15

were recovered, 5 of which appear to have served as flaking tools and 1 as a projectile point. Shell artifacts consist of beads and bead fragments. Eight beads were cut from thick river-mussel shells, and 15 were manufactured from the columellae of conch shells.

Subsurface Artifacts

Most items in the Anderson collection were ceramic vessels from burials, followed by bead necklaces and bracelets. A number of items, especially conch-shell spoons, were found in the vessels, but we deleted items that had questionable proveniences. Most of these were small objects that probably were incorporated as grave fill rather than being primary funerary offerings.

Ceramic Vessels

To the best of our knowledge, 254 of the ceramic vessels excavated by Anderson can be tied to specific burials. Anderson recovered several other vessels—some were photographed by Price and Price (1979), others are in the University of Missouri collection—but they lack intrasite provenience. The 48 vessels associated with burials 1, 2, 4–8, 10–31, and 35 were described in Chapman and Anderson (1955). Based on inspection of the photographs in that publication or on inspection of vessels housed at the university, we can derive the ceramic types and vessel forms for these 48 vessels. Many of the remaining 206 provenienced vessels excavated by Anderson can be identified using Price and Price's (1979) photographs and Anderson's 1945–1961 field notes, which, while seldom mentioning ceramic type, are in many cases sufficiently detailed that the type can be ascertained, as can individual motifs and other characteristics. Of these 206, we can determine the form of 202 vessels. One hundred sixty-six of the 218 burials excavated by Anderson yielded the 254 provenienced vessels, an average of slightly over 1.5 vessels per vessel-producing burial. The vessels are listed by burial number in Appendix 2 (burials followed by a "W" were those from Anderson's western portion of the site; specific burials and burial locations are discussed in a later section).

Vessel Form

One hundred thirty-three (53%) of the 250 vessels for which a form is known are bottles, 98 (40%) are bowls, and 19 (7%) are jars. These percentages are close to those from Nodena (Table 6.2). Bottles exhibit the greatest variation with regard to shape as well as to ceramic type (discussed below), and bowls show the least variation. There is obviously a significant positive correlation between vessel shape and ceramic type, the former often being used in the description of the latter. This pleiotropic relation is evident in the group of vessels labeled "Campbell punc-

Table 6.2
Ceramic Vessels Recovered from Nodena in 1932

		Vessel Form		
Excavator	Location of Burials	Bottle	Bowl	Jar
University of Arkansas[a]	Upper	99 (45%)	73 (33%)	49 (22%)
University of Arkansas[b]	Middle	64 (46%)	59 (43%)	16 (12%)
Alabama Museum of Natural History[c]	Upper	445 (47%)	371 (40%)	123 (13%)

[a] Data from Durham 1989.

[b] Data from Fingers 1989.

[c] Data from Jones 1989.

tated," where, by "definition," the design elements and resulting motif occur only on a certain shape of bottle (see Chapter 2). And, in fact, Campbell punctated bottles are fairly consistent in appearance, with the major difference being in the thickness of the neck midway between the lip and the junction of the neck and the body. Most examples exhibit vertical necks, but on several a clay collar with punctations was added. On a few other examples the neck was channeled on the interior surface opposite the collar (Plate 3a).

Jars encompass a fairly wide range of variation (Figure 6.17). One common form is a wide-mouth, globular vessel that has a vertical, slightly everted neck (Figure 6.17a; Plate 3b) or, more commonly, a convex neck (Figure 6.17c). Carinated jars—some of which probably could be termed deep bowls (e.g., Figure 6.17g; Plate 3d)—are minor constituents of the assemblage. Oftentimes carinated jars/bowls are modeled as frogs or fish (e.g., Figure 6.17g), as are some of the smaller globular jars (e.g., Figure 6.17d). Several examples of compound jar-bottles also exist (Plate 5c).

Bowls, if we exclude effigy vessels, exhibit the least variation in shape, the most notable being rim/lip treatment and wall curvature (Figures 6.17 and 6.18). The most noticeable difference is the presence or absence of a notched fillet of clay at or just below the lip on both plain bowls and effigy bowls (Figure 6.18). The majority of vessels exhibit the fillet, which varies considerably in thickness, depending on the intended depth of the notching. The other major source of variation, degree of wall curvature, probably was tied to vessel function. Some bowls are almost hemispherical, while others have walls that flare from the base at approximately 45° (Plate 3c). Careful reading of Anderson's field notes shows that red-slipped bowls often contained a serrated mussel-shell "spoon," as shown in Plate 4d. The same was true of bowls from Berry (Chapter 7).

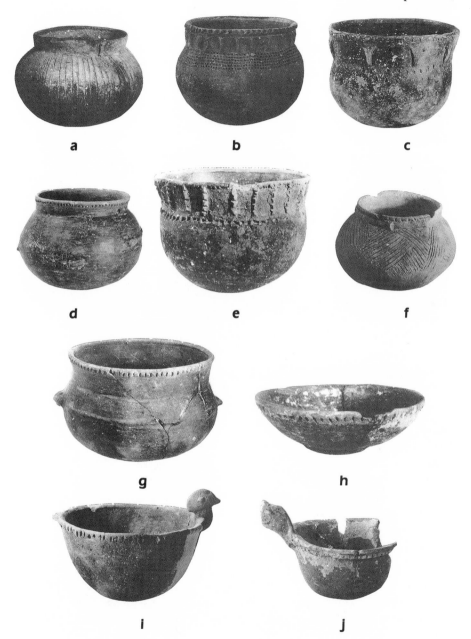

Figure 6.17. Jars (a–g) and bowls (h–j) from Campbell burials: a, burial 108 (Kent incised); b, burial 55 (Campbell punctated); c, burial 92 (Campbell punctated); d, burial 12W (Bell plain); e, burial 101 (Campbell appliquéd); f, burial 49W (Barton incised); g, burial 107 (Bell plain); h, burial 25W (Bell plain); i, burial 75 (Neeley's Ferry plain); j, burial 104 (red-slipped). All originally part of the Anderson collection (Price and Price 1979).

a

c

Figure 6.18. Bell plain bowls (a, b) and Neeley's Ferry plain bowls (c, d) from Campbell burials: a, burial 26; b, burial 97; c, burial 20W; d, burial 91. MU collection.

b

d

One vessel deserves special mention: that included with burial 25W, represented by the skeleton of a 16–20-year-old female (Holland 1991: 256). The vessel in question is a small bowl, about 5 inches in diameter at the rim, that has a short ring base (Figure 6.17h). All other known bowls from Campbell, at least as far as we know, are flat-based. The bowl appears to be quite thick and has a series of notches below the lip. Price and Price (1979) note on the catalog card that the bowl "appears similar to European vessel forms." Two other vessels were included in the burial, a Bell plain bowl with a pinched fillet rim and a Bell plain bottle with a wide mouth and a short, slightly flaring neck. Forty-seven shell beads and a cut-shell spoon were also recovered from the burial fill (discussed in the following section).

As opposed to the plain bowls, effigy bowls exhibit considerable variation. Numerous effigy forms have been recovered from Campbell burials, including a host of animal forms, such as fish, bats, birds, turtles, canines, deer, opossums, and "cat monsters." Some bowls carry stylized animal appendages, such as the specimen in Figure 6.19a, which has wide rim tabs made to resemble fins (compare that specimen to the plain-tab bowl in Figure 6.19b). Quite often, however, the animal is represented in full, with the bowl serving as its body. In some cases the animals are represented by small modeled heads and tails added to hemispherical bowl rims (e.g., Figures 6.17i, j and 6.20; Plate 5d), but in other cases the head and other appendages such as front and hind legs continue down the wall of the vessel (Figure 6.21). Other effigy forms include gourds and conch shells (Figure 6.22a, b; Plate 2b). At least three examples of "bone tabs," created by adding long strips of clay to the bowl rim, are known from Campbell. The vessel shown in Figure 6.22c is red-slipped on the interior and on the strips. Two other bowls, both from the deep-pit burial, are red-slipped on the interior and white-slipped on the exterior, including on the bones.

The most variation in Campbell vessels occurs among what, for lack of a better term, we call "flaring-neck" bottles (Figures 6.22f, j and 6.23–6.24). In fact, the flaring-neck bottle, along with the notched-fillet bowl, characterizes the late-Mississippian Pemiscot Bayou assemblages (see examples from Berry [Chapter 7]). We did not attempt to establish subcategories of the form—limited as we were for the most part only to photographs—but the flaring-neck bottle is ripe for detailed analysis relative to spatial and chronological implications. Although we use the term *flaring-neck,* the actual neck angle ranges from nearly vertical to widely flaring. On some examples the neck flares from the neck-body juncture (e.g., Figures 6.23d and 6.24g) and on others the neck starts up vertically and then begins to flare (e.g., Figure 6.24i). Neck height also varies considerably, perhaps in proportion to the overall height of the vessel or to the shape and height of the body. Bodies range in shape from almost globular to subglobular, often to the point of appearing elliptical (e.g., Figure 6.23h).

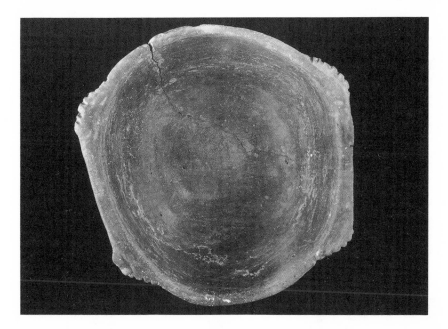

a

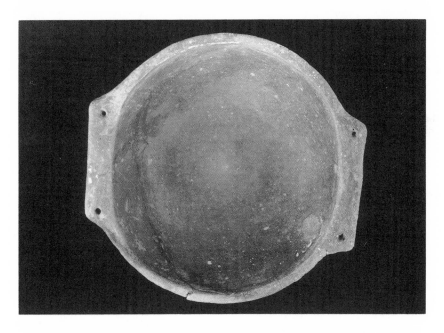

b

Figure 6.19. Wide-tab bowls from Campbell burials: a, burial 13 (Bell plain); b, burial 10B (Neeley's Ferry plain). MU collection.

Figure 6.20. Bell plain effigy bowl from Campbell burial 16 (3½ inches high). MU collection.

Figure 6.21. Bell plain effigy bowl from Campbell burial 45 (3 inches high at rim). MU collection.

Figure 6.22. Bowls (a–c) and bottles (d–j) from Campbell burials: a, burial 109 (red-slipped [interior]); b, burial 39 (red-slipped [interior]); c, burial 71 (red-slipped [interior and on appliquéd strips]); d, burial 25 (Bell plain); e, burial 1W (Bell plain); f, burial 62 (red-slipped); g, burial 36 (Nodena red-and-white); h, burial 7 (Nodena red-and-white); i, burial 64W (type unknown); j, burial 4 (Neeley's Ferry plain). All originally part of the Anderson collection (Price and Price 1979).

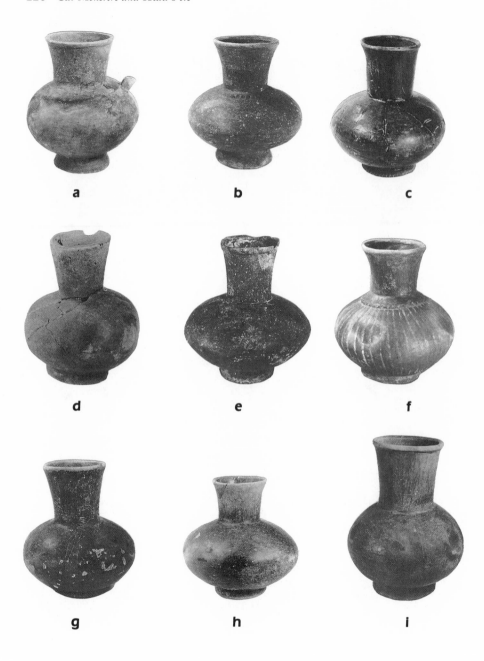

Figure 6.23. Everted-neck, annular-base Bell plain (a, c–i) and Neeley's Ferry plain (b) bottles from Campbell burials: a, burial 90; b, burial 27; c, burial 70W; d, burial 50; e, burial 61; f, burial 80W; g, burial 2W; h, burial 89; i, burial 113. All originally part of the Leo Anderson collection (Price and Price 1979).

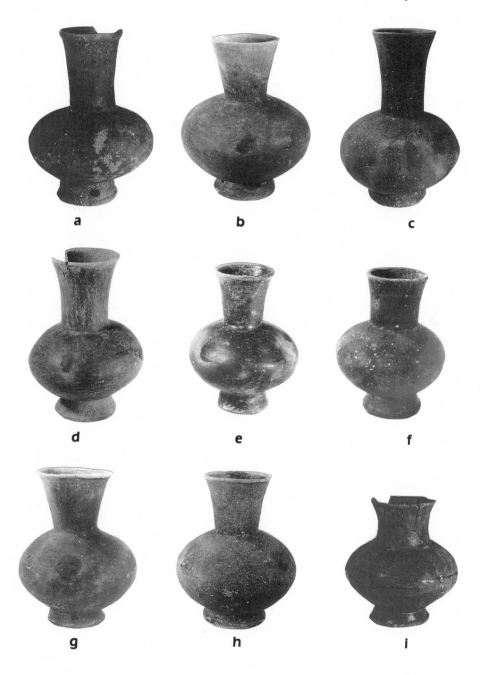

Figure 6.24. Everted-neck, annular-base Bell plain (b–e, g, i) and Neeley's Ferry plain (a, h) bottles from Campbell burials: a, burial 28AW; b, burial 4AW; c, burial 40; d, burial 82W; e, burial 66W; f, burial 68 (type unknown); g, burial 26; h, burial 41; i, burial 83. All originally part of the Anderson collection (Price and Price 1979).

Figure 6.25. Everted-neck, annular-base Bell plain bottle from Campbell showing coiled base. Banks collection.

The majority of Campbell bottles have what is traditionally termed (e.g., Phillips et al. 1951: fig. 103) an "annular base" (Figures 6.23 and 6.24), though technically the base is a vertical or flaring hollow foot ring as opposed to a strip or rounded slab of clay added to the vessel bottom. The foot ring is often perforated by four or more holes, and the lip of the ring is often crenelated. Several examples exhibit a true annular base (a circular strip of clay), and a few contain a rounded slab of clay. On one example (Figure 6.25) the clay strip was spiraled, and on a cat-monster bottle the base was coiled to resemble a snake (Figure 1.2).

The great majority of flaring-neck bottles from Campbell are plain-surface, though a few are decorated with Rhodes engraved swirls (e.g., Figure 6.26) or Walls engraved motifs (e.g., Figures 6.23g and 6.27; Plate 2f). Red-slipped, flaring-neck bottles have been found (Plates 4c and 6c), as have Nodena red-and-white bottles (Plate 6f). Most decoration, however, occurs on squatter vessels with lower necks than those seen on the flaring-neck bottles. One of the two Nodena red-and-white vessels that Anderson excavated—the one associated with burial 7 (Figure 6.22h)—has a wide neck of medium height and a slab base. The other example, from burial 36 (Figure 6.22g), has a short neck and no basal support. By far the most common bottle decoration consists of rows of small punctations on the bottom third to half of the neck (Figures 6.28 and 6.29). The consistent representation of this pattern on Campbell bottles led Chapman and Anderson (1955) to propose the type *Campbell punctated*. The neck areas that were punctated were often thickened considerably by adding a clay collar and then punctating the collar (e.g., Figure 6.29a, c). On most specimens four small appliquéd strips extend from near the lip down to the punctated region.

Another bottle form found at Campbell—the head pot—is by far the most renowned late-Mississippian vessel type (see Hathcock 1988 and Mills 1968).

Figure 6.26. Everted-neck, annular-base Rhodes engraved bottle from Campbell (provenience labeled as "backdirt"; 9 inches high). MU collection.

Figure 6.27. Everted-neck Walls bottle from Campbell with stepped design on the neck and cat-monster designs on opposing faces of the body. Compare with the vessel from Berry in Figure 1.2.

a

c

Figure 6.28. Campbell punctated bottles from Campbell burials: a, burial 48; b, burial 51; c, burial 18; d, burial 45. All from MU collection.

b

d

Figure 6.29. Bottles from Campbell burials: a, burial 24 (Campbell punctated); b, burial 20 (Campbell punctated); c, burial 23W (Campbell punctated); d, burial 30 (Campbell punctated); e, burial 88W (Walls engraved–Campbell punctated); f, burial 87W (Campbell punctated); g, burial 1 (Campbell appliquéd); h, burial 96 (Neeley's Ferry plain); i, burial 43 (Neeley's Ferry plain). All originally part of the Anderson collection (Price and Price 1979).

Head pots have been found at other Pemiscot Bayou sites, such as Brooks and Berry, as well as at sites in northeastern Arkansas, but never in the quantity of that from Campbell (as far as we know). Perhaps the most publicized head pot is the one Anderson found while excavating burial 10A, the remains of a 31–35-year-old female. The vessel is $5\frac{5}{8}$ inches high and has a $2\frac{1}{2}$-inch-diameter orifice (Plate 7a). The natural buff color of the jar is accented by a red slip around the eyes, ears, back of the head, and rim. We identify it as Carson red-on-buff. Incised lines around the eyes and mouth and on the forehead and nose probably represent tattooing. Several lines radiating outward from the eyes depict the weeping-eye motif.

Several other head pots from Campbell and other Pemiscot County sites are shown in Plate 7. The vessels exhibit wide variation in terms of shape and design, especially in the use of incising and color application. Some have incising around one or both eyes as well as in other facial areas such as below the chin. The majority are painted, usually carrying red pigment in the hair regions with the face either left buff color or painted white. Ear perforations range in number from three to five or more, with five being the most common frequency. Some bottles exhibit tall necks, a few hardly any necks at all, and the majority a neck height between 1 and 1.5 inches.

Similar to the head pots are small bottles made to resemble the three-dimensional human form (Figures 6.30 and 6.31). The vessel in Figure 6.31 contains a thickened area on the back on the human form, giving it the appearance of a hunchback. Running down the center of the back is a notched fillet of clay that resembles a vertebral column, leading to the belief among some collectors and archaeologists that spina bifida was prevalent among late Mississippian period groups in the central Mississippi River valley. However, there are no skeletal data to support this notion. The bottle shown in Figure 6.30 was slipped red, except for the face, which was left buff color. The face was incised with lines resembling tattooing, similar to those seen on head pots, and the body was engraved through the red slip to carry the tattooing effect down the torso. The head carries the top knot represented on head pots by the bottle neck, and it also shows the perforated projection on the forehead. Hathcock (1988: 227) states that this vessel is almost identical to one from Mississippi County, Arkansas: "Both vessels were broken at the knees which may suggest the bottle forms were definitely made to be used as utility objects rather than as funerary objects only."

Perhaps the most remarkable vessel ever found at Campbell is the human-effigy bottle shown in Plate 2c. The vessel is 10.5 inches high and contains red and white paint on the head and black paint on the arms and around the eyes. The highly exaggerated ears exhibit six perforations (only five are visible in the left ear in Plate 2c), and another perforation extends through the front of the lip that forms the base of the bottle neck, which is on top of the head. Like the two vessels discussed above, the legs were broken prehistorically (restored in Plate 2c).

Figure 6.30. Human-effigy bottle from Campbell. Compare the facial incising, which represents tattooing, with that on head pots. The tattooing motif has been carried down the body in the form of engraving, which cut through the red slip that covered all but the face. The legs apparently were broken prior to the placement of the object in the ground.

Figure 6.31. "Hunchback" effigy from Campbell. Note the thin strip of clay running down the back of the figure; it has been speculated that this represents the vertebral column and that spina bifida was prevalent among Pemiscot Bayou groups. There is no skeletal evidence of this whatsoever.

Vessel Type

Table 6.3 lists the frequencies of vessel forms by type for the 190 Anderson vessels from Campbell burials for which we know the type. As with the surface-collected material, Bell plain and Neeley's Ferry plain are the predominant types, but others—notably Campbell punctated—are also well represented. As a generalization, bowls are either plain or slipped, bottles are either plain or punctated with some incising/engraving and slipping, and jars are either plain or decorated with appliqués, punctations, or incised/engraved lines.

In contrast to the large percentage of Campbell appliquéd sherds in the surface collection (19%), Campbell appliquéd vessels make only a modest contribution to the burial-vessel assemblage (6%). This does not imply that few vessels exhibit appliqués; the number of vessels listed in Appendix 2 that have small appliqués indicates otherwise. All the statement implies is that our criterion for sorting sherds or vessels into the type is identical to that of Chapman and Anderson: the presence of long, thin, usually notched appliqué strips extending from the lip to the shoulder. Most of the appliqués mentioned in Appendix 2 are short strips, usually four in number, added to a neck to give the appearance of small handles. We do not identify these as Campbell appliquéd.

One ceramic type that occurs with significant frequency in the surface collection that is not represented in the burial-vessel assemblage is Ranch incised. Parkin punctated also occurs repeatedly in the surface collection, but only two vessels were found in a burial context, one of which is unprovenienced. The provenienced vessel, from burial 10C, has a Campbell appliquéd rim and is listed in Table 6.3 as Campbell appliquéd. The types Vernon Paul appliquéd, Hollywood white-slipped, and Kent incised are represented by one vessel each (a Rhodes incised bottle was reconstructed from sherds labeled "back dirt"). Types that occur infrequently in the combined Williams and Chapman-and-Anderson surface collections, such as Carson red-on-buff, Nodena red-and-white, and Walls engraved, also occur in low frequencies in the burial-vessel assemblage.

Nonceramic Artifacts from Burials

Nonceramic artifacts, except for shell, are poorly represented in the burials excavated by Anderson, though several classes of material—iron, brass, and glass—clearly indicate that the Campbell inhabitants were receiving European goods at some point after A.D. 1541. Below we list by material class various artifacts found by Anderson as well as items that we have seen in private collections.

Bone Artifacts

Only five of the burials Anderson excavated contained bone artifacts (Table 6.4), four of which also had other items in association. Perhaps most interesting of the bone artifacts was a "gaming die" made of an elk astragalus found with burial 102 (Figure

Table 6.3
Number and Percentage of Intact Ceramic Vessels
Recovered from Campbell, Listed by Vessel Type and Form

Ceramic Type[a]	Form					
	Bottle		Bowl		Jar	
Neeley's Ferry plain	20	(19%)	16	(23%)	4	(23%)
Bell plain	52	(50%)	39	(57%)	2	(12%)
Campbell punctated	17	(17%)	0	(0%)	0	(0%)
Hollywood white-slipped	1	(1%)	0	(0%)	0	(0%)
Campbell appliquéd	3	(3%)	1	(1%)	7	(41%)
Campbell incised	1	(1%)	0	(0%)	1	(6%)
Barton incised	0	(0%)	0	(0%)	1	(6%)
Vernon Paul appliquéd	0	(0%)	0	(0%)	1	(6%)
Kent incised	0	(0%)	0	(0%)	1	(6%)
Walls engraved	3	(3%)	0	(0%)	0	(0%)
Red-slipped	3	(3%)	12	(17%)	0	(0%)
Carson red-on-buff	1	(1%)	1	(1%)	0	(0%)
Nodena red-and-white	2	(2%)	0	(0%)	0	(0%)
Total	103	(100%)	69	(99%)	17	(100%)

[a] Five "hybrid" vessels are included—1 Campbell punctated–Parkin punctated bottle was included in the Campbell punctated category, 1 Hollywood white-slipped–Campbell punctated bottle was placed in the Hollywood white-slipped type, 1 Campbell appliquéd–Parkin punctated jar was typed as Campbell appliquéd, 1 Campbell appliquéd–Campbell punctated bottle was typed as Campbell appliquéd, and 1 Walls engraved–Campbell punctated bottle was typed as Walls engraved.

6.32). Anderson recovered at least two more bone dice (of white-tailed deer bone), though no provenience was listed (Figure 6.32). Astragalus dice are considered a late Mississippian period trait (Lewis 1988, 1990a; Morse and Morse 1983; see Eisenberg 1989 and Wesler 1991 for an opposing view). As with the astragalus dice associated with the late Mississippian period burials reported by Lewis (1988), the provenienced Campbell specimen was found with a child burial. Dice similar to those from Campbell have been found at Brooks and Denton Mounds (Chapter 7).

Shell Artifacts

At least 44 of Anderson's burials contained shell (39 of these burials also contained other materials), mostly in the form of beads and ear plugs (Table 6.4; Figures 6.33 and 6.34). Anderson's notes and field drawings show the position of most of the beads, which in the majority of cases were around the neck but in a few cases were around one of the ankles. Anderson also found miniature mask pendants

Table 6.4
Distribution of Bone, Shell, and Lithic Artifacts in Campbell Burials

Bone Artifacts		Shell Artifacts, continued	
Burial		Burial	
50	See later discussion	113	Unmodified mussel shell
52	Unidentified tool		Conch-shell beads (10)
60	See Table 6.5	118	Spoon
102	Cube die[a]	121	Beads (18)
17W	Awl	3W	Unmodified mussel shell
Shell Artifacts		4AW	Ear plug
Burial			Beads (212)
5	Ear plugs (2)	4BW	Beads (?)
18	Bead	5W	Spoon
23	Beads (11)	16W	Ear plug
	Conch-shell mask gorget	19W	Unmodified mussel shell
29	Ear plugs (2)	25W	Beads (47)
31	Spoon (1)		Spoon
41	Unmodified mussel shell	26W	Mask gorget
51	Ear plugs (2)	28AW	See later discussion
	Unmodified mussel shell	28BW	Ear plugs (2)
52	Unmodified mussel shells (3)		Beads (27)
54	Ear plugs (2)	36W	Ear plugs (2)
	Buttons (3)	52W	Bead
	Beads (3)	57W	Beads (16)
	Drilled disk	60W	Mask gorget
	Fragment	61W	Mask gorget
57	Conch-shell mask gorget	65W	Beads (17)
59	Spoon	70W	Ear plugs (2)
60	See Table 6.5	77W	Bead, button/gorget
61	Beads (29)	83W	Beads (31)
	Ear plugs (2)	**Lithic Artifacts**	
	Unidentified fragment	Burial	
74	Unmodified mussel shell	20	Nodena point
82	See later discussion	32	Nodena point
83	Beads (15)	60	See Table 6.5
	Ear plugs (2)	112	Discoidals (2)
85	Spoons (2)		Round stone
91	Beads (3)	121	Expanding-stem biface
102	Unmodified mussel shell		Contracting-stem biface
104	Bead		Biface
109	Beads (3)		Unmodified pebble
111	Beads (29)	24W	Geode "bowl"
	Bead fragments (4)	36W	Pipe drills (5)

[a] Two other bone cubes (dice) were recovered, but they lack provenience.

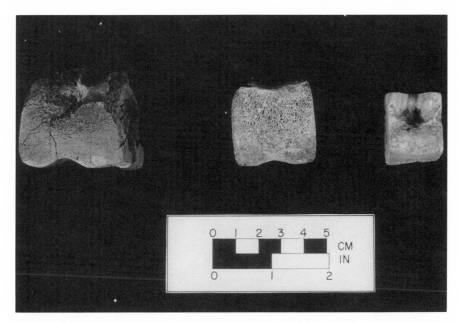

Figure 6.32. Cut-bone astragalus "dice" from Campbell. The specimen on the left, probably of elk, is from burial 102; the other two specimens are unprovenienced. Alan Banks collection (originally part of the Anderson collection [Price and Price 1979]).

(Figure 6.35), spoons, and shell disks, along with engraved "buttons" of the type that S. Williams (1980) holds as horizon markers for the Armorel phase. We also include here pearls, at least one string of which was recovered in the 1970s from a burial (Plate 8d). Future analysis will be aimed at pinpointing the origin of the pearls, which we suspect are from fresh-water species.

Lithic Artifacts

Anderson recovered few lithic artifacts from the Campbell burials (Table 6.4), and burial 60 produced almost 79% of the total. Though small, the assemblage is typical of those from late Mississippian period Pemiscot Bayou sites in that it contains triangular Madison points and teardrop-shaped Nodena points, "snub-nosed scrapers," and "pipe drills." Materials recovered by persons other than Anderson include polished adzes, two polished-chert discoidals—one of kaolin chert (Plate 1f) and the other of a red chert (Plate 1e), and a long, thin blade made of a translucent white chert with red banding. Several catlinite objects, manufactured from raw material from Pipestone, Minnesota, have been found over the years, including the disk pipe shown in Plate 1d and two small pieces, one double-cross shaped and the other fish shaped (Plate 1a, b). As noted by Morse and Morse (1983: 277) and Price and Price (1979: 115), catlinite disk pipes are commonly associated with Siouan groups in the upper Mississippi River valley.

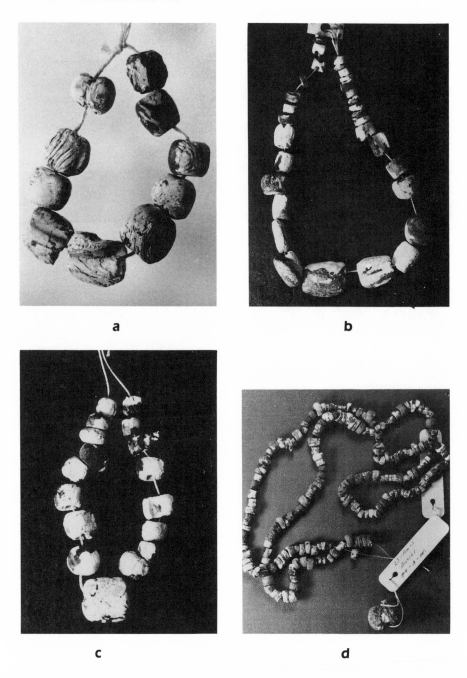

Figure 6.33. Shell artifacts from four Campbell burials: a, burial 113 (necklace of 10 beads); b, burial 83W (necklace of 31 beads); c, burial unknown (necklace of 17 beads); d, burial unknown (1 ear plug and necklace of 212 beads). All originally part of the Anderson collection (Price and Price 1979).

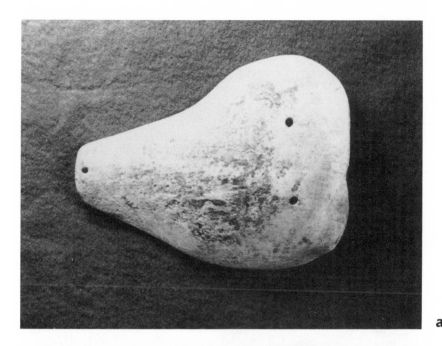

a

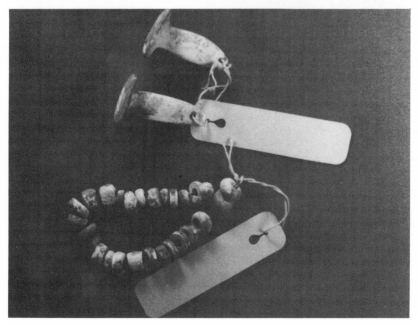

b

Figure 6.34. Shell artifacts from two Campbell burials: a, burial 60W (mask gorget from chest of skeleton); b, burial 28BW (2 ear plugs and necklace [?] of 27 beads). All originally part of the Anderson collection (Price and Price 1979).

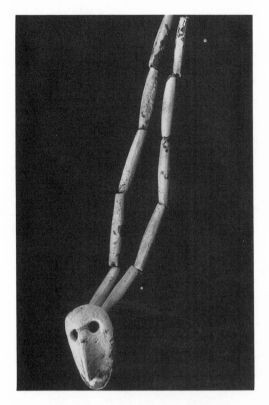

Figure 6.35. Carved-shell mask pendant and 10 tubular bone beads from Campbell. Hathcock collection.

To our knowledge, only two disk pipes have been found in Pemiscot County: the one from a Campbell burial and one collected by Anderson from the surface of McCoy (Chapter 7). The burial that produced the catlinite pipe also produced a large slate disk.

Copper Artifacts

Only five Campbell burials excavated by Anderson contained copper objects, four of which also had other items in association (two other burials that we know of contained green staining and therefore possibly also had copper objects). One additional skeleton from an Anderson excavation exhibited green staining from contact with copper salts on the maxilla and mandible, though no metal was recovered. The items appear to have been manufactured from native ores as opposed to European ores, though it is impossible at this point to determine the source. Copper from the Great Lakes region was being cold-hammered into usable objects by groups across the central United States since at least the Middle Archaic period (ca. 5000–3000 B.C.), though few pieces have been found in southeastern Missouri (the Wulfing plates cache from Dunklin County being a notable exception [Watson 1950]). Future analysis will be aimed at pinpointing the source(s) of the raw materials used to manufacture the artifacts from Campbell and other Pemiscot Bayou sites, which we predict will be the Ste. François Mountains in eastern Missouri. We did not document any Campbell burials that contained both items of copper and items of iron, brass, or glass (discussed in the next section), though at least one burial at Brooks (Chapter 7) contained a combination of brass and copper artifacts.

Burial 50 was that of a child estimated to be 2–5 years old at death (Holland 1991: 254). The burial was located south of the county road (spatial arrangement of burials is discussed later), 18 inches below ground surface—one of the shallower burials at the site. Burial offerings consist of a necklace with 1 rolled-copper bead and 36 beads manufactured from fish vertebrae (Figure 6.36a), a Bell plain bottle, and a fish-effigy bowl. Both vessels lay at the back of the head. Figure 6.37d, which reproduces the page from Anderson's journal describing burial 50, shows the placement of items he recovered.

Burial 81 lay north of the road at a depth of 19 inches, but Anderson did not remove the skeleton from the ground; hence, no information on age or sex is available. The body was interred with 6 tubular copper beads (no photograph), a Bell plain bowl, and a Walls engraved bottle. Figure 6.37c shows the placement of the items.

Burial 82 lay north of the road at a depth of 19 inches, but the skeleton was not removed from the ground; hence, no information on age or sex of the individual is available. The body was interred with 2 shell ear plugs, a necklace of 39 tubular copper beads (apparently hematite-stained on the inside) interspersed with 61 tiny shell-disk beads (Figure 6.36b), a turtle-effigy bottle, and a fish-effigy bowl. Figure 6.37a shows the placement of the items Anderson recovered.

Burial 110 was of a 46–50-year-old male (Holland 1991: 255) and was located south of the road at a depth of 27 inches. Anderson recovered one bottle from the burial; green staining of the maxilla and mandible of the skeleton indicate that at one time copper artifacts had been present.

One other Campbell burial, and possibly two more (discussed below), produced evidence of copper artifacts. A burial excavated in the 1970s contained a thin, 3.9-cm-long rolled sheet of copper; a shell bead from another burial exhibited green staining; and the clavicle of a child from a third burial was stained green.

Iron, Brass, and Glass Artifacts

Few Campbell burials contain artifacts of iron, brass, or glass, but the ones that do contain such artifacts demonstrate conclusively that burials were made at Campbell at least into the 1540s, the time of Spanish incursions into the central Mississippi Valley. Two burials excavated by Anderson—burials 60 and 28AW— produced hammered-iron artifacts, the latter also producing glass beads. Burial 60 was that of a 36–40-year-old male (Holland 1991: 255) and was located north of the road at a depth of 26 inches. Burial inclusions, which far outnumber those in any

a

b

Figure 6.36. Bone, shell, and copper ornaments from two Campbell burials: a, burial 50 (necklace of 36 fish-vertebrae beads and 1 tubular copper bead); b, burial 82 (2 shell ear plugs and necklace of 61 shell-disk beads and 39 tubular copper beads). All originally part of the Leo Anderson collection (Price and Price 1979).

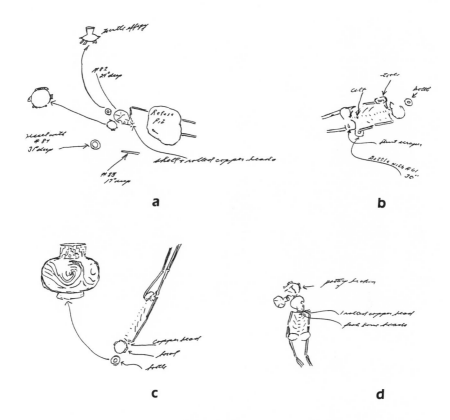

Figure 6.37. Leo Anderson's field drawings of four Campbell burials containing metal: a, burial 82; b, burial 60; c, burial 81; d, burial 50.

other burial at Campbell, are listed in Table 6.5. Three pieces of iron were recovered (Figure 6.38b); Price and Price (1979) state on the catalog card that the pieces "appear to be parts of a knife blade." The bone cylinders (Figure 6.38a) are unique in the burial assemblage; Price and Price note that one exhibited rust stains. They also note that the handle may have been used to socket the beaver's tooth, which could have served as a chisel (the tooth was worked on the distal end). The small triangular point and one of the "blanks" were noted as being "encrusted with rust." The rust on the three objects probably came from being in contact with the iron object that produced the three fragments; all tools were found on the right shoulder of the skeleton except for a polished black celt (Figure 6.38c) that probably had been placed under the body. Anderson noted in his field records that the object had pushed several vertebrae aside from the rear of the skeleton. Figure 6.37b shows the placement of items he recovered.

Burial 28AW was of an 11–15-year-old male who was interred with a neonate (unnumbered by Anderson, who included it as part of burial 28W, but labeled

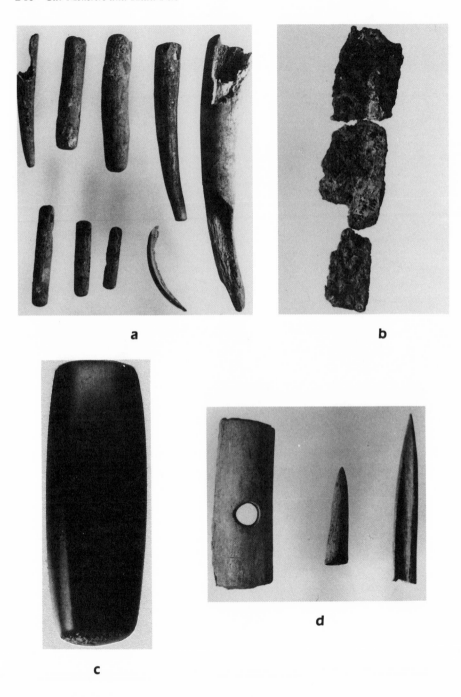

Figure 6.38. Objects associated with Campbell burial 60: a, worked bone; b, three metal fragments, probably of a knife; c, polished celt; d, worked bone. All originally part of the Leo Anderson collection (Price and Price 1979).

Table 6.5
Objects Included with Campbell Burial 60

Bone	Lithic	Shell	Metal	Ceramic
Antler projectile point	Triangular point	Mussel-shell spoon	Iron fragments (3)	Bottles (2)
Awl	Snub-nosed scraper			
Arrow-shaft wrench	Stemmed biface			
Antler flakers (3)	Polished celt			
Handle	Blanks (2)			
Beaver tooth	Chisel			
Cylinders (5)	Hammerstone			
	Sandstone saw			
	Cores/bifaces (8)			
	Pumice abraders (2)			
	Polished pebbles (3)			

by Holland [1991] as burial 28BW). The body had been interred with 2 large shell ear plugs (Figure 6.39b, c), an ankle bracelet of 7 shell beads, and a necklace of at least 175 shell beads (Figure 6.39a). Also recovered from the burial fill were several shell beads, at least 4 clear glass beads (Figure 6.39d), and 4 tubular iron beads (Figure 6.39d). Ceramic items consist of 3 vessels—a tall-neck Neeley's Ferry plain bottle, a bowl, and a bottle (we assigned 2 miniature bottles in association to burial 28BW).

The most significant European items from Campbell came not from Anderson's excavations but from those of relic collectors mining the site in the 1970s. For example, relic collectors have found Clarksdale bells (P. A. Morse 1981; Morse and Morse 1983) similar to the two from a site in western Tennessee shown in Figure 6.40 (see also Klinger 1977b for a Clarksdale bell from Parkin), but the most attention has centered around reports of glass chevron beads found with at least one burial. Rumors that the beads existed have abounded for years, though their whereabouts were unknown. There is no question as to either the authenticity of the beads (Plate 8a, c) or their provenience as being from Campbell. There is, however, some question about the number of necklaces that contained the beads. After they were recovered, the beads were strung in the two necklaces shown in Plate 8, though it is possible that the beads were originally all part of one piece. As currently strung, one necklace contains 18 glass beads, 2 drilled pearls, 11 long shell beads, and 1 carved-shell pendant. The other necklace contains 6 glass beads, 19 bone beads, and 1 large bead of polished quartz (probably from Arkansas). One bone bead exhibits traces of green staining, suggesting that a piece of copper was part of the original necklace. Multicolored, faceted chevron beads have been found across the southeastern United States (e.g., Fairbanks 1968; M. T. Smith 1987; Smith and Good 1982) and, because of their fairly restricted time of usage, are good markers for identifying mid- to late-sixteenth-century sites (M. T. Smith 1983; Smith and Good 1982).

Figure 6.39. Artifacts associated with Campbell burial 28AW: a, shell ornaments (necklace of 175 beads, ankle bracelet of 7 beads, and 1 ear plug); b, c, drilled-shell ear plugs; d, 4 glass beads (top), 2 shell beads (middle), and 4 iron beads (bottom [lower right bead has a third shell bead attached]). All originally part of the Anderson collection (Price and Price 1979).

One of the most remarkable European items ever recovered from Campbell is shown in Plate 8b. It is a brass book clasp that was made into a pendant and was found in association with several large shell beads and a whelk, which together formed a necklace placed in a grave near the mound. A clavicle recovered with the items is from a 5- to 10-year-old child. The pendant has raised strips on one face that partition the surface into compartments. Into these compartments was rubbed finely crushed colored glass mixed with an unknown fixative. The end product closely resembles cloisonné. Similar pieces are unknown from the region.

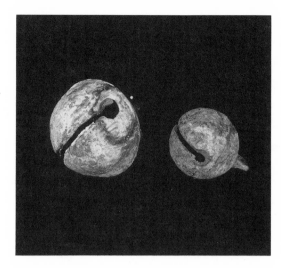

Figure 6.40. Brass Clarksdale bells from western Tennessee. These items, manufactured in Spain during the sixteenth and seventeenth centuries, are similar to those from Campbell and a few other contemporary sites in the tristate region.

In summary, it is fair to say that the European artifacts from Campbell constitute a remarkable set of materials. The quantity of beads is unsurpassed by any other assemblage from the region, though by no means are the beads themselves unique in the central Mississippi River valley. Taken as a whole, and with the exception of the "cloisonné" piece, the assemblage is what one would expect from a site occupied during the time of the de Soto expedition: chevron beads, iron knife fragments, and Clarksdale bells. Unfortunately, the importance of the materials is greatly diminished because of the loss of context. For example, it would be interesting to know if the European-derived items included as burial offerings crosscut all age and sex lines or, based on the skeletons excavated by Anderson, were actually restricted to males. We can, however, use other classes of artifacts to search for possible patterning in burial offerings, a topic taken up below.

Nonspatial Mortuary-Related Dimensions

Several features of the mortuary programs at Campbell are worth noting, if for no other reason than to dispel any uneasiness on the part of the reader who might wonder why certain analyses were not undertaken. One topic that will surely be raised is that of status. Were there large and significant differences among how certain individuals were interred that might reflect social position within the Campbell population? The answer to this question is no. First, as we noted in the Preface, our goal in this volume is to present data, not to speculate about social and political organization. We do not in any way mean to imply that such topics are unimportant, but neither do we believe that the data from Campbell allow us to address the topics. However, we do believe that it is important to search for patterns in the data—data that others may interpret as they see fit. To that end, Holland (1991) compiled a sizable body of information on burial inclusions—who was interred with what—and on burial orientation and location (discussed in the next section).

Figure 6.41 shows that the percentage of burials with artifacts included declines beginning with the 11–15 age group (see Table 6.6 for frequencies). The percentage of males buried with artifacts continues to decline through the 16–20 age group, beginning to recover after 21–25 years of age. Females rebound earlier. While female skeletons also show a decline in the frequency of associated offerings in the 11–15 age bracket, the frequency of included artifacts begins to increase in the 16–20 age group. The percentage of burials with offerings reaches peaks for both sexes around age 31 before beginning a brief decline. This second decline is considerably less severe than the one that occurs in the late-teenage years, with offerings to males beginning to rebound around age 41 and offerings to females continuing to decline until age 46. The percentage of burials with artifacts peaks a third time in the 51–55 age bracket and then declines again. The pattern shown in Figure 6.41 is mirrored by the patterns of specific artifact classes. Ceramic vessels and shell items were less frequently offered to individuals between 11 and 31 years of age than they were to older and younger individuals. Lithic artifacts occur too infrequently to make much out of the distribution. As compelling as these patterns might appear, chi-square tests indicate no statistical significance.

Burials and Vessel Form

Figure 6.42 illustrates both the frequencies of occurrence of single vessels in burials by form and the frequencies of occurrence of multiple vessels in burials by form. For example, there were 53 occurrences of a single bottle—and no other vessels—in a burial. There were 62 occurrences of a bottle-bowl pair—and no other vessels. In all, 85 of the 166 burials (51%) contained only 1 vessel each: 53 contained a bottle, 20 a bowl, 8 a jar, and 4 a vessel of unknown form. Seventy-seven burials contained 2 vessels each: 62 contained a bowl and a bottle, 6 a bowl and a jar, 4 a bottle and a jar, 2 a pair of bottles, 2 a pair of bowls, and 1 a pair of jars. Three burials contained 2 bottles and a bowl each, and 2 contained 2 bowls and a bottle each. Looked at in simplest terms, if a burial had multiple vessels (82 occurrences out of 166 total burials with vessels), the odds were overwhelming (76%) that the combination would be 1 bowl and 1 bottle. There is, however, no statistically significant correlation between vessel-form combinations and any segment of the burial sample, in terms of either age or sex.

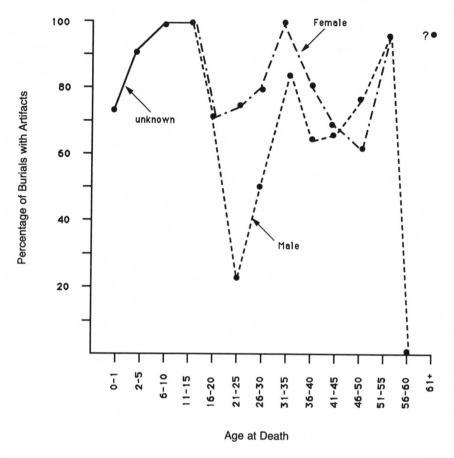

Figure 6.41. Campbell burial offerings distributed by age and sex (after Holland 1991).

Burials and Decorated versus Nondecorated Vessels

In terms of decorated versus nondecorated vessels, females were more likely than males to be buried with a vessel of a type other than Neeley's Ferry plain or Bell plain, but again, the difference is not significant. Neither is the difference between who was buried with and who without effigy vessels significant.

Burials and Vessel Placement

Placement of vessels relative to the corpse varied greatly, and we could find no patterning in the location of a vessel relative to either vessel type or vessel form. Some vessels were placed at the rear of the head, others were placed on or near one of the shoulders, and still others were placed along one of the legs. In a few

Table 6.6
Distribution of Campbell Skeletons with Burial Offerings, by Age and Sex

Age	Sex	With Artifacts	Without Artifacts
0–1	?	6	2
2–5	?	10	1
6–10	?	3	0
11–15	?	4	0
16–20	M	3	1
	F	6	2
21–25	M	1	3
	F	3	1
26–30	M	1	1
	F	4	1
31–35	M	5	1
	F	6	0
36–40	M	9	5
	F	13	3
41–45	M	2	1
	F	9	4
46–50	M	4	1
	F	5	3
51–55	M	3	0
	F	2	0
56–60	M	0	2
	F	0	0
61+	M	0	0
	F	1	0
Total	M	28	15
	F	49	14

instances, a vessel was placed over the face of the corpse. In one case, burial 7 (Chapman and Anderson 1955: fig. 22), a Nodena red-and-white bottle occupied the place where the skull should have been (no skull was recovered).

Method of Interment

Only 5 of the 218 skeletons were interred in a position other than extended and supine. One individual was prone, one was flexed, one was semiflexed, and two adults were bundled. Minor differences among the extended, supine skeletons were noted by Anderson, such as the degree to which the arms were flexed or to

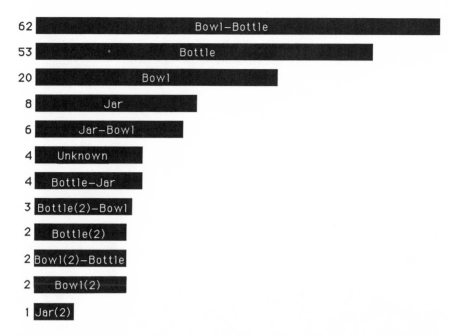

Figure 6.42. Frequency of single-vessel and multivessel burial inclusions at Campbell. For example, there were 62 occurrences of a bowl and a bottle together and 53 occurrences of a bottle only.

which side the head was inclined, but we did not attempt to correlate this with age, sex, or vessel form/type. Several individuals, judging from the constricted appearance of the skeletons, appear to have been wrapped in a covering (such as a blanket) before interment, but without more photographs of burials it is not possible to determine whether this practice was widespread at Campbell. Crews working for Cyrus Thomas (1894) found bark coffins at Pecan Point, which was contemporaneous with Campbell, and in a few places Anderson mentions finding what might have been rotted wood.

Burials and Number of Artifact Classes

Most of the Campbell burials were rather uniform in number of artifact classes present. One hundred thirty-one of the 176 burials that produced artifacts contained a single artifact class (123 of those cases were vessels). Thirty-six burials contained 2 artifact classes (35 of those cases involved ceramic vessels), 7 contained 3 classes, 1 contained 4 classes (burial 50), and 1 contained 5 classes (burial 60). Table 6.7 lists the 9 burials that contained more than 2 classes.

Table 6.7
Campbell Burials Containing More than Two Artifact Classes

Burial	Sex	Age	Ceramic Vessels	Lithic	Shell	Metal	Bone	Clay
23	?	?	2	-	+	-	-	+
50	?	2–5	2	-	-	+	+	+
52	M	30–35	1	-	+	-	+	-
60	M	35–40	1	+	+	+	+	-
82	?	Adult	2	-	+	+	+	-
102	?	6–10	1	-	+	-	+	-
25W	M	16–20	3	-	+	+	-	-
28AW	M	11–15	3	-	+	+	-	-
36W	M	30–35	1	+	+	-	-	-

Skeletal Orientation

The most obvious mortuary aspect at Campbell involves orientation of the skeletons. Drawings of the burials in Anderson's field notes include magnetic-north arrows from which head orientation could be determined for 201 skeletons, though to minimize error we collapsed the bearings into eight compass directions of 45° each: north (338–23°), northeast (23–68°), east (68–113°), southeast (113–158°), south (158–203°), southwest (203–248°), west (248–293°), and northwest (293–338°). Table 6.8 lists the distribution of the skeletons using the eight collapsed compass directions. The majority of skeletons were oriented to the east (40%), followed by north (26%), northeast (8%), southeast (7%), northwest (7%), south (5%), and west (4%). Only two skeletons (1%) were oriented to the southwest.

A Kolmogorov-Smirnov one-sample test confirms the obvious, that is, that the distribution shown in Table 6.8 deviates significantly from random. Figure 6.43 shows the distribution of Campbell skeletons for each point on the compass rose. A similar pattern is evident at the Turner site in nearby Butler County, Missouri, which predated the Campbell site by more than a hundred years. There, almost 78% of the skeletons were oriented east or east-northeast, 8% were oriented west, 7% were oriented west-northwest, 5% were oriented to the southeast, and 2% were oriented to the northwest (Black 1979). In contrast, the pattern of burial orientation at Denton Mounds is almost exactly the opposite. Of the nine burials for which orientation could be determined, four (44%) were oriented to.the west, three (33%) to the northwest, one (11%) to the north, and one (11%) to the east. Likewise, many of the skeletons at Nodena "seem[ed] to be oriented parallel with the nearby slough on the east, on a general north–south axis" (D. F. Morse 1989:

Table 6.8
Frequency of Campbell Skeletons Oriented in Eight Compass Directions

Sex	Orientation of Skeletons' Heads							
	N	NE	E	SE	S	SW	W	NW
Male	8	3	24	1	0	1	3	2
Female	22	5	23	1	4	0	0	5
Undetermined	23	9	34	12	7	1	6	7
Total	53	17	81	14	11	2	9	14

Age Group	Orientation of Burial							
	N	NE	E	SE	S	SW	W	NW
0–1	4	0	1	0	0	0	0	0
2–5	2	0	3	4	0	0	1	1
6–10	0	1	1	1	0	0	0	0
11–15	1	0	2	0	1	0	0	0
16–20	3	0	5	0	0	0	0	3
21–25	1	2	4	0	0	0	1	0
31–35	6	0	5	0	0	0	0	0
36–40	10	2	10	0	1	1	1	2
41–45	4	2	8	0	1	0	0	1
46–50	1	2	6	1	2	0	0	1
51–55	1	0	4	0	0	0	0	0
56–60	0	0	2	0	0	0	0	0
61+	1	0	0	0	0	0	0	0
Total	34	9	51	6	5	1	3	8

102). Coincidentally, most of the Campbell burials, that is, those oriented to the east, also paralleled a slough located adjacent to the site.

But while the orientations of Campbell skeletons were nonrandom, there is no readily discernible pattern of orientation with regard to sex. A higher percentage of females than males were aligned to the north, while more males were oriented to the east (Holland 1991). No males were oriented to the south, and no females were oriented southwest or west. Despite these differences, a chi-square test reveals no statistically significant difference in orientation by sex. Neither is there a discernible nonrandom pattern of orientation by age (Table 6.8), area of the site, stature, cranial deformation versus nondeformation (discussed later), or burial inclusions (Holland 1991).

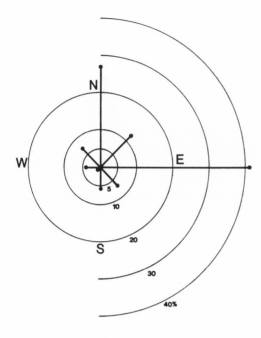

Figure 6.43. Percentage of skeletons at Campbell interred in each of eight directional intervals on the compass rose (determined relative to head position) (from Holland 1991).

Spatial Mortuary-Related Dimensions

Despite the apparent unsystematic nature of Anderson's probing and excavation, we can see several features in the spatial arrangement of interments. As shown in Figures 6.5–6.7, burials tend to cluster together as opposed to being evenly spaced or distributed randomly. Some of the clustering is undoubtedly exaggerated by Anderson's field techniques—probe until a skeleton or ceramic vessel is encountered, then excavate it, in the process perhaps encountering adjacent burials—but some of clustering probably is not. Of the 218 known skeletons excavated by Anderson, 148 were interred within 2 m of another skeleton; 93 of these were oriented in the same direction as at least one neighboring skeleton.

Further, clusters of burials appear to segregate into larger, discrete areas. Figure 6.44a shows the density of burials within a 2-m^2 grid superimposed over the site (burials were counted in the square where the head was located). Aside from obvious clustering brought about through excavation bias, five more or less definable areas of high density are visible. One concentration occurs in the northwestern corner of the site, north of the 534N line; a second is located in the southwestern corner; a third, low-density concentration is centrally located, along the 520N line; a fourth is located in the northeastern corner, north of the 520N line; and a fifth concentration is located south of the road, along the 460N line. The numbers of individuals buried in these areas are similar to the groups of "around 15 to 20 or more" that D. F. Morse (1989: 102) suggests represent "family cemeteries" at Nodena.

Figure 6.44b shows the density of ceramic vessels found at Campbell using the grid system noted above. As expected, squares with the highest density of burials generally also contain the most vessels. Similarly, the distribution of burials with shell artifacts takes on much the same pattern (Figure 6.44d). The pattern changes, however, when the average number of ceramic vessels per burial is plotted by square (Figure 6.44c). The original five large burial concentrations, each centered around one or two dense squares, begins to show some internal patterning, with multiple high-density squares within each group.

Summary

Leo Anderson's excavations of the Campbell skeletons and associated burial goods have allowed us an unparalleled view of a late Mississippian period population in the central Mississippi River valley. We obviously could wish that more care had been exercised in excavating the skeletal sample and that more time had been spent excavating houses and related domestic features such as hearths and pits, but we still have much better knowledge of Campbell than we do of any of the other Pemiscot Bayou sites. The chronological sequence at Campbell possibly extends back into the Late Woodland period, though this assessment is based on the presence of one clay-tempered, Mulberry Creek cordmarked sherd and one Baytown sherd, both in the Chapman-Anderson surface collection. Sherds and complete vessels of Neeley's Ferry plain and Bell plain are abundant, but since those types occurred throughout the Mississippian period, they are not useful in determining the range of years during which the site was occupied. On the other hand, the presence of types that are assumed to date post–A.D. 1400, such as Nodena red-and-white, Hollywood white-slipped, Campbell appliquéd, Campbell incised, Campbell punctated, Ranch incised, Rhodes incised, and Carson red-on-buff, not to mention the head pots and other human forms, indicates a late Mississippian period occupation. And the sheer number of presumed late-period vessels indicates that the post–A.D. 1400 occupation was substantial. The presence of European-derived metal and glass beads indicates that burials were being placed in the ground at Campbell as late as the mid-sixteenth century.

Perhaps the most significant feature of the Campbell assemblages, especially when they are taken in the aggregate, is the tremendous range in material culture generated by late Mississippian period Pemiscot Bayou groups. Certainly no other site discussed in this volume comes close to having produced a comparable group of artifacts in terms of both breadth and depth, although with certain exceptions many if not most of the items from Campbell have been duplicated in collections from sites such as Brooks, Berry, and Denton Mounds. The quantity of material

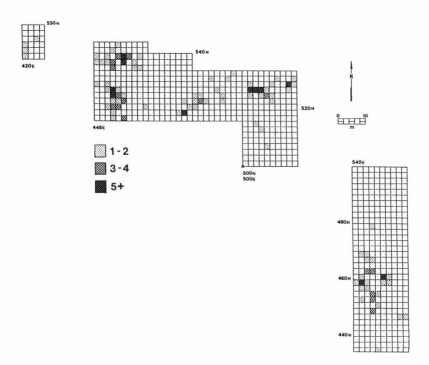

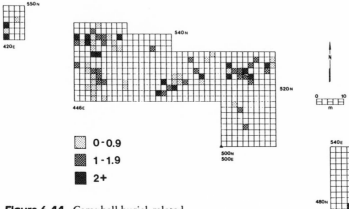

Figure 6.44. Campbell burial-related distributions viewed by 2-m² units: a, burial density; b, ceramic-vessel density; c, average number of vessel inclusions per burial within each unit; d, shell-artifact density. The grid was established during analysis (from Holland 1991) and has nothing to do with Leo Anderson's excavation system.

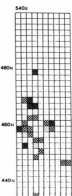

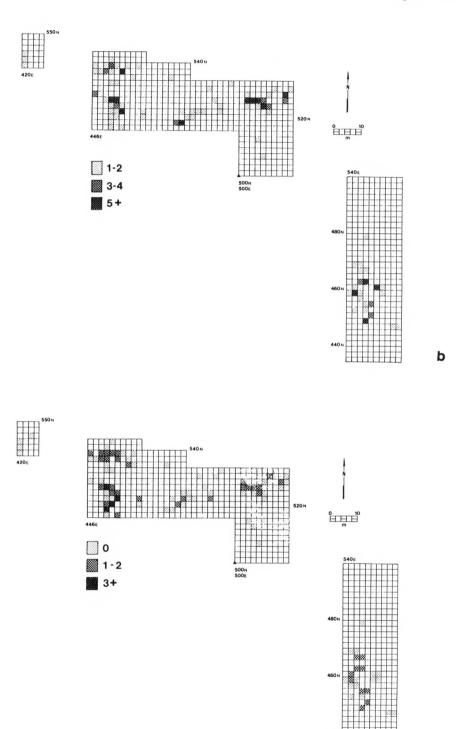

hauled out of Campbell over the past several decades has only strengthened Campbell's reputation as an important late-period archaeological site, but in many ways it has also skewed our understanding of late-period life along Pemiscot Bayou. We strongly suspect that Campbell played no special part in post–A.D. 1400 life as it was played out in the dense swampland of southeastern Missouri, instead being only one of at least a dozen communities similar in size and nature. We simply happen to know much more about it than we do about the others. We examine what we do know about these other communities in the next chapter.

7

OTHER LATE MISSISSIPPIAN PERIOD SITES

Michael J. O'Brien and J. Raymond Williams

Nine other late-period sites in southern Pemiscot County have been investigated archaeologically, though the amount of work conducted at them is substantially less than that undertaken at Campbell, Murphy, and Kersey. Most artifact assemblages from these sites—Berry, Brooks, Cagle Lake, Denton Mounds, Dorrah, Holland, Kinfolk Ridge, McCoy, and Nora Tucker—consist of surface-collected sherds and in some cases materials excavated in advance of land-leveling activities. The University of Missouri houses collections from all nine sites, though in a few instances we lack the dates of collection and the names of the collectors. None of the collections are extremely large, and several are almost too small to be of much analytical interest. In the case of Kinfolk Ridge we are able to augment the sample by using information provided by S. Williams (1954). In several other cases, such as Berry and McCoy, we draw on materials that were in the Leo Anderson collection (as recorded by Price and Price [1979]) and, in the case of Berry, Brooks, Cagle Lake, and Denton Mounds, in private collections.

Seven of the sites—Berry, Brooks, Cagle Lake, Denton Mounds, Dorrah, McCoy, and Nora Tucker—also produced skeletal material, most of which had been exposed through erosion or plowing. Skeletons complete enough and in good enough condition to remove from the sites came from Denton Mounds, Nora Tucker, and Cagle Lake, though only those from Denton Mounds (J. R. Williams 1972) have any provenience assigned to them. Unfortunately, the condition of most of the bone from that site was in the worst condition of any of the seven skeletal assemblages, precluding all but the most superficial of analyses. On the other hand, those skeletons are well documented in terms of general age of individuals, the direction in which the individuals were oriented upon burial, and grave inclusions. No such information exists for skeletons from the other sites. We discuss the burials and, in the case of Denton Mounds, associated grave goods under each site heading but present the skeletal analysis in Chapter 8.

We also illustrate a few items from sites that have never been registered with the Archaeological Survey of Missouri and about which we know very little. Any information we do have comes from artifact collectors and local informants. The artifacts from these sites definitely date to the late Mississippian period and are reminders that there probably are other late-period sites in the Pemiscot Bayou locality that are completely unknown to either archaeologists or relic collectors.

Berry

The Berry site (23PM59) is located on a large, prominent levee remnant, approximately 5 km east of the town of Cooter (Figure 1.4) and just south of an old lake or slough (now called Old Franklin Ditch) shown on the GLO plat of T16N R12E produced in 1854. Soils in the immediate site area are Commerce silt loam and Commerce silty-clay loam. The SCS map made in the 1960s (Brown 1971: sheet 42) marks the site as a "kitchen midden." In 1992 a dense scatter of artifacts covered an area in excess of 3 ha.

The surface collection from Berry housed at the University of Missouri consists of 9 sherds and a handful of lithic items. The sherd assemblage includes the types Neeley's Ferry plain (2 specimens [1 of which probably is from a Campbell appliquéd jar]), red-slipped, Campbell appliquéd (2), Rhodes incised (2), Bell plain, and Baytown plain. However, the pitifully small collection does not reflect the fact that Berry, after Campbell, probably is the best-known late Mississippian period site in southern Pemiscot County, in large part because of the number of elaborate burial vessels that have appeared and continue to appear on the antiquities market. Based on interviews with the landowner, Kenneth Berry Jr., we estimate that close to a thousand vessels have been removed from Berry over the years. The University of Missouri curates 51 vessels from the site, all apparently donated by Leo Anderson except for 2, which were donated by Duff Schult of Caruthersville. We surmise, based on the 1979 date-of-gift to the university, that Anderson gave the vessels to the university shortly before his collection was sold. We know that he did not, however, give all of his vessels from Berry to the university, since Price and Price (1979) recorded an additional 41 vessels[1] in Anderson's private collection just prior to the sale.

Unfortunately, Anderson did not keep the kind of records of his Berry excavations that he did of his work at Campbell. In fact, none of the Berry vessels cataloged by Price and Price (1979) had burial numbers on them, whereas almost all of the Campbell vessels did. Only 12 Berry vessels housed at the University of Missouri have provenience information, and, if Anderson assigned consecutive numbers to the burials he excavated, he encountered at least 76 such vessels. Based on interviews with Anderson, Price and Price (1979: 113) note that "Anderson worked at the site for a brief time in 1965 while it was being looted by others. According to Anderson, because of the rapid pace and extensiveness of the looting, he found it impossible to maintain records." Either Duff Schult joined him for a period of time, or Anderson gave Schult several vessels, since the 2 donated by Schult are numbered "23PM59-25," which is how Anderson numbered his pots.

Several vessels from Anderson's excavations at Berry are shown in Figures 7.1–7.6. The vessels are subdivided by form and type in Table 7.1. It is unknown whether these represent all the vessels removed by Anderson. Many of the forms and types also recovered by Anderson and others at Campbell are represented in the Berry assemblage: Bell plain bottles of all sizes and shapes (Figures 7.1 and 7.2), including the tall, everted-neck bottle with an annular base (Figure 7.1a–d); two Rhodes engraved bottles with Walls engraved designs on the necks (one shown in Figure 7.1c); Campbell punctated bottles with small appliquéd strips on the necks (Figure 7.1h, i); and a tri-faced vessel in which the vessel body is formed by three individually molded human heads (Figure 7.2e). Hathcock (1988: 213) shows two vessels from Campbell (one red-slipped) that are almost identical to the one in Anderson's collection from Berry. The everted-neck jar (Figure 7.2g) is also present, as are small bowls with notched appliquéd strips (Figure 7.3), bowls with effigy rim riders (Figures 7.4 and 7.5), and tab bowls (Figure 7.6).

In point of fact, the vessels recovered by Anderson do little justice to the spectacular range of vessels from Berry, including Walls engraved bottles with two cat-monster faces engraved on the bodies (Figure 1.2), cat-monster bowls (Figures 1.1 and 7.5), a bottle with molded human bones on the vessel body, and a Nodena red-and-white "canoe" bottle (Figure 7.7). At least one head pot also has come from Berry (Plate 7b).

Pieces of at least 12 skeletons, probably excavated by Anderson or Schult, were given to the university at an unknown date. They were heavily damaged, either by plowing or by indiscriminate excavation.

---

1. We have photographs of only 35 of these 41 vessels.

Figure 7.1. Bottles from Berry burials: a, red-slipped; b, Bell plain (note vertical ribbing); c, Rhodes engraved (with Walls engraving on neck); d, Bell plain (with four teardrop-shaped impressions on shoulders); e, Bell plain; f, red-slipped; g, Bell plain; h, Campbell punctated; i, Campbell punctated. All originally part of the Anderson collection (Price and Price 1979).

Figure 7.2. Bottles (a–e), jars (f, g), and bowls (h–j) from Berry burials: a–e, Bell plain; f, Parkin punctated; g, Campbell appliquéd; h, Neeley's Ferry plain; i, Bell plain; j, Neeley's Ferry plain. Specimen d exhibits exterior moldings made to resemble human ulnae and radii and also exhibits scratched forked-eye designs on the exterior. Eight smooth pebbles were found in specimen h; bird bones were found in specimen j. All originally part of the Anderson collection (Price and Price 1979).

a

c

Figure 7.3. Notched-fillet, Bell plain bowls from Berry burials ($2\frac{1}{2}$–3 inches high). MU collection.

b

d

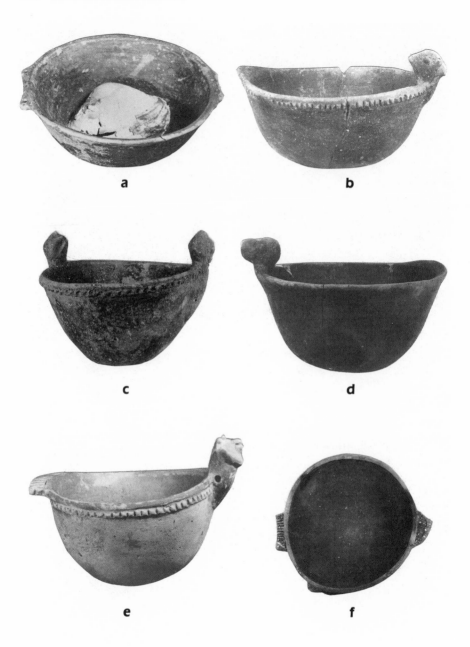

Figure 7.4. Tab (a) and effigy (b–f) bowls from Berry burials: a, red-slipped; b, Bell plain; c, Neeley's Ferry plain; d–f, Bell plain (f with a coarse-paste head and tail). Specimen a contained a large unmodified mussel shell. All originally part of the Anderson collection (Price and Price 1979).

Figure 7.5. Cat-monster effigy bowl (Neeley's Ferry plain paste) from Berry ($3\frac{7}{8}$ inches high at rim). MU collection.

Figure 7.6. Perforated-tab, Neeley's Ferry plain bowl from Berry ($2\frac{1}{4}$ inches high). MU collection.

Figure 7.7. Nodena red-and-white canoe-shaped bottle from Berry (9 inches high). Berry collection.

Table 7.1
Frequency and Percentage of Intact Ceramic Vessels Recovered from Berry, by Type and Form

Ceramic Type	Form					
	Bottle		Bowl		Jar	
Neeley's Ferry plain	4	(9%)	5	(14%)	4	(80%)
Bell plain	32	(73%)	28	(78%)	0	(0%)
Parkin punctated	0	(0%)	0	(0%)	1	(20%)
Campbell punctated	4	(9%)	0	(0%)	0	(0%)
Rhodes engraved	2	(2%)	0	(0%)	0	(0%)
Red-slipped	2	(4%)	2	(5%)	0	(0%)
Carson red-on-buff	1	(2%)	1	(3%)	0	(0%)
Total	45	(99%)	36	(100%)	5	(100%)

Note: Total includes 51 vessels housed at the University of Missouri and 35 vessels in the Anderson collection photographed by Price and Price (1979).

Brooks

Brooks (23PM56) is located approximately 2 km north and slightly west of Cooter and approximately 3 km southeast of Steele, on one of the largest expanses of Commerce silt loam in southern Pemiscot County. The SCS (Brown 1971: sheet 41) mapped the site as a "kitchen midden." Duff Schult reported the site to the

Archaeological Survey of Missouri in 1964. He noted the presence of a single mound, then about 1 ft high, that at one time had supported a modern house, which had been razed prior to his visit. The small surface collection of ceramic material housed at the University of Missouri, probably donated by Schult (year unknown), is listed by type in Table 7.2.

Table 7.2
Frequency and Percentage of Surface-Collected Sherds from Brooks, by Type

Ceramic Type	Frequency	Percentage
Neeley's Ferry plain	7	17
Bell plain	8	21
Red-slipped	8	21
Parkin punctated	3	8
Parkin punctated with red slip	1	3
Campbell appliquéd	2	6
Carson red-on-buff	1	3
Barton incised	3	8
Sand-tempered	1	3
Baytown	4	10
Total	38	100

As is the case with Berry, the small surface collection from Brooks substantially underrepresents the diversity of late Mississippian period vessel forms and types. In fact, Brooks probably is surpassed only by Campbell and Berry in terms of the number of ceramic vessels that have been removed from the site, including several head pots and numerous cat-monster bowls. Hatchcock (1988) illustrates 24 vessels from Brooks, including a red-on-buff head pot (Plate 7e), a red-slipped cat-monster bottle, two gadrooned bottles with annular bases, a square bottle with four slab feet cut in a stairstep design (Figure 7.8), and vessels of the types Campbell punctated, Campbell incised, Fortune noded, and Vernon Paul appliquéd. Figure 7.9 illustrates a bowl with human-effigy rim riders, Plate 6d a thick-slipped Nodena red-and-white bottle with the ogee design, Plate 4a a red-slipped, short-neck bottle, and Plate 7e a head pot.

One unusual item from Brooks is the small, carved-bone owl shown in Figure 7.10. The piece was manufactured from a first phalanx of a white-tailed deer, the artist taking advantage of the natural contours of the bone for the eye orbits, nose, and body.

Perhaps the most important materials from Brooks are not the ceramic vessels or carved bone but rather the European items found in association with the

Figure 7.8. Stepped, slab-footed bottle from Brooks (7$\frac{1}{2}$ inches high). Hathcock collection.

Figure 7.9. Human-effigy bowl from Brooks (4 inches high). Hathcock collection.

Figure 7.10. First phalanx of a white-tailed deer carved into the shape of an owl from Brooks; unmodified phalanx on the right for comparison. Hathcock collection.

skeleton of a child excavated in the 1970s. At least some of the items appear to have been parts of a necklace. Included in the assemblage (Figure 7.11) are an iron belt buckle and tongue (Figure 7.11b, c); two pieces of iron (one probably a knife blade [Figure 7.11d]); a small, brass (rolled) tube (Figure 7.11e); two copper-covered wooden ear plugs; a drilled piece of copper; eight small pieces of rolled sheet copper; and an angled piece of copper (Figure 7.11p). The rolled copper pieces contain plant fibers within the tubes, probably the remnants of the necklace cord. The ear plugs, which appear to be of cypress, are approximately 3 cm long. The extremely thin copper sheets that cover the plugs were folded around the wooden pieces and then hammered down in place. The angled piece of copper was manufactured from a flat sheet that was cut, then was bent, and then had its edges folded over to enclose wood or wood fibers, similar to the ear plugs. Both ends of the fragment exhibit ragged edges, indicating the piece was longer in both directions. Although there is no way of knowing for sure, the piece could have been part of a copper figurine. Compare the piece to the arm of the clay figurine from Campbell in Figure 6.30 in terms of size and shape. Brooks is one of two Pemiscot Bayou sites that, to our knowledge, have produced European goods (the other being Campbell). Future analysis will be aimed at identifying the sources of the materials in the items, especially the copper items.

Several skeletal elements from Brooks, perhaps the remains of three individuals, were donated to the University of Missouri at an unknown date; the remains are so deteriorated that little analysis can be performed on them.

Cagle Lake

Cagle Lake (23PM13; referred to by Leo Anderson in his notes as Kersey II and by S. Williams [1954] as Persimmon Grove) is located approximately 5 km northeast of Steele, on the east bank of a slough of Pemiscot Bayou. The slough

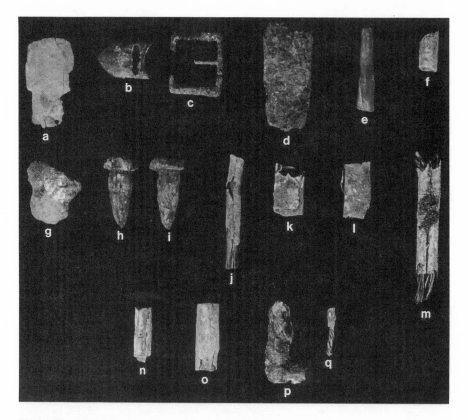

Figure 7.11. Metal artifacts from a single burial at Brooks: a, drilled copper sheet; b, c, brass belt buckle; d, g, iron fragments; h, i, copper-covered wooden ear plugs; e, f, j–o, q, rolled or folded copper (some fragments containing cordage); p, angled copper fragment. Photo courtesy of R. Hathcock.

(today referred to as Ditch 4) is labeled "Pemiscot Bayou" on the GLO plat of T17N R12E produced in 1857, but the main channel was farther to the west, in more or less its current position. Soils in the immediate vicinity are Commerce silt loam and Crevasse loamy sand.

After the site had been chisel plowed to a depth of 15 inches early in 1968, house features, pits, and burials were evident across the surface (J. R. Williams 1968: 106). With help from students and friends, J. Raymond Williams spent a weekend in early spring of 1968 conducting a surface collection and excavating one of the houses. A 6-ft-high mound once stood on the site, as reported by S. Williams (1954: 187), though by 1968 its height had been reduced by bulldozing and years of plowing (J. R. Williams 1968: 106). The mound has subsequently been destroyed; since no map of the site was made, the mound's exact location relative to the artifact scatter is unknown. In 1992 a fairly dense concentration of artifacts extended over about a 2-ha area.

The collection housed at the University of Missouri contains J. R. Williams's surface-collected and excavated materials from Cagle Lake, some of which are shown in Figure 7.12, but the collection also contains four partially recon-structable Neeley's Ferry plain vessels that bear the label "surface level 1/29/65." We have no idea who collected the vessels, but the date suggests that at least three years prior to Williams's visit the site was being plowed deeply. We would also guess that the university does not currently have all of the surface material that Williams collected, since for almost all ceramic types our listing shows lower frequencies than in Williams's original report. We thus reproduce these original counts in Table 7.3. The table lists a number of types, such as Walls engraved and Hollywood white-slipped (with a deep red interior [Plate 2e]), that usually do not appear in surface collections from other late-period sites in the region, a result of the relatively large size of the Cagle Lake collection.

Table 7.3
Frequency and Percentage of
Surface-Collected Sherds from Cagle Lake, by Type

Ceramic Type	Frequency	Percentage
Neeley's Ferry plain	119	27
Bell plain	195	44
Red-slipped	47	11
Barton incised	17	4
Parkin punctated	43	10
Campbell appliquéd with Barton incised shoulder	3	<1
Campbell punctated	1	<1
Walls engraved	2	<1
Mound Place incised	2	<1
Fortune noded	1	<1
Matthews incised	1	<1
Manly punctated	1	<1
Rhodes incised	1	<1
Vernon Paul appliquéd	1	<1
Hollywood white-slipped with red-slipped interior	1	<1
Miscellaneous punctated	1	<1
Miscellaneous incised	1	<1
Miscellaneous engraved	1	<1
Total	438	100

Source: Data from J. R. Williams 1968.

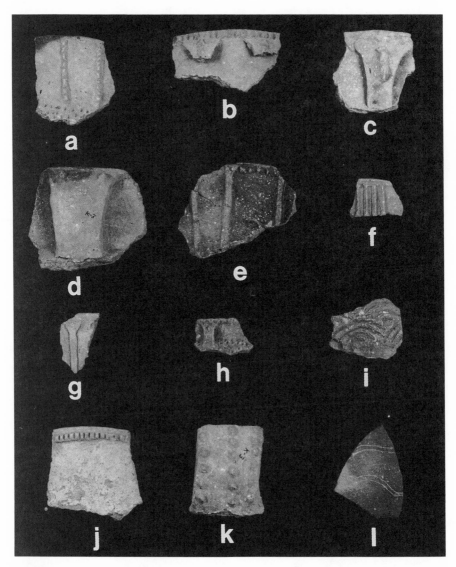

Figure 7.12. Surface sherds from Cagle Lake in the MU collection: a–h, Campbell appliquéd; i, Ranch incised; j, Bell plain (notched-fillet bowl); k, Fortune noded; l, Walls engraved.

Williams's surface collection contains a number of classes of lithic items commonly found on Mississippian sites, including 1 slate celt, 1 basalt celt, 11 adzes and adze fragments, 7 "snub-nosed" scrapers, 7 "pipe drills," 9 Nodena points, 14 triangular projectile points, and 24 triangular points with slightly convex sides.

At some point Leo Anderson acquired two vessels from Cagle Lake that were photographed by Price and Price (1979). One is a small, hooded bottle with the

Figure 7.13. Small bottle with a red-slipped body and white-slipped neck from Cagle Lake. Originally part of the Anderson collection (Price and Price 1979).

hood in the shape of an opossum head. The other (Figure 7.13) is a small bottle with a neck that is greatly exaggerated in terms of its width. The neck is slipped in white, and the body is slipped in red.

Four 10-ft^2 excavation units were placed over one of the houses exposed by chisel plowing. Level 1 was excavated to a depth of 15 inches across the units, at which point the tops of the wall trenches were clearly visible. Level 2 consisted of fill between 15 and 20 inches within the house walls and between 15 and 21 inches outside the house walls (sterile soil was reached at 21 inches). Level 3 consisted of approximately 3 inches of fill directly above the house floor. The square house measured approximately 17.5 ft on each side and had a continuous wall trench around its perimeter (Figure 7.14). The trench, which measured 1–2.5 ft wide, contained the remains of 8 small charred posts (averaging 3.5 inches in diameter), identified by the Forest Products Laboratory at the University of Wisconsin–Madison as red mulberry *(Morus rubra)*. Fired clay (daub), much of it containing cane impressions, was concentrated in the level directly above the top of the wall trench (Figure 7.14). Despite the fact that the fill was not screened, almost 7.4 kg of daub was recovered. Our interpretation of the house construction is as follows:

> The wall trenches were dug, then eight large posts . . . were placed in the center of each wall. A few smaller posts were placed between these. The walls were then covered with split and whole cane mats and clay which fit into the wall trench below ground level. Soil was then placed back into the wall trenches around the posts and bottom edges of the mats. Excavation showed a line of charred cane protruding vertically from the wall trench and daub. When the house burned, the base of the cane mats were charred and preserved in the wall trench. . . .

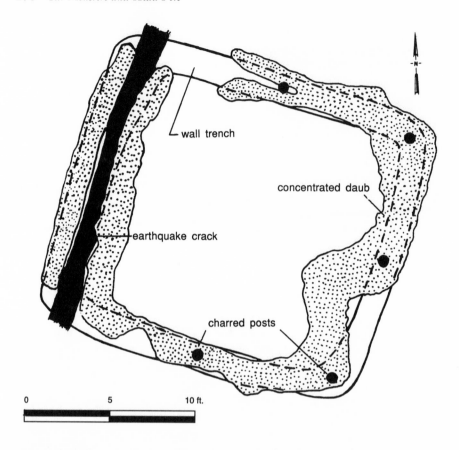

Figure 7.14. Plan of wall-trench house uncovered at Cagle Lake in 1968, showing locations of charred posts, concentrations of daub, and an earthquake crack (after J. R. Williams 1968).

> The New Madrid earthquake was apparently responsible for the disturbance on the west side. There, the daub and wall trench had been broken from the rest of the structure and the area where they had once been, was filled with yellow sand. (Williams 1968: 110)

Table 7.4 lists the frequencies of sherds by type from the three excavation levels at the house. Campbell appliquéd makes up 3% of the excavated assemblage, one of the highest-percentage occurrences of that type on any known site in Pemiscot County. Its relatively large percentage, along with the presence of Nodena red-and-white and Kent incised in the excavated assemblage and Hollywood white-slipped and Walls engraved in the surface assemblage, indicates a late-period component roughly equal in diversity to Campbell.

To determine something about the depositional history of the portion of the site containing the house, we carried out several exercises. Although Williams's

Table 7.4
Frequency of Sherds from House Excavation at Cagle Lake, by Type

Ceramic Type	Level 1	Level 2		Level 3	Total
		Inside	Outside		
Neeley's Ferry plain	189	149	67	54	459
Bell plain	128	65	34	33	260
Red-slipped	5	5	5	10	25
Barton incised	3		15		18
Parkin punctated	23	21	1	5	50
Campbell appliquéd	8	18	3	2	31
Campbell appliquéd with Parkin punctated shoulder		1			1
Campbell punctated		1			1
Mound Place incised	1				1
Kent incised	1	1			2
Ranch incised	1	1	1		3
Nodena red-and-white		1			1
Total	359	263	126	104	852

Note: Data from J. R. Williams 1968.

original report lumped ceramic materials from all excavation units into the levels shown in Table 7.4, the excavation grid can be reestablished using the provenience information on the original artifact bags. We reestablished the grid, and, once we laid out artifacts by horizontal as well as vertical provenience, we attempted to refit sherds from different proveniences to determine whether they came from the same vessels. No refits were made. We then compared all Campbell appliquéd sherds and all Barton incised sherds from the standpoints of paste, surface treatment, and design to determine the minimum number of vessels of each type present within the walls of the house. Examination indicated a minimum of 13 Campbell appliquéd vessels and 9 Barton incised vessels.

Dating the house is problematic, though we suspect that most if not all the ceramic debris was either contemporary with the house or close to it in age. If, and we emphasize the word *if,* most of the excavated assemblage came from the occupants of the house, then the data give us some insight into the ceramic "types" that were in use simultaneously in a late-period site. Certainly other late-period houses in the Pemiscot Bayou locale need to be excavated—houses over which we have better analytical control than the one reported here—but the Cagle Lake house is still an important datum from which to examine contemporaneity of ceramic types.

Somewhat surprisingly, Cagle Lake has produced few intact vessels, perhaps due to the fact that pothunters have concentrated their efforts on the more well known sites. Cagle Lake is known to collectors by the name Anderson used—Kersey II—and when we finally realized this, we did find a few intact vessels in collections, the most elegant of which is shown in Figure 7.15. The vessel shape—a deep, straight-walled jar—is extremely rare in the collections we viewed. This particular vessel, of the Walls engraved type, has two sets of intertwined rattlesnakes with stairstep designs on their backs. Between the snakes in each pair is a swirl broadly engraved into the vessel wall.

Twelve skeletons from Cagle Lake are housed at MU, though no record exists of a donor or a date of donation. The condition of the bone is fair to poor, and few measurements could be made.

Denton Mounds

Denton Mounds (23PM549, also known as Rhoades [Hathcock 1988]) is located near the west bank of Pemiscot Bayou, approximately 5 km west and slightly north of Steele. The site consists of 5 mounds between 3 and 6 ft high (Figure 7.16) and an artifact scatter of at least 6 ha in extent (J. R. Williams [1968: 94] listed the artifact scatter as covering 15 acres). The site is situated almost entirely on Commerce silt loam and was mapped by the SCS (Brown 1971: sheet 35) as a "kitchen midden." As part of the University of Missouri land-leveling project, Williams (1972) excavated three small areas south and slightly west of the mounds in 1967. Excavation areas were selected on the basis of reports of burials and houses made by local artifact collectors and on their potential for land leveling. All three areas apparently were peripheral to the zone of greatest surface debris (south of Area III and east of Area II [Figure 7.16]). Recent plowing and lack of rain decreased the amount of material visible on the surface, and hence only 69 sherds were collected from Area I (35 Neeley's Ferry plain, 7 Bell plain, 8 red-slipped, 1 Barton incised, 3 clay-tempered plain-surface, 9 clay-tempered Bell plain, and 6 listed as mixed tempers). Excavators also collected 12 Nodena points and fragments, 9 Madison points and fragments, 2 celt fragments, and 2 adze fragments.

Excavation of Area I was carried out in 10-ft^2 units (Figure 7.17). Excavation began as a series of 8 units aligned north–south but was expanded as burials and a house outline were encountered. Four vertical levels were used to segregate artifacts: Level 1, the plow zone, went to a depth of 9 inches; level 2 extended to a depth of 14 inches; level 3 to 19 inches; and level 4 to 22 inches, where the artifact deposit ended. Williams (1972) presented artifact counts by level for each of the three excavation areas. We spent considerable time resorting (where

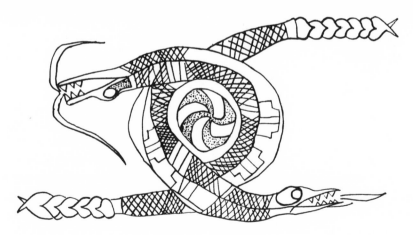

Figure 7.15. Deep vessel from Cagle Lake exhibiting intertwined rattlesnakes engraved on opposing faces (6$^1/_2$ inches high). This vessel form is extremely rare in the Pemiscot Bayou assemblages. Hathcock collection.

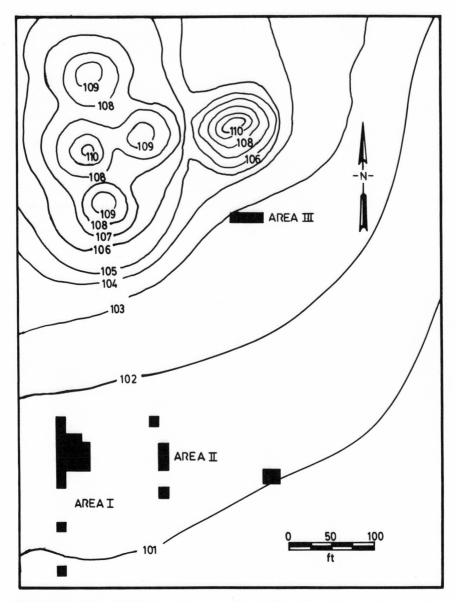

Figure 7.16. Plan of 1967 excavation areas at Denton Mounds in relation to the mounds (after J. R. Williams 1972).

possible) the excavated material into Williams's original 10-m² units to determine whether there was any spatial patterning in the distributional data. Total artifact counts tended to be slightly higher in some levels in the eastern half of the excavated area, but there appeared to be no pattern to the differences. Recounts of sherds from the excavated levels were in all cases slightly higher than those reported by Williams (1972), probably because of sherd breakage while the materials were in storage. We list Williams's original frequencies in Table 7.5.

At the base of the cultural deposit, in lighter-colored subsoil, four more or less continuous lines of charred posts forming a square house were found in the eastern two-thirds of Area I. The rows of posts measured 27 ft, enclosing an area of 729 ft². As Williams (1972: 102) described the outline,

> The wall of the southwest quarter was constructed by placing single posts closely together in a fairly straight line; the other walls were not as exactly built, and often appear to consist of a double row of posts which perhaps indicate repair of the house by adding posts at a later time. A large center post, thirteen inches in diameter, was located exactly in the center of the structure. No other large support posts were located. There was some evidence that the house had at least partially burned as most of the post fragments were charred. The individual wall posts ranged from one and one-half to four inches in diameter.

The Forest Products Laboratory at the University of Wisconsin–Madison identified the charred posts as hackberry *(Celtis occidentalis)*, black locust *(Robinia pseudoacacia)*, and ash *(Fraxinus* sp.); two-thirds of the posts were of black locust. A charred-wood sample from the large center post produced an uncorrected date (M-2217) of A.D. 1290 ± 100 (Crane and Griffin 1972; J. R. Williams 1972). The walls may not have been plastered, since little fired clay was recovered (2,834 g). A diffuse area of burned earth just west of the northwest corner of the structure was interpreted as a hearth, shown in Figure 7.17 in its projected form.

Five 10-ft² units were excavated to the east of Area I, in what Williams (1972) labeled "Area II." The largest amounts of cultural material were contained within a sloping-sided pit that reached a depth of 34 inches below the ground surface. It is unclear at exactly what depth the pit was first recognized, though Williams segregated artifacts from Area II, including plow-zone materials, by pit and nonpit. However, since Williams (1972: fig. 34) originally mapped the contours of the pit beginning at the base of the plow zone (9 inches below ground surface), we used that datum point when we reexamined the materials. We hoped that there might be some stratigraphic breaks in the pit fill in terms of changes in ceramic-type percentages, but the percentages were remarkably consistent throughout the 5-inch-thick levels. Neeley's Ferry plain made up between 75% and 84% of the level assemblages, followed by Bell plain, red-slipped, and other types. The combined pit assemblage is shown in Table 7.6, along with ceramic type frequencies for sherds outside the pit (including all plow-zone materials). The pit also contained 5 complete or fragmentary Nodena points, 6 complete or fragmentary Madison points, 1 adze, 5 bone awls, and 1 bone bead.

Four 10-m² excavation units were placed approximately 50 ft south of the largest mound (Figure 7.16), in what Williams (1972) labeled "Area III," to determine the

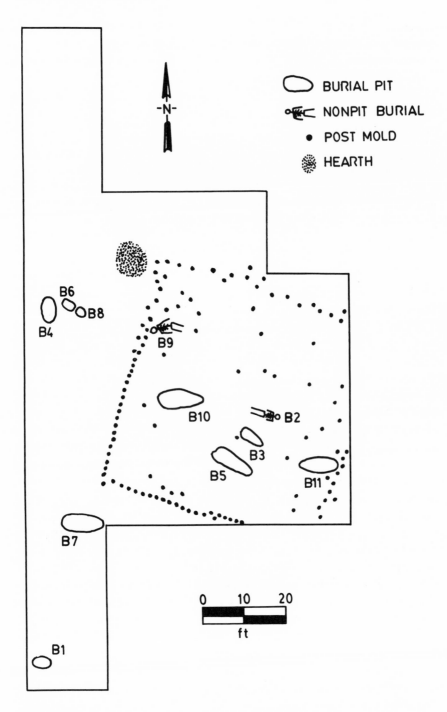

Figure 7.17. Plan of 1967 excavation of Area I at Denton Mounds showing locations of post molds, burials, and hearth area (after J. R. Williams 1972).

Table 7.5
Frequency of Sherds from Excavation Units In Area I at Denton Mounds, by Type

Ceramic Type	Level 1	Level 2	Level 3	Level 4	Total
Neeley's Ferry plain	275	133	89	25	522
Bell plain	24	3	13	3	43
Red-slipped	8	4	9	9	30
Campbell appliquéd	11	3			14
Rhodes incised	2	7			9
Barton incised	1				1
Parkin punctated	7	5	1		13
Shell-tempered, incised and punctated	1				1
Shell-and-clay-tempered, plain-surface	1	1	1		3
Clay-tempered, plain-surface	19	5	5		29
Total	349	161	118	37	665

Source: Data from J. R. Williams 1972.

density of material in a near-mound locale. Material was extremely sparse, leading Williams (1972: 120) to comment that the "lack of material and the absence of any features indicates that the area was not used specifically for living." Sherds of Neeley's Ferry plain (total for all levels = 161) and red-slipped (total for all levels = 34) composed over 95% of the ceramic materials in each of the four excavation levels.

Burials

Eleven burials were found in Area I—9 skeletons in elongate pits and 2 not in pits (Figure 7.18). The skeletal material was in poor condition. Burial 1, of a child, was represented by two teeth and a cranial fragment contained in the west end of a pit 28 x 16 inches and 13 inches deep. Burial 2 was of an extended, supine adult, with the head oriented to the northwest. The skeleton had been damaged through plowing, which had removed some of the bones and had broken a Neeley's Ferry plain bottle that had been placed on the left shoulder. Plowing may have destroyed the pit outline, which was not found.

Burial 3 was of an extended, supine adult placed in a pit (dimensions not given) with the head oriented to the northwest. Two vessels were placed at the head, one

Table 7.6
Frequency of Sherds from Excavation Units in Area II at Denton Mounds, by Type

Ceramic Type	Pit Fill		All Other	
	Frequency	Percentage	Frequency	Percentage
Neeley's Ferry plain	688	78	165	81
Bell plain	123	14	17	8
Red-slipped	22	2	4	2
Campbell appliquéd	16	2	2	1
Campbell punctated	3	<1		
Campbell incised	7	<1		
Ranch incised	2	<1		
Rhodes incised			1	<1
Parkin punctated	7	<1	4	2
Vernon Paul appliquéd	1	<1		
Clay-tempered, plain-surface	2	<1	8	4
Sand-tempered, plain-surface			2	1
Sand-tempered, cordmarked	2	<1		
Total	873	100	203	100

Source: Data, with modifications, from J. R. Williams 1972.

a large clay-and-shell-tempered bowl with a notched rim fillet (Figure 7.19a) and the other a clay-and-shell-tempered, complex-contour jar with vertical appliquéd strips. Burial 4 was of a supine, semiflexed juvenile placed in a pit with the head oriented to the north (Figure 7.18b). The left humerus was extended, and the right humerus lay on the pelvis.

Burial 5 was of an extended, supine adult placed in a cone-shaped pit with the head oriented west-northwest (Figure 7.18a). The pit fill contained over 30 lbs of cane-impressed daub; one long piece of charred cane lay alongside the left femur. Two vessels were found with the skeleton, one a shell-tempered Campbell appliquéd jar lying on the left humerus and the other a clay-tempered bowl on the left clavicle. Burial 6 was of a supine, semiflexed juvenile placed in a pit with the head oriented to the northwest. Grave goods consisted of two square bone "dice" placed beside the left humerus, a Neeley's Ferry plain bottle on the left pelvis and femur (Figure 7.19c), and a Campbell appliquéd jar beside the right femur. Burial 7 was of a supine, extended adult placed in a cone-shaped pit with the head oriented to the west. Two vessels were associated with the interment, one a Carson red-on-buff (Williams [1972: 108] originally labeled it as Nodena

a

b

c

d

Figure 7.18. Burials excavated at Denton Mounds: a, burial 5; b, burial 4; c, burial 10; d, burial 9.

Figure 7.19. Burial vessels from Denton Mounds: a, Bell plain bowl (clay- and shell-tempered) with notched rim fillet (burial 3; $3\frac{3}{4}$ inches high); b, Bell plain bottle (clay- and shell-tempered) (burial 9; $7\frac{1}{4}$ inches high); c, Neeley's Ferry plain bottle (burial 6; $6\frac{3}{4}$ inches high); d, Bell plain fish-effigy bowl (clay- and shell-tempered) (burial 9; $3\frac{7}{8}$ inches high). MU collection.

red-and-white) bottle (Plate 6a) on the left clavicle and the other a clay-and-shell-tempered bowl to the left of the sternum. Burial 8 was of an infant placed beneath an inverted clay-and-shell-tempered bowl within a pit.

Burial 9 was of a supine, semiflexed juvenile interred with the head pointing west-southwest (Figure 7.18d). The arms were parallel to the upper body, and the legs were semiflexed. Two vessels were associated with the skeleton, one a clay-and-shell-tempered fish-effigy bowl (Figure 7.19d) located to the left of the sternum and the other a clay-and-shell-tempered bottle (Figure 7.19b) that lay on the right humerus. Burial 10 was of a supine, extended adult placed in a cone-shaped pit with the head oriented to the west (Figure 7.18c). Two vessels had been placed adjacent to the left clavicle, one a large, shell-tempered bowl with a rim fillet and the other a small, shell-tempered, composite-contour jar. Burial 11 was of a supine extended adult placed in a pit with the head oriented to the east. The left arm had been bent at the elbow and the lower half of the arm draped across the torso near the abdomen. The pit had been widened on the left side of the body to accommodate two vessels that were placed next to the humerus. One is a clay-and-shell-tempered, composite-contour bottle, and the other is a clay-tempered, frog-effigy bowl with a horizontal rim fillet. In addition, two Nodena points and a Madison point were found on the right side of the pelvis, and another Nodena point was found near the left knee. Burial data are summarized in Table 7.7; profiles of all burial vessels are shown in Figure 7.20.

Table 7.7
Summary of Characteristics of Burials from Denton Mounds

Burial	Direction of Head	Interment Type			Age	Vessels
		Extended	Flexed	Unknown		
1	W			X	Small Child	None
2	E	X			Adult	Bottle
3	NW	X			Adult	Jar, bowl
4	N		X		Juvenile	None
5	WNW	X			Adult	Jar, bowl
6	NW		X		Juvenile	Jar, bottle
7	W	X			Adult	Bowl, bottle
8	?			X	Infant	Bowl
9	WSW		X		Juvenile	Jar, bottle
10	W	X			Adult	Jar, bowl
11	E	X			Adult	Jar, bottle

Source: Data from J. R. Williams 1972.

Discussion

Denton Mounds is an important site from a number of standpoints, not the least of which is the kind of grave goods that were recovered. For example, burial 6 contained a Campbell appliquéd jar and two bone dice, which S. Williams (1980) uses as a temporal marker for his late Markala horizon. The co-occurrence of the dice and the Campbell jar suggests that if the ceramic type Campbell appliquéd is a late manifestation, then the dice are as well. J. R. Williams's (1972) analysis of the burial inclusions called attention to the different types of tempers added to late-Mississippian vessels. Among the 15 vessels removed from burial contexts, 6 are tempered with coarse shell, none with fine shell, 2 with clay, and 7 with a

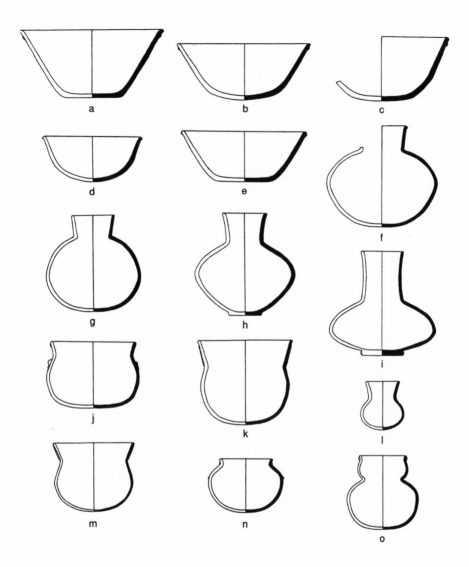

Figure 7.20. Profiles of burial vessels from Denton Mounds: a, o, burial 3; b, l, burial 10; c, burial 8; d, burial 1; e, i, burial 7; f, j, burial 11; g, k, burial 6; h, n, burial 9; m, burial 5.

mixture of clay and shell (J. R. Williams 1972: 132). The bowl found with burial 5 and the frog-effigy bowl found with burial 11 are examples of the clay-tempered type. The former occurred with a Campbell appliquéd jar and the latter with a mixed shell-and-clay-tempered, short-necked bottle.

J. R. Williams (1972: 126) made several comments about the small assemblage of vessels from Denton Mounds relative to the much larger assemblage then available from Campbell (the 35 burials and vessels discussed in Chapman and

Anderson [1955]), though in some cases his conclusions were probably biased because of differences in sample size. For example, he noted that, unlike many of the Campbell bottles, the Denton Mounds bottles on the whole have shorter necks and shorter ring bases (Figures 7.19 and 7.20). But the Denton Mounds bottle sample comprises only four specimens, while the Campbell sample is much larger. He also noted that no Bell plain vessels were included as mortuary offerings at Denton Mounds, though a high percentage of offerings at Campbell were of that type. Based on the published information from Campbell (Chapman and Anderson 1955), Williams's comment was correct, but it is quite apparent from examining the available collection from Campbell (Chapter 6) that Chapman and Anderson identified vessels as Bell plain that Williams would have placed in his *clay-tempered plain* category. He also noted that at Denton Mounds no duplication in vessel shape (e.g., bottle, bowl, or jar) occurred in any single burial, which, based on evidence available in 1972, he viewed as a phenomenon parallel to that at Campbell. However, this pattern is not repeated at Campbell, as demonstrated in Chapter 6. Williams (1972: 153) further noted that, unlike at Campbell, where the majority of skeletons had their heads pointing between north and east, at Denton Mounds 8 of the 10 skeletons for which position could be determined had their heads pointing north, west, or northwest.

Williams (1972: 155–56) made a fairly strong, though, as he realizes, not totally convincing, claim that the structure excavated in Area I served a mortuary-related purpose. The strongest part of his argument that the structure served a purpose other than as a domicile (whether mortuary-related or not) lay with (a) its size (27 feet on a side, 729 ft^2), which is larger than most Mississippian houses in southeastern Missouri (almost 10 ft longer on a side than the house at Cagle Lake); (b) the small size of the wall posts relative to the overall size of the structure; (c) the absence of an interior hearth; and (d) the presence of very little daub (excluding the 30 lbs included in the pit fill associated with burial 5), even though the house was partially burned. Williams also noted that 6 skeletons of adults were found within the confines of the walls (Figure 7.17); children were often buried under Mississippian house floors, but adults were not. He went on to state that the house might actually postdate the burials, which is a reasonable assumption. However, although he did not give the depths at which the burials or pit outlines were first encountered during excavation, numerous photographs in the University of Missouri Museum of Anthropology archives clearly indicate that the tops of the burial pits as well as the two skeletons that were not in pits lay within inches of the level at which the post molds were first encountered (at the base of the plow zone).

In favor of the argument that the burials and the structure were contemporary is the fact that the double line of posts running up to the northwest corner of the structure completely missed the cranium of burial 9. In fact, the inside row of posts curves around the skeleton. Likewise, the posts that formed the southeastern side of the house bypassed (barely) the eastern end of the pit containing burial 11. These facts strongly suggest that either the interments postdate the erection of the structure or the persons who erected the structure knew precisely where the interments were located and took precautions not to disturb them.

The date derived from the charred post in the center of the structure excavated in Area I—A.D. 1290 ± 100 (uncorrected)—is not an unreasonable assessment, keeping in mind (a) that the date is tied to the death of the tree that produced the log (not necessarily to when the log was used) and (b) that at the 95% confidence interval the date range is A.D. 1090–1490. Based on the tight association of ceramic types at the site—types that in the absence of radiocarbon dates are presumed to have occurred late in the ceramic sequence—we would guess that a date in the range of A.D. 1400–1500 is not unreasonable for the structure and the burials. Unfortunately, the date from Denton Mounds is not only the single assay from that site but also the only radiometric date for any site in Pemiscot County.

Items recovered from Denton Mounds subsequent to Williams's work further support a late-fifteenth- or sixteenth-century date of occupation. These include a Nodena red-and-white bottle with a perforated, expanding annular base (Plate 6f), a red-slipped compound vessel (Figure 2.6), and two dog effigies (Figure 7.21), one with Rhodes incised spirals on its side and a Campbell punctated neck. The latter piece was recovered from a burial that also contained two copper-covered wooden (cypress?) ear plugs (Plate 1c) that are almost identical to those found at Brooks (Figure 7.11). Another burial produced the five adzes shown in Plate 1h, which had been placed near the right hand of an adult. The adzes are similar to the four examples from burial 55 at Murphy (Figure 5.24), which also had been placed near the right hand of the deceased. Also found in the Denton Mound burial were a bowl and a bottle, the hindquarter of a deer, and a large bird, which had been placed on the chest of the deceased (R. Hathcock, pers. comm., 1993).

Dorrah

Dorrah (23PM11; also known to collectors as Matthews) is located approximately 7 km northeast of Steele, on the west side of a slough of Pemiscot Bayou. The slough (today referred to as Ditch 4) is labeled "Pemiscot Bayou" on the GLO plat of T17N R12E produced in 1857, but actually the main channel was farther to the west, in more or less its current position. Soils in the site vicinity are Commerce silt loam and Steele sandy loam, both of which commonly occupy areas on the tops of young levees (Brown 1971). The survey form submitted to the Archae-ological Survey of Missouri sometime in the 1950s shows a small mound located on the site, but no trace remains of it. In 1992 a light artifact scatter was evident over an area of approximately 2 ha.

a

b

Figure 7.21. Dog-effigy bottles from Denton Mounds: a, Rhodes incised with a Campbell punctated neck ($7\frac{1}{2}$ inches high); b, Bell plain ($5\frac{1}{8}$ inches high). The incised-punctated bottle came from a burial that also contained two copper-covered wooden ear plugs. Hathcock collection.

No professional excavations have been carried out at Dorrah, and the site has never been reported in the archaeological literature. Our knowledge of the site comes primarily from a surface collection housed at the University of Missouri (at least some of these sherds apparently were collected by Leo Anderson and R. A. Marshall in 1963). Frequencies of ceramic types are listed in Table 7.8, and several of the sherds are shown in Figure 7.22.

The collection from Dorrah spans at least a portion of the Late Woodland period and probably all of the Mississippian period, that is, from before ca. A.D. 900 to after A.D. 1400–1500. The collection is large enough that most of the late Mississippian period types represented in the large collection from Campbell are present in the Dorrah assemblage, including all the incised types. Interestingly, the assemblage contains no Bell plain sherds, which we suppose is attributable to collector bias.

Table 7.8
Frequency and Percentage of Surface-Collected Sherds from Dorrah, by Type

Ceramic Type	Frequency	Percentage
Neeley's Ferry plain	109	40
Red-slipped	7	2
Barton incised	8	3
Parkin punctated	49	18
Campbell appliquéd	23	8
Campbell incised	5	2
Campbell punctated	4	1
Hollywood white-slipped	1	<1
Ranch incised	1	<1
Kent incised	2	<1
Walls incised	2	<1
Wallace incised	1	<1
Mound Place incised	3	1
Fortune noded	1	<1
Shell-tempered, cordmarked	5	2
Baytown plain	12	4
Mulberry Creek cordmarked	20	7
Sand-tempered, plain-surface	14	5
Sand-and-clay-tempered, plain-surface	5	2
Sand-tempered, plain-surface, gadrooned	1	<1
Clay-tempered, plain-surface, gadrooned	1	<1
Total	274	~100

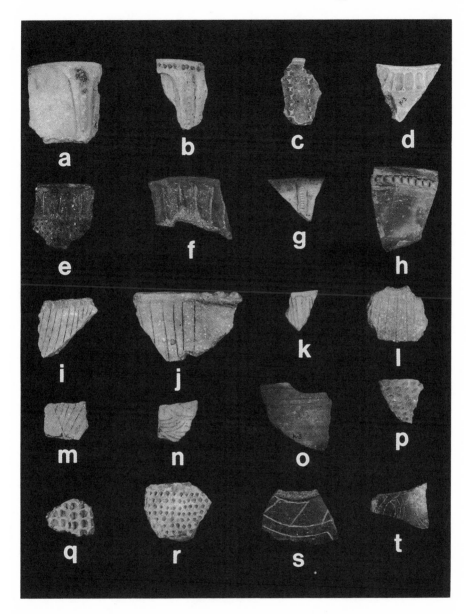

Figure 7.22. Surface sherds from Dorrah in the MU collection: a–g, Campbell appliquéd; h, Bell plain (notched-fillet bowl); i–k, Campbell incised; l, Kent incised; m, Barton incised; n, Ranch incised; o, Mound Place incised; p–r, Parkin punctated; s, t, Walls engraved.

Two skeletons from Dorrah were donated to the University of Missouri sometime in the 1960s. They apparently were included with a surface collection of sherds, which was given by an unknown donor.

Holland

The Holland site (23PM2; also referred to as Machlin and Cooter-Holland Junction [Marshall 1965]) is located on an eroded levee remnant on the east bank of Pemiscot Bayou, approximately 2 km east of the town of Holland (Figure 1.4). Soils in the site vicinity are Commerce silt loam and Commerce silty-clay loam, portions of which have dark-colored surfaces "caused by waste and refuse from Indian camps or by decay of grass vegetation" (Brown 1971: 6). The SCS (Brown 1971: sheet 41) marks the site as a "kitchen midden." Marshall (1965: 16) predicted that borrow areas connected with the construction of Interstate 55 might remove a portion of the site, but they did not. Agricultural activities, however, have substantially modified the site surface, flattening the few sandy rises in the area and exposing a light scatter of artifacts across an area of about 4 ha.

S. Williams (1954: 190) noted that remnants of five mounds were still visible in the early 1950s, but writing several years later Marshall (1965: 16) stated, "It is reported that the mounds associated with this site were bulldozed about ten years ago." Unfortunately, no professional excavation of the site ever occurred, and the only information available is contained in the surface collection made by S. Williams (1954) and in a small surface collection housed at the University of Missouri (collector and date unknown). Williams (1954: 190–91) noted the occurrence of Fortune noded and Vernon Paul appliquéd sherds as well as snub-nosed scrapers and Nodena points, but he presented no totals. Table 7.9 lists the number of sherds in the University of Missouri collection by type. The presence of Baytown plain and Mulberry Creek cordmarked (clay-tempered types) indicates a date of occupation of before ca. A.D. 900, and the presence of Campbell appliquéd indicates a terminal occupation late in the Mississippian sequence.

Kinfolk Ridge

Kinfolk Ridge (23PM15) is located approximately 3 km south-southeast of Caruthersville on an extremely large expanse of Commerce silt loam. The SCS (Brown 1971: sheet 34) marks the site as a "kitchen midden." Very little is known about the site, with the only published reference of which we are aware being S. Williams's (1954: 189) short description: "Two mounds are present on this site. One has skeletons being ploughed out of it so it is assumed to be a burial mound."

Table 7.9
Frequency and Percentage of Surface-Collected Sherds from Holland, by Type

Ceramic Type	Frequency	Percentage
Neeley's Ferry plain	16	40
Red-slipped	4	10
Barton incised	3	8
Barton incised with red-slipped exterior	1	2
Parkin punctated	2	5
Ranch incised	1	2
Campbell appliquéd	2	5
Baytown plain	1	2
Clay-tempered with appliquéd rim	1	2
Mulberry Creek cordmarked	3	9
Sand-tempered, plain-surface	4	10
Sand-tempered, plain-surface, red-slipped interior	2	5
Total	40	100

Note: Includes only sherds in the University of Missouri collection.

No traces of the mounds are visible today, though a light scatter of pottery and bone is still evident across about a 2-ha area. Williams made a sizable surface collection from the site, which is presented in Table 7.10. The only sherds in the University of Missouri collections are five pieces of Walls engraved, which, based on type of design and method of engraving, apparently represent individual vessels. Current residents in the area describe large numbers of vessels, including Nodena red-and-white bottles, that have been removed from burials at Kinfolk Ridge.

McCoy

McCoy (23PM21; also referred to as Chute [S. Williams 1954]) is located along the crest and slope of a large levee remnant, approximately 4 km southeast of Caruthersville. Soils in the site vicinity are Caruthersville very fine sandy loam, which includes dark-surfaced areas "caused by waste and refuse from Indian camps" (Brown 1971: 6). The SCS (Brown 1971: sheet 34) mapped McCoy onto their field sheets as a "kitchen midden." The site was examined archaeologically in the winter of 1968 as part of the University of Missouri land-leveling project (J. R. Williams 1968), though inclement weather allowed the party little opportunity to accomplish more than to produce a sketch map and conduct a surface

Table 7.10
Frequency and Percentage of Surface-Collected Sherds from Kinfolk Ridge, by Type

Ceramic Type	Frequency	Percentage
Neeley's Ferry plain	411	81
Bell plain	40	8
Matthews incised	2	<1
Red-slipped	11	2
Parkin punctated	38	7
Wickliffe plain	1	<1
Unidentified punctated	4	1
Unidentified noded	1	<1
Total	508	~100

Source: Data, with a few modifications in terminology, from S. Williams 1954.

collection. Deep chisel plowing had exposed numerous house outlines and burials, and the locations of these were plotted relative to the contours of the sand ridge (Figure 7.23). The houses formed a U-shaped pattern along the toe of the sand ridge, with the open end to the southwest (J. R. Williams 1968). Thirty-eight house stains were identified, 22 of which could be measured. The measurable stains averaged about 12 by 18 ft, with the long axes oriented northeast–southwest. Some of the houses showed evidence of having burned; others were distinguishable because of the dark organic staining against the lighter soil of the sand ridge. The densest concentration of house stains was on the northwest side of the mapped area, where 10 house stains occurred within an area of approximately 100 by 50 ft. A small mound 2–3 ft high was still present on the ridge in 1968 (Figure 7.23), and a local resident told the field crew that the mound had once been 7–8 ft high and had been pyramidal in shape (J. R. Williams 1968: 102).

When S. Williams (1954: 193) visited the site in the early 1950s, that mound was 6 ft high and 100 ft in diameter. During his visit the field crew was hard-pressed to find many sherds on the surface, and in fact he reports only the presence of Mississippi plain, Bell plain, red-slipped, and Parkin punctated. J. R. Williams, on the other hand, because of recent chisel plowing, collected a wider range of material (Figure 7.24). In his report (1968) he combined his collection with that made by Leo Anderson; the ceramic type frequencies and percentages of assemblage are shown in Table 7.11 (after we examined Williams's collection, we added 1 sherd of Hollywood white-slipped to the list and decreased the Bell

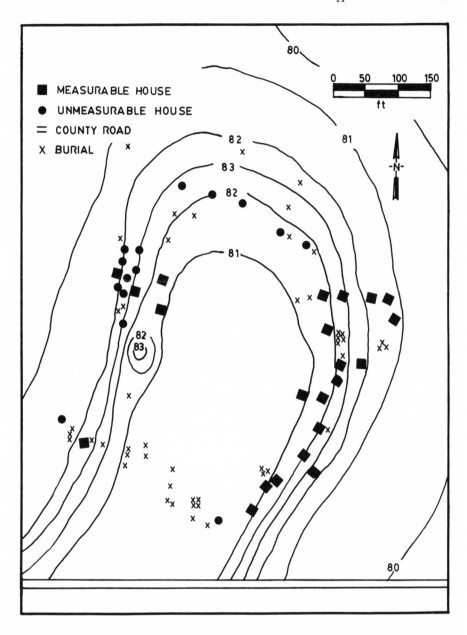

Figure 7.23. Site plan of McCoy made in 1968 showing locations of burials and house stains (after J. R. Williams 1968).

plain count by 1 sherd). Williams's list is one of the few from southeastern Missouri that point out the hybrid nature of the ceramic types. Usually investigators do not make mention of the fact that, for example, a sherd exhibits characteristics of Campbell appliquéd as well as of Manly punctated, or that a Parkin punctated sherd was slipped on the interior side; rather, they usually assign the specimens to one type or another. The problems that Williams encountered in sorting the sherds from McCoy underscore the problem with using the central Mississippi Valley type system devised and revised over the years. For example, two sherds illustrated in Figure 7.24 (h and i) are identified as Bell plain, though they exhibit designs molded in relief. On the specimen shown in Figure 7.24h, small appliquéd strips were added to form a human long bone; the specimen in Figure 7.24i contains two appliquéd strips that form an X.

The assemblage contains no Late Woodland ceramic types (e.g., Baytown plain or Mulberry Creek cordmarked [but see below]), and the 15 established types listed in Table 7.11, comprising 250 sherds (ignoring for the moment the category "miscellaneous punctated"), point to the appearance of McCoy late in the Mississippian period. It is impossible to state unequivocally that all the sherds date to

Table 7.11
Frequency and Percentage of Surface-Collected Sherds from McCoy, by Type

Ceramic Type	Frequency	Percentage
Neeley's Ferry plain	64	25
Bell plain	85	34
Barton incised	3	1
Fortune noded	1	< 1
Walls engraved	2	1
Hollywood white-slipped	1	< 1
Ranch incised	1	< 1
Rhodes incised	1	< 1
Kent incised	1	< 1
Nodena red-and-white	1	< 1
Manly punctated	1	< 1
Red-slipped	15	6
Parkin punctated	49	19
Parkin punctated (red-slipped inside)	16	6
Campbell punctated	3	1
Campbell appliquéd (with Manly punctated shoulder)	3	1
Campbell appliquéd	3	1
Miscellaneous punctated	1	< 1
Total	251	~100

Source: Data, with a few modifications, from J. R. Williams 1968.

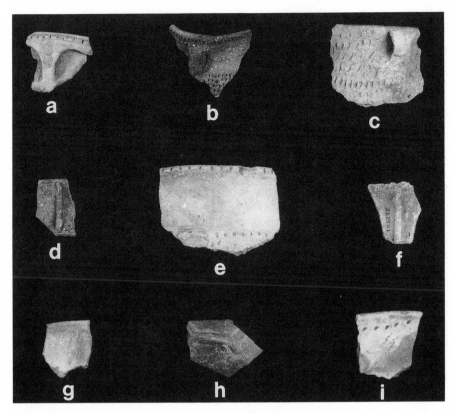

Figure 7.24. Surface sherds from McCoy in the MU collection: a–c, e, Parkin punctated (a, b, and e with nonpunctated necks except for a row of small punctations around the rim); d, f, g, Campbell appliquéd; h, Bell plain with bone-shaped appliqué; i, Bell plain.

the final third of the Mississippian period, though with the exception of Barton incised, Manly punctated, and red-slipped, all the sherds with surface treatment date after ca. A.D. 1350.

J. R. Williams (1968) also listed other artifact categories that were surface collected by his crew and by Anderson, including 5 Nodena points and 7 Madison points, 3 "snub-nosed scrapers," and 14 adzes and adze fragments. Photographs taken of Anderson's collection prior to sale (Price and Price 1979) indicate that he had collected hundreds of Madison and Nodena points from McCoy, along with adzes, shell masks, and numerous bone items (Figure 7.25). His collection also contained several large, presumably Late Woodland points as well as a broken Hardin barbed point, which dates to the Early Archaic period (ca. 7000–5000 B.C.). Early Archaic remains are rarely found in southern Pemiscot County, and we would not have expected to find such remains at McCoy, given its location in what at the time was in the active meander-belt region. We would have guessed that channel movements associated with the meandering Mississippi River would have eradicated levees and bars that dated to that early period. Several possibilities could account for the presence of the point: (a) the levee remnant containing McCoy is substantially unmodified from the early Holocene; (b) the point was found elsewhere by later occupants and reused at McCoy; or (c) the point was redeposited on the ridge by natural forces.

J. R. Williams (1968: 104), as did S. Williams (1954: 193), mentioned a catlinite disk pipe that Anderson found on the site (S. Williams stated that the pipe was fragmentary and that Anderson collected the pieces at different times). Price and Price (1979: 115) note that the pipe is the only known example of its kind from southeastern Missouri, though at the time they were unaware of the specimen from Campbell (Chapter 6). They also document a "sun disc" made from what appeared to be micaceous shale, noting, "These discs are more commonly associated with the large Mississippian temple mound centers such as Moundville in Alabama" (115). It is also almost identical to a disk from Campbell.

J. R. Williams (1968: 102) stated that 48 burials at McCoy were recorded in 1968, though apparently only 4 skeletons were brought back from the field. The burials occurred either as single interments or as clustered interments of 2–5 individuals, arranged in a ring that more or less mirrored the pattern exhibited by the house stains (Figure 7.23). The major difference between the two patterns was the presence of numerous burials across the slightly lower relief area at the southwest end of the mapped area. The large area between the 81-ft and 82-ft contour lines contained 8 individuals and only 4 structures, all within a few feet of that contour line or at the southwest end of the open area.

Nora Tucker

Nora Tucker (23PM552) is located approximately a mile northeast of the Kersey site, on Caruthersville sandy loam. The SCS map (Brown 1971: sheet 32) marks the site as a "kitchen midden." Today, a scatter of artifacts covers an area of about 2 ha. We do not know when the site was recorded or who donated the small collection of materials from it to the university. The large size of the sherds and the fairly intact condition of the human bone, including reconstructable remains of four skulls, leads us to suspect that the material was excavated. All sherds are labeled "G. Fill," which supports this notion.

The collection consists of sherds that span the Late Woodland and Mississippian periods, including Baytown plain, Neeley's Ferry plain, Bell plain, red-slipped, and five decorated types (Table 7.12). Several sherds are from late Mississippian period vessels, including a bowl with a notched rim fillet, small jars with arcaded

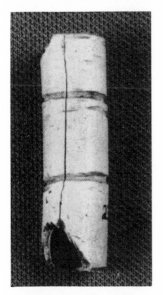

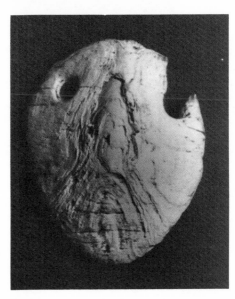

Figure 7.25. Artifacts from McCoy: a, Mound Place incised (left) and Walls engraved sherds; b, cut-bone tube; c, shell-mask pendant; d, small pebble ground and pecked to resemble a human face. All originally part of the Anderson collection (Price and Price 1979).

handles, an annular-based bottle, and two bowls with molded effigies on the exterior walls. The Hollywood white-slipped sherd is from a large jar.

Table 7.12
Frequency and Percentage of Surface-Collected Sherds from Nora Tucker,

Ceramic Type	Frequency	Percentage
Neeley's Ferry plain	10	20
Bell plain	17	32
Red-slipped	7	14
Barton incised	5	10
Parkin punctated	5	10
Campbell appliquéd	2	4
Manly punctated	2	4
Hollywood white-slipped	1	2
Baytown plain	2	4
Total	51	100

Undocumented Sites

Artifacts in several private collections carry provenience information that indicates that other late Mississippian period sites exist in the Pemiscot Bayou locality. We use the term *undocumented* to indicate that we have never seen the sites, not to imply that they do not exist. One site, termed "State Line," is located almost directly south of Campbell on, as the name indicates, the Missouri-Arkansas state line. Vessels from the site include two dog-effigy bottles with Campbell punctated necks (see Figure 7.21a for an almost identical specimen from Denton Mounds) and at least four head pots (Plate 7g; see also Hathcock [1988: 217]). At least one piece of rolled copper has also been found.

Another site, informally referred to as either McKesskell or Braggadocio, the latter after the small town of the same name, lies about 5 mi northwest of Dorrah. It has produced numerous late Mississippian period artifacts, including expanding annular-base Nodena red-and-white bottles (Plate 6e), the red-slipped fish-effigy bowl shown in Plate 5a, the red-and-white conch-shell bowl shown in Plate 5b, at least two head pots (Plate 7d), and a long, thin blade of Kay County, Oklahoma, chert (Plate 1g), similar in shape to at least two blades from Campbell.

Berry II is another locale that has produced numerous vessels, including two head pots, one of which is shown in Figure 1.3. The site is located slightly north of Holland.

A fourth site, unnamed, that is south and slightly west of the town of Cooter (J. Cherry, pers. comm., 1993), produced the head pot shown in Plate 7h.

Although we currently have little information on the size of these prehistoric communities, they have been described to us as roughly the same size as Campbell. From what we have been able to learn, none of these sites had a mound. Undoubtedly, future research will yield evidence of still other late Mississippian period sites in and around Pemiscot Bayou.

8

SKELETAL ANALYSIS

Thomas D. Holland

At one time or another, skeletal remains from 9 late Mississippian period Pemiscot Bayou sites were placed into curation at the University of Missouri, though in a few cases (see Chapter 6) no information exists on who made the collections. All 9 skeletal assemblages were examined for this study, though the type and amount of information derived from the analysis vary considerably among assemblages. The Campbell collection is the largest and best-documented skeletal series, with 138 skeletons and field notes on 218 skeletons. Because of its size, it allows an unparalleled view of the paleodemographic composition of a late Mississippian period group residing in the central Mississippi River valley. This is not to say that the sample is unbiased, as I discuss below, but its size far exceeds anything known from the region with the exception of the combined sample from Middle and Upper Nodena (northeastern Arkansas) analyzed by Powell (1989).

Questions commonly asked about prehistoric populations include: Was there a balanced sex ratio? What was the birth rate? How long did they live? What was the infant mortality rate? What effects did diet have on general health? I attempt to answer these questions relative to the late Mississippian period inhabitants of the Pemiscot Bayou locality. My primary focus is on the Campbell population, though the remains from other Pemiscot Bayou sites offer important clues as well. Where possible I compare my findings with those obtained from examination of other skeletal series from neighboring areas, especially Powell's (1989) analysis of skeletons from Middle and Upper Nodena.

Biases in the Skeletal Series

Any image of a prehistoric population that emerges from skeletal analysis is necessarily colored by a variety of biases. Bias in the skeletal assemblages discussed here has occurred via at least five pathways—burial, preservation, excavation, curation, and analysis—though each has contributed differentially to the findings. The five types of bias and their effects on specific series are discussed below.

Burial-Related Bias

Bias introduced at the time of burial is the most intriguing and potentially confounding type of bias and is based on the fact that, as Saxe (1971: 39) and others have pointed out, "treatment at death is a reflection of the position occupied in a status system in life." Thus any cemetery population, by its very nature, is an imperfect reflection of the living population. Not everyone in a community necessarily warrants disposal in the same fashion or in the same locale. High-status individuals along with social pariahs might be interred away from average individuals, and newborns in particular might not be afforded the same treatment as established members of the community. It is impossible for the archaeologist to control this type of directional bias, yet it is incumbent on the researcher not to be led astray by it.

Preservation Bias

The second source of bias—preservation of skeletal elements—is related closely to the first in that individuals buried in different ways and in different areas may be subjected to different agents of decay. Gordon and Buikstra (1981), for example, have demonstrated the effect on bone of even subtle differences in soil chemistry. Bone of reduced mineral content, such as is found in young children and senescent adults (especially females), may be the most adversely affected. Soil samples taken from the interior of three Campbell crania ranged in pH from 6.4 to 6.6, and no doubt the low acidity of the soil contributed to the fairly good preservation of the skeletons, which, though broken, could be restored in the laboratory (Figure 8.1). Still, Anderson's field notes clearly indicate that many burials uncovered were in too poor a condition to remove. Soil conditions at many of the other Pemiscot Bayou sites, especially Murphy and Denton Mounds, were such that frequently bone could not be removed from the ground without it falling apart.

Differential preservation may also bias a sample by affecting different elements within a single skeleton at different rates. Bones with large surface areas, such as scapulas and ribs, can be subjected to greater chemical damage than those with

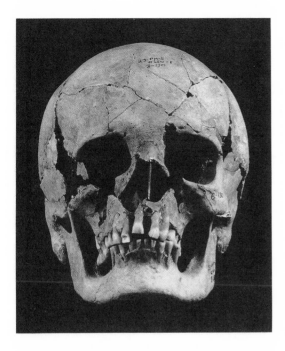

Figure 8.1. Campbell burial 65 W showing excellent condition of the bone and type and amount of restoration.

more compact elements. Smaller bones, such as phalanges and loose teeth, while resistant to chemical breakdown, may be disassociated from the skeleton through the action of burrowing animals and penetrating plants. Anderson's field notes also indicate that a number of Campbell burials were disturbed by later interments (see Figure 6.9). In addition, some bones may be gnawed preferentially by animals. Fragile elements such as ethmoids are more likely to be damaged than are more robust elements such as femurs. Fortunately, most smaller, fragile bones are of less importance in gross biological analysis than are the larger bones.

Differential preservation results not only from conditions of the physical environment but also from conditions brought on by the social environment, that is, how living peoples disposed of the dead. It seems fairly clear from excavations at Campbell, Murphy, and Denton Mounds that by the late Mississippian period the vast majority of the dead were interred soon after death, usually by extending the body in a pit. Chronologically earlier burials, however, such as those at Kersey and some at Murphy, were handled differently. In some cases bodies were allowed to decompose, after which the bones were gathered and either placed in a pit (vertically or horizontally) or, as evidence from Kersey suggests, placed in an above-ground box. The notes from the excavations at Murphy clearly show, as do some of the photographs, that not all bones were necessarily interred when the remains of an individual were placed in the ground. In several cases only the arm and leg bones and the cranium were buried. Additionally, the remains of numerous individuals at Kersey and Murphy were cremated, in most cases leaving behind perhaps a few scraps of bone and a pit full of ashes. Obviously, there is no method of determining the age or sex of cremated individuals. Further, if cremation was, for a time, the most-used method of disposing of the dead, regardless of age and sex, then we are missing a large piece of information for that time period.

Excavation Bias

The third, and perhaps most serious, form of bias is that introduced by the excavator (see Schiffer 1987). Archaeologists attempt to minimize and control this form of bias through the use of probability sampling, but no Pemiscot Bayou skeletal assemblage was recovered through a probabilistic sampling program. Certainly at Campbell male and female skeletons had an equal probability of being detected with a probe, as did burials with and without ceramic-vessel burial inclusions (53 of the 218 burials had no grave associations).[1] However, the age of individuals recovered appears to be strongly biased by the probing technique, with infants and children, because of their small size, being underrepresented (Holland 1991: 91). The Campbell skeletal assemblage thus represents a sample of unknown proportion and representativeness, drawn from a much larger cemetery population. Likewise, there appears to be no reason to suspect that the second-largest assemblage, that from Murphy, is biased toward individuals of either sex, since large areas were opened and all visible skeletons were excavated.

Removal and Curation Bias

The fourth bias, introduced through activities associated with the removal and curation of skeletal material, clearly affects all the skeletal series. For example, not all of the 218 Campbell skeletons excavated by Anderson were removed and curated. Many were left in the ground, and only portions of others were removed. In addition, it is not altogether clear how many skeletons were at one time curated at the University of Missouri. Records are imprecise, and in many cases skeletons were commingled so that two individuals were assigned a single collection accession number. In 1965, when Cole (1965) examined the Campbell crania, Anderson had excavated 144 burials, but only 104 skeletons were available for study. Presently, parts of 138 (63% of the skeletons Anderson excavated) provenienced skeletons are curated. Anderson's field records do not indicate any pattern to which skeletons were removed and which were left in the ground, and I assume the curated remains are representative of the total.

Powell (1989) faced a similar, though more exaggerated, problem in her analysis of skeletal material from Nodena. Over 1,775 burials had been excavated

---

1. This figure was erroneously reported as 46 in Holland 1991.

at Upper Nodena, but only 159 skeletons (9%) were available for analysis. Combined with the skeletal material from Middle Nodena, the total sample available to Powell was 228 (12%) out of 1,844 skeletons. Of those 228, 49 (22%) were represented by crania only. One hundred twelve (81%) of the 138 curated skeletons from Campbell have cranial elements. Forty individuals (29%) are represented by skulls (occasionally with cervical vertebrae) alone. Eighty-four (61%) have lower-limb elements, and 80 (58%) have upper-limb members. Similarly, 71% of the skeletons from Murphy have cranial elements (26% of all Murphy skeletons are represented only by crania or cranial fragments), 66% have lower-limb elements, and 57% have upper-limb elements.

Larger bones are more likely to be deemed important and thus to be collected, and it is clear that crania and limb bones were the elements most likely to be removed from the Pemiscot Bayou sites. For the Campbell series, we might expect that since Anderson did not employ a screen during excavation, smaller elements would have been recovered less frequently than larger bones. However, at least 42 skeletons have hyoid bones associated with them, and at least 4 produced fragments of ossified thyroid cartilage—small, nondescript elements commonly overlooked under the best of conditions.

An additional bias has been introduced into at least the Campbell assemblage, in this case by an unidentified agent. Of 81 intact femurs (the largest bone in the human body) in curation, 59 (73%) are from the right side, while only 22 (27%) are from the left. This is in sharp contrast to the 112 tibias, 57 (51%) of which are right and 55 (49%) left (Holland 1991: table 5.7). If we assume that Anderson recovered femurs and tibias from both right and left sides in approximately equal proportions, then we are left with the conclusion that femurs in general, and left femurs in particular, have been culled from the curated specimens, probably for use as laboratory specimens in human-osteology classes[2] or for use in research.

Analytical Bias

Effects of the fifth bias, that introduced during analysis, can be minimized by applying the same procedures to all skeletons equally and by taking a conservative approach to estimates of such dimensions as age, sex, and stature. For the most part, the Pemiscot Bayou skeletons show a marked dimorphism in secondary sex-linked characteristics, which greatly facilitated analysis. Skeletons of males often are as exceptionally robust as those of females are gracile. Sex determination could generally be made on the basis of two or more elements, especially the cranium and the pelvis. Age estimates used here are conservative: No individual was assessed an age unless the indicators were relatively unambiguous, and age

---

2. This practice has subsequently been prohibited under curation policy.

estimates were placed within 5-year intervals (e.g., 21–25 years of age) to bracket error. For most skeletons, age could be assessed from several indicators; however, dental wear was weighted most heavily for three reasons: (a) a majority of the provenienced, curated skeletons contain teeth; (b) the dental wear patterns appear to be fairly uniform; and (c) dental wear has been shown to be a reliable indicator of age (e.g., Lovejoy 1985). I employed Black's (1979) attrition table, established for a nearby Mississippian population, in age assessment.

The Skeletal Sample

Table 8.1 lists the number of known skeletons (many are not complete) from each of the 9 sites and the number of skeletons used in this analysis. It is important to understand exactly what this last number represents. For example, Anderson's notes indicate that he excavated at least 218 skeletons at Campbell, though there are currently only 138 skeletons in the University of Missouri collections (Chapter 6). J. R. Williams (1972) excavated 11 skeletons at Denton Mounds (Chapter 7), but only 2 were complete enough that they could be used in this analysis. Likewise, notes and excavation forms, along with analysis of the forms, indicate that the remains of 89 individuals were uncovered at Murphy (Chapter 5). However, the great majority of these bones were left in the ground because of their poor condition, and thus I examined only 35 skeletons, all of which were greatly deteriorated. At McCoy, J. R. Williams (1968) plotted the locations of 48 "burials" (Chapter 7), which I am taking to be individuals. The remains of four individuals are in the University of Missouri collections, and I assume they were part of Williams's 48 burials. I have no information on the other sites in terms of numbers of skeletons excavated, so the entries under the categories "number of skeletons" and "number analyzed" are the same.

It is also important to note that because of the poor condition of much of the skeletal material and the fact that not all elements of each skeleton were recovered, the number of individual skeletons (more precisely, the number of skeletal elements) available for different analyses varies considerably. For example, the Campbell assemblage contains the remains of 138 individuals, but I restricted my determinations of sex to adults, that is, individuals aged 16 and up (106 individuals), thus excluding 32 skeletons. Of the remains of the 106 adults, only those from 72 individuals could be used reliably to examine stature. Further, only 90 of those 106 skeletons had retained enough crania to be useful in examining cranial deformation. In short, samples used in each analysis are subsets of the larger skeletal assemblages.

In the following discussion I focus on the skeletal series from Campbell simply because it is the largest assemblage. Under many of the topics I present two tables, one exclusively for the Campbell series and one that includes the Campbell

Table 8.1
Number of Skeletons from Pemiscot Bayou Sites and Number Used in Analysis

Site	Number Documented	Number Used
Berry	12	12
Brooks	1	1
Cagle Lake	9	9
Campbell	218	138
Denton Mounds	11	2
Dorrah	2	2
McCoy	48	4
Murphy	89	35
Nora Tucker	6	6
Total	396	209

skeletons along with those from other Pemiscot Bayou sites. In some places I include a table that compares a trait frequency within the Pemiscot Bayou series against frequencies in other Mississippian-period skeletal series, especially those from Middle and Upper Nodena (Powell 1989). Most of the Campbell data are excerpted from Holland's (1991) in-depth examination of the skeletons, and interested readers are urged to consult that treatment for specific details on measurements of individual skeletal elements and especially on pathological indicators.

Demographic Profile

Paleodemographic analysis depends on a fairly large sample, accurate and unbiased age and sex estimates, and some knowledge of the rate of increase in the population. The resulting model is only as accurate as those demographic estimates. Of the nine Pemiscot Bayou assemblages, only the Campbell sample begins to meet these three criteria, though even it probably is biased against children and perhaps, given the possibility that a few individuals were buried in the mound (Chapter 6), is biased against elite individuals as well. One way to measure the degree to which a sample—here the Campbell assemblage—meets a normal distribution is to plot its profile and then compare the profile to profiles of other samples that are judged to be less biased. Pronounced deviations between the profile under study and the external baseline profile then can be attributed either to sample bias or to some "culturally induced" bias of which we are unaware. If it can somehow be demonstrated that the profile is not a result of sample bias—and in the Pemiscot Bayou samples this would, in most cases, be difficult to demon-strate—then further site examinations should be centered on understanding the reasons for the bias (e.g., segments of the population were being cremated or disposed of in off-site areas).

When constructing a model of a population from a skeletal series, it can be assumed that the living population was stable at the time the skeletons entered the ground. The theory of stable populations assumes that a population is infinitely large, is closed to migration, and has fixed rates of fertility and mortality at each age (Weiss 1973). The model developed below further assumes a growth rate of zero, so the birth rate equals the mortality rate. Even if the actual growth rate was not zero but merely close to it, the stationary model will not be much in error, especially if the sample is drawn from several generations (Sattenspiel and Harpending 1983; Weiss 1973; Weiss and Smouse 1976).

Age and Sex Distribution

Given the excellent state of bone preservation and Anderson's thoroughness in recovery, 128 of the 138 skeletons from Campbell include enough elements to allow me to place the individuals in 5-year age brackets. I determined the sexes of the 106 individuals aged 16 and over; the distribution of analyzed skeletons by sex and age is shown in Figure 8.2. The most striking feature of the composite profile is the low number of adult males (43) compared to that of adult females (63) (a sex ratio of 68.25). Table 8.2 lists the adult sex ratio by age group (males/females x 100) and the sex ratios for a Campbell population standardized to a radix of 100 females and 100 males. As noted above, Weiss (1973) argues that an unbiased sex ratio should approximate 50%, that is, a sex ratio of 100.00, but the Campbell population is biased systematically in favor of females. Inter-estingly, Powell (1989) obtained an adult sex ratio almost identical to that from Campbell for the Upper and Middle Nodena sites (71.43; 80 males to 112 females). The Nodena sample yields a sex ratio of 56.45 for adults aged 18–30 and 85.37 for adults over 30 years of age. This compares to 64.71 and 71.74 for the same age classes at Campbell. Based on examination of sample bias in the Nodena assemblage, Powell concluded that the Nodena sex ratio is probably accurate. Powell (1988) also found a lower sex ratio at Moundville, Alabama, though not as low as those at Campbell or Nodena. Of 536 adults that could be sexed reliably, 296 were classed as females, compared to 240 classed as males—a sex ratio of 81.08. It remains a distinct possibility, then, that the sex ratio seen at Campbell may be a result of the Campbell population's lifeway rather than a result of bias introduced through excavation, curation, or analysis.

The skeletal samples from the other seven sites are too small to model any demographic profiles, though a few basic parameters can be generated, such as

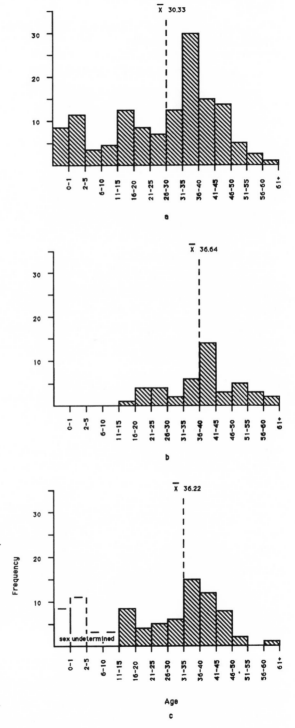

Figure 8.2. Demographic profiles of the Campbell skeletal sample population: a, total sample population (n = 128); b, adult males (n = 43 [the individual in the 11–15-year range was included as an adult since it was judged to be on the line between that range and the 16–20-year range); c, adult females (n = 63) and juveniles (sex undetermined [n = 28]) (after Holland 1991).

Table 8.2
Adult Sex Ratio and Standardized Sex Ratio for the Campbell Skeletal Series, by Age Group

Age Group	Males	Females	Ratio	Standardized[a] Males	Standardizeda Females	Ratio
16–20	4	8	50.00	9	13	69.23
21–25	4	4	100.00	9	6	150.00
26–30	2	5	40.00	5	8	62.50
31–35	6	6	100.00	14	10	140.00
36–40	14	16	87.50	33	25	132.00
41–45	3	13	23.08	7	21	33.33
46–50	5	8	62.50	12	13	92.31
51–55	3	2	150.00	7	3	233.33
56–60	2	0	. . . .	5	0	. . . .
61+	0	1	0.00	0	2	0.00

[a] Assumes a radix of 100 females and 100 males.

Table 8.3
Average Adult Age at Death and Male Sex Ratio for Seven Pemiscot Bayou Skeletal Series

Site	Number	Age	Standard Deviation	Sex Ratio
Berry	12	37.1	5.82	140.0
Cagle Lake	9	35.8	10.00	125.0
Campbell	106	36.3[a]	11.10	68.2
Dorrah	2	46.3	12.40	100.0
McCoy	4	35.0	2.89	300.0
Murphy	20	38.3[b]	8.90	81.8
Nora Tucker	6	36.7	10.70	500.0

[a] Compare the age at death for Campbell adults (36.3) with the average age at death of all Campbell individuals (30.3).

[b] Compare the age at death for Murphy adults (38.3) with the average age at death of all Murphy individuals (31.1).

mean adult age at death (discussed in the following section) and the adult-male sex ratio (Table 8.3).

Survivorship and Mortality

Several features are readily apparent in the age-sex profile shown in Figure 8.2, which is reproduced in Figure 8.3 in terms of percentage for only those individuals

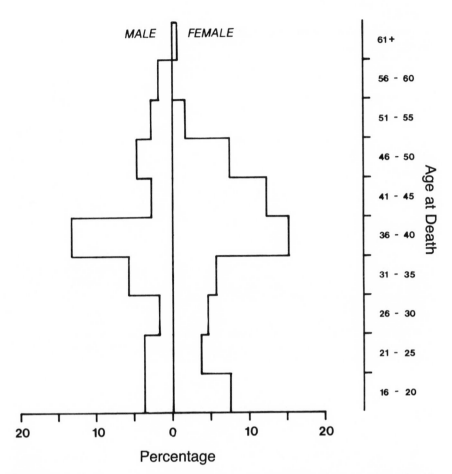

Figure 8.3. Population pyramid constructed from Campbell adult skeletons (after Holland 1991).

aged 16 or older at death. Mortality appears to have been high during the first several years of life at Campbell, again in the late teenage years—especially for females—and again in the late thirties. While females outnumber males after the 36–40 age group, a Kolmogorov-Smirnov test indicates no statistical significance to this pattern. Population parameters that are more specific, such as life expectancy, can be drawn from the life table assembled for the Campbell population (Table 8.4).

Table 8.3 compares the average adult ages at death for 7 of the Pemiscot Bayou skeletal assemblages (those from Denton Mounds and Brooks are excluded). Of those, only the assemblage from Dorrah exhibits a mean age at death above 38.3. All the sites, however, have overlapping mean ages at one standard deviation, and

Table 8.4
Abridged Life Table Based on the Campbell Skeletal Series

x[a]	D(x)	d(x)	l'(x)	l(x)	L(x)	T(x)	e(x)	q(x)	C(x)
0	19	14.8	128	100.0	462.9	2988.3	29.9	.148	15.5
5	3	2.3	109	85.2	419.9	2525.4	29.7	.028	14.1
10	4	3.1	106	82.8	406.3	2105.5	25.4	.038	13.6
15	12	9.4	102	79.7	375.0	1699.2	21.3	.118	12.6
20	8	6.3	90	70.3	335.9	1324.2	18.8	.089	11.2
25	7	5.5	82	64.1	306.6	988.3	15.4	.085	10.3
30	8	6.3	75	58.6	277.3	681.6	11.6	.107	9.3
35	30	23.4	67	52.3	203.1	404.3	7.7	.448	7.0
40	16	12.5	37	28.9	113.3	201.2	7.0	.432	3.8
45	13	10.2	21	16.4	56.7	87.9	5.4	.619	1.9
50	5	3.9	8	6.3	21.5	31.2	5.0	.626	.7
55	2	1.6	3	2.3	7.8	9.8	4.2	.667	.3
60	1	0.8	1	0.8	2.0	2.0	2.5	1.000	.1
65	0	0.0	0	0.0	0.0	0.0	0.0	1.000	0

[a] Symbols: x, age in years; D(x) absolute number of individuals dead at age x; d(x) percentage of individuals dead at age x; l'(x) absolute number of survivors to age x; l(x) number of survivors to age x with a radix of 100; L(x) number of person years in age class x; T(x) total person years lived by population to age x before all are dead; e(x) life expectancy at age x; q(x) probability of death in succeeding age class for individuals reaching age x; C(x) percentage of individuals in age class x.

the differences probably reflect small samples and inherent sample biases rather than any demographic reality.

More interesting is Table 8.5, which shows computed population parameters for the general population at Campbell and compares them to those from four other populations (discussed below). Examining just the statistics for Campbell, we see that the crude mortality rate is 33.5 per 100 individuals. Life expectancy at birth is approximately 30 years, close to the average age at death, declining to just over 21 years at age 15 (in other words, a 15-year-old could expect to live another 21 years). The survivorship curve for Campbell (Figure 8.4) shows a steep initial drop followed by a less steep decline between ages 6 and 19. There then follows a moderately steep decline until age 35, when the curve dips rapidly. Separating the curve into adult male and adult female components (Figure 8.5) reveals that survivorship is similar for the sexes, with females outsurviving males between the ages of 35 and 45, when the curve for females dips below that for males. Life expectancy at age 15 for females is 20.8 and for males is 21.6. Life expectancy for males in their late thirties and forties likewise is greater than that for females. Only from age 50 on do females have an appreciably greater life expectancy.

Table 8.5
Comparison of Demographic Parameters for Campbell, Moundville, Carlston Annis, Klunk-Gibson, and Turner

Demographic Parameter	Campbell	Moundville	Carlston Annis	Klunk-Gibson	Turner
Adult sex ratio (M:F)	68.2	81.1	98.0	100.6	47.8
Fertility					
Crude birth rate	33.5	37.0	45.0	33.9	43.5
Mean family size	2.5	2.5	3.3	3.0	3.3
Gross reproductive rate	1.8	1.9	2.7	1.7	2.6
Generation length	27.2	26.1	26.6	27.8	26.7
Mortality					
Crude death rate	33.5	37.0	45.0	33.9	43.5
Life expectancy at birth	29.9	28.1	22.4	29.5	23.0
Life expectancy at age 15	21.3	18.8	19.4	26.7	20.4
Proportion <15 years	20.3	19.5	38.4	32.4	39.1
Proportion 15–50 years	73.5	74.7	52.8	47.2	52.1
Proportion >50 years	6.3	5.9	8.8	20.4	8.8
Proportion D30+/D5+	0.7	0.6	0.5	0.7	0.5
Adult survivorship	7.8	7.3	14.3	30.2	14.5
Dependency ratio	0.4	0.3	0.9	1.2	0.9

Sources: Moundville data from Powell 1988; Carlston Annis data from Mensforth 1990; Klunk-Gibson data from Buikstra 1976; Turner data from Black 1979.

The Campbell mortality curve (plotted logarithmically in Figure 8.6), on the other hand, reveals that female mortality begins a gradual increase at age 20, while male mortality assumes a typical pattern—dropping between ages 20 and 25 before accelerating dramatically over the subsequent decade. After age 35 male mortality drops shortly and then increases steadily. Why female mortality fails to show a strong peak at the onset of the childbearing years (rather than a slow increase) is unclear.

The other 4 sites against which the Campbell demographic parameters are contrasted in Table 8.5 are diverse in geographical and chronological terms, and all have yielded large skeletal samples. Moundville is a large Mississippian ceremonial center in west-central Alabama and is exceeded in size only by Cahokia, located in the American Bottom area of western Illinois. Of the over 3,000 burials excavated at Moundville, Powell (1988) used 564 skeletons to construct her demographic tables. Carlston Annis, in western Kentucky, is a large Archaic site radiocarbon dated to ca. 2500–1000 B.C. The associated cemetery yielded 354 individuals ranging in age from 7 months to over 70 years (Mensforth 1990). Another sizable, well-documented skeletal series is that from Klunk-Gibson, a Middle Woodland Havana cemetery in the lower Illinois River valley that dates to the first few centuries A.D. The site produced 528 burials (Buikstra 1976). The

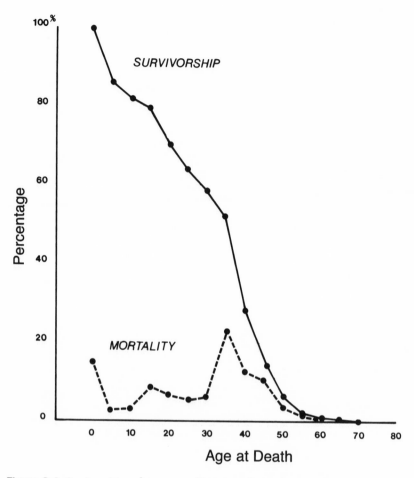

Figure 8.4. Survivorship and raw-mortality curves for the Campbell population (after Holland 1991).

Turner site is a small, Mississippian cemetery in the Western Lowlands dated to ca. A.D. 1300. One hundred eighteen individuals were contained in 54 burials there (Black 1979). With the exception of adult sex ratio, a strong similarity exists between the demographic parameters for Carlston Annis and for Turner, while Campbell compares most favorably with the Moundville and, to a lesser extent, the Klunk-Gibson samples. When the adult mortality curve for Campbell (ages 15–55) is plotted logarithmically against adult mortality curves for 7 western prehistoric populations compiled by Weiss (1973), the anomaly is striking (Figure 8.7). Even allowing that gaps in Weiss's data create some artificial smoothing, the dramatic increase in Campbell mortality at age 30–40 is still unexplained.

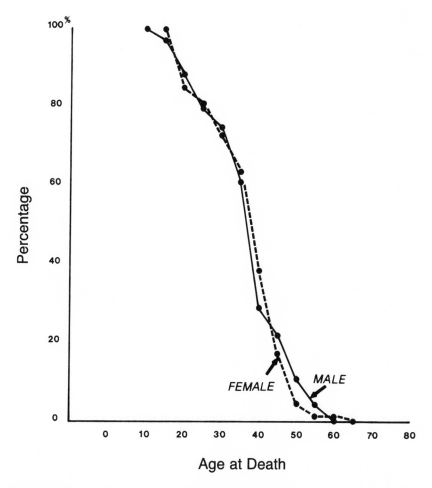

Figure 8.5. Survivorship curves for Campbell adult females versus adult males (after Holland 1991).

Fertility

The values shown in Tables 8.4 and 8.5 can be used to calculate additional demographic figures. Given the assumptions of the stable-population model with zero growth, the crude birth rate must equal the crude death rate. Thus, just over 33 children per 1,000 adults would have been born annually at Campbell. A more specific measure of fertility, the gross reproduction rate, that is, how many females will be born to a female from a cohort of 1,000 females during her lifetime, is slightly under 2, with a generation length of 27.2 years.

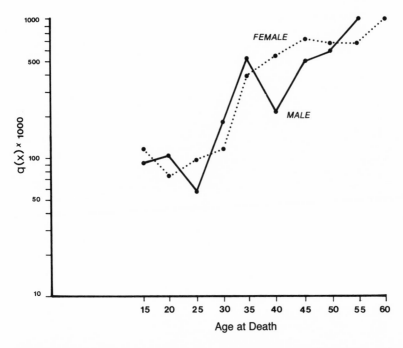

Figure 8.6. Logarithms of mortality curves for Campbell adult females versus adult males (after Holland 1991).

Physical Characteristics

I examined several physical characteristics of the Pemiscot Bayou populations, including cranial deformation, stature, sexual dimorphism, dental abnormalities, and pathological disturbances. Again, the Campbell assemblage provided the majority of insights into the physical makeup of the late Mississippian period peoples along Pemiscot Bayou, though evidence from the other assemblages now demonstrates that the presence of characteristics such as auditory exostoses was not unique to the Campbell population.

Cranial Deformation

Perhaps the most visible characteristic of the skeletal series is the presence of a large number of artificially deformed crania. Intentional deformation of skulls is not uncommon in prehistoric populations, especially among Mississippian populations in the middle and lower Mississippi River valley. D. F. Morse (1989), for example, reports that of the 123 skulls in the Hampson collection—primarily

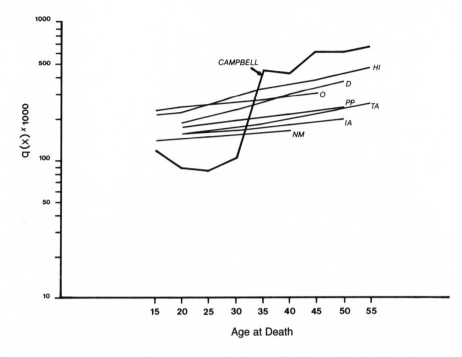

Figure 8.7. Logarithms of mortality curves for Campbell adults and for 7 prehistoric groups compiled by Weiss (1973). D = Dickson Mounds (western Illinois); HI = Hiwassee Island (Tennessee); IA = Illinois Archaic; NM = Norton Mound (Illinois); O = Occaneechi (Virginia); PP = Pecos Pueblo (New Mexico); TA = Texas "aboriginals" (after Holland 1991).

collected from Upper and Middle Nodena and contemporaneous sites in Arkansas and Tennessee—only 6 (4.9%) could be considered nondeformed. Powell (1989: 73) reports that "numerous female crania" from the Nodena site exhibit fronto-occipital deformation, while males are "less frequently and less severely deformed." Identification of cranial deformation is not a recent phenomenon in central Mississippi River valley archaeology. For example, Conant (1878: 362–64) described occipital flattening on skulls from the Sikeston site in New Madrid County.

I made determinations of deformation present on Pemiscot Bayou crania conservatively in that I did not count any deformation possibly attributable to postmortem processes. To further standardize information on artificial deformation, I employed types outlined by Neumann (1942). Using this system, I classified deformed crania into two categories: occipital and fronto-vertico-occipital. Both types result from binding an infant's head to a flat cradleboard. Occipital flattening is restricted to deformation of the occipital bone, while fronto-vertico-occipital deformation includes the flattening of the frontal bone as well as the occipital (Figure 8.8).

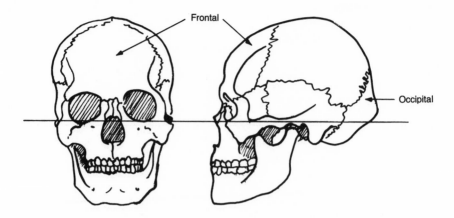

Figure 8.8. Front and lateral views of the cranium showing locations of frontal and occipital bones.

Ninety adult and subadult crania from Campbell and 41 adult crania from the other Pemiscot Bayou sites were included in the sample of 131 crania. Table 8.6 shows the distribution across the sites by deformation type. Campbell produced 24 deformed skulls (Figure 8.9), 21 of females and only 3 of males (discussed in more detail below). Murphy produced 5 deformed male skulls and 7 deformed female skulls; Berry produced 2 deformed male skulls; Cagle Lake produced 2 deformed female skulls; McCoy produced 2 deformed male skulls and 1 deformed female skull; and Nora Tucker produced 1 deformed male skull. Forty-four crania, or 34% of the total of 131 crania, exhibit deformation. Thirteen of the 57 male skulls (23%) and 31 of the 70 female skulls[3] (44%) are culturally deformed, though 12 of the 13 deformed male crania (the exception being at Murphy) display only slight flattening of the occipital, typical of "cradleboarding." Female crania, in contrast, generally show severe fronto-vertico-occipital deformation, including 1 cranium from McCoy and 6 from Murphy. The occurrence of cranial deformation varies from 0% at Denton Mounds, Dorrah, and Brooks to a high of 75% at McCoy and Murphy. Table 8.6 shows the incidence and type of cranial deformation for the 9 sites that produced crania. These extremes, though, may once again be reflecting sample bias. However, when all the crania listed in Table 8.6 for which the sex is known are considered as a single population, the distribution by sex displays a high degree of statistical significance.

3. Four skulls are of unknown sex (see Table 8.6).

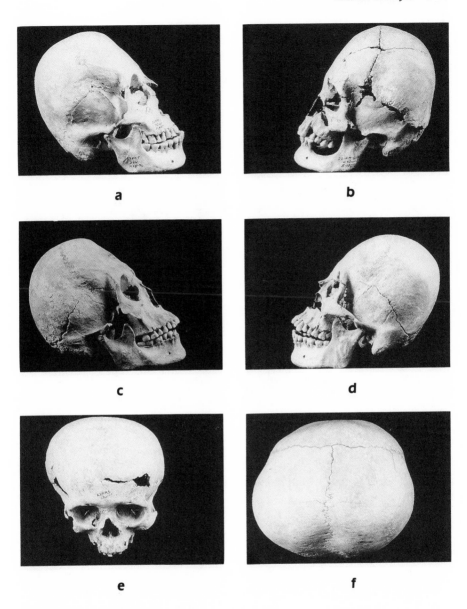

Figure 8.9. Culturally deformed crania from Campbell: a–d, frontal deformation; e, f, occipital deformation (two views of the same cranium). Specimen a is from burial 30W; b is from burial 65W; c is from burial 47W; d is from burial 11W; e and f are from burial 20W.

Table 8.6
Cranial Deformation in Nine Skeletal Series from Pemiscot Bayou, by Sex and Type

Site	Sex	Number Examined	Normal	Occipital Deformation	Fronto-Vertico-Occipital Deformation	Total Number Deformed
Berry	M	5	3	2	0	2
	F	2	2	0	0	0
Cagle Lake	M	3	3	0	0	0
	F	3	1	2	0	2
Campbell	M	36	33	3	0	3
	F	54	33	5	16	21
Denton Mds.	?	2	2	0	0	0
Dorrah	M	1	1	0	0	0
	F	1	1	0	0	0
McCoy	M	3	1	2	0	2
	F	1	0	0	1	1
Murphy	M	8	3	4	1	5
	F	8	1	1	6	7
Nora Tucker	M	1	0	1	0	1
	F	1	1	0	0	0
	?	1	1	0	0	0
Brooks	?	1	1	0	0	0

Table 8.7
Distribution of Cranial Deformation among Campbell Skeletons, by Age Group

Crania	Age Group									
	16–20	21–25	26–30	31–35	36–40	41–45	46–50	51–55	56–60	61+
Deformed	1	0	1	0	8	7	2	3	1	1
Normal	8	6	6	10	20	5	8	1	1	1
Total	9	6	7	10	28	12	10	4	2	2

Table 8.7 shows the distribution of deformation types at Campbell by age. Since deformation begins soon after birth, the incidence of deformed crania should be the same for all age groups. But note that no individual under the age of 20 was identified positively as having an artificially deformed cranium (the one case in the 16–20 age group was estimated at 20 years of age). Likewise, older adults

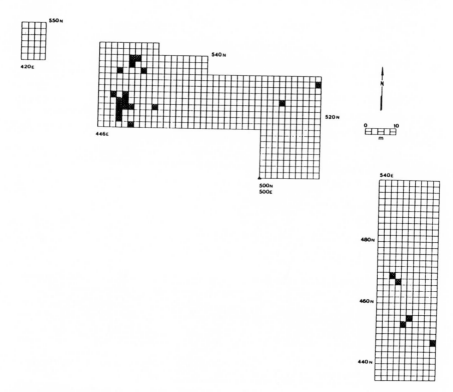

Figure 8.10. Distribution of Campbell burials with culturally deformed crania (from Holland 1991).

account for most cases of deformed crania. Only 2 individuals under the age of 31 at death had deformed crania, compared to 22 individuals over the age of 31. This disparity is statistically significant and suggests that individuals with deformed skulls may have immigrated to the Campbell site as adults.

The presence of artificially deformed crania may well have contributed to Chapman and Anderson's (1955) speculation as to the existence of a moiety kinship system at Campbell. The distribution of burials with deformed crania does, in fact, show nonrandom patterning (Figure 8.10). Two-thirds of the deformed crania were recovered from the western half of the site, and only 12.5% of the deformed skulls were found in the northern area. Chi-square analysis indicates that this pattern is significant at the $p < .05$ level, but whether this pattern results from status or kin distinctions or from temporal differences on the site is unclear.

Table 8.8 shows the distribution of cranial deformation among Murphy skeletons by age group. As with the Campbell assemblage, no subadult skulls show evidence of deformation. The majority of individuals with deformed crania were in the 31–40 age group. Interestingly, all 12 skeletons exhibiting deformed crania were vertically or horizontally bundled (6 of each) upon interment. Two of the nondeformed skulls also came from bundle burials, and one came from an undetermined type of interment. Unfortunately, the small sample (further complicated by the fact that no skulls from extended burials could be analyzed because of poor condition) precludes taking this analysis any further. What the data do suggest is that, if our temporal placement of interment methods is correct, that is, if bundling as a method predated extending the skeleton, then cranial deformation was practiced as far back as at least the middle portion of the Mississippian period. Further evidence of this comes from examination of the Kersey skulls (see below).

Table 8.8
Distribution of Cranial Deformation among Murphy Skeletons, by Age Group

Crania	Age Group									
	16–20	21–25	26–30	31–35	36–40	41–45	46–50	51–55	56–60	61+
Deformed	0	1	2	3	5	0	1	0	0	0
Normal	0	0	0	1	1	1	0	0	0	0
Total	0	1	2	4	6	1	1	0	0	0

Stature

Data on stature, derived from measurements of femurs and tibias, are presented in Table 8.9. The results show a marked sexual dimorphism. Estimated average male statures exceed those calculated for females by 8.0 to 16.2 cm (3.2–6.4 inches) (see footnotes to Table 8.9 for sources of techniques used). Males ranged in height from approximately 174.7 cm (68.8 inches) at Murphy to 167.0 cm (65.8 inches) at Berry. The tallest females were found at Cagle Lake (162.8 cm [64.1 inches]) while Murphy—in contrast to its tallest males—produced the shortest females (158.5 cm [62.4 inches]). These stature estimates and sexual differences are comparable to those observed for the late-prehistoric sites of Turner and Nodena (Table 8.9).

Sexual Dimorphism

Work on nonhuman primates as well as on human groups suggests that female size is limited by two factors, the most powerful of which is lactation. Females

Table 8.9
**Estimated Adult Stature for Skeletal Series from Five Pemiscot
Bayou Sites, Nodena, and Turner**

Site	Sex	Number	Stature (cm)			
			TG[a]	S.D.	G[b]	S.D.
Berry	M	7	167.0	5.96	164.6	5.99
	F	4	159.0	5.27	156.5	4.77
Cagle Lake	M	1	172.3	0.00	170.3	0.00
	F	2	162.8	3.25	161.8	1.34
Campbell	M	31	170.4	3.73	167.3[c]	3.14
	F	41	159.9	4.83	158.3	4.71
Murphy	M	3	174.7	5.17	172.8	5.00
	F	2	158.5	0.67	157.2	0.57
Nora Tucker	M	4	170.1	1.43	169.7	1.41
	F	0	. . . .	. . . .	. . . .	. . . .
Nodena	M	20	171.8	4.01	. . . .	. . . .
	F	13	160.0	18.94	. . . .	. . . .
Turner	M	16	. . . .	. . . .	168.3	4.00
	F	20	. . . .	. . . .	156.8	3.78

Sources: Nodena data from Powell 1989; Turner data from Black 1979.

[a] Based on Trotter and Gleser's (1958) formula for white male femurs and white female femurs and tibias.

[b] Based on Genovés's (1967) formula for male femurs and female tibias.

[c] Only 29 males were estimated using the Genovés method.

require substantially larger amounts of energy during pregnancy and the ensuing period of nursing. Since women in nonindustrial societies can expect to spend the majority of their adult lives either pregnant or lactating, selection has favored a smaller body size with lower energy requirements (Hamilton 1982). At the same time, however, small female body size engenders increased risks at childbirth. The result is that female size is held near an optimal size for reproduction and thus females should demonstrate less variation in size than males, whose body size is unrestrained by the requirements of childbirth. Relying on this theory, Steele and Powell (1990) have used variation in adult stature to infer stress. Populations in which females display larger standard deviations for stature than males (such is the case at Campbell [Holland 1991]) can be interpreted as undergoing some form of stress.

Yet there is no consensus on exactly how to interpret changes in sexual dimorphism. Indeed, one reason that analysis of sexual dimorphism is so popular is that it can be used to support almost any model. In early studies, the issue seemed rather clear: A decrease in dimorphism is indicative of stress (see Stini 1969, 1972). Some studies (see Holland 1991) suggest that males are less able to buffer environmental and nutritional insults and, as a consequence, can be developmentally stunted by stress. With males failing to reach growth potential to the same degree as females, the gap between the two sexes is narrowed. Haviland (1967) used such a pattern of decreasing sexual dimorphism with arguable success in his explanation of the Mayan collapse. On the other hand, Larsen (1984) has argued that increased stress associated with a shift to agriculture affects females more, resulting in an increase in sexual dimorphism. The confusion may, in part, result from "long-term selection on the genotype and short-term fluctuation of the phenotype" within a particular population (Hamilton 1982: 147), as well as the "likelihood that males are more protected from stress in many societies" (Goodman et al. 1984: 20). (It should not be overlooked that immigration, perhaps in the form of mates, might also increase dimorphism.) Lacking a "consistent trend," Cohen and Armelagos (1984: 588) conclude that "the meaning of dimorphism itself as an index appears to be ambiguous."

Although the meaning of sexual dimorphism may be somewhat ambiguous, it warrants attention nonetheless. I employed Hamilton's (1982) method of examining gross difference between the sexes for a given measurement, which uses the formula

$$\frac{Male\ mean - Female\ mean}{Female\ mean} \times 10$$

Table 8.10
Comparison of Sexual-Dimorphism Scores from Campbell, Murphy, and Nodena

Measurement	Site		
	Campbell	Murphy	Nodena
Humerus			
Maximum length	8.3	. . . .	7.0
Maximum head diameter	15.2	8.2	15.0
Femur			
Bicondylar length	6.6	10.7	8.0
Vertical head diameter	11.6	11.7	13.8

Source: Nodena data from Powell 1989.

Table 8.10 compares selected scores from Campbell and Murphy with those from Nodena. Humeral scores from Campbell compare favorably with those from Nodena, but the Murphy scores differ markedly from the others with the exception of femoral-head-diameter scores.

Dentition

Teeth are subject to two major processes: buildup, in the form of calculus deposits, and breakdown, either in the form of mechanical abrasion or chipping or in the form of chemical decay. Both processes lend themselves to inferences regarding diet and food-processing techniques. For example, calcified dental plaque, that is, dental calculus (or tartar), results when the sticky layer of food residue and bacteria coating the teeth mineralizes. Mineralization may be catalyzed when an alkaline environment, resulting from oral bacteria metabolizing protein or from alkaline drinking water, acts on calcium in the plaque. Thus, diets rich in animal protein may predispose an individual to the production of calculus. On the other hand, ingestion of carbohydrates promotes the growth of lactic-acid-forming bacteria. If left unneutralized, lactic acid serves to dissolve not only the recently crystallized plaque but the tooth surface as well, resulting in dental caries. There is, therefore, an inverse relation between plaque and caries, and each is an indicator of a different type of diet (Hillson 1979), though this relation can be complicated by cultural modifications to food, such as when, for example, lime is used to process maize. I examined dental arcades from 137 adults (97 from Campbell), represented by 2,979 individual teeth, for caries, attrition, calculus, and abnormalities (see Holland 1991 for additional analyses of teeth from Campbell).

Calcified Dental Plaque

My scoring for calculus deposits was conservative in that I only scored teeth with definite calculus incrustations as positive (scores 2–4, depending on severity), while I scored those teeth simply discolored by plaque as negative (score of 1). Table 8.11 shows the distribution of plaque among teeth from the Pemiscot Bayou sites. The teeth of Campbell males on average exhibit higher scores than do the teeth of the females, though this pattern does not hold true at all the other sites. Only at Cagle Lake, Murphy, and Nora Tucker do males exhibit higher calculus scores on average, and often the differences (relative to those of females) are insignificant.

Table 8.11
Mean Calcified Dental Plaque Scores of Skeletal Series from Pemiscot Bayou Sites

Site	Sex	Number	Mean Score	S.D.
Berry	M	6	1.25	0.23
	F	2	1.47	0.25
	All	8	1.31	0.24
Cagle Lake	M	4	1.30	0.23
	F	4	1.25	0.17
	All	8	1.27	0.19
Campbell	M	39	1.41	0.43
	F	58	1.32	0.37
	All	97	1.36	0.40
Dorrah	M	1	1.11	....
	F	1	2.95	....
	All	2	2.03	1.30
McCoy	M	2	1.71	0.84
	F	2	1.74	0.71
	All	4	1.72	0.64
Murphy	M	8	1.92	0.66
	F	6	1.37	0.57
	All	14	1.68	0.69
Nora Tucker	M	3	1.62	0.54
	F	1	1.04	....
	All	4	1.47	0.53

Table 8.12 compares the Campbell dentition by age group—those under 35 versus those over 35. There are no significant differences between the two groups in terms of dental plaque. Table 8.12 also compares the Campbell dentition to the Nodena dentition examined by Powell (1989). Considerable difference exists between the calculus scores from Campbell skeletons and those from Nodena skeletons. Undoubtedly, some of the difference can be attributed to the conservative approach taken in scoring the Campbell teeth, but no conservative scoring will account for all the discrepancy shown in Table 8.12. There is almost a reversal of the two calculus distributions, with the majority of the Campbell teeth showing no accumulation and the majority of the Nodena teeth exhibiting the greatest accumulation. Even if all the Campbell teeth in stages 3 and 4 and two-thirds of those in stage 2 were combined, the resulting group would still contain less teeth

Table 8.12
Distribution of Calcified Dental Plaque for Campbell and Nodena Skeletons, by Age

Site	Age	Number of Teeth Examined	Scores of Teeth			
			1	2	3	4
			Maxilla			
Campbell	<35	481	326 (67.8%)	135 (28.1%)	18 (3.7%)	2 (0.4%)
Campbell	>35	650	437 (67.2%)	193 (29.7%)	14 (2.2%)	6 (0.9%)
Nodena	<35	637	88 (13.8%)	273 (42.9%)	161 (25.3%)	115 (18.1%)
Nodena	>35	512	13 (2.5%)	263 (51.4%)	123 (24.0%)	113 (22.1%)
			Mandible			
Campbell	<35	498	326 (65.5%)	154 (30.9%)	16 (3.2%)	2 (0.4%)
Campbell	>35	625	390 (62.4%)	179 (28.6%)	52 (8.3%)	4 (0.6%)
Nodena	<35	600	70 (11.7%)	185 (30.8%)	96 (16.0%)	249 (41.5%)
Nodena	>35	420	26 (6.2%)	119 (28.3%)	96 (22.9%)	179 (42.6%)

Source: Nodena data from Powell 1989.

than the 656 Nodena teeth in stage 4. The reason for the great difference, which I assume was related to diet, is unclear.

Dental Caries and Antemortem Tooth Loss

Dental caries, along with its associated abscesses and tooth loss, probably is the most common pathology identified on a skeleton, though it is "uncertain as to how much [it] add[s] to the disease load of prehistoric populations" (Goodman et al. 1984: 37; see also Calcagno and Gibson 1991). Increasingly, archaeologists are using dental-caries rates as indicators of dietary shifts, going so far as to assign caries rates to specific diets (e.g., Rose et al. 1984). Goodman et al. (1984) warn, however, of attempting to do too much with dental evidence. For example, circularity may be introduced into one's analysis if caries rates are used to identify dietary shifts and then used again to assess the impact of that shift. This is not a problem with the Campbell material, at least, since there is independent evidence for diet in the form of isotopic analysis of bone samples (Boutton et al. 1991; Lynott et al. 1986).

One hundred eleven of the 135 skeletons (82%) where both maxillas and mandibles are present have at least one carious tooth (Table 8.13). The average number of lesions per individual is 4.0, a figure comparable to those obtained from Nodena (Powell 1989). Individual caries rates range from 2.5 lesions per individual at Nora Tucker to a staggering 6.8 per individual at Cagle Lake. Rose et al. (1984) argue that values higher than 2.0 caries lesions per individual are indicative of a high-carbohydrate diet, with values higher than about 2.6 indicating maize dependency. Caries rates for the Pemiscot Bayou sites, relative to other late-prehistoric sites in the central Mississippi Valley (Table 8.14), suggest a high degree of carbohydrate intake, consistent with that associated with other late Mississippian period populations. Since the mean number of caries is in part a

Table 8.13
Prevalence of Dental Caries and Antemortem Tooth Loss in Pemiscot Bayou and Nodena Skeletal Series

Site	Percentage of Carious Individuals	Number[a] of Carious Teeth per Individual	Percentage of Carious Teeth	Lesions per Tooth	Lesions per Individual	Total Carious and Lost Teeth per Individual
Berry	100.0	4.2	18.5	0.27	6.0	7.3
	(6/6)	(25/6)	(25/135)	(36/135)	(36/6)	(44/6)
Cagle Lake	83.3	5.0	17.9	0.24	6.8	5.7
	(5/6)	(30/6)	(30/168)	(41/168)	(41/6)	(34/6)
Campbell	84.5	3.5	14.9	0.18	4.2	5.6
	(82/97)	(336/97)	(336/2254)	(408/2254)	(408/97)	(539/97)
Denton Mounds	100.0	2.5	26.3	0.89	3.5	2.5
	(2/2)	(5/2)	(5/19)	(7/19)	(7/2)	(5/2)
Dorrah	100.0	3.0	12.8	0.17	4.0	6.5
	(2/2)	(6/2)	(6/47)	(8/47)	(8/2)	(13/2)
McCoy	50.0	3.3	15.5	0.20	4.3	4.8
	(2/4)	(13/4)	(13/84)	(17/84)	(17/4)	(19/4)
Murphy	69.2	3.3	15.3	0.19	3.7	5.7
	(9/13)	(10/3)	(26/170)	(32/170)	(11/3)	(17/3)
Nora Tucker	50.0	2.3	10.7	0.12	2.5	3.8
	(2/4)	(9/4)	(9/84)	(10/84)	(10/4)	(15/4)
Brooks	100.0	4	22.2	0.28	5.0	4.0
	(1/1)	(4/1)	(4/18)	(5/18)	(5/1)	(4/1)
Nodena[b]	77.4	2.8	18.3	0.23	3.5	4.1
	(120/155)	(426/155)	(426/2331)	(543/2331)	(543/155)	(635/155)

[a] Carious teeth per individual, lesions per individual, and carious and lost teeth per individual calculated only from individuals with matching maxilla and mandible.

[b] Data from Powell 1989.

Table 8.14
Mean Number of Dental Caries per Individual in Skeletal Series from Pemiscot Bayou and Selected Other Mississippi River Valley Sites

Site	Period	Number of Individuals	Mean Caries per Individual
Berry	L. Mississippian	6	6.0
Cagle Lake	L. Mississippian	6	6.8
Campbell	L. Mississippian	97	4.2
Denton Mounds	L. Mississippian	2	3.5
Dorrah	L. Mississippian	2	4.0
McCoy	L. Mississippian	4	4.3
Murphy	M./L. Mississippian	13	3.7
Nora Tucker	L. Mississippian	4	2.5
Brooks	L. Mississippian	1	5.0
Nodena	L. Mississippian	155	3.5
Hazel	L. Mississippian	33	2.6
Parkin	L. Mississippian	8	5.9
Wapanocca	L. Mississippian	209	3.5
Johnny Wilson	M. Mississippian	7	2.6
Mangrum	M. Mississippian	2	1.0
Burris	M. Mississippian	1	1.0
Floodway Mounds	M. Mississippian	1	3.0
Zebree	M. Mississippian	2	0.0
Zebree	E. Mississippian	13	2.4
Owls Bend	E. Mississippian	1	1.0
Banks	L. Baytown	7	0.9
Hyneman 2	L. Baytown	1	0.0
Little Cypress Bayou	L. Baytown	3	2.7
Powell Canal	Baytown	4	0.5
Gold Mine	Baytown	89	1.1

Sources: Data from Rose et al. 1984, 1991; Nodena data from Powell 1989.

function of mean age and rate of wear, Table 8.14 must be interpreted with caution unless the populations can be shown to be demographically similar. However, the mean caries rate for Nodena individuals (3.5) is less than the rate of 4.2 for those from Campbell and probably relates to the significantly higher incidence of dental plaque on Nodena teeth.

Table 8.15 lists the distribution of caries by age group for the Campbell skeletal series. Although Hildebolt et al. (1988) argue that caries rates from Campbell reflect the influence of ingested trace elements, the high frequency of caries indicated at Campbell is consistent with the high ratio of carbon-13 to carbon-12 ($^{13}C/^{12}C$) obtained by Lynott et al. (1986) from bone samples from the site and interpreted as a marker of intensive use of maize (see also Boutton et al. 1991). As

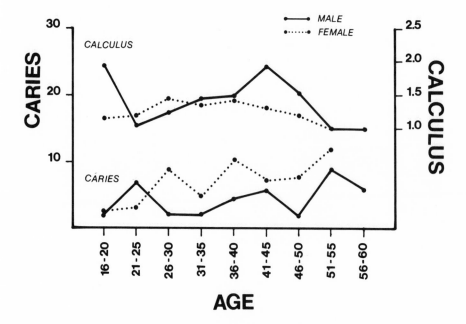

Figure 8.11. Distribution of caries and calculus among Campbell skeletons (after Holland 1991).

Table 8.15
**Prevalence of Dental Caries and Antemortem Tooth Loss
at Campbell, by Age Group**

Age Group	Number of Individuals	Number of Carious Individuals	Number of Caries	Percentage of Total Caries	Number of Teeth Lost	Percentage of Total Lost
11–15	3	2	3	0.74	0	0.00
16–20	11	10	32	7.84	0	0.00
21–25	7	6	38	9.31	0	0.00
26–30	7	5	26	6.37	6	2.96
31–35	11	9	42	10.29	7	3.45
36–40	28	24	126	30.88	65	32.02
41–45	12	12	79	19.36	30	14.78
46–50	11	8	48	11.76	35	17.24
51–55	4	4	12	2.94	30	14.78
56–60	2	1	1	0.25	11	5.42
61+	1	1	1	0.25	19	9.36

might be predicted, the Campbell population displays the high-caries, low-cal-culus rate expected with maize consumption. Figure 8.11 illustrates that an inverse relation between caries and calculus exists at Campbell. Males, for the most part, have higher calculus scores than do females while at the same time exhibiting less caries and antemortem tooth loss. It *might* be inferred from this pattern that males were consuming more animal protein than females, who were more reliant on maize, though there is no evidence of a sexually dimorphic pattern to dental wear (Holland 1991).

Table 8.16
Frequency of Linear Enamel Hypoplasia among Skeletal Series from Pemiscot Bayou Sites and Nodena

Site	With LEH	Without LEH
Berry	6	0
Cagle Lake	6	0
Campbell	46	51
Denton Mounds	2	0
Dorrah	2	0
McCoy	3	1
Murphy	6	7
Nora Tucker	3	1
Brooks	1	0
Nodena	68	8

Source: Nodena data from Powell 1989.

Linear Enamel Hypoplasia

Linear enamel hypoplasia (LEH), which is manifest as faint lines in the teeth, is a marker of acute growth disruption, such as would occur during seasonal starvation, in contrast to the chronic nature of cribra orbitalia (discussed later). Seventy-five of 135 Pemiscot Bayou skeletons (56%) examined exhibited LEH (Table 8.16). The incidence ranges from 46% at Murphy to 100% at Berry, Cagle Lake, Denton Mounds, Dorrah, and Brooks. In general, the incidence of LEH seen in the Missouri material is comparable to that observed at Moundville (Powell 1988) and Nodena (Powell 1989). The combination of medium to high LEH rates and high cribra-orbitalia rates suggests that severe, short-term stress episodes (such as starvation) were alleviated only partially and at the expense of long-term health concerns.

Nondental Pathologies and Abnormalities

Nondental pathologies can be grouped into one of three categories: mechanical damage (e.g., degenerative arthritis and fractures), physiological damage (e.g., cribra orbitalia, spina bifida, and osteomas), and disease.

Degenerative Arthritis

By far the second most common pathology of any type (after dental caries) noted on prehistoric skeletons is degenerative arthritis. Degenerative arthritis is age-progressive, so much so that Stewart (1979a) suggests it can be used as an aid to estimating age at death. In addition, degenerative arthritis may be activity related (Tainter 1980). Larsen (1984), for example, has shown a decrease in degenerative joint disease between prehistoric hunter-gatherers and successive agriculturists in Georgia.

I scored degenerative arthritis on the Campbell skeletons simply as present or absent.[4] I considered arthritis to be present if any element displayed pitting, eburnation, lipping, or osteophytic growths. Further, if I scored any element positive, then I considered all elements of that bone type to be positive. For example, if an individual displayed arthritis on either tibia, then I scored the individual positive for tibias. Overall, 27 males out of 44 (61%) display evidence of arthritis, compared to 33 out of 63 females (52%). In addition, I detected no

Table 8.17
Incidence of Degenerative Arthritis among Campbell Skeletons

Bone	Males	Females	Total
Mandible[a]	5/35 (14%)	7/53 (13%)	12/88 (14%)
Humerus	12/30 (40%)	16/40 (40%)	28/70 (40%)
Radius	2/27 (7%)	9/40 (23%)	11/67 (16%)
Ulna	6/27 (22%)	5/39 (13%)	11/66 (17%)
Vertebra			
Cervical	7/32 (22%)	5/40 (13%)	12/72 (17%)
Thoracic	1/12 (8%)	2/15 (13%)	3/27 (11%)
Lumbar	6/14 (43%)	7/20 (35%)	13/34 (38%)
Sacrum	4/23 (17%)	10/28 (36%)	14/51 (28%)
Femur	5/29 (17%)	9/40 (23%)	14/69 (20%)
Tibia	6/26 (23%)	10/38 (26%)	16/64 (25%)
Fibula	0/25 (0%)	1/37 (3%)	1/62 (2%)
Patella	3/19 (16%)	2/27 (7%)	5/46 (11%)

[a] Mandibular condyles.

4. Only skeletons from Campbell were examined.

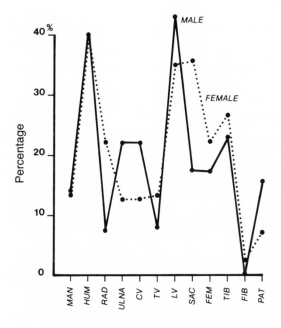

Figure 8.12. Distribution of arthritis among Campbell skeletons. Man = mandible; Hum = humerus; Rad = radius; CV = cervical vertebrae; TV = thoracic vertebrae; LV = lumbar vertebrae; Sac = sacrum; Fem = femur; Tib = tibia; Fib = fibula; Pat = patella (after Holland 1991).

statistically significant relation between cultural deformation of the skull and the distribution of arthritis. Table 8.17 shows the distribution of degenerative arthritis by element at Campbell (percentages represent the percentage of individuals with the affected element out of the total number of individuals for which that element is present). As can be seen, the humerus is the most commonly affected area, followed by the lumbar vertebrae, the sacrum, the tibia, and the femur. Males show a different pattern than females with regard to areas affected (Figure 8.12), though the difference is not statistically significant (Holland 1991: 159).

Neural-Arch Defects

One of the most common types of physiological abnormality observed on the Campbell skeletons is neural-arch defects. While I observed no cases of spina bifida on cervical, thoracic, or lumbar vertebrae, I identified 3 examples of sacral spina bifida. In addition, 30 other sacra display one or more defects on their dorsal surface. These defects are manifest either as a sacral aperture—a small circular opening in the neural arch—or as a sacral hiatus—a "tear" in the neural arch. Thirty-three of the 40 (82%) sacra for which the dorsal surface could be examined are defective. Nineteen of the 40 (47%) sacra have defects of a single segment, 6 (15%) have defects in 2 segments, 5 (12%) in 3 segments, and 3 (7%) have complete cleavage of all 5 segments. Eighteen of the 19 (95%) male sacra are defective, compared to only 15 of the 21 (71%) female sacra. Not all sacral segments are affected equally. In fact, a defect in the fifth segment is so common as to almost be considered normal. Sixteen of the 19 (84%) male sacra and 10 of the 21 (48%) female sacra have defective fifth segments. The effects of neural-arch defects on the general health of the Campbell population is unknown.

Cranial Osteoblastic Tumors

Another common pathology was the development of benign osteoblastic tumors on the cranial vault, generally on the frontal bone or anterior portion of the parietals. Nine of 79 (11%) Campbell crania and 2 of 10 (20%) Murphy crania exhibit button osteomas. Generally, these osteomas occur singly, though 1 Campbell female crania displays over 30.

Auditory Exostoses

A second form of benign osteoma (actually an exostosis) often identified in archaeological specimens is the small bony growth in the external auditory meatus, a condition commonly referred to as "ear exostoses." Following Hrdlička's (1935: 1) definition, ear exostoses are "all distinct bony excrescences or tumors within the external auditory canal that can definitely be recognized as an abnormal formation." The etiology of these growths is unknown, though Hrdlička (1935: 85) notes that they are "neither a constitutional, nor infectious, nor malignant disease." Instead, the formation of ear exostoses appears to be a response to mechanical or chemical irritation (Hrdlička 1935). Indeed, it has been proposed (e.g., Adams 1951) that ear exostoses are caused by frequent, long-term exposure to cold water—what has been called the "aquatic theory" (DiBartolomeo 1979). Kemink and Graham (1982: 105) go so far as to state that ear exostoses "are invariably associated with a history of cold water exposure over long periods of time." More recently, Kennedy (1986) examined the relation between the frequency of exostoses and latitude and found that exostoses are rare in 0–30° north and south latitudes as well as above 40°. The highest frequencies are found in middle latitudes, that is, 30–40° north and south, among populations exploiting marine and fresh-water resources. (The Pemiscot Bayou sites are located at 36° north.) Thus, Kennedy (1986) believes sufficient evidence exists for the relation between exostoses formation and cold water to eliminate exostoses from the list of nonmetric variables used in population-distance studies.

Twenty-four of the 129 skulls examined (19%) had exostoses (Table 8.18). The incidence among the study samples ranges from 0% at Berry to 50% at Dorrah. Furthermore, the distribution of exostoses by sex suggests that at Campbell, Cagle Lake, Dorrah, McCoy, Murphy, and Nora Tucker males are more likely than females to exhibit the condition (Table 8.19). Whether this condition results from fishing, musseling, or some other subsistence-linked activity is unknown, but the

Table 8.18
Incidence of Auditory Exostoses in Skeletal Series from Pemiscot Bayou Sites

Site	Number of Skulls	Affected Skulls	Percentage
Berry	7	0	0.0
Cagle Lake	9	1	11.1
Campbell	88	17	19.3
Dorrah	2	1	50.0
McCoy	4	1	25.0
Murphy	13	3	23.1
Nora Tucker	5	1	20.0
Brooks	1	. . . .	. . . .

pattern (significant at the $p < .05$ level) does suggest that late-Mississippian males were spending more time in cold water than were females.

We can examine the crania from Campbell to gain a more in-depth perspective on the distribution of the condition across a particular population. Seventeen of 88 (19%) Campbell adults with at least one intact temporal bone display auditory exostoses. Eleven of 37 (30%) adult Campbell males and 6 of 51 (12%) adult Campbell females exhibit the trait, a statistically significant difference ($p < .05$). Eight of the eleven males (73%) exhibit bilateral development, while the remaining 3 exhibit right-side involvement only. Four (67%) of the 6 females likewise were bilaterally affected, with the remaining two also affected on the right side only. Combined, the right side accounts for 17 of 29 (59%) exostoses, a pattern that is not statistically significant.

All but 2 of the affected Campbell adults were over age 30. Two affected female skeletons fall into the 21–25 age group, 1 affected male skeleton falls into the 31–35 age group, 10 affected adults (6 males and 4 females) were aged 36–40, 1 male was aged 41–45, 2 males were aged 51–55, and 1 male skeleton falls into the 56–60 age group. The average age for affected males is 42.6, while females average 32.8. The average age for the combined sexes is 39.1. This suggests that it requires some time for auditory exostoses to form and is in keeping with DiBartolomeo's (1979) observation, based on examination of modern humans (mostly swimmers), that auditory exostoses are painless until approximately the tenth year of exposure (to water), at which time the auditory canal becomes occluded.

Porotic Hyperostosis and Cribra Orbitalia

Porotic hyperostosis and cribra orbitalia may or may not be related (Stewart 1979b), and they certainly do not have to appear together. Both conditions have

Table 8.19
Distribution of Auditory Exostoses in Skeletal Series
from Pemiscot Bayou Sites, by Sex

Site	Sex	Temporal Bones	Total Skulls	Side Affected			Percentage of Temporal Bones	Percentage of Skulls
				R	L	Bilateral		
Berry	M	10	5	0	0	0	0.0	0.0
	F	4	2	0	0	0	0.0	0.0
Cagle Lake	M	7	4	1	1	1	28.6	25.0
	F	9	5	0	0	0	0.0	0.0
Campbell	M	73	37	11	8	8	26.0	29.7
	F	98	51	6	4	4	10.2	11.8
Dorrah	M	2	1	1	0	0	50.0	100.0
	F	2	1	0	0	0	0.0	0.0
McCoy	M	6	3	1	1	1	33.3	33.3
	F	2	1	0	0	0	0.0	0.0
Murphy	M	14	7	3	3	3	42.9	42.9
	F	10	6	0	0	0	0.0	0.0
Nora Tucker	M	4	2[a]	1	1	1	50.0	50.0
	F	1	1	0	....	....	0.0	0.0

[a]The number of skulls shown in Table 8.18 includes 2 of unknown sex.

been linked to thalassemia, sickle-cell anemia, and iron-deficiency anemia, and most researchers (e.g., Hengen 1971; Mensforth et al. 1978) now agree that porotic hyperostosis and cribra orbitalia are linked to iron deficiency. Both have also been linked traditionally to nutritional insults that result from a maize-staple diet, though the dietary link is increasingly being called into question. That both conditions are indicative of chronic stress is not at issue, however.

Anemia appears to have afflicted approximately half (44%) of the 144 Pemiscot Bayou individuals whose skeletons could be examined for diagnostic lesions (both active and healed). In addition, numerous skulls that were judged to not exhibit porotic hyperostosis did display the "pin-prick pitting" of cribra orbitalia (Figure 8.13) that has been reported at Nodena (Powell 1989), Moundville (Powell 1988), and other sites in the southeast (e.g., Webb and Snow 1974). Table 8.20 shows that the frequency of skulls affected with one or the other or both kinds of damage ranges from 29% at Berry to 100% at both Dorrah and Brooks. Cribra orbitalia is present on 46 (32%) of the skulls, while 31 (22%) exhibit porotic hyperostosis. Affliction rates for cribra orbitalia range from 0% at Dorrah and McCoy to 100% at Brooks, while porotic hyperostosis ranges from 0% at Brooks to 100% at Dorrah. These rates are somewhat higher than those at Nodena (Table 8.20).

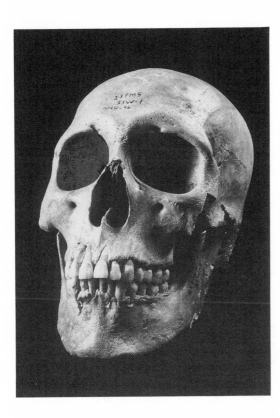

Figure 8.13. Pin-prick pitting of cribra orbitalia around the orbits of Campbell burial 31W cranium.

Table 8.20
Incidence of Cribra Orbitalia and Porotic Hyperostosis among Skeletal Series from Pemiscot Bayou and Nodena

Site	Number	Cribra Orbitalia	Porotic Hyperostosis	Individuals with Both	Total Affected
Berry	7	2	1	1	2
Cagle Lake	7	1	2	0	3
Campbell	104	33	17	8	42
Dorrah	2	0	2	0	2
McCoy	4	0	2	0	2
Murphy	14	5	4	3	7
Nora Tucker	5	4	3	3	4
Brooks	1	1	0	0	1
Middle Nodena	53	5	1	1	5
Upper Nodena	118	7	4	2	9

Source: Middle and Upper Nodena data from Powell 1989.

Tuberculosis-Like Disorder

One skeleton from Campbell, representing a woman aged 36–40 at death, exhibits large lytic lesions of the vertebral bodies of the eleventh and twelfth thoracic and third lumbar vertebrae. The lesions resemble those resulting from tuberculosis. Ortner and Putschar (1981) note that vertebral tuberculosis lesions—particularly of the lower thoracic and lumbar—are the most common and characteristic kind of bone lesions. In addition, in approximately 80% of the cases at least two adjacent vertebrae are affected. Ortner and Putschar (1981) also note that generally in these cases the condition begins in early childhood and follows a chronic course. Left untreated, the lytic nature of the disease leads to the destruction of the vertebral centra and a condition known as cavitation, resulting in angular kyphosis (twisting). The Campbell specimen, an older adult, displays no kyphosis.

Another skeleton from Campbell—the one Chapman and Anderson (1955) believed was of a shaman because of skeletal deformity—presents evidence of a tuberculosis-like disorder. The right humerus, of a male aged 36–40, exhibits a large cloaca on the medial surface of the proximal end, similar to those associated with tuberculosis. The sinus measures approximately 17 mm in diameter and is surrounded by reactive bone. The humeral shaft is shortened and twisted, possibly in response to an earlier compound fracture, though there is no evidence of a healing callous. Tuberculosis of the shoulder is less common than of the hip or knee, but when it does occur it affects males preferentially, and the right side is three times more likely to be involved than the left. Chapman and Anderson (1955) reported that the skeleton exhibited a twisted spine in the ground, though the vertebrae were not removed and hence are unavailable for examination.

Powell (1989) reports no cases of tuberculosis from Nodena, though her sample of postcranial bones is small. Powell (1988) did, however, report several suspected cases from Moundville. Others (e.g., Buikstra and Cook 1981; Perzigian et al. 1984; Widmer and Perzigian 1981) have identified possible tuberculosis-like pathologies on Mississippian populations throughout the central and southeastern United States. Further, it appears that these tuberculosis-like diseases were unknown in the Midwest prior to the population aggregation that characterized the Mississippian period (Buikstra 1981, 1984). Additional support for the presence of pre-Columbian tuberculosis is found in artifacts. Hump-backed effigy vessels that began to show up in late Mississippian period sites in the central Mississippi River valley (Arkansas, Tennessee, Mississippi, and Missouri) have been interpreted as evidence for spinal tuberculosis in pre-Columbian North America (e.g., Webb 1936). Several hump-backed effigy vessels have come from Pemiscot County sites, including Campbell (Figure 6.31). D. Morse (1978) notes that the spines of most hump-backed vessels are smooth, with evenly spaced vertebrae throughout their curvatures. If these effigies were based on live models, the artisans took some artistic license.

It should be noted that a variety of diseases and conditions mimic the symptoms of tuberculosis. These include chronic pyogenic osteomyelitis (D. Morse 1978) and fungal infections such as blastomycosis and coccidioidomycosis (Shadomy 1981). Nevertheless, Buikstra (1981: 18), after reviewing the available evidence, concludes that there is support for the "notion that there existed a tuberculosis-like pathology in the New World prior to 1492." Thus the possibility of a tuberculosis-like disease at Campbell cannot be ruled out. No similar condition was observed on any skeletons from the other Pemiscot Bayou sites.

Summary

Our understanding of health and diet that emerges from analysis of the skeletal remains of the Pemiscot Bayou inhabitants is still far from adequate, though the picture that develops is one of maize-reliant populations with marked sexual dimorphism and relatively light disease loads. There is some evidence for crowd diseases—two possible cases of a tuberculosis-like condition at Campbell—but overall the populations appear to have been in good health. Average age at death for males and females alike is the late 30s or even early 40s—an average that many modern developing countries would do well to match. Life expectancy at birth (29.9 years at Campbell) is high relative to many other prehistoric populations of comparable size, as is the proportion of the population (at least at Campbell) between 15 and 50 years of age. In contrast, the gross reproductive rate as well as the crude birth rate are slightly low relative to other prehistoric midwestern groups. One anomaly in the demographic profile (based on the Campbell sample) is a sharp increase in mortality between the ages of 30 and 35. Males actually show the sharpest rise in mortality between 25 and 35 years of age. Females, on the other hand, show an increase in mortality starting at age 20 and increasing rapidly between ages 30 and 35. No doubt this reflects females' entrance into the childbearing years—a hazardous enterprise for both mother and child—but childbirth obviously cannot explain male mortality.

The Campbell population also displays a pronounced bias in favor of females so that the adult sex ratio stands at 69.8—a figure close to, but still lower than, that calculated for the Nodena population (the Murphy sample also displays a sex ratio of less than 100.0). It would appear that either males were somehow being removed from the mortuary population (perhaps by dying away from the site) or that excess females were being added to it (or both). Interestingly, the distribution of individuals with artificial cranial deformation suggests that females were being added to the Campbell population as adults (conceivably as wives). Variation in anthropometric measurements supports this inference, though it is not conclusive.

A surplus of females (or dearth of males), combined with a sharp increase in mortality during the third decade for both sexes, might be indicative of warfare, but such conjecture is not supported strongly by the rather scanty evidence for traumatic injuries. Only nine fractures were identified in the Campbell sample, though two of the nine were healed compression fractures of the skull—the type that would result from having one's head struck with a blunt instrument. No fractures were noted on skeletal material from the other Pemiscot Bayou sites, though the poor condition of the bone and low recovery rates probably contributed to the lack of evidence. Additionally, of the seven Campbell individuals with fractures, at least five are males (the remaining two are one female and one individual of unknown sex). D. F. Morse (1989) notes that the Casqui Indians who accompanied de Soto when he entered the chiefdom of Pacaha engaged in wholesale slaughter of any males within reach. Nor was this an isolated event, for it seems that the Pacaha and the Casqui had been engaged in a protracted war. Morse further entertains the possibility that a predominance of male skeletons at Nodena may reflect a similar type of raiding.

Dentally, the late-prehistoric inhabitants of the Pemiscot Bayou locality suffered from mouths ravaged by caries. On average, individuals had lost or suffered carious lesions in one out of every six teeth. While the mean number of caries per individual is staggeringly high at Berry and at Cagle Lake, the average for the whole Pemiscot Bayou assemblage is consistent with the figures reported for other maize-dependent cultures in the region. Whatever differences the populations in the region had, their dietary staple was the same. Skeletons of females over the age of 25 show a higher incidence of caries compared to those of males. Males, on the other hand, show a higher incidence of calcified dental plaque. The inverse pattern of caries development and calculus deposition suggests that at least at Campbell females ingested greater amounts of carbohydrates than did males and that males ingested more animal protein than did females—a situation that may account for the greater variation in stature seen in the females.

The animal protein available to the Pemiscot Bayou groups almost certainly included fish and other riverine animals. Not only were the sites located on or near abandoned channels of the Mississippi, but they were also very near the main river channel. Skeletal analysis shows that males had a markedly greater incidence of ear exostoses than did females (e.g., 30% versus 12% at Campbell), suggesting that males spent more time in the water than females, perhaps engaged in fishing-related activities.

But full stomachs were bought at a price, and the skeletal samples (especially those from Campbell) exhibit indicators of stress associated with sedentary agriculturists. Cribra orbitalia—generally regarded as an indicator of chronic stress, such as that associated with heavy reliance of adults on calorie-rich but nutrient-poor maize—is present on almost 40% of the crania examined. The exact extent to which this phenomenon is dietary versus environmental is unclear, but the implication of chronic stress is unambiguous. Surprisingly, acute-stress markers are widespread as well, suggesting that the late-prehistoric peoples of

Pemiscot Bayou faced more insults than merely seasonal starvation. On the other hand, there is a low frequency of linear enamel hypoplasia—commonly regarded as an indicator of acute (often cyclical) stress, as is found in the fetuses and children of hunter-gatherer groups that regularly experience resource depletion. Stress does not appear to have been equally distributed, with females experiencing more stress than males. Female stature exhibits a larger variance than that of males—a condition that perhaps reflects a response to stress—though the practice of importing wives from other populations may produce the same pattern.

Other pathologies and abnormalities are less easy to interpret. There is no clear (or statistically significant) pattern to the distribution of arthritis between sexes. Females show a higher (though not significant) incidence of cranial button osteomas than do males.

9

CONCLUDING REMARKS
Michael J. O'Brien

The Late Mississippian Period archaeological record of the Pemiscot Bayou locality presents us with a glimpse into the lifeways of prehistoric groups in one small portion of the central Mississippi River valley just prior to and during the arrival of the Spanish into the region. The natural environment of the locality was one of diversity in terms of flora and fauna, attributable in large part to its unique Holocene and terminal Pleistocene geomorphological history. Based on the locations of archaeological sites and on data generated from General Land Office records and modern soil surveys, we know that late Mississippian period communities were confined primarily to large, heavily forested natural-levee remnants left behind as the Mississippi River constantly cut and recut its course across the landscape of eastern Pemiscot County. These levee remnants often were islands in an otherwise low-lying expanse of backwater that housed some of the densest stands of cypress and cottonwood found in the Mississippi Valley. It was in this ecologically complex environment that the prehistoric inhabitants began producing some of the most impressive ceramic vessels ever manufactured in what is now the United States.

Unfortunately, the glimpse that we have been afforded into the lifeways of these prehistoric peoples, fascinating as it is, lacks many details. Decades of digging, most of it nonsystematic and uncontrolled, some of it clandestine, have produced abundant evidence of how the Pemiscot Bayou inhabitants manufactured and decorated their vessels but little or no data on other important aspects of everyday life. For example, we know almost nothing about the plant and animal resources that were consumed or in what proportions, though based on skeletal evidence the health of the prehistoric groups was such that many individuals, if they made it past childhood, enjoyed fairly long lives. The disease load appears to have been consistent with that of contemporary groups in the central Mississippi River valley.

What the admittedly biased archaeological remains do allow us to state is that there were *at least* 11 locations (including State Line and Braggadocio) in southeastern Pemiscot County that were occupied between ca. A.D. 1400 and 1545. Interestingly, all the locations are in the meander-belt portion of the ancient Mississippi River system as opposed to on the older braided surfaces to the west, between the meander-belt system of the Mississippi and Little rivers. Although systematic survey across all portions of Pemiscot County is needed before it can be stated categorically that late Mississippian period remains do not occur on the older surface, available evidence indicates that by ca. A.D. 1400 indigenous groups were highly focused on the heavily forested backswamp areas around Pemiscot Bayou and between that watercourse and the Mississippi River.

Many if not all of the communities probably were occupied simultaneously, though systematic dating of the artifacts and their contexts is needed to demonstrate this conclusively. I base the supposition solely on the co-occurrence at the different sites of certain artifacts and intricate decorative motifs, some of which are listed in Table 9.1. For example, Campbell, Brooks, Berry, and Denton Mounds have all produced astragalus dice; Campbell, Berry, Braggadocio, Holland, Brooks, and State Line have yielded head pots; and Campbell, Brooks, Denton Mounds, and State Line have produced copper artifacts such as beads, hair ornaments, and ear plugs. Campbell and Brooks are almost identical in terms of artifact assemblages, including the presence of Spanish glass, brass, and iron artifacts. If all the communities were not occupied simultaneously, there was at least considerable temporal overlap among many of them.

Murphy and Kersey give us important insights into earlier Mississippian-period life in the Pemiscot Bayou locality, especially relative to how the dead were treated before and at the time of burial. Both sites contained numerous cremations and bundled burials, neither of which has been recognized at the later sites. Murphy and Kersey also both contained funeral-related structures—a crematory pit and walled structure at Murphy and charnel houses at Kersey. Both also contained extended burials, though it is difficult to place the ones at Kersey in time. Certainly Kersey witnessed a major occupation during the Late Woodland period and the early portion of the Mississippian period. What is interesting about the site is its large size during those periods and the fact that the extended burials do not appear to be late-occurring phenomena. I cannot state conclusively that they are not as late as the extended burials at sites such as Campbell, Berry, Brooks, or Denton Mounds, but they do not contain the typical vessels or other items found in burial contexts at those sites.

On the other hand, I suspect that the extended burials at Murphy were contemporaneous with the late-period burials at many if not all of the other

Table 9.1
Known Occurrences of Certain Late Mississippian Period Artifacts in Pemiscot Bayou Assemblages

Artifact	Site							
	Berry	Braggadocio	Brooks	Campbell	Denton Mds	Holland	McCoy	State Line
Head pots	X	X	X	X				X
Human figures	X			X				
Conjoined pots	X		X	X				
Copper			X	X	X			X
Bone dice	X		X	X	X			
Bone buttons				X				
Nodena points	X	X	X	X	X	X	X	X
Catlinite				X			X	
Brass			X	X				
Iron			X	X				
Glass			X	X				
Gadrooned pots				X				
Nodena red-and-white pots	X	X	X	X	X			
Cat-monster pots	X		X	X				

Pemiscot Bayou sites. Of all the sites examined here, Murphy exhibits the longest and most complete post–A.D. 1200 occupational history. The large mound at Murphy probably dates to the period ca. A.D. 1200–1300, based on its similarity to other large mounds in southeastern Missouri that date to that period. Most sites containing large mounds, such as Beckwith's Fort (also known as Towosahgy) in Mississippi County and Lilbourn in New Madrid County, were palisaded (J. R. Williams 1964), a feature not documented at Murphy.[1] But accepting for the moment that Murphy was occupied during the heyday of the fortified centers, then we can, on the basis of the presence of later material, assign it a temporal range of perhaps 300–400 years or more. The presence of Baytown plain and Mulberry Creek cordmarked sherds in the excavated deposits suggests an even longer occupational span.

Dating the occupation spans represented at the other sites is, in a very real sense, more problematic than it is at Murphy and Kersey. Because of the nonsystematic nature of work conducted at the sites and because of our lack of knowledge of

---

1. Langdon, situated on the edge of the Malden Plain in Dunklin County (Dunnell n.d.), was also palisaded, though its large mound was not in the league with those at sites such as Murphy, Beckwith's Fort, and Lilbourn. Its height relative to its base is more like the dimensions of the Parkin mound.

when certain vessel shapes and designs made their appearances, it is impossible to state precisely when the sites were first occupied. The lack of absolute dating for established ceramic types is particularly vexing. As pointed out in Chapter 2, the received wisdom is that certain types such as Nodena red-and-white, Rhodes incised/engraved, and Walls engraved occurred late in the ceramic sequence, but the lack of either radiocarbon or thermoluminescence dates for those types leaves open the possibility that at least in some localities they began earlier than suspected. On the other hand, most of the available surface collections from the sites contain a few sherds of types that, based on dated contexts elsewhere, predate the Mississippian-period occupations—types such as Mulberry Creek cordmarked and Baytown plain. Unless those types persisted for much longer periods than is normally assumed, we are left with the conclusion that the levee remnants containing the late Mississippian period sites were occupied as early as the Late Woodland period (Figure 4.10). I cannot determine the nature of those early occupations, but I *can* document that the debris left behind was sparse.

Despite the obvious similarities among the Pemiscot Bayou assemblages, one of the major points of this volume is to examine the differences among them. Any meaningful examination of variation rests on certain assumptions about the representativeness of the samples—a point on which the Pemiscot Bayou assemblages fall short. No two of the sites received equal amounts of excavation, nor were any of the deposits screened. Although many small objects, including beads, were recovered from burial contexts, I have no way of assessing how representative the samples are. Also, many of the surface collections are highly biased toward certain ceramic types. In many cases our knowledge that particular artifacts came from particular sites is serendipitous, being based mainly on the willingness of informants to share their knowledge with us. For example, the fact that I cannot document the presence of copper artifacts at Berry is probably based on nothing more than my lack of knowledge as opposed to the fact that copper items were not used there. It is more than a little sobering to contemplate the number of artifacts from the Pemiscot Bayou sites about which we know nothing.

The Pemiscot Bayou Communities in Regional Perspective

It is also sobering to realize that the efforts aimed at identifying and measuring variation among the late Mississippian period archaeological assemblages from the Pemiscot Bayou locality—much of which still remains to be accomplished—is really only the first step toward a larger goal, namely, understanding how those assemblages fit into a broader regional framework. The second step involves extending the study of variation geographically, especially into northeastern Arkansas and western Tennessee—areas that are especially rich in sites containing late Mississippian period artifacts that appear at first glance to be similar if not identical to artifacts from the Pemiscot Bayou locality. In Chapter 3, Greg Fox and I examined similarities and dissimilarities in excavated and surface-collected Mississippian assemblages, and we found that there were marked contrasts between the late Pemiscot Bayou assemblages and the presumably earlier assemblages from the Cairo Lowland. But with the exception of Parkin, we did not examine the question of similarity or dissimilarity between the Pemiscot Bayou sites and other late Mississippian period sites to the south, due primarily to the lack of published sherd frequencies by type.

The remainder of this chapter takes up the question of similarity/dissimilarity between the Pemiscot Bayou sites and other Mississippian sites, especially as those issues relate to two questions. The first question is, If large enough samples from southeastern Missouri, northeastern Arkansas, and western Tennessee could be ordered temporally, and if variation within certain artifact classes could be measured reliably and consistently, would we be in a position to examine the origins of the people(s) who inhabited the meander-belt portion of the alluvial valley? Were they simply the descendants of earlier peoples who exploited the dense, swampy terrain, or were they new groups who entered the region from elsewhere, bringing with them the array of beautiful and often bizarre ceramic items that found their way into mortuary contexts? This question has been asked repeatedly by archaeologists working in the central Mississippi River valley, and it seems appropriate to pose it here. At the other end of the spectrum is the equally interesting question, Can we link any portion of the late Mississippian period archaeological record to ethnohistorically known groups, especially those mentioned in the de Soto accounts? This has become a much-debated issue in archaeological circles, though discussions tend to focus on the route of the de Soto expedition and not on underlying archaeological principles of analysis.

The two questions, although at opposite ends of the temporal spectrum, are really one question, namely, Are there, at the regional level, perceptible differences among assemblages that can be used to group certain assemblages while simultaneously segmenting them from other assemblages or groups of assemblages? Note that I am not asking whether the late Mississippian period phases that have been formulated for the central Mississippi River valley are valid constructs; rather, I am asking whether it is even possible to use certain dimensional attributes to define spatially isolated clusters. And, of course, the answer is yes. But, and this is a big but, to have any usefulness, the sorting exercise must proceed in an orderly fashion using comparable and representative samples. I examine below some of the schemes that have been proposed for partitioning the late-period archaeological record of the tristate region, expanding the discussion of a few of the late-period phases presented in Chapter 2.

The discussion is organized around the two questions posed above—the one regarding origins and the one regarding ethnohistorical groups. Both questions have temporal and spatial implications, and few if any answers provided thus far are particularly satisfying. The problems lie not in the questions themselves but in the methods and materials used to answer them. I propose a few analytical methods that could provide answers to the questions posed here. Importantly, the applicability of the methods crosscuts any spatial or temporal boundaries that are arbitrarily set. In other words, they are as important for measuring variation among only the Pemiscot Bayou sites as they are for examining variation across the tristate region. Some of the analyses can be undertaken using existing materials, but others will take new materials collected using appropriate sampling designs.

The Question of Origins

Who were the people who inhabited the meander-belt region after ca. A.D. 1400? There would seem to be two possible answers to this question: (1) they were simply the descendants of earlier peoples who occupied the region or (2) they were Mississippian peoples who immigrated to the area from somewhere else. Many archaeologists (e.g., Morse and Morse 1983) have opted for the second explanation, tying the late Mississippian period occupation of the meander-belt region to population movements from farther north in the central Mississippi River valley. Key to the argument is the apparent disappearance of residential groups in the Cairo Lowland after ca. A.D. 1400—the "vacant-quarter" hypothesis proposed by S. Williams (1983), which was discussed in Chapter 1. If the large, fortified communities of the Cairo Lowland were abandoned, then the people, unless they died, had to go somewhere:

> This population did not simply disappear. It shifted into the meander belt areas of the Mississippi and St. Francis rivers, the Little River–Pemiscot Bayou crevasse channel of the Mississippi, and the alluvial soils of the White River [of Arkansas]. These particular regions experienced significant increases in population. Trying to determine which particular site population went where specifically is not really possible at this time. The Cairo Lowland population almost certainly went south to Mississippi County, Arkansas, and the immediate environs to help form the Nodena phase. Many of the other Eastern Lowlands populations presumably nucleated together as the Parkin phase [along the St. Francis and lower Tyronza rivers]. Probably, many of the Western Lowlands populations nucleated to form the Greenbrier phase [along the lower reaches of the White River]. (Morse and Morse 1983: 282–83)

The archaeological record for the Cairo Lowland and the Western Lowlands clearly indicates that ca. A.D. 1350–1375 many if not all of the large, fortified centers either were abandoned or witnessed significant declines in population. Many of the smaller communities peripheral to the centers also were abandoned. In at least two instances—Turner and Snodgrass, adjacent communities located in the Western Lowlands—the communities were burned, apparently deliberately (Price and Griffin 1979). What is unclear is the reason behind abandonment. However, it is also unclear what the relations were between the fortified centers and the outlying communities, though received wisdom indicates that there were settlement hierarchies with the centers at the top and tiers of progressively smaller communities extending downward from the center (e.g., Price 1978). Most of the population attached to this settlement hierarchy spent most of the year away from the major centers engaged in agriculture. During various times of the year, especially in times of danger, the people congregated behind the safe walls of the centers. Many of the centers and their supposed satellite communities were sited on high sand ridges, and it is these landforms that figure prominently in the Morse and Morse scenario of the origins of the meander-belt populations.

As the story goes, the sand ridges on the braided surfaces of the Western Lowlands and the Cairo Lowland could support sizable communities as long as during most of the year the populace maintained a dispersed settlement system, that is, living in small communities located away from the centers. But when the need arose to change their system to one that was more nucleated, the sand ridges were not large enough in terms of available crop acreage to support the communities. So the groups packed up and moved south. Some went to the floodplain of the White River, some to the St. Francis River, and some between the Little River and the Mississippi River—the area that includes Pemiscot Bayou–Left Hand Chute. But why did they move south? The answer, according to Morse and Morse, is that the tristate area offered large expanses of silt and sandy loam that could support nucleated settlements.

And what about the "sudden" need to nucleate? Morse and Morse (1983: 284) offer the following explanation: "The Nodena phase seems to have been the main reason for this nucleation, as it apparently was expanding at the expense of other phases." This is confusing in light of the fact that Morse and Morse had just stated (282–83) that it was the Cairo Lowland population that moved south and helped form the Nodena phase. How could those groups help form the Nodena phase if it was against the Nodena expansion that they were defending themselves? Who was protecting themselves from whom? Also, Morse and Morse's explanation belies the fact that northeastern Arkansas already had a sizable population during the period in which the Cairo Lowland groups were supposedly immigrating. Also missing is mention of the fact that, as noted earlier, many of the Cairo Lowland "civic-ceremonial" centers were heavily fortified. Thus, the Western Lowlands and Cairo Lowland groups had been used to protecting themselves for several centuries before they decided to give it all up and head south.

What can we make of these scenarios? Is there any evidence that suggests a southward migration by Mississippian peoples during the late fourteenth and early fifteenth centuries? Not much, though there is one point in the Morses' favor, and one that has been noted throughout this volume—the apparent lack or paucity of earlier material at many of the late Mississippian period sites in the tristate region. I have noted this phenomenon for the Pemiscot Bayou sites, and Morse and Morse (1983: 283) indicate that it holds true for some of the northeastern Arkansas sites as well: "Many of the sites in the Nodena phase are single Mississippian component sites, probably an indication of a sudden increase in population. Although many Parkin phase sites involve the resettlement of older civic-ceremonial centers, there appears to be a temporal gap between the two populations." In the absence of a large suite of radiometric assays, is there any method of determining (a) whether there was an in situ development of late Mississippian period cultural remains as opposed to an import from the north, and (b) if there was an import, where it came from?

Several field and analytical methods discussed earlier would at least allow us to begin to address these questions. For example, to my knowledge no one has ever made direct comparisons between Cairo Lowland materials and materials from the Pemiscot Bayou–Left Hand Chute region in anything other than the most cursory of fashions (e.g., S. Williams 1954). Large surface collections generated through systematic and intensive methods would probably yield data sets appropriate for the types of analyses needed. Importantly, three types of sites should be examined: (1) early and middle Mississippian period sites in the Cairo Lowland—the purported homeland of some of the Nodena people; (2) late Mississippian period sites in the Pemiscot Bayou–Left Hand Chute locality—the area to which the Cairo Lowland groups supposedly immigrated; and (3) early and middle Mississippian period sites in the Pemiscot Bayou–Left Hand Chute locality. The collections are going to differ in terms of ceramic types represented as well as percentage of representation of other types, but are there certain analytical dimensions that would demonstrate technological or decorative continuity between the Cairo Lowland and the Pemiscot Bayou–Left Hand Chute locality? Or, on the other hand, are there definite continuities in terms of technological and decorative dimensions between early and middle Mississippian period ceramic assemblages in the Pemiscot Bayou–Left Hand Chute locality and later ceramic assemblages from the same locality?

Nonceramic artifacts could also provide important data. For example, are there clear continuities or discontinuities in lithic raw materials on early and late sites in Pemiscot County, Missouri, and Mississippi County, Arkansas? Continuity in raw materials between early and late assemblages from the Pemiscot Bayou–Left Hand Chute locality would at least suggest an in situ development of late Mississippian period "culture"; discontinuity between raw materials in earlier Mississippian-period assemblages and those dating post–A.D. 1400 might indicate that Cairo Lowland immigrants to the area continued to rely on sources of material they had used previously—sources that were different than those used by their predecessors along Pemiscot Bayou. Currently, information on stone-tool manufacture, especially relative to raw materials used, is erratic at best. The absence of naturally occurring stone resources in the meander-belt region meant that the inhabitants, regardless of their origin, either traded for raw material or procured it themselves from distant sources. From what I have observed in the Pemiscot Bayou assemblages, it appears materials were obtained from Crowley's Ridge and from streams flowing off the Ozark Escarpment, but I have little or no information on the relative percentages of different types of material in any single assemblage. Pemiscot Bayou groups also received such materials as catlinite from Minnesota, Knife River flint from central North Dakota, kaolin chert and Mill Creek chert from southern Illinois, Dover chert from western Tennessee, Kay County chert from northern Oklahoma, and quartz and chalcedony from Arkansas. These exotic materials show up in the sites as finished products and not as cores or chipping debris, strongly suggesting that the Pemiscot Bayou groups were receiving the materials in finished form. The same is true for Mississippian-period groups who were living on the Malden Plain to the west (Dunnell et al. 1994).

Connections with Ethnohistorical Groups to the South

At the opposite end of the chronological spectrum from the question of origins is a series of related questions: How were the late-fifteenth-century and sixteenth-century communities in the Pemiscot Bayou locality related to those in northeastern Arkansas and western Tennessee? Are there acceptable grounds upon which to geographically partition the sites in the tristate region? Can any such subdivisions be linked to groups identified through early historical period accounts? The third question has been treated extensively in the archaeological literature by numerous authors (e.g., Clayton et al. 1993; D. F. Morse 1989, 1990; P. A. Morse 1981, 1990; Morse and Morse 1983; G. P. Smith 1990; M. T. Smith 1987; Hudson et al. 1990) who have examined the various de Soto accounts and attempted to match landmarks with historical descriptions of the landmarks. The second question has also been examined in considerable depth by several authors (e.g., Morse and Morse 1983; G. P. Smith 1990). It is well beyond the scope of this volume to document all the pertinent research, especially that regarding the de Soto expedition, but I can examine a few aspects of it that have provided important information concerning the link between ethnographically known groups and the archaeological record, and I can point out some of the problems that have plagued research. Not surprisingly, inadequate data and inappropriate analytical measures, especially the shoehorning of ceramic-type percentages into definitions of phases, have clouded the issue considerably. These problems, as we shall see, leave us somewhat out on a limb when it comes to examining connections between the late-period Pemiscot Bayou communities and contemporary communities to the south.

In one of the more ambitious attempts to subdivide the late-period archaeological record of the tristate region, G. P. Smith (1990) subdivides the Mississippi

Valley from Pemiscot County, Missouri, on the north to Helena, Arkansas, on the south into 12 phases or districts. Smith's goal is to derive meaningful cultural units from material remains:

> Combining the results of these studies implies that sociocultural units at the tribal (or chiefdom) level can be distinguished by contrasting configurations of material culture within larger groupings, not a particularly novel idea. Further implied, however, is that frequency patterns of shared elements may be crucial to making such distinctions. Of particular importance in this regard is the steep gradient of frequencies at cultural boundaries. It is this latter implication that is here taken as a working hypothesis, applied primarily to ceramics, in defining local phases of Mississippian culture. (G. P. Smith 1990: 138)

This rationale, of course, is the same as that used by Willey and Phillips (1958): Sites containing similar frequencies of artifact types—here ceramic types—are assumed to have been part of a temporally and spatially distinct culture-historical unit. Intuitively this is an acceptable proposition; the problem is (a) in demonstrating similarities among assemblages so as to construct meaningful culture-historical units and (b) in documenting differences between those assemblages on one hand and all other assemblages on the other. Smith used surface collections to define his phases, noting, "One may not like to rely so heavily on surface collections but must in the end face the fact that there is still very little else to work with in the Mississippi Alluvial Valley" (G. P. Smith 1990: 168). He relied heavily on percentage of occurrence as an analytical tool, explaining, "The use of ceramic frequency configurations is intended to permit use of smaller collections than those necessary to produce enough marker-type or mode specimens for phase assignment" (G. P. Smith 1990: 168).[2] There is nothing inherently wrong with using either surface-collected sherds or type-frequency data in archaeological analysis; the problem is in using highly biased collections and in using sherd types that are totally inappropriate for the purpose of chronological ordering. Almost all schemes that subdivide the archaeological record of the tristate region into phases contain a fatal flaw—the use of percentages of Neeley's Ferry plain and Bell plain. What archaeologists have done is to confuse the very dissimilar dimensions *style* and *function,* using the latter to order deposits temporally and spatially. In essence, they have succumbed to the weakness of the data sets that Smith identified, that is, the small size. Since the small size of the assemblages can often result in the failure of "marker types" to show up, archaeologists rely on the two most frequently occurring types to make their assemblage assignments.

Conflation of style and function is nothing new in archaeology, but failure to recognize the differences can significantly alter the results of time-ordering

---

2. For a discussion of sample size relative to central Mississippi River valley surface collections, see various discussions in Phillips 1970 and Phillips et al. 1951.

exercises (see Dunnell [1978] for an extended discussion). Archaeologists from the time of Phillips et al. (1951) have been preoccupied with using ceramic types to seriate artifact assemblages from the Mississippi Valley and to draw geographic boundaries around like assemblages, and the two types that often figure prominently in these schemes are Neeley's Ferry plain and Bell plain. Recall from discussion in Chapter 2 that these two "ware"-based types will outweigh the percentages of decoration-based types in almost any Mississippian-period assemblage. In fact, the central Mississippi Valley ceramic type system is built around those two wares. For example, Old Town red is distinguished from Varney red by the type of ware on which the red slip occurs—Old Town red on a Bell plain paste and Varney red on a Neeley's Ferry plain paste—as well as by the kind of slipping (R. C. Dunnell, pers. comm., 1993). But the size of shell particle included as temper in a vessel is a *functional* dimension, not a *decorative* one. As such, it is not a neutral trait and therefore does not exhibit the stochastic distribution typical of features such as decoration (see Dunnell 1978; O'Brien and Holland 1990, 1992; O'Brien et al. 1994). It is the stochastic nature of decorative features that renders them ideal for use in chronological-ordering exercises such as seriation. Shell tempering, on the other hand, exhibits a distribution expected of a polymorphic trait that is under selective control. Recent work on the functional characteristics of shell-tempered pottery (e.g., Dunnell and Feathers 1991; Feathers 1989, 1990; Feathers and Scott 1989) has given us an entirely new set of insights into the technological history of shell tempering, including the important interrelation of temper size and firing regime. It has also demonstrated that shell-particle size is not a good basis for temporal partitioning of data sets. I would argue that it is not much better for spatial partitioning.

Based on their survey results, Phillips et al. (1951: 126) concluded that Bell plain occurred much more commonly around Memphis, where it became the dominant type in the late Mississippian period, than it did in the St. Francis River drainage, where "it never is numerically strong and is noticeable in the last period and at sites with other connections to the Memphis area." Ever since then, archaeologists have used percentages of Neeley's Ferry plain and Bell plain as phase criteria, employing "marker-type or mode specimens" (G. P. Smith 1990: 168) as needed on an ad hoc basis. For example, Figure 9.1, reproduced from Smith (1990: fig. 8-5), shows his configuration of sherd-type frequencies for five late Mississippian period phases. Notice that, as Phillips et al. (1951) proposed, the Memphis-area Walls-phase sites exhibit larger percentages of Bell plain than they do of Neeley's Ferry plain. But look at the percentages for the Commerce phase, which lies to the south of the Walls phase. The percentages are reversed from those for the Walls-phase sites. Now examine the distributions for the Nodena and Horseshoe Lake phases. Is there really much of a difference? Even when the percentages of the "marker types" such as Barton incised and Parkin punctated are factored in, no less than 14 different site arrangements can be derived from

Smith's data, and none of them violate the percentage ranges discussed by Smith for each phase. For example, many of the Nodena sites can be interchanged with many of the Horseshoe Lake sites without destroying the trends. Can we really make the case that we are dealing with different "culture-historical" units here?

The Parkin and Nodena Phases

In a similar but more restricted analysis, Morse and Morse (see also D. F. Morse 1989, 1990; P. A. Morse 1981, 1990), following suggestions made by Phillips et al. (1951), attempt to link two of the central Mississippi River valley phases—Parkin and Nodena—to aboriginal provinces mentioned in the de Soto chronicles. The two phases, especially Nodena, are important here because of their proximity to the Pemiscot Bayou locality. As discussed in Chapter 2, Phillips (1970) lumped three of the Pemiscot Bayou sites—Campbell, Holland, and McCoy (Chute)—into the Nodena phase, which he extended from Pemiscot County southward into Arkansas and western Tennessee, almost to Memphis. Morse and Morse (1983: fig. 12.1) also include the Pemiscot Bayou sites in the Nodena phase. If the Parkin and Nodena phases are in actuality useful constructs, meaning that there are significant differences between a Parkin component and a Nodena component, and if the Pemiscot Bayou assemblages are more like Nodena assemblages than they are like Parkin assemblages, then perhaps we have a sixteenth-century link between the Pemiscot Bayou locality and an ethnohistorically known group. Campbell, of course, because of the Spanish goods recovered there, has often been labeled (e.g., Morse and Morse 1983) as a community contacted directly by a small Spanish contingent sent northward by de Soto during his stay in the Pacaha provincial capital (see below).

Morse and Morse make a rather convincing claim that Parkin, a 6.9-ha village near the confluence of the St. Francis and Tyronza rivers in Cross County, Arkansas, is the main town of the Casqui province that figured prominently in the de Soto chronicles. Various points of reference in the chronicles can be verified on the Parkin landscape, as can landmarks along a route from the point at which de Soto crossed the Mississippi River northwest toward Parkin. Morse and Morse (1983: 311) speculate that the now-destroyed site of Pecan Point in southern Mississippi County, Arkansas, was the capital town of Pacaha, a province to the east of Casqui and that province's chief rival.[3] I see no reason to doubt either the validity of the chronicles or the relative placement of the provinces of Casqui and Pacaha. Neither am I in a position to cast doubt on the assignment of Parkin and Pecan Point (or Bradley [see note 3]) as provincial capitals. What concerns me is the equation of provincial territories with archaeological phases. For example,

3. D. F. Morse (pers. comm., 1993) states that he and P. A. Morse have now decided that Bradley was the capital of Pacaha.

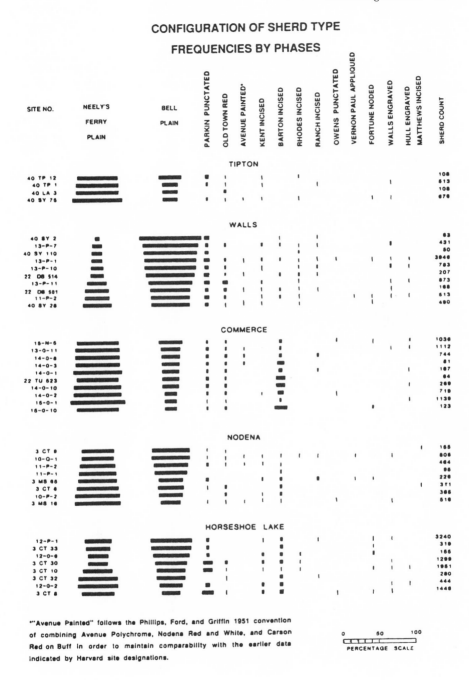

Figure 9.1. Configurations of ceramic type percentages for sites in five late Mississippian period phases in the central Mississippi River valley (used by permission from G. P. Smith 1990 [©1990 The University of Alabama Press]).

Morse and Morse (1983: 313) state: "To summarize, the De Soto expedition crossed the Mississippi near Commerce Landing in the province of Quizquiz (east Walls phase), crossed to Aquixco (west Walls phase), went inland to Casqui (Parkin phase), back east to Pacaha (Nodena phase), visited the Ste. François Mountains and the Greenbrier phase, retraced their steps to Casqui, and went south to Quigate (Kent and/or Old Town phases) and then farther west to the Ozarks (Quapaw phase) before turning south toward Little Rock." Amazingly, de Soto traversed either seven or eight archaeological phases during his short foray into Arkansas (see Figure 2.8). It is unfortunate that he did not make better note of the percentages of different types of pottery used by the inhabitants, especially pottery of the types Neeley's Ferry plain and Bell plain.

There have been repeated attempts to separate the Parkin and Nodena phases in terms of ceramic-type percentages. P. A. Morse (1981: 26), for example, states, "Sites in the Nodena, Walls, and Kent phases have similar pottery types in their assemblages (Phillips 1970: 931), but the percentages of these types differ greatly enough to assume there are corresponding cultural differences." One characteristic used implicitly by P. A. Morse (1981) to distinguish Parkin sites is the high percentage of Neeley's Ferry plain (70% or more) and the low percentage of Bell plain (apparently only a few percentage points). Conversely, Nodena-phase sites contain larger percentages of Bell plain (Morse and Morse [1983] place the range at 25–35% of total decorated sherds and rim sherds), lower percentages of Neeley's Ferry plain (around 45%), and low percentages of painted types other than Old Town red. Morse and Morse (1983: 285) make an interesting notation relative to the occurrence of two ceramic types—Barton incised and Parkin punctated—on Nodena sites: They are fairly common at some sites and rare at others. Given that Parkin punctated is one of the hallmarks of the Parkin phase, it thus appears that the type is common both on Parkin sites and on some Nodena sites. As an aside it might be noted that if those two types fluctuate widely in percentage on sites assigned to the same phase, then they are not very useful as phase designators.

Phillips (1970), of course, was one of the leading proponents of using the cumulative-curve graph to demonstrate similarities and differences among ceramic assemblages. And, I must admit, some of his graphs appear quite convincing. For example, Figure 9.2, reproduced from Phillips's (1970) report, shows his cumulative graphs for sites in the Parkin, Nodena, Walls, and Kent phases. With the exception of the Upper Nodena site on the Nodena-phase graph (see discussion in Chapter 2), the graphs appear orderly. For example, six Parkin-phase sites contain roughly equal percentages of Neeley's Ferry plain, Barton incised, and Parkin punctated—the dominant ceramic types. Even the three Nodena-phase sites exhibit similarities, especially in the sizable percentages of Bell plain rims and low percentages of Barton incised and Parkin punctated. Based on a comparison of the two graphs, we would have little trouble separating sites of the two phases. But what even Phillips (1970: 930–31) has to say about the graphs is

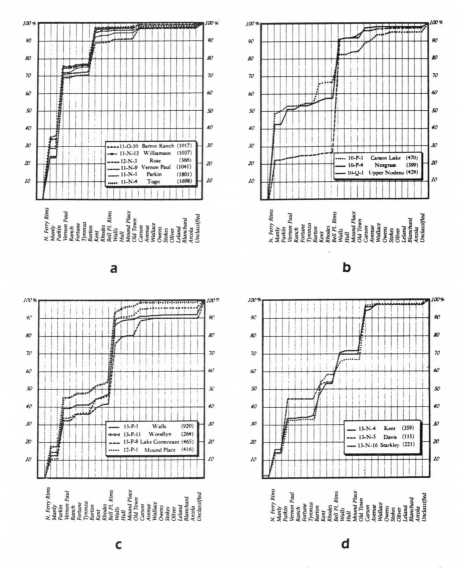

Figure 9.2. Cumulative ceramic type percentages for sites in four late Mississippian period phases in the central Mississippi River valley: a, Parkin; b, Nodena; c, Walls; d, Kent (used by permission from Phillips 1970 [Copyright 1970 by the President and Fellows of Harvard College]).

interesting: "The graphs in fig. 448 [reproduced here as Figure 9.2] are not offered as proof of the validity of the phases in question, or even as a demonstration of method. . . . These particular examples (again excepting Nodena) are *only the most successful of a large number of tries, not confined to the Mississippi period*" (emphasis added). Given the ranges in sample size with which Phillips was working, it is a wonder he got the degree of fit that he did.

Unfortunately, instead of arguing for more-rigorous sampling, Phillips (1970: 932) emphasized a change in perspective relative to phase formation: "The positive outcome was the realization that the failure [of the graphing method] was in the data and the reliance on quantitative to the neglect of qualitative criteria, not in the idea that small-scale culture-historical phases can be distinguished by means of their pottery complexes." In other words, Phillips is arguing that we should place less analytical emphasis on frequency distributions and more emphasis on whether a vessel looks or feels as if it should be Parkin rather than Nodena.

In summary, it is difficult to find in the literature any well-grounded criteria for differentiating between Parkin and Nodena sites. If one clings to the large percentage of Neeley's Ferry plain pottery as a Parkin-phase marker, it becomes difficult to make the case even at the type site. P. A. Morse (1981: fig. 7) plotted sherd frequencies in two different samples from Parkin—the one used by Phillips (1970), shown in Figure 9.2 (1,801 sherds), and one collected over a period of time by the University of Arkansas (15,926 sherds). In the Phillips sample, sherds of Neeley's Ferry plain contribute about 23% of the total, those of Parkin punctated about 49%, and those of Barton incised about 13%. In the University of Arkansas sample, however, sherds of Neeley's Ferry plain contribute about 82% of the total, those of Parkin punctated about 10%, and those of Barton incised only 2–3%. These are staggering differences, especially when viewed against the six-site cumulative graph for the Parkin phase presented in Figure 9.2a.

In light of the extensive discussion of assemblage similarity/dissimilarity in Chapter 3, we might ask how well multidimensional scaling would segregate Nodena-phase sites from Parkin-phase sites. Recall that in Chapter 3 Fox and I showed how multidimensional scaling, after sherds of Neeley's Ferry plain and Bell plain were removed from the assemblages, separated Parkin and the Pemiscot Bayou sites from the Cairo Lowland sites. If Phillips (1970) and Morse and Morse (1983) are correct that the late Pemiscot Bayou sites are more similar to the Nodena-phase sites than they are to the Parkin-phase sites, then perhaps multidimensional scaling will separate the type site of Parkin from the late Pemiscot Bayou sites. Figure 9.3 shows the results plotted in two dimensions and, for comparative purposes, a two-dimensional plot of just the Pemiscot County sites. In Chapter 3 Fox and I presented a three-dimensional plot of the Pemiscot County sites, but two dimensions are clear enough for our purposes here. Notice that as in the three-dimensional plots shown in Figure 3.9, Campbell is an extreme outlier in both Figures 9.3a and 9.3b. Dorrah and Cagle Lake are outliers from the central group, though neither is as far removed as Campbell. But notice the location of Parkin (number 12 in Figure 9.3a) relative to the central group of sites. It is, in fact, as close as or closer to many of the Pemiscot County sites as are Kinfolk Ridge and McCoy. Does this suggest that Parkin is different from the majority of the Pemiscot County sites? The answer is obviously no. But suppose, for the sake of argument, that we are biasing the analysis somehow by including two early sites—Kersey and Wardell—and one site—Murphy—that has an earlier component in it. If we exclude those samples, would Parkin be distinguishable from the late Pemiscot Bayou sites? Again, as shown in Figure 9.4, the answer is no. It appears, *given the current data sets and all the problems with them,* that no amount of statistical manipulation can sort out Parkin from Nodena.

Future Research Directions

Will it ever be possible to sort out the late Mississippian period sites of northeastern Arkansas and southeastern Missouri into those culture-historical units of which Phillips spoke? Possibly, though given the highly biased condition of the existing database, one is going to have to regard the results with considerable caution. It would greatly enhance such analyses, however, if fresh sets of materials were collected in a systematic manner. But beyond statistical applications, there are several research directions that might provide highly informative information. Several of these are discussed briefly below.

Source and Provenience of Ceramic Materials

I would begin by taking a closer look at the ceramic materials with an eye to pinpointing subtle variation and plotting that variation spatially. For example, looking at the ceramic vessels from the Pemiscot Bayou sites, one is struck by the *apparent* standardization of production, especially in terms of form and decoration. This apparent standardization can be extended to include vessels from neighboring regions in western Tennessee and northeastern Arkansas, and is, of course, one of the main bases for establishing the late Mississippian period phases used to categorize sites and assemblages in the central Mississippi River valley. But what about the not-so-obvious differences in the vessels—differences that heretofore have been relegated to the category of "noise" in a rush to find similarities? It is entirely possible that some of the clays used to manufacture vessels, as well as the pigments used to paint them, are different enough from each other that they can be identified as to locality of manufacture. There is also a possibility, not necessarily a remote one, that some of the late Mississippian period vessels were being traded from one or more production centers. If so, and the vessels can be traced to points of origin, we should, after a time, be able to develop a clear picture of which groups were exchanging vessels with which other groups. Prime candidates for this analysis are the 100-plus head pots from the region. Qualitative assessment of design characteristics suggests that the work of individual craftsmen can already be identified and that in at least one instance a single craftsman was responsible for a head pot from Campbell and one from Cross County, Arkansas

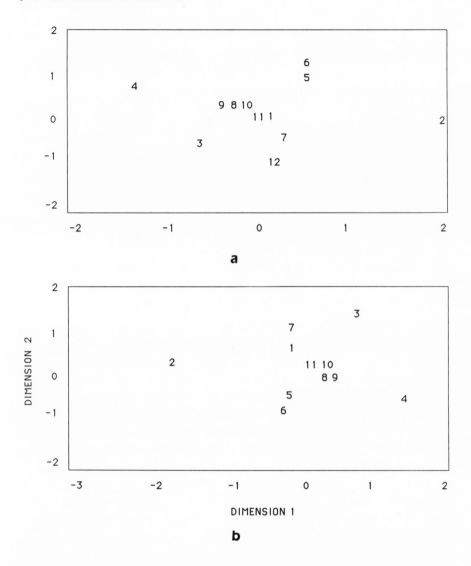

Figure 9.3. Results of multidimensional scaling of surface-collected and excavated ceramic assemblages from (a) 11 Pemiscot County sites and Parkin and (b) only the 11 Pemiscot County sites. Note the small degree of difference in positioning of the sites relative to each other regardless of whether Parkin is included. Key to sites: 1, Holland; 2, Campbell; 3, Dorrah; 4, Cagle Lake; 5, Kinfolk Ridge; 6, McCoy; 7, Wardell; 8, Kersey; 9, Murphy; 10, Brooks; 11, Denton Mounds; 12, Parkin.

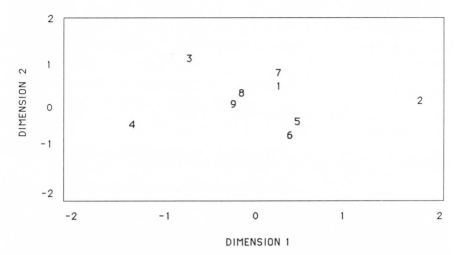

Figure 9.4. Results of multidimensional scaling of surface-collected and excavated ceramic assemblages from eight late Mississippian period Pemiscot County sites and Parkin. Key to sites: 1, Holland; 2, Campbell; 3, Dorrah; 4, Cagle Lake; 5, Kinfolk Ridge; 6, McCoy; 7, Brooks; 8, Denton Mounds; 9, Parkin.

(J. Cherry, pers. comm., 1993). Empirical evidence, however, is needed to make this more than an impression.

One method of determining location of manufacture is through the sourcing of clays and paints by means of x-ray analysis (for clays) and neutron-activation analysis (for clays and pigments). In one project currently under way, I am using neutron activation to examine large samples of sherds of Campbell appliquéd not only from Pemiscot Bayou sites but also from several sites in western Tennessee. Campbell appliquéd occurs almost exclusively on jars, which I assume were not traded or exchanged. I am using the sherds, in conjunction with daub samples, to establish a series of clay-composition fingerprints of clays local to each site. The program can be expanded to include sherds of types that I suspect might have been traded, such as Nodena red-and-white and the other polychromes.

A parallel exercise will be aimed at identifying pigments used to decorate the vessels, following on work initiated by Dunnell and Jackson (1992). As they note, different recipes may have been used by different groups to produce the pigmented designs, and the pigments might have been traded even if the vessels were not (Dunnell and Jackson 1992: 14). Dunnell and Jackson use energy-dispersive x-ray analysis to estimate the major and minor elements in the pigments, where I plan to use neutron-activation analysis. To date, Dunnell and Jackson's analysis has produced interesting results, the most interesting of which are based solely on visual inspection of decorative techniques. There are three techniques for applying red and white slips to a vessel: red applied next to white; red applied over white; and white applied over red. Recall that in Chapter 2, under the discussion of Nodena red-and-white, Fox and I cited Chapman's notation that in southeastern Missouri there occur examples of red slip on top of white slip, a reason he gave for shortening the type name to Nodena red. In their survey of paint-application technique in southeastern Missouri and northeastern Arkansas, Dunnell and Jackson (1992) found examples of all three techniques, though red-on-white was limited to a single occurrence. The other two techniques strongly sorted geographically. With a single exception, samples from north of the Missouri-Arkansas line contained white slip over red slip; Arkansas samples contained separate panels of red and white slip, perhaps overlapping a bit where the panels met. A single Arkansas sherd exhibited a red slip over a white slip. Dunnell and Jackson also found strong geographical sorting by type of vessel. With one exception, red-and-white-slipped vessels in their sample from north of the state line are bowls; those from south of the line are bottles.

Red-and-white-slipped vessels and sherds from the Pemiscot Bayou locality should yield interesting results when compared with future results obtained by Dunnell and Jackson. Currently, their sample is restricted to 25 sherds from 11 sites—four in Missouri and 7 in Arkansas. Importantly, the Missouri sites all are located on the older braided-stream deposits of Malden Plain and Commerce Hills; the Arkansas sites are located in the meander-belt portion of the alluvial valley. Sherds and vessels from the Pemiscot Bayou sites will significantly expand their sample, though my impression is that their results, at least relative to vessel form, will hold up. I have seen many more red-and-white bottles than bowls in the collections I have examined, and *all* of the bowls are either red on the interior and white on the exterior or vice versa. I have seen no bowls with red and white together on the same vessel exterior or interior. I have, however, noted examples of all three application techniques on bottles, though red-beside-white appears to be the most common of the three, followed by red-on-white. Future work will be aimed at quantifying the variation among the Pemiscot Bayou assemblages.

Vessel Form

When decoration is the primary dimension of focus, the results have been encouraging, though there are many late Mississippian period vessel forms·that also appear to be useful chronological markers. One is the annular, expanding-base (often perforated) bottle with a flaring neck that is so prominent in the large assemblages from Berry and Campbell (chapters 6 and 7). Based on his assessment of burial vessels from Denton Mounds, J. R. Williams (1972), in fact, was inclined to place that site earlier than Campbell because of observed differences in neck and ring height. It may turn out that that particular bottle form underwent changes in shape through time, but there is no doubt that it is a later form than the narrower-necked bottle. Methods of decorating the annular, expanding-base bottle varied considerably, and these might also be temporally diagnostic. For example, the bottle can be red-slipped, red-and-white-slipped, incised, or engraved. But to concentrate *only* on decoration precludes the possibility that form-related characteristics are also temporally sensitive. Other vessel forms that appeared late in the sequence (at least as currently understood) include the head pot, which certainly exhibits spatial variation; square bottles; conch-shell bowls; and standing-dog effigy bottles.

Vessel Function

In a related vein, efforts could be directed toward understanding how late Mississippian period vessels were used and how, through time, vessel forms changed relative to function. We can no longer simply assign vessels the function of "funerary wares," since literally all bowls, jars, and bottles recovered from burial contexts exhibit extensive evidence of use-wear, especially on the bases (e.g., Plate 4b). I have also noticed extensive wear on vessel interiors, especially bowls, caused by scraping, cutting, and other activities. We need to establish classes of wear so that we can better understand how the vessels were used prior to their inclusion as burial offerings.

Absolute Dating

Despite the encouraging results that decoration and form provide, there is still the problem that the changes we can document are free-floating, that is, the decorative and formal dimensions show time in a relative as opposed to an absolute sense. And even if decorative or formal change is rendered in an absolute sense for one geographic area, how do we know that that change was contemporary across the region? I contend that no archaeologist knows precisely when any of the myriad ceramic types came into being in the tristate region, when they ended, or how long they persisted. We may know *roughly* when certain types came into being and when they died out, but these rough approximations may be accurate to something on the order of 100–200 years. There appears to be no way out of this dilemma except through implementation of a large-scale dating program across the tristate region (e.g., Dunnell 1989, 1993; Dunnell and Feathers n.d.). More than enough materials currently exist in collections for a thermoluminescence-dating program, except for the fact that soil samples for background counts do not exist. Thermoluminescence dating is an expensive proposition, but it offers the advantage of dating the artifacts themselves as opposed to dating the contexts containing the sherds and vessels. Ideally, intact vessels containing sediments can be treated as single analytical units, using the sediments for background counts and small plugs from the vessels as the objects to be dated. Complementary analysis could involve dating pieces of the skeletons found associated with the vessels.

Sources of Lithic Materials

Another promising area of research is in the sourcing of materials, especially copper. I earlier mentioned the examination of raw-material-procurement patterns relative to determining whether patterns changed through time, but it is also germane to pinpointing regional differences among late-period assemblages. Many of the raw materials are identifiable macroscopically, but some are not. Compositional studies would greatly expand our knowledge of where some materials were being derived, especially the brown chert typically labeled as "Crowley's Ridge gravel." Analysis of the copper pieces is crucial to determining whether they were manufactured from native ores or whether they are Spanish in origin.

Cranial Deformation

One of the intriguing features of the Pemiscot Bayou burials is the high incidence of cranial deformation, especially among adult females. In the Campbell sample of 90 crania, 33 of 54 female skulls exhibited deformation as opposed to only 3 of 36 male skulls. No individual with an estimated age at death of less than 20 years exhibited a deformed cranium. Where did the individuals with deformed crania come from? Apparently they immigrated to Campbell as adults, but their places of origin are unknown. Individuals with deformed crania have been recovered from other late Mississippian period sites in Arkansas and Tennessee, leading one to suspect that at least some of the communities in the tristate region were exchanging females, as well as a few males, as marriage partners. Powell (1989), for example, indicates that among the skeletal assemblage from Nodena, females with deformed crania outnumbered males exhibiting the trait. How widespread was cranial deformation? Was it only practiced by groups living in the region between Pemiscot Bayou–Left Hand Chute and the Mississippi River, or was it practiced by people along the St. Francis River as well? The presence of some cranial deformation among the Kersey and Murphy skeletal samples indicates that the practice of deforming the cranium was not exclusively a post–A.D. 1400 occurrence, but comparative data are lacking.

Closing Comment

This chapter can be closed with the same caveat raised in the Preface: The present volume presents a considerable amount of information, but it leaves many questions unanswered. In fairness, perhaps I should say that many of the questions are unanswered in *my* mind, not necessarily in the minds of other archaeologists working in the region. These include questions such as, How long were the Pemiscot Bayou communities occupied? Where did the people come from who inhabited the relict levees along former courses of the Mississippi River? Why are there different numbers and kinds of goods interred with different individuals? Was Campbell, along with the other Pemiscot Bayou communities, part of the province of Pacaha? Did the Spanish actually contact any of the inhabitants of the Pemiscot Bayou communities? Maybe someday we will be able to answer these questions, as well as others that are equally important, but that day is not yet here. Regrettably, one has to agree with Phillips (1970: 934) when he laments that "we haven't even begun to understand the nuances of variation, particularly in the chronological dimension, of our insufficiently specific cultural units such as Nodena." Things haven't changed much in the last two decades, and they never will until we drop those "insufficiently specific cultural units" and get on with the real work of identifying and measuring variation in the assemblages from the late Mississippian period communities. I hope this volume has set the tone for that work, in the meantime bringing to light an extraordinary set of materials that are ripe for further analysis.

APPENDIX 1

Burials and Burial Inclusions from Murphy

Burial	Type of Interment	Description of Inclusions
Area F		
UB1	Horizontal bundle	Everted-neck Neeley's Ferry plain bottle; Neeley's Ferry plain bowl with cat-monster rim rider
UB2	Horizontal bundle	None
UB3	Extended	Bell plain bottle with short, everted neck
Area H		
6	In a post hole	None
Area I		
UB4	Cremation	None
UB5	Cremation	None
UB6	Cremation	None
UB7	Cremation	None
8	Horizontal bundle	Small Neeley's Ferry plain jar; Neeley's Ferry plain bowl
13	In a post hole	None
16	Cremation	None
20	Cremation	None
24	Cremation	None
25	Horizontal bundle	Small Bell plain bottle with 3 crude engraved lines below neck/body juncture
Area J		
UB8	?	Nodena point
UB9	?	None
UB10	?	None
UB11	?	None
7	Vertical bundle	None
26	Vertical bundle	None
27	Vertical bundle	None
28	Horizontal bundle	None
29	Vertical bundle	None
30	Vertical bundle	None
31	Horizontal bundle	None
32	Horizontal bundle	None
33	Vertical bundle	None

Continued on next page

34	Vertical bundle	Bowl with interior red slip
35	Vertical bundle	None
36	Horizontal bundle	None
37	Horizontal bundle	None
38	Horizontal bundle	None
39	Vertical bundle	None
40	?	
41	Horizontal bundle	Small bottle with polychrome red and orange exterior slips
42	Vertical bundle	
43	Extended	Small quartzite hammerstone
44	Horizontal bundle	2 bowls (unknown type) stacked one inside the other; Bell plain bottle with strongly flaring neck, raised annular base, and incised stepped "cloud" decoration on rim
45	Horizontal bundle	
49	?	Expanding-neck Bell plain bottle with raised, annular base; Vernon Paul everted-rim bowl with entwined appliqué strips at neck-body juncture and interior red slip
50	Extended	Neeley's Ferry plain bottle with slightly flaring neck; Neeley's Ferry plain bowl with animal-effigy rim rider
54	Extended	Neeley's Ferry plain bowl with owl-effigy head and tail rim riders
55	Extended	Rhodes incised bottle with strongly flaring neck and annular base; 4 brown-chert adzes
56	Horizontal bundle	None
57	Vertical bundle	None
58	Horizontal bundle	None
60	Extended	None
62	Horizontal bundle	None
63	Extended	None
65	Horizontal bundle	None
66	Vertical bundle	Chert adze; Nodena point
67	Horizontal bundle	Three coarse-paste pottery disks
68	Horizontal bundle	None
69	Horizontal bundle	None

70	Extended	Bell plain bottle with exterior reddish-brown slip (typed as red-slipped); Campbell punctated bottle with vertical appliquéd strips below lip
75	Extended	Rhodes incised bottle; everted-rim bowl (type unknown) with 4 stepped "cloud" cutouts around rim; 2 thin 4-cm-diameter copper disks with wooden backings (located on parietal)
76	Extended	Restricted-orifice bowl with nicked rim (missing from collection)
77	Horizontal bundle	Bell plain bottle molded into body of a turtle, with head, tail, and 4 legs protruding; Parkin punctated jar; bowl with interior red slip
Area K		
UB14	?	Bell plain bottle with incised line at neck-body juncture
11	Cremation	None
14	?	None
17	Cremation	2 drilled conch-shell beads; pipe bowl with human face; miniature polychrome bottle with exterior orange slip with black banding overslip
18	Vertical bundle	Bones smeared with red ochre.
19	Cremation	Fortune noded jar with 2 noded handles; vessel of unknown type and form; fragment of fine-paste bottle exhibiting bird wing modeled in relief
23	?	8 conch-shell beads
Area L		
1	Horizontal bundle	Bell plain flat-base bottle
2	Horizontal bundle	Small Walls engraved, coarse-paste jar with engraved weeping-eye motifs, circles, and cross-hatched bands on exterior
3	?	None
4	?	Bottle of unknown type and form
9	Horizontal bundle	Neeley's Ferry plain bowl with (fragmentary) animal-effigy rim rider
10	Horizontal bundle	Bell plain bottle with short, straight neck

Continued on next page

12	Horizontal bundle	Neeley's Ferry plain everted-rim bottle; miniature Neeley's Ferry plain bottle
21	Extended	Coarse-shell-tempered elbow pipe; vessel of unknown type and form
22	?	Walls engraved bottle with cross-hatched bands and concentric circles on the body

Area P

UB12	Vertical bundle	None
UB13	Horizontal bundle	None
46	Vertical bundle	None
47	Vertical bundle	None
48	Horizontal bundle	None
51	Extended	Bell plain bottle with medium-height, slightly everted neck; small Neeley's Ferry plain bowl with two pairs of holes near lip
52	Horizontal bundle	None
53	Extended	None
59	Horizontal flexed	Small Neeley's Ferry plain jar with opposing loop handles and crude appliquéd medallions on the exterior
61	?	Neeley's Ferry plain bowl with (missing) effigy rim rider; Neeley's Ferry plain jar with loop handles
64	Urn	Large Neeley's Ferry plain jar (urn) with a row of punctations around the lip and another row at the neck-body juncture and 4 strap handles; small Neeley's Ferry plain conjoined bottles
71	?	Coarse-paste pottery disk
72	Vertical bundle	None
73	Extended (infant)	None
74	Horizontal bundle	Coarse-paste pottery disk

Unknown

11A	?	Walls engraved bottle with stepped and eccentric designs on body
11B	?	Walls engraved bottle with cross-hatched area outlining serpent form

APPENDIX 2

Known Ceramic Vessels Associated with Burials at Campbell

Burial	Ceramic Type	Form	Comments
1	Campbell appliquéd	Bottle	Vertical appliquéd strips on neck
2	Bell plain	Bottle	Short neck, slightly flaring
4	Neeley's Ferry plain	Bottle	Tall neck, flaring near rim; small ring base
	Bell plain	Bowl	Notched rim fillet
5	Bell plain	Bottle	26 vertical gadroons; raised, flat pedestal base
7	Nodena red-and-white	Bottle	Alternating wide, vertical bands from rim
8	Red-slipped	Bowl	Notched rim fillet
10A	Bell plain	Bowl	Notched rim fillet
	Carson red-on-buff	Bottle	Effigy head pot
10B	Neeley's Ferry plain	Bowl	Miniature vessel with 2 wide rim lugs
	Neeley's Ferry plain	Bottle	Miniature hooded "lemon squeezer" type
10C	Neeley's Ferry plain	Bottle	Miniature
	Campbell appliquéd/ Parkin punctated	Jar	Miniature
11	Campbell punctated	Bottle	Slightly everted neck
12	Neeley's Ferry plain	Bottle	Medium-height, everted neck; annular base
13	Bell plain	Bowl	Several notched protuberances below lip to give appearance of fish fins
	Campbell appliquéd	Jar	Eight vertical appliqués on everted rim
14	Neeley's Ferry plain	Jar	Vessel molded in shape of fish with head, tail, and fins; row of nodes below rolled lip
	Bell plain	Bowl	Notched-lip vessel with bird-head rim rider and tab tail opposite; smaller bird rides on tail
15	Bell plain	Bottle	Short, straight neck

Continued on next page

	Bell plain	Bowl	Notched fillet below lip
16	Bell plain	Bowl	Bird-head rim rider, tab tail opposite; notched rim fillet
	Campbell punctated	Bottle	Rows of punctations below angled-notches on lip
17	Bell plain	Bowl	Notched rim fillet
	Bell plain	Bottle	Medium-height, slightly flaring neck; annular base
18	Campbell punctated	Bottle	
19	Red-slipped	Bottle	Dog head and tail protrude from vessel wall, which is elongate parallel to animal's body; 4 feet had been broken off
20	Campbell punctated	Bottle	4 appliquéd strips above punctations
21	Campbell punctated	Bottle	17 appliquéd strips above 4 rows of punctations
22	Bell plain	Bowl	Bat head extends above bowl lip, tail opposite; stylized wings appliquéd to exterior wall
23	Campbell punctated	Bottle	
	Campbell appliquéd	Jar	
24	Red-slipped	Bowl	Notched rim
	Campbell punctated	Bottle	4 appliquéd strips above thickened neck with vertical punctations
25	Neeley's Ferry plain	Bowl	No treatment
	Bell plain	Bottle	2 small bottles joined by 2 horizontal beams
26	Bell plain	Bottle	Tall, strongly flaring neck; flaring, perforated annular base
	Bell plain	Bowl	Notched rim fillet
27	Neeley's Ferry plain	Bowl	Notched rim fillet
	Neeley's Ferry plain	Bottle	Medium-height flaring rim; notches around neck-shoulder juncture; flaring annular base
28	Bell plain	Bowl	Small notches on lip
	Bell plain	Bottle	
29	Bell plain	Bottle	Medium-height slightly flaring rim; flaring annular base
30	Bell plain	Bowl	Notched rim fillet
	Campbell punctated	Bottle	Medium-height compound neck caused by constriction of area con-

			taining 5 rows of punctations; 4 appliquéd strips below lip
31	Neeley's Ferry plain	Bottle	Short, straight neck; globular body
	Bell plain	Bowl	Notched rim fillet; mussel shell inside
35	Campbell punctated	Bottle	Medium-height compound neck caused by constriction of area containing 5 rows of punctations; 4 appliquéd strips below lip
	Bell plain	Bowl	Bat effigy
36	Nodena red-and-white	Bottle	Alternating vertical bands from rim; edges of hole in vessel side ground smooth
38	Neeley's Ferry plain	Bowl	Miniature; notched lip
39	Neeley's Ferry plain	Bottle	Squat body; short, flaring neck
	Red-slipped	Bowl	Molded in shape of conch shell; red-slipped on interior
40	Bell plain	Bowl	Notched rim fillet
	Bell plain	Bottle	Extremely tall neck, slightly flaring near lip; annular base
41	Neeley's Ferry plain	Bottle	Tall flaring neck; annular base
42	Campbell punctated	Bottle	4 appliquéd strips above punctations
	?	Bowl	
43	Campbell incised	Jar	Everted rim; incisions limited to rim area
	Neeley's Ferry plain	Bottle	"Bottle-in-a-bowl" form; bowl portion has notched fillet rim
44	Campbell punctated	Bottle	Miniature; 4 appliquéd strips above punctations
45	Campbell punctated	Bottle	Straight neck, flaring lip; annular base
	Bell plain	Bowl	Bird head protruding from vessel wall; tail and feet opposite
46	?	Bowl	
48	Bell plain	Bottle	Short, straight neck
50	Bell plain	Bottle	Medium-height, strongly flaring neck; annular base
	?	Bowl	Fish effigy
51	Bell plain	Bottle	Short, flaring neck

Continued on next page

52	Campbell punctated	Bottle	4 appliquéd strips above 4 rows of punctations
53	?	Bowl	
54	Neeley's Ferry plain	Bowl	Everted rim
	Neeley's Ferry plain	Bottle	Miniature
55	Neeley's Ferry plain	Jar	Pinching below notched rim to resemble vertical appliquéd strips; 6 rows of punctations below
	Bell plain	Bowl	Notched rim fillet and notched base
56	Neeley's Ferry plain	Bottle	
58	Neeley's Ferry plain	Bowl	Noded rim
	?	Bottle	Fish head, tail, and fins protrude from exterior
59	Red-slipped	Bowl	Single band of punctations on thickened rim; mussel shell inside
	?	Bottle	
60	?	Bottle	
61	Bell plain	Bottle	Tall neck, everted near rim
	Bell plain	Bowl	Cat-monster effigy with pinched-fillet rim; mussel shell inside
62	Red-slipped	Bottle	Medium-height neck, annular base (unpainted)
63	Bell plain	Bottle	Horizontal incisions on neck; 5 small handles descending from just below lip
64	Bell plain	Bottle	Medium-height, everted neck; perforated annular base
	?	Bowl	Bat effigy
65	Bell plain	Bottle	Medium-height, everted neck; 4 evenly spaced nodes on shoulder with vertical incision below each
	?	Bowl	
66	Bell plain	Bottle	Medium-height, straight neck; perforated annular base
67	Red-slipped	Bottle	Fish head, tail, and fins protrude from exterior
68	?	Bottle	Medium-height, slightly everted neck; thickened annular base
70	Bell plain	Bottle	Tall, everted neck

	Red-slipped	Bowl	
71	Red-slipped	Bowl	Single row of punctations on lip exterior; 4 molded "sticks" below punctations; slipped interior and over "sticks"
	?	Bottle	Medium-height, everted neck; perforated, expanding annular base
72	?	Bottle	Tall, everted neck; perforated, expanding annular base
74	Bell plain	Bottle	Medium-height, slightly everted neck; notched annular base
75	Neeley's Ferry plain	Bowl	Crested duck on rim, tab tail opposite; notched rim
76	?	Bottle	
77	Campbell punctated	Bottle	9 appliquéd strips above vertical punctations
78	Campbell appliquéd	Jar	
81	Bell plain	Bowl	Notched rim containing 2 bifurcate lugs
	Walls engraved	Bottle	Engraved swirls on shoulder and body; symmetrical stair-step design on straight neck, which had been cut down 1–2 inches; expanding annular base
82	?	Bottle	Body molded in shape of turtle, with four legs below and head and tail protruding from walls; flared neck on vessel
	?	Bowl	Vessel molded in shape of fish with head, tail, and dorsal fins protruding from just below lip
83	Bell plain	Bottle	Medium-height everted neck; 4 evenly spaced nodes on shoulder with incised line around each; notched annular base
	Red-slipped	Bowl	Deer effigy
84	Bell plain	Bottle	Short, slightly everted neck
85	Bell plain	Bottle	Tall, straight neck; flaring annular base
	?	Bowl	Notched rim fillet; 2 mussel shells inside

Continued on next page

86	Bell plain	Bowl	Notched rim fillet; 2 mussel shells inside
	Bell plain	Bottle	Medium-height, everted neck; 4 evenly spaced nodes around lip, punctations below
88	?	Bowl	Fish effigy
89	Bell plain	Bottle	Medium-height, slightly flaring neck; annular base
90	Bell plain	Bottle	Medium-height, slightly flaring neck; molded turtle features around shoulders; annular base
	Bell plain	Bowl	Notched rim fillet
91	Neeley's Ferry plain	Bottle	Miniature
	Neeley's Ferry plain	Bowl	Notched rim fillet
92	Campbell appliquéd	Jar	8 appliquéd strips on neck above 2 rows of large punctations; 1 row of punctations around lip
93	?	Bottle	
94	?	Bottle	Flaring rim; flaring annular base
95	Bell plain	Bowl	Medium-height, slightly everted neck; flaring, punctated, and notched annular base
	Bell plain	Bottle	Short neck; flaring, notched annular base
96	Neeley's Ferry plain	Bottle	"Bottle-in-a-bowl" form; bowl portion has notched rim fillet
97	Bell plain	Bowl	Notched rim fillet
98	Bell plain	Bottle	Medium-height neck, flaring near lip; punctated annular base
99	Neeley's Ferry plain	Bowl	No treatment
	?	Bottle	Tall, slightly everted neck; flaring, punctated, and notched annular base
101	Campbell appliquéd	Jar	Notched appliquéd strips above single row of punctations
102	Bell plain	Bowl	Notched rim fillet
103	Bell plain	Bottle	Tall neck, slightly flaring near lip; broken and reground annular base
	?	Bowl	Bat/bear effigy
104	Red-slipped	Bowl	Cat-monster effigy

	?	Jar	Miniature
105	?	?	
107	Bell plain	Bowl	Molded fish features around shoulder; notched rim
108	Bell plain	Bowl	Molded fish features around shoulder; notched rim
	Kent incised	Jar	Appliquéd handles near lip
109	Red-slipped	Bowl	Molded in shape of conch shell; slipped on interior
110	?	Bottle	Tall, everted neck; flaring, notched annular base
111	?	Bottle	Tall, flaring neck with expanding, perforated annular base
113	Neeley's Ferry plain	Bowl	4 handles below lip; mussel shell inside
	Neeley's Ferry plain	Bottle	Short neck, slightly flaring near lip
	Bell plain	Bottle	Tall neck, slightly flaring near lip; annular base
114	?	Bowl	Vessel molded in shape of fish with head, tail, and fins
	?	Bottle	
115	?	Bottle	
116	Red-slipped	Bowl	Elaborate vessel molded in shape of fish with head, tail, and fins below row of lip nodes; red-slipped interior
	?	Bottle	Slightly everted neck; expanding annular base
118	Red-slipped	Bowl	Red-slipped interior
	Campbell punctated	Bottle	
119	Bell plain	Bottle	Squat body; short, everted neck
	?	Bowl	Vessel molded in shape of fish with head, tail, and fins
123	Campbell punctated	Bottle	4 handles below lip; 5 rows of punctations below and above handles
124	?	Bowl	
	?	Bottle	
1W	Neeley's Ferry plain	Bowl	Angled notching on lip
	Bell plain	Bottle	Short, slightly flaring neck

Continued on next page

	Walls engraved	Bottle	Tall, flaring rim; zig-zag design on shoulder
2W	Bell plain	Bottle	Everted neck; short, squat body; raised, flat base
3W	Bell plain	Bowl	Notched rim fillet; mussel shell inside
	?	Bottle	Tall, everted rim; annular base missing
4AW	Bell plain	Bottle	Squat body; tall, strongly flaring neck; perforated annular base
5W	?	Bowl	Vessel had been elongated to form animal body; oppossum head, ears, and tail protrude from exterior
6W	Hollywood white-slipped/Campbell punctated	Bottle	5 appliquéd strips extending down into rows of punctations; neck unslipped
	Bell plain	Bowl	Notched rim fillet
8W	?	Bottle	Gadrooned body; expanding annular base
9W	Neeley's Ferry plain	Jar	4 handles extending down from lip
	?	Bowl	Bat effigy
11W	Bell plain	Bowl	Bird-head rim rider, tab tail opposite; notched lip
12W	Bell plain	Jar	Molded fish features around shoulders; single row of punctations below lip
13W	Bell plain	Bowl	Lopsided vessel; single row of closely spaced nodes below lip
14W	Bell plain	Bowl	Notched rim fillet
16W	Neeley's Ferry plain	Bottle	Medium-height, slightly flaring neck; annular base
19W	Bell plain?	Bottle	Miniature vessel with thickened lip
	?	Bowl	Vessel molded to resemble fish
20W	Neeley's Ferry plain	Bottle	Medium-height, slightly flaring neck; annular base
	Neeley's Ferry plain	Bowl	Notched lip
21W	Bell plain	Bowl	Notched lip
	?	Bottle	Everted neck; expanding annular base

23W	Campbell punctated	Bottle	4 appliquéd strips above thickened neck-shoulder juncture containing punctations
24W	Bell plain	Bottle	Medium-height, flaring neck
25W	Bell plain	Bowl	Pinched fillet below lip
	Bell plain	Bowl	Small vessel with notches just below lip; short annular base; C. R. Price and J. E. Price state on catalog card, "appears similar to European vessel forms"
	Bell plain	Bottle	Wide, short, slightly flaring neck
26W	?	Bowl	
28AW	Neeley's Ferry plain	Bottle	Very tall, slightly flaring neck; notched annular base with 4 perforations
	?	Bowl	
	?	Bottle	
28BW	Bell plain	Bottle	Miniature vessel, straight neck; expanding annular base
	Bell plain	Bottle	Miniature vessel, straight neck; engraved arrow design around body
30W	Neeley's Ferry plain	Bowl	Notched rim fillet
34W	Neeley's Ferry plain	Jar	4 handles below lip
35W	?	Bottle	
36W	?	Bottle	
37W	?	Bowl	
43W	Vernon Paul appliquéd	Jar	3 handles below lip; 6 notched appliquéd strips on body
44W	Campbell appliquéd	Bowl	Miniature vessel; 10 vestigial handles below lip
	Neeley's Ferry plain	Bowl	Notched rim fillet
45W	Bell plain	Bottle	Short, everted neck
46W	?	Bowl	
48W	?	?	
49W	Barton incised	Jar	Notched lip; handles on rim
	?	Bowl	Duck effigy
50W	?	Bowl	
	?	Bottle	Mussel shell in mouth
52W	Neeley's Ferry plain	Bottle	

Continued on next page

	Campbell appliquéd/ punctated	Bottle	Arcaded handles above thickened strip containing punctations
53W	?	Bowl	Bat head and tail below lip
54W	Campbell incised	Bottle	5 appliquéd handles below lip; handles and areas between incised with vertical lines
	Carson red-on-buff	Bowl	Red-slipped exterior; red-on-buff swirls interior; appliquéd nodes below lip
56W	?	?	
57W	Bell plain	Bowl	Small, thick vessel; bird rim rider, tab tail opposite; rim notched; red slip in places
	Bell plain	Bowl	Small, oval vessel; small lugs on rim
	Bell plain	Bottle	Squat body; wide, tall, everted neck
59W	?	Bottle	
	?	Bowl	
60W	Bell plain	Bowl	Notched lip
	Bell plain	Bottle	Short, everted neck
62W	?	Bottle	Short, straight neck
64W	Bell plain	Bottle	Hooded "lemon-squeezer" type
65W	Bell plain	Bottle	Extremely tall, everted neck; flat, raised, notched base
	Red-slipped	Bowl	Angled notching on lip
66W	Bell plain	Bottle	Highly polished; tall, everted neck; annular base
	?	Bowl	Vessel molded in shape of fish with head, tail, and fins
67W	Bell plain	Jar	Small vessel; fish elements, including mouth and fins, molded on shoulder
	Neeley's Ferry plain	Jar	Miniature vessel; notches on shoulder
68W	Bell plain	Bottle	Miniature vessel; body molded into 4 lobes
70W	Bell plain	Bottle	Tall, everted neck; annular base
72W	?	?	Miniature vessel
75W	?	Bowl	
	?	Bottle	
76W	?	Bowl	

	?	Bottle	
80W	Bell plain	Bottle	Tall, everted neck; incisions radiate from below neck-shoulder juncture to base, giving the appearance of gadrooning; annular base
82W	Bell plain	Bottle	Extremely tall, slightly everted neck; tall, flaring annular base
83W	?	Bottle	
84W	Bell plain	Bowl	Lopsided vessel; notched rim fillet
	Bell plain	Bottle	Tall, slightly flaring neck that was broken and ground smooth; raised, notched base
86W	Bell plain	Bottle	
87W	Neeley's Ferry plain	Bowl	Row of small punctations below lip
	Campbell punctated	Bottle	4 appliquéd handles below lip
88W	Walls engraved/ Campbell punctated	Bottle	5 appliquéd strips above punctations; engraved spiral design on one side only
	?	Bowl	
89W	Bell plain	Bowl	Notched rim fillet
	Bell plain	Bottle	Medium-height, slightly everted neck; flaring, punctated, and notched annular base
90W	?	Bottle	
	Campbell appliquéd	Jar	4 equally spaced nodes midway down body
91W	Bell plain	Bottle	Short, straight neck
	Bell plain	Bowl	Notched rim fillet
92W	?	Bowl	Notched rim fillet
	Neeley's Ferry plain	Bowl	

REFERENCES

Adams, W.
   1951. The etiology of swimmer's exostoses of the external auditory canals and of associated changes in hearing. *Journal of Laryngology and Otology* 65:133–53, 232–50.

Ahler, S. A.
   1973. Post-Pleistocene depositional change at Rodgers Shelter, Missouri. *Plains Anthropologist* 18:1–26.

Asch, D. L., and N. A. Sidell.
   1992. Archeobotany. In *Early Woodland occupations at the Ambrose Flick site in the Sny Bottom of west-central Illinois,* edited by C. R. Stafford. Center for American Archeology, Kampsville Archeological Center, Research Series, no. 10:177–93.

Asch, N. B., R. I. Ford, and D. L. Asch.
   1972. *Paleoethnobotany of the Koster site: The Archaic horizons.* Illinois State Museum, Reports of Investigations, no. 24.

Autin, W. J., S. F. Burns, B. J. Miller, R. T. Saucier, and J. I. Snead.
   1991. Quaternary geology of the Lower Mississippi Valley. In *Quaternary nonglacial geology: Coterminous U.S.,* edited by R. B. Morrison, 547–82. Vol. K-2 of *The geology of North America.* Boulder, Colo.: Geological Society of America.

Bernabo, J. C., and T. Webb III.
   1977. Changing patterns in the Holocene pollen record of northeastern North America. *Quaternary Research* 8:64–96.

Black, T. K., III.
   1979. *The biological and social analyses of a Mississippian cemetery from southeast Missouri: The Turner site, 23BU21A.* University of Michigan, Museum of Anthropology, Anthropological Papers, no. 68.

Boutton, T. W., M. J. Lynott, and M. P. Bumsted.
   1991. Stable carbon isotopes and the study of prehistoric human diet. *Critical Reviews in Food Science and Nutrition* 30:373–85.

Brackenridge, H. M.
   1962. *Views of Louisiana.* Chicago: Quadrangle.

Brainerd, G. W.
   1951. The place of chronological ordering in archaeological analysis. *American Antiquity* 16:301–13.

Brown, B. L.
  1971. *Soil survey of Pemiscot County, Missouri.* Washington, D.C.: U.S. Department of Agriculture, Soil Conservation Service.

Buikstra, J. E.
  1976. *Hopewell in the Lower Illinois Valley.* Northwestern University Archeological Program, Scientific Papers, no. 2.
  1981. Introduction to *Prehistoric tuberculosis in the Americas,* edited by J. E. Buikstra, 1–23. Northwestern University Archeological Program, Scientific Papers, no. 5.
  1984. The lower Illinois River region: A prehistoric context for the study of ancient diet and health. In *Paleopathology at the origins of agriculture,* edited by M. N. Cohen and G. J. Armelagos, 215–34. New York: Academic Press.

Buikstra, J. E., and D. C. Cook.
  1981. PreColumbian tuberculosis in west-central Illinois: Prehistoric disease in biocultural perspective. In *Prehistoric tuberculosis in the Americas,* edited by J. E. Buikstra, 115–39. Northwestern University Archeological Program, Scientific Papers, no. 5.

Butzer, K. W.
  1977. *Geomorphology of the lower Illinois Valley as a spatial-temporal context for the Koster Archaic site.* Illinois State Museum, Reports of Investigations, no. 34.

Calcagno, J. M., and K. R. Gibson.
  1991. Selective compromise: Evolutionary trends and mechanisms in hominid tooth size. In *Advances in dental anthropology,* edited by M. A. Kelley and C. S. Larsen, 59–76. New York: Wiley-Liss.

Chapman, C. H.
  1957. Middle Mississippi burial mound. In *A report of progress, archaeological research by the University of Missouri, 1955–1956,* edited by C. H. Chapman. Missouri Archaeological Society, Special Publication.
  1980. *The Archaeology of Missouri, II.* Columbia: University of Missouri Press.

Chapman, C. H., and L. O. Anderson.
  1955. The Campbell site: A late Mississippi town site and cemetery in southeast Missouri. *The Missouri Archaeologist* 17.

Christenson, A. L., W. E. Klippel, and W. Weedman.
  1975. An archaeological survey of the proposed William L. Springer Lake Greenbelt project. Manuscript on file, Illinois State Museum.

Clayton, L. A., V. J. Knight, Jr., and E. C. Moore, eds.
  1993. *The de Soto chronicles: The expedition of Hernando de Soto to North America in 1539–1543.* 2 vols. Tuscaloosa: University of Alabama Press.

Cohen, M. N., and G. J. Armelagos.
  1984. Editors' summation in *Paleopathology at the origins of agriculture,* 585–601. New York: Academic Press.

Cole, K. W.
  1965. Cranial analysis of a late Mississippian population from southeast Missouri. Master's thesis, Department of Anthropology, University of Missouri–Columbia.

Conant, A. J.
  1878. Archaeology of Missouri. *Transactions of the Academy of Science of St. Louis* 3:353–68.

Connolly, T. J.

1986. Cultural stability and change in the prehistory of southwest Oregon and northern California. Ph.D. diss., Department of Anthropology, University of Oregon.

Cottam, G.

1949. The phytosociology of an oak woods in southwestern Wisconsin. *Ecology* 30:271–87.

Cottam, G., and J. T. Curtis.

1956. The use of distance measures in phytosociological sampling. *Ecology* 37:451–60.

Cowgill, G. L.

1990. Why Pearson's r is not a good similarity coefficient for comparing collections. *American Antiquity* 55:512–20.

Crane, H. R., and J. B. Griffin.

1972. University of Michigan radiocarbon dates XIV, XV. *Radiocarbon* 14:155–222.

Delcourt, H. R., P. A. Delcourt, G. R. Wilkins, and E. N. Smith, Jr.

1986. Vegetational history of the cedar glades regions of Tennessee, Kentucky, and Missouri during the past 30,000 years. *Association of Southeastern Biologists Bulletin* 33:128–37.

DiBartolomeo, J.

1979. Exostoses of the external auditory canal. *Annals of Otology, Rhinology, and Laryngology,* 88, supp. no. 61:1–17.

Doran, J. E., and F. R. Hodson.

1975. *Mathematics and computers in archaeology.* Cambridge: Harvard University Press.

Dunnell, R. C.

1978. Style and function: A fundamental dichotomy. *American Antiquity* 43:192–202.

1989. Four new TL dates for southeast Missouri. *Missouri Association of Professional Archaeologists Newsletter* 1(1):7–9.

n.d. *The Langdon site.* Manuscript on file, Museum of Anthropology, University of Missouri–Columbia.

Dunnell, R. C., and J. K. Feathers.

1991. Late Woodland manifestations of the Malden Plain, southeast Missouri. In *Stability, transformation, and variation: The Late Woodland Southeast,* edited by M. S. Nassaney and C. R. Cobb, 21–45. New York: Plenum Press.

n.d. Thermoluminescence dating of surface archaeological materials. In *The dating of archaeological surfaces,* edited by C. Beck. Albuquerque: University of New Mexico Press (in press).

Dunnell, R. C., M. Ikeya, P. T. McCutcheon, and S. Toyoda.

1994. Heat treatment of Mill Creek and Dover cherts on the Malden Plain, southeast Missouri. *Archaeomaterials* (in press).

Dunnell, R. C., and M. K. Jackson.

1992. Technology of late Mississippian polychromes. Paper presented at 49th annual meeting of the Southeastern Archaeological Conference, Little Rock.

Durham, J. H.

1989. Excavations at Nodena in 1932. In *Nodena,* edited by D. F. Morse, 23–29. Arkansas Archeological Survey, Research Series, no. 30.

Eisenberg, L. E.

1989. On gaming pieces and culture contact. *Current Anthropology* 30:345.

Fairbanks, C. H.
   1968.   Early Spanish colonial beads. *The Conference on Historic Site Archaeology Papers 1967* 2:3–21.

Feathers, J. K.
   1989.   Effects of temper on strength of ceramics: Response to Bronitsky and Hamer. *American Antiquity* 54:579–88.
   1990.   An evolutionary explanation for prehistoric ceramic change in southeast Missouri. Ph.D. diss., University of Washington. Ann Arbor, Mich.: University Microfilms.

Feathers, J. K., and W. D. Scott.
   1989.   Prehistoric ceramic composite from the Mississippi Valley. *Ceramic Bulletin* 68:554–57.

Finger, C. J., Jr.
   1989.   The University of Arkansas Museum excavations at Middle Nodena. In *Nodena,* edited by D. F. Morse, 31–32. Arkansas Archeological Survey, Research Series, no. 30.

Fisk, H. N.
   1944.   *Geological investigation of the alluvial valley of the Lower Mississippi River.* Vicksburg, Miss.: U.S. Army Corps of Engineers.

Fisk, H. N., and E. McFarlan, Jr.
   1955.   *Late Quaternary deltaic deposits of the Mississippi River.* Geological Society of America, Special Paper No. 62, 279–302.

Flint, T.
   1832.   *History and geography of the Mississippi Valley.* 2d ed. Cincinnati: Farnsworth.

Ford, J. A.
   1954.   The type concept revisited. *American Anthropologist* 56:42–54.
   1961.   In favor of simple typology. *American Antiquity* 27:113–14.

Fox, G. L.
   1992.   A critical evaluation of the interpretive framework of the Mississippi period in southeast Missouri. Ph.D. diss., Department of Anthropology, University of Missouri–Columbia.

Frest, T. J., and L. P. Fay.
   1980.   Peoria loess mollusc faunas and Woodfordian biomes of the upper Midwest. *AMQUA Abstracts.* Sixth biennial meeting of the American Quaternary Association, Orono, Maine.

Geier, C. R.
   1975.   *The Kimberlin site: The ecology of a Late Woodland population.* Missouri Archaeological Society, Research Series, no. 12.

Genovés, S.
   1967.   Proportionality of long bones and their relation to stature among Mesoamericans. *American Journal of Physical Anthropology* 26:67–78.

Goodman, A. H., D. L. Martin, G. J. Armelagos, and G. Clark.
   1984.   Indications of stress from bone and teeth. In *Paleopathology at the origins of agriculture,* edited by M. N. Cohen and G. J. Armelagos, 13–49. New York: Academic Press.

Gordon, C. C., and J. E. Buikstra.
   1981.   Soil pH, bone preservation, and sampling bias at mortuary sites. *American Antiquity* 46:566–71.

Griffin, J. B., and A. C. Spaulding.

1952. The central Mississippi River valley archaeological survey, season 1950: A preliminary report. In *Prehistoric pottery of eastern United States,* edited by J. B. Griffin. Ann Arbor: University of Michigan Museum of Anthropology.

Guccione, M. J.

1987. Geomorphology, sedimentation, and chronology of alluvial deposits, northern Mississippi County, Arkansas. In *A cultural resources survey, testing, and geomorphic examination of ditches 10, 12, and 29, Mississippi County, Arkansas,* by R. H. Lafferty III, M. J. Guccione, L. J. Scott, D. K. Aasen, B. J. Watkins, M. C. Sierzchula, and P. F. Bauman, 67–99, D1–D38. Report submitted to the U.S. Army Corps of Engineers, Memphis District.

Guccione, M. J., and L. H. Hehr.

1991. Origin of the "Sunklands" in the New Madrid seismic zone: Tectonic or alluvial drowning? *Geological Society of America Abstracts with Programs* 23(5):88–89.

Guccione, M. J., R. H. Lafferty III, and L. S. Cummings.

1988. Environmental constraints on human settlement in an evolving Holocene alluvial system, the Lower Mississippi Valley. *Geoarchaeology* 3:65–84.

Hamilton, H. W., J. T. Hamilton, and E. F. Chapman.

1974. *Spiro Mound copper.* Missouri Archaeological Society Memoir, no. 11.

Hamilton, M. E.

1982. Sexual dimorphism in skeletal samples. In *Sexual dimorphism in Homo sapiens,* edited by R. L. Hall, 107–63. New York: Praeger.

Hathcock, R.

1976. *Ancient Indian pottery of the Mississippi River valley.* Camden, Ark.: Hurley Press.

1988. *Ancient Indian pottery of the Mississippi River valley.* 2d ed. Marceline, Mo.: Walsworth.

Haviland, W. A.

1967. Stature at Tikal, Guatemala: Implications for ancient Maya demography and social organization. *American Antiquity* 32:316–25.

Hengen, O. P.

1971. Cribra orbitalia: Pathogenesis and probable etiology. *Homo* 22:57–75.

Hildebolt, C. F., S. Molnar, M. Elvin-Lewis, and J. K. McKee.

1988. The effect of geochemical factors on prevalences of dental diseases for prehistoric inhabitants of the state of Missouri. *American Journal of Physical Anthropology* 75:1–14.

Hill, F. C.

1975. Effects of the environment on animal exploitation by Archaic inhabitants of the Koster site. Ph.D. diss., Department of Biology, University of Louisville.

Hillson, S. W.

1979. Diet and dental disease. *World Archaeology* 11:145–61.

Holland, T. D.

1991. An archaeological and biological analysis of the Campbell site. Ph.D. diss., Department of Anthropology, University of Missouri–Columbia.

Holmes, W. H.

1886. Ancient pottery of the Mississippi Valley. *Bureau of American Ethnology, Fourth Annual Report,* 361–436.

1903. Aboriginal pottery of the eastern United States. *Bureau of American Ethnology, Twentieth Annual Report.*

Hopgood, J. F.
  1969a. Continuity and change in the Baytown pottery tradition in the Cairo Lowland,
          southeast Missouri. Master's thesis, Department of Anthropology, University
          of Missouri–Columbia.
  1969b. *An archaeological reconnaissance of Portage Open Bay in southeast Missouri.* Missouri
          Archaeological Society Memoir, no. 7.

Houck, L.
  1908.   *A history of Missouri.* Vol. 1. Chicago: Donnelley.

Hrdlička, A.
  1935.   Ear exostoses. *Smithsonian Miscellaneous Collections* 93(6):1–100.

Hudson, C., M. T. Smith, and C. B. DePratter.
  1990.   The Hernando de Soto expedition: From Mabila to the Mississippi River. In
          Towns and temples along the Mississippi, edited by D. H. Dye and C. A. Cox,
          181–207. Tuscaloosa: University of Alabama Press.

Jones, W. B.
  1989.   The Alabama Museum of Natural History excavations at Nodena. In *Nodena,*
          edited by D. F. Morse, 33–35. Arkansas Archeological Survey, Research Series,
          no. 30.

Kemink, J., and M. Graham.
  1982.   Osteomas and exostoses of the external auditory canal—medical and surgical
          management. *Journal of Otolaryngology* 11:101–6.

Kennedy, G. E.
  1986.   The relationship between auditory exostoses and cold water: A latitudinal
          analysis. *American Journal of Physical Anthropology* 71:401–15.

King, J. E., and W. H. Allen, Jr.
  1977.   A Holocene vegetation record from the Mississippi River valley, southeastern
          Missouri. *Quaternary Research* 8:307–23.

Klein, W. M., R. H. Daley, and J. Wedum.
  1975.   Environmental inventory and assessment of navigation pools 24, 25, and 26,
          upper Mississippi and lower Illinois rivers: A vegetational study. Report
          submitted to the U.S. Army Corps of Engineers, St. Louis District, St. Louis.

Klinger, T. C.
  1977a. An exceptional example of carved bone technology from the lower Mississippi
          Valley. *Arkansas Archeologist* 16–18:93–98.
  1977b. Parkin archeology: A report on the 1966 field school test excavations at the
          Parkin site. *Arkansas Archeologist* 16–18:45–80.

Klippel, W. E., G. Celmer, and J. R. Purdue.
  1978.   The Holocene naiad record at Rodgers Shelter in the western Ozark Highland
          of Missouri. *Plains Anthropologist* 23:257–71.

Kuchler, A. W.
  1964.   *Potential natural vegetation of the coterminous United States.* American Geographical
          Society Special Publication No. 36.

Lafferty, R. H., III.
  1984.   Predictive models. In *A cultural resources survey and evaluation in the Tyronza River
          Watershed phase I area, Mississippi County, Arkansas,* by R. H. Lafferty III, L. G.
          Santeford, P. A. Morse, and L. M. Chapman, 79–132. Mid-Continental Re-
          search Associates (Lowell, Ark.) Report of Investigation, no. 84-2.
  1987.   Predictive model and the distribution of archeological sites. In *A cultural
          resources survey, testing, and geomorphic examination of ditches 10, 12, and 29,*

Mississippi County, Arkansas, by R. H. Lafferty III, M. J. Guccione, L. J. Scott, D. K. Aasen, B. J. Watkins, M. C. Sierzchula, and P. F. Bauman. Mid-Continental Research Associates (Lowell, Ark.) Report of Investigation, no. 86-5.

Lafferty, R. H., III, and R. F. Cande.

1989.   *Cultural resources investigations in the proposed Peacekeeper Rail Garrison, Eaker Air Force Base, Mississippi County, Arkansas.* Mid-Continental Research Associates (Lowell, Ark.) Report of Investigation, no. 88-5.

Larsen, C. S.

1984.   Health and disease in prehistoric Georgia: The transition to agriculture. In *Paleopathology at the origins of agriculture,* edited by M. N. Cohen and G. J. Armelagos, 367–92. New York: Academic Press.

Lewis, R. B.

1974.   *Mississippian exploitative strategies: A southeast Missouri example.* Missouri Archaeological Society, Research Series, no. 11.

1982.   Two Mississippian hamlets: Cairo Lowland, Missouri. Illinois Archaeological Survey, Special Publication, no. 2.

1986.   *Mississippian towns of the western Kentucky border: The Adams, Wickliffe, and Sassafras Ridge sites.* Frankfort: The Kentucky Heritage Council.

1988.   Old World dice in the protohistoric southern United States. *Current Anthropology* 29:759–68.

1990a. On astragalus dice and culture contact: Reply to Eisenberg. *Current Anthropology* 31:410–13.

1990b. The late prehistory of the Ohio-Mississippi rivers confluence region, Kentucky and Missouri. In *Towns and temples along the Mississippi,* edited by D. H. Dye and C. A. Cox, 38–58. Tuscaloosa: University of Alabama Press.

Little, E. L., Jr.

1953.   *Check list of native and naturalized trees of the United States (including Alaska).* U.S. Forest Service, Agriculture Handbook, no. 41.

Lovejoy, C. O.

1985.   Dental wear in the Libben population: Its functional pattern and role in the determination of adult skeletal age at death. *American Journal of Physical Anthropology* 68:47–56.

Lynott, M. J., T. W. Boutton, J. E. Price, and D. E. Nelson.

1986.   Stable carbon isotopic evidence for maize agriculture in southeast Missouri and northeast Arkansas. *American Antiquity* 51:51–65.

McKern, W. C.

1939.   The Midwestern Taxonomic Method as an aid to archaeological study. *American Antiquity* 4:301–13.

McMillan, R. B., and W. E. Klippel.

1981.   Environmental changes and hunter-gatherer adaptation in the southern Prairie Peninsula. *Journal of Archaeological Science* 8:215–45.

Marshall, R. A.

1965.   An archaeological investigation of Interstate Route 55 through New Madrid and Pemiscot counties, Missouri. Missouri State Highway Department, Highway Archaeology Report, no. 1.

n.d.   Highway salvage archaeology at two village sites in Pemiscot and New Madrid counties, Missouri, 1965. Report on file, University of Missouri, Museum of Anthropology.

Meltzer, D. J., and R. C. Dunnell, eds.
   1992.   *The archaeology of William Henry Holmes.* Washington, D.C.: Smithsonian Institution Press.

Mensforth, R. P.
   1990.   Paleodemography of the Carlston Annis (Bt-5) Late Archaic skeletal population. *American Journal of Physical Anthropology* 82:81–99.

Mensforth, R. P., C. O. Lovejoy, J. W. Lallo, and G. J. Armelagos.
   1978.   The role of constitutional factors, diet, and infectious disease in the etiology of porotic hyperostosis and periosteal reactions in prehistoric infants and children. *Medical Anthropology* 2:1–59.

Michaux, F. A.
   1819.   *The North American sylva, a description of the forest trees of the United States, Canada and Nova Scotia.* Translated by A. L. Hillhouse. Paris: d'Hautel.

Million, M. G.
   1975.   Ceramic technology of the Nodena phase people (ca. A.D. 1400–1700). *Southeastern Archaeological Conference Bulletin* 18:201–8.
   1980.   The Big Lake phase pottery industry. In *Zebree Archaeological Project: Excavations, data interpretation, and report on the Zebree Homestead site, Mississippi County, Arkansas,* edited by D. F. Morse and P. A. Morse, 18-1–18-42. Fayetteville: Arkansas Archeological Survey.

Mills, L.
   1968.   Mississippian head vases of Arkansas and Missouri. *The Missouri Archaeologist* 30.

Moore, C. B.
   1910.   Antiquities of the St. Francis, White and Black rivers, Arkansas. *Journal of the Academy of Natural Sciences of Philadelphia* 14:255–364.
   1911.   Some aboriginal sites on Mississippi River. *Journal of the Academy of Natural Sciences of Philadelphia* 14:367–478.

Morse, D.
   1978.   *Ancient disease in the Midwest.* Illinois State Museum, Reports of Investigations, no. 15.
   1980.   Pathology and abnormalities of the Hampson skeletal collection. In *Nodena,* edited by D. F. Morse, 41–60. Arkansas Archeological Survey, Research Series, no. 30.

Morse, D. F.
   1989.   The Nodena phase. In *Nodena: An account of 90 years of archeological investigation in southeast Mississippi County, Arkansas,* edited by D. F. Morse, 97–113. Arkansas Archeological Survey, Research Series, no. 30.
   1990.   The Nodena phase. In *Towns and temples along the Mississippi,* edited by D. H. Dye and C. A. Cox, 69–97. Tuscaloosa: University of Alabama Press.

Morse, D. F., and P. A. Morse.
   1983.   *Archaeology of the central Mississippi Valley.* New York: Academic Press.

Morse, P. A.
   1981.   *Parkin.* Arkansas Archeological Survey, Research Series, no. 13.
   1990.   The Parkin site and the Parkin phase. In *Towns and temples along the Mississippi,* edited by D. H. Dye and C. A. Cox, 118–34. Tuscaloosa: University of Alabama Press.

Neumann, G. K.
   1942.   Types of artificial deformation in the eastern United States. *American Antiquity* 7:306–10.

Nuttall, T.
 1905. Journals of travels into the Arkansas Territory during the year 1819. In *Early western travels, 1748–1846,* vol. 13, edited by R. G. Thwaites. Cleveland: Clark.

O'Brien, M. J., and T. D. Holland.
 1990. Variation, selection, and the archaeological record. In *Archaeological method and theory,* vol. 2, edited by M. B. Schiffer, 31–79. Tucson: University of Arizona Press.
 1992. The role of adaptation in archaeological explanation. *American Antiquity* 57:36–59.

O'Brien, M. J., T. D. Holland, R. J. Hoard, and G. L. Fox.
 1994. Evolutionary implications of design and performance characteristics of prehistoric pottery. In *Journal of Archaeological Method and Theory* (in press).

O'Brien, M. J., R. L. Lyman, and T. D. Holland.
 1989. Geoarchaeological evidence for prairie-mound formation in the Mississippi Alluvial Valley, southeastern Missouri. *Quaternary Research* 31:83–93.

Ortner, D. J., and W. G. J. Putschar.
 1981. *Identification of pathological conditions in human skeletal remains.* Smithsonian Contributions to Knowledge, no. 28.

Perzigian, A. J., P. A. Trench, and D. J. Brown.
 1984. Prehistoric health in the Ohio River valley. In *Paleopathology at the origins of agriculture,* edited by M. N. Cohen and G. J. Armelagos, 347–66. New York: Academic Press.

Phillips, P.
 1958. Application of the Wheat-Gifford-Wasley taxonomy to eastern ceramics. *American Antiquity* 24:117–25.
 1970. *Archaeological survey in the lower Yazoo Basin, Mississippi, 1949–1955.* Harvard University, Peabody Museum, Papers, no. 60.

Phillips, P., J. A. Ford, and J. B. Griffin.
 1951. *Archaeological survey in the lower Mississippi Alluvial Valley, 1940–1947.* Harvard University, Peabody Museum, Papers, no. 25.

Porter, D. A., and M. J. Guccione.
 n.d. The Charleston alluvial fan: Evidence for a Pleistocene/Holocene flood(s) in the lower Mississippi Alluvial Valley. Paper on file, University of Arkansas Department of Geology.

Potzger, J. E., M. E. Potzger, and J. McCormick.
 1956. *The forest primeval of Indiana as recorded in the original U.S. land surveys and an evaluation of previous interpretations of Indiana vegetation.* Butler University, Botanical Studies, no. 13, 95–111.

Powell, M. L.
 1988. *Status and health in prehistory: A case study of the Moundville chiefdom.* Washington, D.C.: Smithsonian Institution Press.
 1989. The people of Nodena. In *Nodena,* edited by D. F. Morse, 65–95. Arkansas Archeological Survey, Research Series, no. 30.

Price, J. E.
 1978. The settlement pattern of the Powers phase. In *Mississippian settlement patterns,* edited by B. D. Smith, 201–31. New York: Academic Press.

Price, J. E., and J. B. Griffin.
 1979. *The Snodgrass site of the Powers phase of southeast Missouri.* University of Michigan, Museum of Anthropology, Anthropological Papers, no. 66.

Price, J. E., and C. R. Price.
   1979.   *An inventory and assessment of the Leo Anderson collection of archaeological and historical specimens.* Southwest Missouri State University, Center for Archaeological Research, Reports of Investigations, no. 256.
   1990.   Protohistoric/early historic manifestations in southeastern Missouri. In *Towns and temples along the Mississippi,* edited by D. H. Dye and C. A. Cox, 59–68. Tuscaloosa: University of Alabama Press.

Purdue, J. R.
   1980.   Clinal variation in some mammals during the Holocene in Missouri. *Quaternary Research* 13:242–58.

Robertson, P. A., G. T. Weaver, and J. A. Cavanaugh.
   1978.   Vegetation and tree species patterns near the northern terminus of the southern floodplain forest. *Ecological Monographs* 48:249–67.

Robinson, W. S.
   1951.   A method for chronologically ordering archaeological deposits. *American Antiquity* 16:293–301.

Rose, J. C., B. A. Burnett, and M. W. Blaeuer.
   1984.   Paleopathology and the origins of maize agriculture in the lower Mississippi Valley and Caddoan culture areas. In *Paleopathology at the origins of agriculture,* edited by M. N. Cohen and G. J. Armelagos, 393–424. New York: Academic Press.

Rose, J. C., S. C. Anton, A. C. Aufderheide, L. Eisenberg, J. B. Gregg, E. J. Neiburger, and B. Rothschild.
   1991.   *Skeletal Database Committee recommendations.* Detroit: Paleopathology Association.

Royall, P. D., P. A. Delcourt, and H. R. Delcourt.
   1991.   Late Quaternary paleoecology and paleoenvironments of the central Mississippi Alluvial Valley. *Geological Society of America Bulletin* 103:157–70.

Rutledge, E. M., L. T. West, and M. Omakupt.
   1985.   Loess deposits on a Pleistocene age terrace in eastern Arkansas. *Soil Science Society of America* 49:1231–38.

Sattenspiel, L., and H. Harpending.
   1983.   Stable populations and skeletal age. *American Antiquity* 48:489–98.

Saucier, R. T.
   1964.   *Geological investigation of the St. Francis Basin, lower Mississippi Valley.* U.S. Army Engineer, Waterways Experiment Station, Technical Report, no. 3-659.
   1968.   A new chronology for braided stream surface formation in the Lower Mississippi Valley. *Southeastern Geology* 9:65–76.
   1970.   Origin of the St. Francis Sunk Lands, Arkansas and Missouri. *Geological Society of America Bulletin* 81:2847–54.
   1974.   *Quaternary geology of the Lower Mississippi Valley.* Arkansas Archeological Survey, Research Series, no. 6.
   1978.   Sand dunes and related eolian features of the Lower Mississippi Alluvial Valley. *Geoscience and Man* 19:23–40.
   1981.   Current thinking on riverine processes and geologic history as related to human settlement in the southeast. *Geoscience and Man* 22:7–18.

Saxe, A. A.
   1971.   Social dimensions of mortuary practices in a Mesolithic population from Wadi Halfa, Sudan. In *Approaches to the social dimensions of mortuary practices,* edited by J. A. Brown, 39–57. Society for American Archaeology, Memoir, no. 25.

Schiffer, M. B.
1987. *Formation processes of the archaeological record.* Albuquerque: University of New Mexico Press.

Scott, L. J., and D. K. Aasen.
1987. Interpretation of Holocene vegetation in northeastern Arkansas. In *A cultural resources survey, testing, and geomorphic examination of ditches 10, 12, and 29, Mississippi County, Arkansas,* by R. H. Lafferty III, M. J. Guccione, L. J. Scott, D. K. Aasen, B. J. Watkins, M. C. Sierzchula, and P. F. Bauman. Report submitted to the U.S. Army Corps of Engineers, Memphis District.

Scully, E. G.
1953. Extinct river channels as a method of dating archaeological sites in southeast Missouri. *The Missouri Archaeologist* 15(1–2):84–91.

Shadomy, H. J.
1981. The differential diagnosis of various fungal pathogens and tuberculosis in the prehistoric Indians. In *Prehistoric tuberculosis in the Americas,* edited by J. E. Buikstra, 25–34. Northwestern University Archeological Program, Scientific Papers, no. 5.

Shelford, V. E.
1963. *The ecology of North America.* Urbana: University of Illinois Press.

Shennan, S.
1988. *Quantifying archaeology.* San Diego: Academic Press.

Smith, B. D.
1981. The division of mound exploration of the Bureau of (American) Ethnology and the birth of American archaeology. *Southeastern Archaeological Conference Bulletin* 24:51–54.
1986. The archaeology of the southeastern United States: From Dalton to de Soto, 10,500–500 B.P. *Advances in World Archaeology* 5:1–92.

Smith, F. L., and R. T. Saucier.
1971. *Geological investigation of the Western Lowlands area, Lower Mississippi Valley.* U.S. Army Engineer Waterways Experiment Station, Technical Report, no. S-71-5.

Smith, G. P.
1990. The Walls phase and its neighbors. In *Towns and temples along the Mississippi,* edited by D. H. Dye and C. A. Cox, 135–69. Tuscaloosa: University of Alabama Press.

Smith, M. T.
1983. Chronology from glass beads: The Spanish period in the Southeast, 1513–1670. In *Proceedings of the 1982 Glass Bead Conference,* edited by C. Hayes, 147–58. Rochester Museum, Research Records, no. 16.
1987. *Archaeology of aboriginal culture change in the interior Southeast: Depopulation during the early historic period.* Gainesville: University Presses of Florida.

Smith, M. T., and M. E. Good.
1982. *Early sixteenth-century glass beads in the Spanish colonial trade.* Greenwood, Miss.: Cottonlandia Museum.

Smith, R. E., G. R. Willey, and J. C. Gifford.
1960. The type-variety concept as a basis for the analysis of Maya pottery. *American Antiquity* 25:330–40.

Steele, D. G., and J. F. Powell.
1990. An osteological examination of prehistoric hunters and gatherers of the southern desert and semi-desert regions of North America. Paper presented at the 55th Annual Meeting of the Society for American Archaeology, Las Vegas.

Steponaitis, V. P.
  1983. *Ceramics, chronology and community patterns: An archaeological study at Moundville.*
      New York: Academic Press.

Stewart, T. D.
  1979a. *Essentials of forensic anthropology.* Springfield, Ill.: Thomas.
  1979b. Patterning of skeletal pathologies and epidemiology. In *The first Americans:*
      Origins, affinities, and adaptations, edited by W. S. Laughlin and A. B. Harper,
      257–74. New York: Gustav Fischer.

Steyermark, J.
  1963. *Flora of Missouri.* Ames: Iowa State University Press.

Stini, W.
  1969. Nutritional stress and growth: Sex differences in adaptive response. *American*
      Journal of Physical Anthropology 31:417–26.
  1972. Reduced sexual dimorphism in upper arm muscle circumference associated
      with protein-calories deficient diet in South American populations. *American*
      Journal of Physical Anthropology 36:341–52.

Tainter, J. A.
  1980. Behavior and status in a Middle Woodland mortuary population from the
      Illinois Valley. *American Antiquity* 45:308–13.

Teller, J. T.
  1987. Proglacial lakes and the southern margin of the Laurentide Ice Sheet. In *North*
      America and adjacent oceans during the last deglaciation, edited by W. F. Ruddiman
      and H. E. Wright, Jr., 39–69. Vol. K-3 of *The geology of North America.* Boulder,
      Colo: Geological Society of America.
  1990. Volume and routing of late-glacial runoff from the southern Laurentide Ice
      Sheet. *Quaternary Research* 34:12–23.

Teltser, P. A.
  1988. *The Mississippian archaeological record on the Malden plain, southeast Missouri: Local*
      variability in evolutionary perspective. Ph.D. diss., Department of Anthropology,
      University of Washington.

Thomas, C.
  1894. Report of the mound explorations of the Bureau of Ethnology. In *Bureau of*
      American Ethnology, Twelfth Annual Report, 163–97.

Trotter, M., and G. C. Gleser.
  1958. A re-evaluation of estimation based on measurements of stature taken during
      life and of long bones after death. *American Journal of Physical Anthropology*
      16:79–123.

Walker, W. M., and R. M. Adams.
  1946. Excavations in the Matthews site, New Madrid County, Missouri. *Transactions*
      of the Academy of Science of St. Louis 31(4):75–120.

Warren, R. E.
  1982a. The historical setting. In *The Cannon Reservoir Human Ecology Project: An*
      archaeological study of cultural adaptations in the southern Prairie Peninsula, edited
      by M. J. O'Brien, R. E. Warren, and D. E. Lewarch, 29–70. New York:
      Academic Press.
  1982b. Holocene dynamics. In *The Cannon Reservoir Human Ecology Project: An*
      archaeological study of cultural adaptations in the southern Prairie Peninsula,
      edited by M. J. O'Brien, R. E. Warren, and D. E. Lewarch, 71–84. New
      York: Academic Press.

Watson, V. D.
1950. *The Wulfing plates: Products of prehistoric Americans.* Washington University Studies (n.s.), Social and Philosophical Sciences, no. 8.

Webb, G. B.
1936. *Tuberculosis.* New York: Hoeber.

Webb, T., III, and R. A. Bryson.
1972. Late- and postglacial climatic change in the northern Midwest, USA: Quantitative estimates derived from fossil pollen spectra by multivariate statistical analysis. *Quaternary Research* 2:70–115.

Webb, W. S., and C. E. Snow.
1974. *The Adena people.* Knoxville: University of Tennessee Press.

Weiss, K. M.
1972. On systematic bias in skeletal sexing. *American Journal of Physical Anthropology* 37:239–49.
1973. *Demographic models for anthropology.* Society for American Archaeology Memoir No. 27.

Weiss, K. M., and P. E. Smouse.
1976. The demographic stability of small human populations. In *The demographic evolution of human populations,* edited by R. H. Ward and K. M. Weiss, 59–74. New York: Academic Press.

Wesler, K. W.
1991. Ceramics, chronology, and horizon markers at Wickliffe Mounds. *American Antiquity* 56:278–90.

Wheat, J. B., J. C. Gifford, and W. W. Wasley.
1958. Ceramic variety, type cluster, and ceramic system in Southwestern pottery analysis. *American Antiquity* 24:34–47.

White, J. K.
1976. *Pottery techniques of native North America.* Chicago: University of Chicago Press.

Whittaker, F.
1993. Lowland adaptation during the Late Archaic in the central Mississippi River valley. Paper presented at the 58th Annual Meeting of the Society for American Archaeology, St. Louis.

Widmer, L., and A. J. Perzigian.
1981. The ecology and etiology of skeletal lesions in late prehistoric populations from eastern North America. In *Prehistoric tuberculosis in the Americas,* edited by J. E. Buikstra, 99–113. Northwestern University Archeological Program, Scientific Papers, no. 5.

Willey, G. R., and P. Phillips.
1958. *Method and theory in American archaeology.* Chicago: University of Chicago Press.

Williams, J. R.
1964. A study of fortified Indian villages in southeast Missouri. Master's thesis, Department of Anthropology, University of Missouri–Columbia.
1967. Land leveling salvage archaeological work in southeast Missouri: 1966. Report submitted to the National Park Service, Midwest Archeological Center, Lincoln, Neb.
1968. Southeast Missouri land leveling salvage archaeology: 1967. Report submitted to the National Park Service, Midwest Archeological Center, Lincoln, Neb.
1971. A study of the Baytown phase in the Cairo Lowland of southeast Missouri. Ph.D. diss., Department of Anthropology, University of Missouri–Columbia.

1972.   Land leveling salvage archaeology in Missouri: 1968. Report submitted to the National Park Service, Midwest Archeological Center, Lincoln, Neb.

1974.   The Baytown phases in the Cairo Lowland of southeast Missouri. *The Missouri Archaeologist* 36 (whole volume).

Williams, S.

1954.   An archeological study of the Mississippian culture in southeast Missouri. Ph.D. diss., Department of Anthropology, Yale University.

1980.   Armorel: A very late phase in the lower Mississippi Valley. *Southeastern Archaeological Conference Bulletin* 22:105–10.

1983.   Some ruminations on the current strategy of research in the Southeast. *Southeastern Archaeological Conference Bulletin* 21:72–81.

1990.   The vacant quarter and other late events in the lower valley. In *Towns and temples along the Mississippi,* edited by D. H. Dye and C. A. Cox, 170–80. Tuscaloosa: University of Alabama Press.

Wood, W. R.

1976.   Vegetational reconstruction and climatic episodes. *American Antiquity* 41:206–7.

Wright, H. E., Jr.

1971.   Late Quaternary vegetational history of North America. In *Late Cenozoic glacial ages,* edited by K. K. Turekian, 425–64. New Haven: Yale University Press.

1976.   The dynamic nature of Holocene vegetation; a problem in paleoclimatology, biogeography, and stratigraphic nomenclature. *Quaternary Research* 6:581–96.

1981.   Vegetation east of the Rocky Mountains 18,000 years ago. *Quaternary Research* 15:113–25.

Yarnell, R. A.

1964.   Aboriginal relationships between culture and plant life in the upper Great Lakes region. University of Michigan, Museum of Anthropology, Anthropological Papers, no. 23.

Zawacki, A. A., and G. Hausfater.

1969.   *Early vegetation of the lower Illinois Valley.* Illinois State Museum, Reports of Investigations, no. 17.

INDEX

dchmitt